Violence, Identity, and Self-Determination

Contributors

GIORGIO AGAMBEN

ALI BEHDAD

CATHY CARUTH

JACQUES DERRIDA

MICHAEL DILLON

PETER FENVES

STATHIS GOURGOURIS

WERNER HAMACHER

BEATRICE HANSSEN

ANSELM HAVERKAMP

MARIAN HOBSON

PEGGY KAMUF

M. B. PRANGER

SUSAN M. SHELL

PETER VAN DER VEER

CORNELIA VISMANN

HENT DE VRIES

SAMUEL WEBER

Violence, Identity, and Self-Determination

EDITED BY HENT DE VRIES
AND SAMUEL WEBER

STANFORD UNIVERSITY PRESS

Stanford, California 1997

Stanford University Press

Stanford, California

© 1997 by the Board of Trustees of the Leland Stanford Junior University

Printed in the United States of America

CIP data appear at the end of the book

Acknowledgments

This volume collects the proceedings of an international workshop held during the summer of 1995 in Amsterdam under the auspices of the newly founded Amsterdam School for Cultural Analysis, Theory, and Interpretation (ASCA), in cooperation with UCLA's Paris Program in Critical Theory. Although its central theme, "Violence, Identity, and Self-Determination," had been chosen in response to recent changes in the geopolitical landscape in central Europe and elsewhere, the conference was not intended to focus primarily upon contemporary events. Rather than concentrate on the socioeconomic or political backgrounds of these historical changes, participants were invited to rethink the concept of violence, both in itself and in relation to the formation and transformation of identities, whether individual or collective, political or cultural, religious or secular. In particular, the notion of self-determination was to be subjected to stringent scrutiny: was it to be understood as a value that excludes violence, in principle if not always in practice? Or was its relation to violence more complex and, perhaps, more sinister?

Reconsideration of the concept, the practice, and even the critique of violence would have to explore the implications, ramifications, and limitations of the more familiar interpretations of the term that have dominated the history of Western thought. To this end, contributors were invited to address the concept of violence from a variety of perspectives: in relation to different forms of cultural representation, and not in Western culture alone; in literature and the arts, as well as in society and politics; in philosophical discourse, psychoanalytic theory, and so-called juridical ideology, as well as in colonial and postcolonial practices and power relations.

In the introduction to this volume we endeavor to retrace some of the major arguments that informed many of the following contributions.

With two significant exceptions, all of the texts published in this volume were delivered at the Amsterdam colloquium. The two exceptions are, first, Jacques Derrida's contribution and, second, the essay by Werner Hamacher. Derrida's text, ". . . and pomegranates," which comprises the third and final section of a meditation upon "religion" and its "return," was initially presented at a conference held not in Amsterdam but in Capri. This fact is not without significance: acutely attentive to a certain "isolation" of its island site, which could hardly be further in spirit from the continental centrality of the Dutch metropolis, Derrida's essay nevertheless addresses and redefines the concerns to which the Amsterdam conference owed its existence. Werner Hamacher's remarks were initially written for the Amsterdam conference, which he was then unable to attend. The editors are therefore grateful and delighted to be able to include both of these texts in this volume.

The workshop in Amsterdam was made possible by the combined support of a number of institutions: the Albert and Elaine Borchard Foundation in Los Angeles, the UCLA Paris Program in Critical Theory, the Belle van Zuylen Institute, the Philosophy Department of the University of Amsterdam, ASCA, the Board of Directors of the University of Amsterdam, and the cultural center "De Rode Hoed." We would like to thank these institutions for their generous financial assistance.

Contents

Contents

Contributors

GIORGIO AGAMBEN is Professor of Philosophy at the University of Verona and is the general editor of the Italian edition of the works of Walter Benjamin. His books to have appeared in English include, most recently, *Homo Sacer: Sovereign Power and Bare Life* (forthcoming), *The Idea of Prose* (1995), *The Coming Community* (1993), and *Stanzas: Word and Phantasm in Western Culture* (1993).

ALI BEHDAD is Associate Professor of English and Comparative Literature at the University of California, Los Angeles. He is the author of *Belated Travelers: Orientalism in the Colonial Dissolution* (1994) and is currently completing a book entitled *National Culture and Immigration*.

CATHY CARUTH is Associate Professor of Comparative Literature and English Director of the Program in Comparative Literature at Emory University. She is the author of *Unclaimed Experience: Trauma, Narrative, and History* (1996) and of *Empirical Truths and Critical Fictions: Locke, Wordsworth, Kant, Freud* (1990). She is also the editor of *Trauma: Explorations in Memory* (1995) and the co-editor, with Deborah Esch, of *Critical Encounters: Reference and Responsibility in Deconstructive Writing* (1994).

JACQUES DERRIDA is Director of Studies at the Ecole des Hautes Etudes and Professor of Humanities at the University of California, Irvine. Among his most recent publications are *Echographies: De la télévision* (with Bernard Stiegler, 1996), *Résistances de la psychanalyse* (1996), and *Le monolinguisme de l'autre* (1996). (All three books are forthcoming in English translation.)

MICHAEL DILLON is Professor of Politics and Executive Director of the Institute for Cultural Research at the University of Lancaster, England. He is also a managing editor of its journal *Cultural Values*. His latest book is *Politics of Security: Towards a Political Philosophy of Continental Thought* (1996). He is currently working on *An Anthology of Continental Political Thought* and *A Critical Companion to Continental Thought*.

PETER FENVES is Professor of German at Northwestern University and the author of *"Chatter": Language and History in Kierkegaard* (1993) and of *A Peculiar Fate: Metaphysics and World History in Kant* (1991). He is also the editor of *Raising the Tone of Philosophy: Late Essays by Immanuel Kant, Transformative Critique by Jacques Derrida* (1993).

STATHIS GOURGOURIS is Assistant Professor of Comparative Literature at Princeton University. He is the author of *Dream Nation: Enlightenment, Colonization, and the Institution of Modern Greece* (1996), as well as various articles on literature and modernity, psychoanalytic theory, and music.

WERNER HAMACHER is Professor of German and Humanities at the Johns Hopkins University. He is the author of *pleroma—Reading in Hegel* (forthcoming) and of *Premises: Essays on Philosophy and Literature from Kant to Celan* (1996). He is co-editor of the series Meridian: Crossing Aesthetics.

BEATRICE HANSSEN is Associate Professor of German at Harvard University, where she also teaches in the Program of Literature. A cultural critic and scholar of the Frankfurt School, she is the author of a study entitled *Walter Benjamin's Other History: Of Stones, Animals, Human Beings, and Angels* (1997). In 1995–96, she was a Mellon Faculty Fellow at Stanford University. She is currently completing a study on critiques of violence.

ANSELM HAVERKAMP is Professor of English at New York University and Chair of Western European Languages at the European University Viadrina. His recent publications include edited volumes *Die Sprache der Anderen* (1997), *Leaves of Mourning* (1996), *Memory Inc* (1996), and *Deconstruction Is/In America: A New Sense of the Political* (1995), and he is the author of *Gewalt und Gerechtikeit: Derrida-Benjamin* (1994).

MARIAN HOBSON is Professor of French at Queen Mary and Westfield College, University of London, and is currently president of the Comité Scientifique of the Collège International de Philosophie, Paris. She is the author of *The Object of Art* (1982) and is completing *Opening Lines: On Jacques Derrida* (forthcoming). Her current project is a book entitled *Why Did Hegel Like Diderot's 'Neveu de Rameau'?*

PEGGY KAMUF is Professor of French and Comparative Literature at the University of Southern California. She is the author of *The Division of Literature: On the University in Deconstruction* (1997), *Signature Pieces: On the Institution of Authorship* (1988), and *Fictions of Feminine Desire: Disclosures of Heloise* (1982).

M. B. PRANGER is Professor of the History of Christianity at the University of Amsterdam. In his publications, which are mainly on medieval monasticism, he focuses on the relationship between religion and literature. His last book is *Bernard of Clairvaux and the Shape of Monastic Thought: Broken Dreams* (1994).

SUSAN M. SHELL is Professor of Political Science at Boston College. She is the author of *The Embodiment of Reason: Kant on Spirit, Generation, and Community* (1996) and of *The Rights of Reason: A Study of Kant's Philosophy and Politics* (1980).

PETER VAN DER VEER is Professor of Comparative Religion, Director of the Research Center on Religion and Society, and the Dean of the Faculty of Social Sciences at the University of Amsterdam. He has taught at the University of Pennsylvania and is the author of *Gods on Earth: The Management of Religious Experience and Identity in a North Indian Pilgrimage Centre* (1988) and *Religious Nationalism: Hindus and Muslims in India* (1994). He is the editor of *Conversion to Modernities: The Globalization of Christian Modernities* (1995) and of the series Zones of Religion.

CORNELIA VISMANN is a lawyer in Berlin and teaches Western European literatures at the European University Viadrina. She has written articles on legal and literary matters and is about to finish *Writing and the State.* She is the editor of *Geschichtskörper: Zur Aktualität von E. H. Kantorowicz* (1997).

HENT DE VRIES is Professor of Philosophy at the University of Amsterdam. He is the author of a comparative study on the work of

Adorno and Levinas, entitled *Theologie im Pianissimo* (forthcoming in English translation) and the co-editor, with Harry Kunneman, of *Die Aktualität der 'Dialektik der Aufklärung': Zwischen Moderne und Postmoderne* (1987) and *Enlightenments: Encounters Between Critical Theory and Contemporary French Thought* (1993). He has completed a book-length study on the work of Jacques Derrida, entitled *Philosophy and the Turn to Religion* (forthcoming).

SAMUEL WEBER is Professor of English and Comparative Literature at the University of California, Los Angeles, and Director of its Paris Program in Critical Theory. He is the author of *Mass Mediauras: Form, Technics, Media* (1996), *Return to Freud: Jacques Lacan's Dislocation of Psychoanalysis* (1991), *Institution and Interpretation* (1987), *The Legend of Freud* (1982), and *Unwrapping Balzac: A Reading of 'La peau de chagrin'* (1979).

Violence, Identity, and Self-Determination

Introduction

HENT DE VRIES AND SAMUEL WEBER

With the collapse of the bipolar system of global rivalry that dominated world politics after the Second World War, the question of violence, in all of its multiple ramifications, notably in relation to national identity and self-determination, imposes itself with renewed urgency. The Manichaean frame of mind that prevailed during the past half century attempted to resolve the issue of violence by associating it with the *other*, generally understood as the *adversary*. The resulting tendency has been to construe violence as the intrusion of an external other upon whatever group, institution, or category one chooses to identify with. Violence, in short, has been widely understood as violation of the self-same in its purity by an external other. In the political value system of the West, the idea of freedom seemed to justify as a corollary the almost universally held belief that self-determination—whether of peoples or of individuals—was an ideal that could and should be implemented without reservation. Indeed, the very notion of democracy was held to be largely identical with self-determination.

Since the breakup of the former Soviet Union, the disintegration of the former Yugoslavia, and the spread of civil strife throughout much of Eastern Europe, the ideal of self-determination and the value system of which it has long been the cornerstone can no longer be accepted as self-evident. It becomes more difficult to consider violence to be an act perpetrated by others when in an increasing number of cases it is being practiced in the name of self-determination. Determination of the Self now reveals itself to be what it probably always has been: determination of the Other. Values based upon the ontological or deontological priority of identity over difference, of sameness over alterity—and such priorities

I

are perhaps inseparable from the notion of value itself—are demonstrating in practice what thinkers from Nietzsche through Adorno to Levinas and Derrida have long suspected: that violence is not necessarily the exclusive characteristic of the other but rather, and perhaps even above all, a means through which the self, whether individual or collective, is constituted and maintained.

Such a suspicion need not imply, to be sure, that the other, however it is conceived—whether as empirical or transcendental, cultural or ethnic, human or inhuman, absolute or relative—is thinkable as pure nonviolence. Nor must it imply that a simple inversion of the established hierarchy of the selfsame and the other as such would suffice radically to transform the intellectual or political landscape. What is at issue here, above all, is the facile ascription of violence to *either* the self *or* the other, either the determination of the self *by the self* or the determination of that self by whatever other. Instead of formulating the question in terms of a simple, but undoubtedly also simplistic alternative—stating or implying that violence stems either from the other or from the self—we would suggest that violence leaves its indelible mark precisely in the *mutual exclusivity* of such binary oppositions, all of which are overdetermined: geographically, historically, culturally, psychoanalytically, politically, religiously, sexually, and otherwise. Along these lines, then, violence would come to pass not in the passage *from* self *to* other, much less in that from other to self, but perhaps in the very attempt to delineate the borders that separate self *from* other. If so, then "violence" could no longer be considered simply to "befall" its victims from without, but rather would be related to what is generally presupposed to be its other: the "inviolate" self. If this were so, then, the most mystified sort of "violence" might even turn out, paradoxically perhaps, to be what seeks to eliminate or to delegitimize violence entirely.

These are troubling suspicions, with implications that are anything but academic. But not only awareness of the profoundly ambivalent dynamics of violence calls into question traditional academic approaches to the problem. Just as the binary logic of either-or, true-false, right-wrong breaks down before the multifaceted dimensions of "violence, identity, self-determination," so too do the traditional disciplines reveal their limitations. The contributions to this volume, however diverse they may be, all demonstrate practically that the *question* of violence must be approached in a distinctly transdisciplinary manner, drawing on resources from a variety of fields and, perhaps even more, from their intersections. Historical, philosophical, political, psychoanalytic, ethnographic, literary, postcolonial, deconstructive perspectives—the list is by no means exhaustive—diversely inform the discussions collected in the following pages. No general theory underlies all of the contributions, nor does any one dominant perspective emerge from them. Rather, facets and dimensions of the problem of violence are explored and avenues of further study opened.

Hent de Vries opens the volume by reviewing discussions by Derrida, Levinas, and Eric Weil concerning whether violence is endemic to discourse and to the advent of being. If violence is in effect universal and universalizing is violent, he asks, does this not trivialize the concept of violence, vitiating the intensity of any ethico-political response? Through a reading of Derrida's account of the sacrifice of Abraham in his *The Gift of Death*, de Vries argues that this is not necessarily the case. Examining the figures of sacrifice, responsibility, and obligation, he demonstrates that the prerequisite of any genuine ethico-political act is a singular and secret decision, an act of testimony that "passionately resists the realms of the 'ethical,' the 'political,' or even the 'act.'" As such, it involves a place of relation that either touches upon violence or is touched by it, a *horror religiosus*. To be wakeful to this proximity of the best and the worst is to rediscover Mount Moriah, to which Abraham was called to sacrifice his son, as the everyday place of our relation to everybody—even to everything. This is not to return to religion per se, but, perhaps, to embark on an "ongoing project" that, as Derrida has shown, entails a "doubling" of God that is neither theistic nor atheistic, but that lies at the source of all responsible discourse on responsibility.

Moving from Mount Moriah to a twelfth-century Benedictine monastery, M. B. Pranger asks whether institutions that phrase their identity in terms of separation from physical violence may nonetheless be intrinsically violent. Pranger's question—like many of the other contributors—suggests that the roots of violence may often be found precisely in discourses and value systems that explicitly claim to exclude or reduce violence. Through a discussion of the twelfth-century abbot Bernard of Clairvaux, Pranger concludes that "monastic, angelic language, which is supposedly innocent and peaceful, manifests itself in the shape of a heightened sense of violence and passion." Christian monasteries were not so much "safe havens" foreshadowing paradise by excluding intra- and extramural forces as places characterized by an intensification of violence. Once again, we find an insight that returns to mark many of the contributions to this volume, namely, that the cultural construction of an identity or place which defines itself *in opposition to* violence often turns out itself to be intrinsically violent.

Yet another dimension of this suspicion is elaborated by Marian Hobson in her essay "Characteristic Violence; or, The Physiognomy of Style." She investigates how eighteenth-century European thinkers like Lavater sought to establish a science of physiognomy at a time when the heightened value placed upon individuality and personal identity brought to light the submerged violence manifest in the desire to classify and thereby to identify the other as an example of a more general rule. Exemplification itself, upon which much of what we even today think of as "reason" and "rationality" depends so heavily, thus emerges as the more or less violent subsumption of the particular under the general. Hobson concludes by demonstrating how these issues continue to occupy contemporary thought, as in Levinas's thematics of the Other and Derrida's discussion of the originary violation of articulation. "Recognition that articulation is violent," she argues, "prevents our amalgamating it in our thought with determinate political violence or political classification. The naturalization of the category, the normalization of the specification, is thus disallowed. Articulation and syntax constitute a 'violence,' but this is an 'anguish' . . . through which the indeterminate passes into concepts. It is the price of any discourse at all."

In his discussion of Freud's 1915 essay "Thoughts for the Times on War and Death," Samuel Weber analyzes what happens when hidden violence suddenly erupts and reveals itself to be a product of the very social and intellectual order that claims to "civilize" it. Until quite recently, Weber observes, Freud's observations might have seemed definitively out of date, but events of the last decade have made them once again disturbingly "timely." Freud's point of departure is the collapse of the traditional self-perception of European civilization as a vehicle of progress in the face of the unprecedented technological violence and mass destruction of the First World War. The self-destructive reality of the First World War irrevocably refuted the universalist (and imperialist) pretensions of the European nations to cultural, cognitive, and moral superiority. Freud's reflections on war and death strengthen the suspicion that the principle of self-determination, long held to be an inviolate and self-evident right of peoples, holds within it an aggressive, destructive potential. It thereby raises the question of the relation of national and individual identity to the other and thus indirectly enjoins us to rethink the whole status of the concept and the practice of violence.

That the urgency of such rethinking has only grown in the past century also underlies the provocative thesis of Giorgio Agamben, who argues that the concentration camp, far from being a historical anomaly, is the hidden model of today's political space. The ambivalence of the defenders of the twelfth-century monastery toward the value of internal and external and their relation to one another returns with a vengeance in Agamben's portrayal of the camp as a zone of indetermination between law and violence, an indetermination which, at least since Carl Schmitt and Walter Benjamin, has been indissociably linked to the concept of sovereignty. Benjamin, in *The Origins of the German Mourning Play*, already described a situation in which the "state of exception" had "become the rule"; Agamben extends and develops this analysis by applying it to contemporary political reality. The state of exception has become the *rule* in contemporary political life, and this has led to the increasing suspension of the rule of law, with the result that anything becomes possible. In a certain sense, Agamben's argument takes up and inverts that of Marian Hobson: instead of the particular being subordinated to the universal as its exemplification, the universal is subordinated to an utterly exceptional particularity. As with all such reversals or inversions, this produces a mirror image of what it inverts: what emerges for Agamben out of this suspension of law in the camp is an indeterminate (and perhaps indeterminable) abstraction, which Agamben takes from Walter Benjamin—"bare life." "Politics is now literally the decision concerning the unpolitical (that is, concerning bare life)." At this point, anything becomes possible. Although death is one of these possibilities, it is not the only one, and Agamben extends his discussion to cover more modern and less lethal "camps," such as those established in modern airports to hold indefinitely displaced "aliens" whose legal and national status is unclear. As a site and symptom of "dislocation," the camp, Agamben concludes, "is the new biopolitical *nomos* of the planet."

Stathis Gourgouris elaborates a related point, examining a shift in "social symbolization" that occurred when, in the Age of Revolution, law was instituted as the "primary agent of social organization." He counters the usual Enlightenment story of progress from *mythos* to *logos* by unraveling the transition from *nomos* to *mythos*, from law to myth, thereby uncovering the intertwining of violence and law at the heart of Enlightenment *nomos*—its "intrinsic outlaw nature, its *paranomia*." Modern societies (his primary example is contemporary American society) thus find themselves caught up in a drama where "fascination with the business of law and order, which is also a celebration of violence, cannot be disentangled from the fascination with law and order's underside: the violence of criminality." He concludes with an appeal to re-examine myth—a polytheistic context in which the sacred is abolished rather than replaced, as modern civic codes replaced the heteronomy of the Holy Scriptures—as an alternative institution of the social community, a social imaginary where "truth and falsehood co-exist, not as antagonistic partners, but as mutually negotiable possibilities without guarantee." Here, on this outlaw side of Enlightenment law, he encounters "the moment of ethical decision, the moment of *krisis*. . . . not *before the law*, but *beside the law*, the moment of *paranomia*."

From a very different perspective, Susan M. Shell also addresses the question of the problem of internal violence as it informs the argumentation of Kant in his essay on "perpetual peace"—*Zum ewigen Frieden*. In a conference in which relatively few speakers were disposed to defend a liberal world order, Susan Shell argues that at the center of Kant's political argument is the question: "Can human aspiration reach beyond the grave?" The problem of finitude is therefore hardly absent from the thinkers of the liberal tradition, and Kant's response to this question is figured in the title of his essay: he insists, not on the realization of perpetual peace as such, but rather on a movement *toward* it—*Zum ewigen Frieden*. Shell's remarks come as a salutary reminder not to let widespread disillusion with political and economic liberalism obscure the untapped resources of its most powerful thinkers. "A few years ago," she concludes, "most thoughtful students of politics found Kant laughably naïve. Today, fewer are laughing." Like Freud, Kant has once again become timely.

"Timely," however, is not necessarily synonymous with "contemporary." This thought, which has gained momentum from Nietzsche's *Untimely Meditations* to the most recent writings of Derrida, is at the origin of the contribution by Michael Dillon. Although most of his scholarly work to date has been in the field of international relations, Dillon takes this opportunity to turn away from both modernity and the dominant discourse of his discipline to examine the possibility of an alternative politics through a re-reading of *Oedipus Rex*. In the tragic situation of Oedipus, Dillon, whose discussion is explicitly informed by the thought of Heidegger, sees an alternative to the subject-oriented worldview that has dominated modern political thinking and practice. Oedipus, he argues, emerges as "the paradigmatic figure of the immanence of alterity in every human being." "The question of the political," Dillon concludes, must be "addressed not in terms of how human being can be ordered and domesticated, nor in terms of mere self-determination, but in terms of what is required of a civilizing movement" so that the "uncanniness of . . . freedom" may be deployed. Freedom, Dillon concludes, is less freedom "of" the self than *from* the self; or, as the title of his contribution, echoing Levinas, succinctly suggests, mortal freedom must be understood "otherwise than [as] self-determination."

The principle of "self" and of "subject" as cornerstones of reality, world, and value is the hallmark of Western civilization in the modern period. A shift in focus from Europe and North America to Asia and Africa involves foregrounding the "other" not just as a shadow or function of the "self," but as a figure in its own right. Peter van der Veer's contribution, "The Victim's Tale: Memory and Forgetting in the Story of Violence," explores the "narrativization" of communal riots between Hindus and Muslims in 1990 in India. Van der Veer analyzes how colonial and postcolonial power seeks to establish truth discursively through accounts of civil violence in archives and the media. Any attempt, however, to find the truth by appealing *directly* to "the victims' story" overlooks the fact that this "story" has already been framed in terms informed either by an essentialist humanism or by a notion opposing the "people" to "the state." Such an opposition must be seen, argues van der Veer, as an attempt to exorcise the violence that affects the community by assigning it an external source. At the same time, van der Veer cautions against the widespread tendency, especially in the West, to interpret religion and religious nationalisms merely as relapses into "fundamentalisms," since this overlooks the fact that they are also "sites of difference," not to be measured exclusively according to the criteria of modern Christians or present-day liberals. Such standards fail to "account for the central role of power and violence in religious discourse, as well as in religious expansion and conversion over the centuries." This violence shows itself both in the emphasis on sacrifice, which is never far from an obsession with killing the other, and in the pursuit of a politics of space and of sacred places, which easily translates into the modern preoccupation with national territory. The fact that van der Veer concludes his discussion with the translation of a poem by a Muslim teacher in Bhagalpu, Manazir Aashiq Harganvi, can serve as a reminder that the totalizing tendencies of narrative discourse may not comprise the only way of articulating or understanding violence, which, van der Veer concludes, must be approached less as a "true story" than as a fragment.

If van der Veer leaves us with the question of a possible complicity between narrative discourse and violence, Ali Behdad explores another aspect of this relation in his reading of J. M. Coetzee's 1980 novel *Waiting for the Barbarians*. He argues that colonialism should be understood as a "violent ritual of erotic dissolution" that simultaneously disrupts and disperses the alterity of the colonized, in order thereby to produce a "sense of continuity" between colonizer and colonized. The question that Behdad raises, at least implicitly, is whether the semblance of "continuity" articulated through the dispersal of the bodily alterity of the colonized other—a female body, it should be noted, in the text—by the (male) colonizer, does not depend in an essential way upon narrative discourse in imposing the "sense of continuity" through which colonial violence effectively dissimulates itself. In short, once again we find ourselves confronted with the possible complicity of narrative discourse and violence.

The problematic relation of narration and violence has long been a concern of those working within the domain of psychoanalysis. What is the role of narrative in establishing the "case study"? (In German medical parlance, this is the *Krankengeschichte*, the "patient's story," which, however, is rarely told by the patient.) What is involved in the move from the discontinuous notes scribbled by an analyst to the coherent, often dramatically structured plot lines of the published case history? What is the relation between the nonnarrative ambiguities and ambivalences, the unresolved violence and conflicts of unconscious desire as articulated in the "primary processes" of dreams, and the dissimulation of that violence through the specious transparency and rationality, through the pseudo-coherence of the "manifest dream" constructed by the "secondary processes" of thought?

In recent analytical writing, this noncontinuous, incoherent dimension of psychic experience has tended to focus upon the status of the trauma as, paradoxically, the founding experience of psycho-analysis. Cathy Caruth's contribution, "Traumatic Awakenings," extends this line of thought to the thought and writing of Freud himself. Whereas Samuel Weber emphasizes Freud's openness and sensitivity to the disorientation brought about by the First World War, Cathy Caruth extends the notion of trauma to the "paradox: that the most direct seeing of a violent event may occur as an abso-lute inability to know it, that immediacy, paradoxically, may take the form of belatedness." The conventional conception of the har-monious relation between "seeing and knowing" is thus put radi-cally into question, a question Caruth explores by rereading a cele-brated dream discussed by Freud in his *Interpretation of Dreams*: the dream of the father whose child has just died. Reading Freud in part through the perspective of Lacan, Caruth argues that the notion of trauma marks a radical disjunction between seeing and knowing, one which introduces an "ethical" relation to the "real," and out of which emerges the obligation to write, think, and bear "ethical witness."

The ethical imperative of bearing witness thus emerges as a possible response to the resurgence of the most brutal and immedi-ate physical violence that characterizes our time, and the century now drawing to a close. Today, perhaps more than ever before, it is impossible to ignore the fact that, as Anselm Haverkamp and Cornelia Vismann remind us in their essay, "Habeas Corpus: The Law's Desire to Have the Body," violence is first of all violence against bodies, and that this circumstance continues to determine the enforcement of the law as well as modern Western juridical ide-ology. "Without the body there is no act, although the desire for the body is *not* the desire to have the act executed. . . . Rather, the body is to focus the decision." The body furnishes this "focus," they ar-gue, both scenically, by helping to organize the proceedings in the courtroom, and systemically, by providing a stable referent for the verdict. In both of these functions, however, it is the discursive ar-ticulation of the "body" that is the decisive operator. Vismann and Haverkamp conclude by calling for "an economy of [legal] discourse rather than a sociology of its effects."

Benjamin's "Critique of Violence" stands in the background of much of the foregoing discussion, and that text is subjected to di-rect scrutiny by Beatrice Hanssen, who interrogates the possibility introduced by Benjamin of considering language to be "a realm of *pure* means, unalloyed by mythical violence." Benjamin's critique of instrumental violence, unlike liberal theories of violence or those of Hannah Arendt, could, Hanssen suggests, be "credited for having attempted to think the paradoxical politics not of a legal but of a potentially legitimate form of violence, one that no longer relapses into the circularity of means and ends." Although such an attempt can ultimately be said to fail, Hanssen concludes, it serves to remind us why strategies that content themselves with globalizing or universalizing interpretations of violence are more dubious than so-called local ones. Hanssen's analysis of Benjamin thus sheds new light on what might be called the "nominalist" suspicion also apparent in other contributions, that the generalization of violence into a universal or transcendental concept runs the risk of legitimating the very violence it seeks to delimit and contain.

Peter Fenves addresses a deceptively simple question to Jacques Derrida, to whose *Specters of Marx* one of the sessions of the Amsterdam Colloquium was devoted: "How is mourning related to the messianic?" Fenves's paper, "Marx, Mourning, Messianicity," reveals that the problem of violence is involved not only in the two poles that define the terms of his question, but above all, in the interplay of mourning and messianism. Fenves approaches the question of this interplay through a reading of the conclusion of *Hamlet*: a play that plays a crucial role both in *Specters of Marx* and in Benjamin's discussion of mourning in *The Origin of the German Mourning Play*. As figured in *Hamlet*, Fenves argues, the play of mourning comes to an end in "sheer 'havoc,' in brutal violence, in near-total devastation." The question of the relation of mourning to messianism thus entails the distinction between two kinds of violence: the demand for revenge and for vengeance that characterizes mourning as Benjamin describes it, and the more radical violence associated with a messianism based in the utter transience of creation. Between these two forms of violence, between a mourning that acknowledges its indebtedness to the other, and a messianism that announces that "the rest is silence," there is, argues Fenves, no common ground. And yet, without contradicting this assertion, one could ask whether it is not precisely for this reason that Derrida insists, in *Specters of Marx*, on distinguishing the "messianic" from "messianism": whether his "messianic" shares the radical nihilism of Benjamin's "messianism," or whether it shatters all such "radicality" to its very roots.

In another paper dealing with *Specters of Marx*, Peggy Kamuf demonstrates how "spectrality" is deployed by Derrida as that *against which* traditional conceptions of identity, political and otherwise, react with more or less violence. Whereas identity politics sees only a threat in the power of spectrality to "disadjust" identity, Derrida demonstrates how such dislocation opens the very possibility of doing justice to the other: to the dead, to the past, but also to the future. The impossibility of ever predetermining or presituating the advent of the ghost conjures the alterity of history, and perhaps of politics. To use this word in a univocal manner, as either to conjure up or to conjure away, is perhaps, Kamuf suggests, to promote or to further the worst violence. Only when these two violently contradictory gestures are thought in their inseparable interdependence can the threat of totalitarian violence perhaps be averted.

The potentiality for violence inherent in identity politics is also the concern of Werner Hamacher, whose essay resituates current notions of "multiculturalism" in the broader context of discussions of selfhood and self-determination in Kant, Nietzsche, Marx, Freud, and Adorno, as well as more contemporary thinkers such as Taylor and Habermas. Hamacher thereby rearticulates the aporetic relation of culture to barbarism. All culturalisms, Hamacher argues, are caught in a logic conjoining idealization to subjugation, universalism to hostility, self-production to self-sacrifice, but also to sacrifice of the other, of the other in (and to) the self. The very pursuit of identity thus remains steeped in a history of violence and of violations, and this holds true for the politics of identity no less than for the culturalist presuppositions that underlie many of the positions assumed in today's debates on multiculturalism. By contrast, the elaboration of an alternative "structure of abstraction and idealization . . . of empiricization and socialization," Hamacher writes, can help us to rethink a form of democracy that would be founded in the abstract equation of individual vote (*Stimme*) and self-determination (*Selbstbestimmung*).

The aporia of identity politics is also one of the subtexts of Jacques Derrida's contribution to this volume, ". . . and pomegranates."[1] In this third and final section of a text entitled "Faith and Knowledge: The Two Sources of 'Religion' In the Limits of Simple Reason,"[2] Derrida argues that the more violent aspects of the "return" to, and of, "religion" must be seen, in part at least, as a reaction against the dislocating, deracinating effects of the apparatus of contemporary technoscience and, in particular, the telematic media, which are one of its most important parts. It is in the perspective of such a reaction that the "new cruelty" is to be situated, which Derrida interprets as a kind of "vengeance of the body proper against an expropriatory and delocalizing tele-technoscience," identified in turn "with the globality of the market, with military-capitalist hegemony and the globalatinization [*mondialatinisation*] of the European democratic model, in its double form: secular and religious."

Derrida's text does not merely address the questions that the Amsterdam conference had defined as its primary set of concerns, it reinscribes and transforms them. Instead of approaching the question of violence in terms of "identity" and "self-determination," Derrida introduces the notion of auto-immunization to describe the manner in which a system, bent on defending itself against external intervention, ceases to distinguish between itself and the other, between internal and external, and enters into a spiral of self-destructive auto-indemnification. Self-determination manifests itself as blind automaticity, as a self-regulating machine out of control, seeking to "indemnify itself" for losses that it simultaneously imposes upon itself while at the same time ascribing their origin to an external other. One could see in this development a bitterly ironic return of the excluded other: but its consequences for those determined henceforth as "other" are anything but reassuring. The other returns but as an object to be eliminated. Et cetera . . .

At the same time, however, the "return of religion" merely brings to the fore what a long tradition of secular rationalism sought to conceal: the ineluctable disjunction of knowledge and belief, of certitude and trust, of the "fiduciary" and the "holy" or the "intact" (*indemne*). What the return of the religious demonstrates, in the perspective of this analysis, is the necessity and impossibility of full indemnification: "The auto-immunity of religion can only indemnify itself without assignable end." Interminable assignation . . .

If this impossibility of ever reaching an "assignable end" is responsible for the worst violence, it also can provide the conditions for something else: the chance of the "plus d'Un": a One-no-more that is simultaneously a More-than-One. It is in assuming or accepting the one-no-more-than-one, and in relinquishing the effort to master or control number—which is to say, to name it and to hold it accountable—that the fatal spiral of self-destructive violence perpetrated in the name of the self, of the priority of the familiar over the alien, of the native over the stranger, can *perhaps* be dislodged.

In thus echoing the Nietzschean "perhaps" at the end of his

essay, Derrida's naming of the unnameable brings a certain anonymity to light. It is the anonymity of the place which, like Moriah,
ranges and deranges our every decision: "This place is unique, it is
the One without name. It makes way [*il donne lieu*], perhaps."

Thus, the trajectory of the Amsterdam conference, extending
beyond the actual meeting and the papers presented at it, concludes
with questions rather than answers. Not the least of these, as Derrida's discussion of "auto-immunization" suggests, concerns the relation of the interpretive and analytic effort to an "object" such as
violence. If the latter seems inextricably bound up with the structurally ambivalent relation of self and other, then this relationship
cannot but affect the nature of the knowledge that takes violence
as its object. Indeed, the Nietzschean suspicion that violence is
never just the object, but always also the medium of all cognitive
discourse suggests that its structural ambivalence may call for new
kinds of discourses prepared to take into account the ambiguous
relationship between conceptualization and violence.

Thus, as the contributions to this volume make clear, although
violence determines the structure of everyday life, of the individual
and collective self, from within, its very ground, manifestation,
and effects are often more elusive than can be grasped by cognitive or hermeneutical procedures for establishing and understanding reality. In that sense, violence—whether past or present, hidden or manifest, excessive or mitigated—can be said to impose a
certain difficulty of articulation. Its catastrophic and traumatic aspects call for more than moral indignation, theoretical cognition,
or even aesthetic imagination. What seems to be required, in excess
of these categories, is a sensitivity to the indeterminate "feelings,"
"signs of history," "ruins," and "silences" for which no generally accepted or accessible idioms are ready at hand. The following texts
can be read as an effort to contribute to the development of such a
sensitivity and thereby to the multifaceted critique of violence so
urgently needed today.

Violence and Testimony: On Sacrificing Sacrifice

HENT DE VRIES

In "Violence and Metaphysics," Derrida discusses the question, raised by Emmanuel Levinas and Eric Weil, of whether "violence" should be ascribed to the philosophical *logos*, to the identity and totality aspired to in its very concept, or whether it should be seen as a violation of this order by some singular and anarchic "other" whose alterity has (thus far) not been appropriated and pacified by rational and coherent discourse. Should one think of violence as a transcendental category—the very introduction of a "category" or "concept" of violence being the first act or declaration of war—or should one restrict this term to the interruptions or ruptures that mark the contingent historical and political or psychological and symbolical instances of all empirical conflict? And does this distinction constitute a genuine alternative? Could the meaning of "violence," as Levinas argued, be expanded to whatever takes place in the realm of beings: to ontology or, more precisely, to whatever it "is" that "lets beings be," namely, to Being, as Heidegger would have it, or to *Seyn*, whether crossed out or not? Or should it be reserved, as Weil claimed, for occurrences that disturb the coherence of philosophical discourse, less in abstract acts of negation than in the most enigmatic yet persistent ways? Is "violence" philosophy's other?

In 1963, the year before Derrida published his essay, Levinas had paid tribute to Weil in no uncertain terms, if not without reservation. Of Weil's *magnum opus*—entitled *Logics of Philosophy* (*Logique de la philosophie*) and published over a decade earlier, in 1951—Levinas wrote, in his *Difficult Freedom* (*Difficile liberté*): "We owe to Mr. Eric Weil's great thesis—whose philosophical importance and tenacity of logic will impose themselves—the systematic and vigorous use of the term 'violence' in its opposition to discourse. . . . We, however, give it a different meaning."[1]

What is this other meaning of "violence" and how is it to be distinguished from and opposed to "discourse"? In determining violence as the other of discourse, Levinas gives the first term an extremely wide-ranging meaning, whereas the latter is taken in a much stricter ethico-religious sense. Indeed, Levinas allows the semantic field of the possible connotations of "violence" to expand until it includes virtually every situation and concept not comprised in the intersubjective relation to the other. This relation to the other, to the other (*l'autre* or *l'Autre*) as neighbor (*autrui*) as well as to God, the *illeité* that leaves His trace in the other's face, is described as "discourse" (as *le Discours* and as *le Dire*). Discourse is thought to be somehow without (or beyond and before) violence: "The Other, the Exteriority, do not necessarily signify tyranny and violence. *An exteriority without violence is the exteriority of discourse.*"[2] It comes to interrupt violence, brings it to a halt, if not empirically, then at least ethically, through an appeal that is a judgment, a judgment over history, independent of its purported end(s).

Violence, by contrast, is said to take place whenever the other is not welcomed or addressed as such. This is so, Levinas claims, wherever discourse attempts to subtract itself from the realm of interlocution and interpellation—whether to achieve a rational coherence or an irrational chaos—or where the terms of this relation are exposed to each other, not as totally other (as they should be), but as alter egos, as each other's mirror images, each other's negations or, what amounts to the same thing, each other's (rational or irrational, diffuse or anonymous and neutral) totality. Wherever the self relates the other to the sameness of its own horizon, the other's singularity will be effaced. But conversely, wherever the self is overtaken or absorbed by the other—by an otherness, that is, or by an obscure, diffuse, anonymous, neutral totality—violence has taken place. Levinas claims that it is only between these two poles—which are extremes bound to collapse into each other—that one can envision the drama of a genuine "spiritual life."

What is meant by this expression? How do the life and the spirit it promises succeed in distancing or demarcating themselves from violence, from death, from the "absolute violence" to which I am "exposed" in death, to wit: "murder in the night?"[3] According to Levinas, "Nothing is more ambiguous than the term 'spiritual life.' Could we not make it more precise by excluding it from any relation to violence? But violence is not to be found only in the collision of one billiard ball with another, or the storm that destroys a harvest, or the master who mistreats his slave, or a totalitarian State that vilifies its citizens, or the conquest and subjection of men in war. Violence is to be found in any action in which one acts as if one were alone to act; as if the rest of the universe were there only to *receive* the action; violence is consequently also any action which we endure without at every point collaborating in it."[4]

In this passage, Levinas seems to determine "violence" as any force or power that characterizes natural phenomena, as well as forms of human interaction in which the self, the other, or all others are not treated as free or as ends in themselves, but rather as objects subjected to an end outside themselves, to which they have not consented. Levinas stretches the definition even further by stating that almost "every causality is violent in this sense: the fabrication of a thing, the satisfaction of a need, the desire and even the knowledge of an object. Struggle and war are also violent." As if this list were not already inclusive enough, he concludes by observing that, last but not least, there is also violence "in the poetical delirium and enthusiasm displayed when we become a mouthpiece of the muse who uses it to speak through us, and in *the fear and trembling through which the Sacred carries us away*; there is violence in passion, be it the passion of a love, wounded by a perfidious arrow."[5]

Thus, violence can be found in whatever narcissistic strategy the self adopts to capture, thematize, reduce, use, and thus annul or annihilate the other. Violence can likewise be found wherever some otherness engulfs or seizes upon the self and forces it to participate in what it—in and of itself and, precisely, as other—is not. Transcendental violence, on the one hand, and empirical or ontic (including mythical and sacred) violence, on the other, secretly correspond, if only because the former—while expressing itself through the power of argument and the force of the concept—could be said to neutralize, elevate, displace, and guard the latter. Here, one totality or, for that matter, one identity comes to substitute for another, sublating the frenzy and anxiety that stigmatize the latter into the tranquil serenity that is the trademark of the former. In sum, this is the logic of our tradition, of philosophy in its relation to myth and religion. Nonetheless, the latter still cast their shadow across the former, haunting it with possibilities that cold reason declares obsolete or would prefer simply to forget. As a consequence, the philosopher's "second violence" resembles or even repeats the

16

"first violence"[6] that precedes it and that, in a sense, calls it into being. More precisely, the philosopher uses a mitigated (not a pure) violence against an already mitigated or transformed violence in order to prevent the latter from becoming pure (again).

As the only exception to this rule, Levinas seems to present the absolute relation to the absolute, the one that withdraws, by its very definition (or rather infinition) from every totality, from all identity, and, ultimately, from all being, from all *Sein*, from all *Seyn*, from its gift, its time, its *Ereignis*, and so on. Other or otherwise than Being, the emplotment and insinuation of the *In*-finite in the finite charges the latter with a sense at once of inspiration, prophecy, election, or holiness, and of obsession, persecution, and trauma. But then is this extreme possibility not somehow haunted and haunting—and, in that sense, violent—in turn? Does it not draw on the prephilosophical experience of a "fear and trembling" that it seeks to flee?

Kierkegaard's *Fear and Trembling* is arguably the most painful example, in the history of religion, of the violence of the other as it announces itself in the breaches of a sacred and sacrificial order. The binding (*Akedah*) of Isaac in Genesis 22 is its touchstone, as it will be the touchstone of this essay on "violence" in relation to notions of testimony, death, and sacrifice, as articulated by Levinas and Derrida.

This topos focuses the process of generalization, even universalization, one sees in Levinas's expansion of the meaning of "violence" and shows how such an expansion does not trivialize the concept, but intensifies its meaning. Although philosophically and theoretically it is impossible to distinguish between the two alternatives of trivialization and intensification, the distinction between them marks all that matters (ethically, politically, and otherwise).

Throughout the history of Western metaphysics—long understood as a linear progression from *mythos* to *logos*—philosophical thought has not only studied violence in all its diffuse and often inarticulate manifestations but, some claim, has contributed to it. The affinity between the totality aspired to by the philosophical concept and the totalitarianism of "the state" has been noted by thinkers as different as Foucault and Levinas. Can one conceive other philosophical or theoretical approaches that escape or at least thematize this complicity? If so, should they not recognize the disturbing lesson of the sacrifice of Abraham: that only a suspension of the ethical (which risks a certain violence and even monstrosity) can open the possibility of responsibility in both practical and intellectual matters? In the following, I argue that this is how we could interpret the testimony of Derrida's essay *The Gift of Death*, which, following Kierkegaard and Levinas, reads the testimony of Abraham's sacrifice and the violence it entails as the paradigm for what is at stake in every genuine ethico-political decision.

Unlike Weil, who claims a connection between discursive coherence and nonviolence, Levinas regards "coherence in ontology," whatever form it assumes, to be "violence itself."[7] Not even the concept of relationship—dialectical, dialogical, or even religious—not even the appeal to alterity in general or as such can help. What escapes coherence is the singularity of a certain gesturing, in the beginning that of language, of the saying that precedes and enables all that is said. As if anticipating his own later analyses of the gift, Derrida reconstitutes this thrust of Levinas's argument: "The ego and the other do not permit themselves to be dominated or made into totalities by a concept of relationship. And first of all because the concept, . . . which is always *given to the other*, cannot encompass the other, cannot include the other. The dative and vocative dimension, which opens the original direction of language, cannot lend itself to inclusion in and modification by the accusative or attributive dimension of the object without violence."[8]

Yet do not the dative and vocative dimensions of language convey theories and philosophies as well as the violence of ontological coherence as they give, address, or expose them to the other? Are not all these performative gesturings "violent" in some respect? Can one give without violence, without the possibility or the risk or the danger of violence? What would it mean to think of violence as an inescapable horizon or inherent potentiality of any act, or of any refraining from action?

In the central thesis of *Totality and Infinity*, Levinas recalls that the violence of the concept, like that of ontological coherence, is not just a "contingent defect of man." Rather, this transcendental violence should be seen as the condition of possibility of all other —empirical, historical, psychological, or physical—real violences and, equally, of their opposite: not eternal peace, but ceaseless suspension of war. Against the background of this ambiguity—that violence is at once transcendental ideality and empirical reality, at once fatal and enticing, necessary and haphazard—Levinas notes: "I am referring to works . . . by Kojève, Hyppolyte, and Eric Weil, just as to a much older wisdom that has never disregarded the necessity of the State. But the fundamental contradiction of our situation (and perhaps of our condition), which is called hypocrisy in my book, is the simultaneous necessity of the hierarchy taught by Athens and of the *abstract* and somewhat *anarchic* ethical individualism taught by Jerusalem in order to suppress violence. Each of those principles, left to itself, only accelerates the opposite of what it wishes to guarantee."[9]

The historical articulation of this antinomy does not lead toward some dialectical mediation or reconciliation, whether distant or imminent. On the contrary, the force of this opposition does not allow for any future ontological coherence. Yet, paradoxically, precisely this dispiriting unity of its differences and differends constitutes the drama of finitude and of history.

Levinas endorses Weil's insistence on the contrast between violence and discourse. Yet he interprets quite differently the meaning of both these terms and the possibilities and the realities for which they stand. Though the predominance of violence in the work of both thinkers may be inextricable from their historical experiences in the Second World War, their different interpretations of "violence" and "discourse" reveal different appreciations of central categories in the tradition of Western philosophy, notably ones linked to the speculative dialectics and the absolute idealism of Hegel.

Weil is not simply Hegelian, Levinas an anti-Hegelian. For Weil, the pursuit of reason is only *one* possibility open to man, what is more, *only a possibility*, never a necessity. In this respect, as in many others, this pupil of Ernst Cassirer is closer to Kant than to Hegel: a post-Hegelian Kantian.[10] For him, the concept of necessity applies only to the domain of "hypothetico-deductive" reasoning, not to the reality that concerns philosophy: "philosophy *obliges itself*, in a free and primary decision, to cohere."[11] Yet, though philosophy may pursue the "idea" of absolute knowledge and thereby postulate an intelligible structure of reality, it should not forget the difference between this structure and what it structures. To neglect this was Hegel's mistake.[12]

According to Weil, at least one other, ineradicable possibility exists. That is violence, the refusal of discourse—the discourse of the other, the infinite striving for its infinite coherence—in favor of a merely individual or personal discourse, which is deemed unique and whose purported "unicity" is superimposed on all other discourses.[13] Only "free choice" can decide between these two possibilities of reason and "non-reason," or violence (in Weil's universe, the alternative to "truth"). From the viewpoint of discourse and its intended or implied coherence, this choice can only appear "absurd."[14] Weil stresses that no coherent or discursive reason can be given for being coherent or for entering discourse. The decision to be just is, in the final analysis, unjustifiable and a priori incomprehensible. For Weil, the choice for *either* violence *or* discourse is neither violent nor discursive, but free. The choice for reason instead of violence cannot be deduced by reason nor reconstructed on the basis of empirical, that is to say, psychologistic or anthropological, phylo- or ontogenetic, generalizations. Although in his *Kantian Problems* (*Problèmes kantiens*, 1963) Weil compares the possibility of violence to the Kantian understanding of "radical evil" as an ineradicable propensity, he does not consider the choice for discourse to be the affirmation (or, for that matter, reaffirmation) of a *Faktum* of reason. On the contrary, being a free choice, it is a possibility to be realized. For Weil, discourse is "good" (*bon*) because it allows man to arrive at the *désintéressement* that is the "silence of the gaze [*regard*]."[15] Discourse and reason are man's "highest aspiration," the "expression of the last desire," which is the paradoxical "desire to be free, not of need [*besoin*], but of desire."[16] To realize and relinquish this desire marks the transition from *homo faber* to *homo theoreticus*. The latter, the "being" that "sees," has a regard for the "presence" that lies beyond "becoming" and "destruction," for the *nunc stans*, the "true eternity," which is to be distinguished from "infinite duration." His gaze "grasps the totality [*le tout*] in its unity" and is ineffable, not because of its ephemeral character, but thanks to its "transcendent force [*force*]," which makes it escape the inherent "negativity" of language, not by one stroke, but through the ironic deployment of this negativity against itself.[17]

Here, one would ultimately have to touch—and rely—upon the theological category of God, which is given in "sentiment" alone: on a Truth that rejuvenates and "purifies" in a "beyond of existence" that is "not necessarily an existence in the beyond"; on a Truth, moreover, that does not "appear," that "*is* not," strictly speaking, but of which it can only be said that "there is," *il y a*, that it gives and "creates."[18] Toward this Truth, this God, the most appropriate attitude would be one of calm confidence, obedience, comprehension, and love, which, as Weil explains, should be seen as more than a mere "*means* of salvation," since whoever possesses it has found a "resting place" (*repos*) in which he is freed from his "solitude" and faces an Other whose "absolute existence" is able to give him absolute recognition.[19]

Once coherence is chosen, it can at any moment be interrupted and thus destroyed by the violence of "silence," "incoherent language," an "act of negation," the deployment of a "'technical' discourse" that loses sight of its end, or, finally, the sheer idiosyncracy of "personal sentiment," which expresses and seeks itself as such.[20] The affirmation that this violence is irreducible, that its possible recurrence cannot be excluded, marks the difference between what Weil wishes to establish as philosophy and, say, theology, metaphysics, absolute idealism, and the most dogmatic forms of dialectical materialism. Yet, we should not forget, Weil suggests, that nonviolence (or truth) is not only the "point of departure" but also "the final end [*le but final*] of philosophy."[21] Whenever discursive coherence is chosen—and in any moral situation it has always already been chosen—it demands nothing less than the reiteration of the (essentially incomplete) totality of the history of thought.[22] In any concrete history, this choice between violence and coherence already lies behind us: "the fact even of the possibility of pure violence appears only at the end." Even the slightest form of organizational life already presupposes a choice for coherence, more or less. And yet, though the diabolical seems a limit-idea, the total absence of moral sense is not unimaginable. Throughout the history of ideas it has loomed behind most distinctions, and not only those between good and evil, God and the devil. Weil affirms that the very structure of discourse, its coherence and its telos, can only be understood "on the basis [*sur le fond*] of what is radically opposed to discourse."[23] Interestingly enough, he compares this logic of presupposition with the structure of Aristotelian metaphysics, which affirms that one can comprehend "form" only on the basis of "matter," of a matter, moreover, that in itself cannot be thought positively, without referring to what is radically opposed to it, namely form.

As Derrida reminds us, Weil's project of discursive coherence is, for Levinas, the project of ontology, and thus violence itself. For Levinas, Weil's thinking leads toward an "end of history" that, in its possession of a telos and its emphasis on cessation or sublation, could be identified with "the absolute coherence of the Logos with itself in itself," or some sort of "harmony in the absolute System." On the contrary, Levinas's own version of the "end of history"—if a logic of opposition is at all pertinent here—is that of a "Peace in separation, the diaspora of absolutes."[24] But in this peace or diaspora, is not the violence of the concept—the "hierarchy taught by Athens" that domesticated and appropriated the different violence (in Levinas's term, the "anarchy") of the realm of notion and appearance, of myth and the sacred—in turn violated, displaced and held at a distance, in the relation called "ethical"? Does the truth of monotheism, wherever it reveals itself as a "religion of adults," as a relation to the totally other that removes itself from all idolatry, from all superstition and imagery, from all rites and incarnation, force and enforce a separation between this peace of absolutes and the reign of empirical and transcendental violence that Levinas ascribes to mythology and ontology? Could the immediacy or the enigma of the relation to the absolute ever put an end to violence and, moreover, do so nonviolently?

Levinas chooses this question as his point of departure, not only in the opening pages of *Totality and Infinity* but also elsewhere. The first article of *Difficult Freedom* formulates it thus: "But is a cause without violence possible? Who welcomes without being shocked? Let mystics be reassured: nothing can shock reason. It collaborates with what it hears. Language acts without being subdued, even when it is the vehicle for an order. Reason and language are external to violence. They *are* the spiritual order. If morality must truly exclude violence, a profound link must join reason, language and morality. If religion is to coincide with spiritual life, it must be essentially ethical. Inevitably, a spiritualism of the Irrational is a contradiction. Adhering to the Sacred is infinitely more materialist than proclaiming the incontestable value of bread and meat in the lives of ordinary people. . . . The intervention of the unconscious and, consequently, the horrors and ecstasies which it feeds—all this is linked ultimately to violence."[25]

But is the relation to the other not violent in its own right? Levinas leaves no doubt that the absolute other (or Other) affects me without absorbing or effacing me and without becoming integrated into me. The relation of self to other, he writes, "while remaining one of the more in the less, is not transformed into the relationship in which, according to the mystics, the moth drawn to the flame is consumed in it."[26] In other words, the relation does "not sink into participation, against which the philosophy of the same will have the immortal merit to have protested."[27] Nor can the other be reduced to an intentional object or an alter ego, to a being among beings that is part of my world and thus enters my horizon.

What remains, then? Is there a thinkable, livable, practicable, or even desirable relation that could respect the other as independent, separate, indeed ab-solute, discharged, in the etymological sense of the Latin verb *absolvere*? Could the Other withdraw from all the violent determinations that tie or bind "Him" to the order of beings, to the present and the present-at-hand, but also to history, historicity, and ultimately to *logos* and Being as such? Could "He" ever do so without some, however minimal or sublime, divine violence? Would this absolute relation to the absolute not be the end of all reason, of all *logon didonai*, of all discussion?

Levinas is of course not unaware of the violence of the sacred, of its diffuse, anonymous, and neutral heteronomy (its invocation of forces and gods, of powers and raptures). His condemnation of it is to some extent an endeavor to demarcate two heterogeneous experiences of the heterogeneous, one violent and one marked by the "peace of absolutes." Yet this attempt is not without some violence of its own. Even without succumbing to the temptation to erase this difference, one might surmise that violence would not peaceably let itself be banned on one side of the line held to separate the ethical "relation without relation" to the other (as absolute) from the nonrelation that immerses the self in the other as the Same or, conversely, reduces this other to the self-same. A certain possibility of violence and violation remains inscribed on the very face of the face, of the *vis-à-vis* that characterizes the encounter with the other as other, as the *tout autre* and the *autrui* irreducible to any form of the Same or the Selfsame. This possibility is acknowledged by Levinas and described or, rather, evoked in vivid, shocking, and uncanny figures, especially in his later works, which speak of responsibility in terms of a "trauma," a "pure burning," the subject's "gnawing away at itself," "hollowing itself out," "turning itself inside out."

By articulating this possibility, Levinas seems to prepare an answer to the questions Derrida formulates implicitly in "Violence and Metaphysics" by remarking that both Levinas and Weil, in their common preoccupation with violence, whether that of the concept, the finite totality, or the totally other who comes to unsettle the concept, the totality, and their coherence, point to the discourse of the infinite and the absolute as what either escapes, or substitutes and sublates, or defers and interrupts the reign of violence. Derrida asks whether this dilemma, in which violence is identified *either* with the order of the finite *or* with the realm of its other (whether with the finite order's negation or otherwise), constitutes a true alternative.

Notwithstanding their differences, Levinas and Weil share sufficient premises to be counted among the philosophers of a certain, metaphysical epoch whose end is, perhaps, not yet in sight—whose end might, perhaps, never come—but whose delimitations and limitations of thought are becoming increasingly clear, especially in light of the question of violence. Derrida writes: "One should examine the common presuppositions of this convergence and divergence. One should ask whether the predetermination, common to these two systems, of violation and pure logos, and, above all, the predetermination of their incompatibility, refers to an absolute truth, or perhaps to an epoch of the history of thought, the history of Being."[28]

This reading would suggest that violence cannot be restricted to any single metaphysical predetermination, whether as self or as other, as totality or as alterity, as coherence or as its absence. Nor can nonviolence be said to be the prerogative or privilege of the infinite or Infinite and the peace it is said to inspire. To the extent that these determinations could be seen as belonging to the history of thought *as* ontology—of "Being thinking itself"[29]—and of metaphysics, neither the finite nor the infinite could aspire to remove itself from the differential notion called "violence." They are carried and traversed by a history whose worst memories continue to haunt their best moments. No rupture with this intermittent interruption of the tradition of violence, whether by the In-finite (Levinas) or by the infinite coherence of discourse (Weil), could ever hope to be total. What is other than violent is somehow violent, or is unable to express (Levinas) or realize (Weil) itself without resorting to the order it seeks to escape or invoking some violence of its own. Discourse, whether infinite or not, whether ethical or not, demands some negotiation with its other—namely, violence—if it is to minimize the risk of allowing the worst violence to come to pass.

With an oblique reference to Levinas's definition of "religion" as the relation to the other that does not close itself off in a totality, Derrida explains this risk as follows: "if one calls this experience of the infinitely other Judaism (which is only a hypothesis for us), one must reflect upon the necessity in which this experience finds itself, the injunction by which it is ordered to occur as logos, and to reawaken the Greek in the autistic syntax of his [or its] own dream. The necessity to avoid the worst violence, which threatens when one silently delivers oneself into the hands of the other in the night."[30]

Thus "Violence *and* Metaphysics"—as in Levinas's title *Totality and Infinity*, the conjunction is not trivial or simply enumerative—leaves no doubt that "*within history* . . . every philosophy of nonviolence can only choose the lesser violence within an *economy of violence.*"[31] Consequently, *within history*—and strictly speaking, Derrida notes, no critique of violence could ever be meaningful, effective, or relevant and responsible elsewhere—nonviolence is somehow violent: "Like pure violence, pure nonviolence is a contradictory concept. . . . Pure violence, a relationship between beings without a face, is not yet violence, is pure nonviolence. And inversely: pure nonviolence, the nonrelation of the same to the other (in the sense understood by Levinas) is pure violence. Only a face can arrest violence, but can do so, in the first place, only because a face can provoke it."[32]

But, Derrida continues, if one accepts this Levinasian proposition, one should take it one step further by showing that this provocation and interruption of violence—*in* and *by* the face—can never take place without, outside of, or beyond a certain metaphysically overdetermined history of Being, which *lets* beings be and, in that sense, can also be said to "open" or "free" or "allow" the face to face. Without this history, without the thought of Being, there would only be the impossible experience of a pure nonviolence that is indeterminate to the point of being interchangeable or confused with its alleged counterpart of pure violence. By contrast, the history and the thought of Being, while never without a certain relation to violence—nothing is without a certain relation to violence—would come "as close as possible to nonviolence": "A Being without violence would be a Being which would occur outside the existent: nothing; nonhistory; nonoccurrence; nonphenomenality. A speech produced without the least violence would determine nothing, would say nothing, would offer nothing to the other; it would not be *history*, and it would *show* nothing; in every sense of the word, and first of all the Greek sense, it would be speech without a *phrase.*"[33]

But, since speech is what, according to *Totality and Infinity*, singles out the relation to the other—the face does not just glance at us, first it speaks—since, moreover, there can be no speech without phrasing, the denunciation of violence must engage in an intricate negotiation with violence itself. Can it do so without using it in return or without mobilizing a violence of its own that is incomparable or incommensurable with the first, but can only counter it by, paradoxically, measuring itself against it? Can it do justice without doing violence to this justice? Derrida does not think so: "there is no phrase which is indeterminate, that is, which does not pass through the violence of the concept. Violence appears with *articulation*. And the latter is opened by the . . . circulation of Being. The very elocution of nonviolent metaphysics is its first disavowal."[34]

Since one cannot avoid speaking, since there can be no denunciation of violence without the act or gesture of a certain *phrazein*, one must oppose violence, if not in the name, then at least with the help of another—less violent—violence. To invoke violence against violence would mean to enter an "economy" of violence, to wage war on war, and thus to be truly responsible, historically speaking—that is to say, *in* and *for* history, indeed *in* and *for* the history of Being: "Hence, only in its silent origin, before Being, would language be nonviolent. But why history? Why does the phrase impose itself? Because if one does not uproot the silent origin from itself violently, if one decides not to speak, then the worst violence will silently cohabit the *idea* of peace?"[35]

What imperative might summon this nonviolent origin to betray itself violently (in and through the medium of the concept and of history) to avoid being confused with the "worst violence"? Whence comes the force, the need, or the injunction to escape cohabitation with *le pire* of absolute or pure (or divine?) violence and to enter the mediated, mitigated, relative or differential, deferred and deferring violence of history? What is the systematic, ontological, or deontological necessity or force by which the "silent origin" of language is called outside itself by itself? Derrida answers:

> If light is the element of violence, one must combat light with a certain other light, in order to avoid the worst violence, the violence of the night which precedes or represses discourse. This *vigilance* is a violence chosen as the least violence by a philosophy which takes history, that is finitude, seriously; a philosophy aware of itself as *historical* in each of its aspects (in a sense which tolerates neither finite totality, nor positive infinity), and aware of itself . . . as *economy*. . . . The philosopher (man) *must* speak and write within this war of light, a war in which he always already knows himself engaged; a war which he knows is inescapable, except by denying discourse, that is, by risking the worst violence. This is why the avowal of this war within discourse, an avowal which is not yet peace, signifies the opposite of bellicosity; the bellicosity—and who has shown this better than Hegel?—whose best accomplice *within history* is irenics. . . . If, in this sense, the movement of metaphysical transcendence is history, it is still violent, for—and this is the legitimate truism from which Levinas always draws inspiration—history is violence.[36]

Do we know, then, precisely where violence comes from, precisely where it begins, resides, or ends, and what (or whom), exactly, it is directed at? Is it a fact, a *Faktum* of reason, in Kant's sense, as much as, say, a "fact of life," even of "spiritual life"? If violence seems thereby to lose its specificity as physical, psychological, political, colonial, structural, domestic, sexual, or even verbal violence—do we have a clear idea of what it is that would bring violence to a halt and mark its cessation? Is the silent individual or collective gesture or is the utopian end-state of nonviolence the absolute opposite of violence, its annihilation, mitigation, its repression, negation or sublation? Is nonviolence nonviolent, in the strict sense of the word? If it is not, how would its "violence" differ from the former's more brutal and manifest empirical (physical, social, or personal) effects, to say nothing of "the worst violence"? Could one retrace the most elusive or remote aspects of violence— for example, the violence in and of nonviolence—without turning them into metaphysical, ontological or, for that matter, theological categories? Without doing them violence in turn?

Critiques of violence are not without violence. They are successful only if they turn violence inside out, if they are somehow violent *in turn*, turning good violence against bad or the worst violence. No one has analyzed this complementary, supplementary, complicity—and its intrinsic dangers—at greater length and with more consequence than Derrida, as a glance at his recent *Of Spirit* (*De l'esprit*), "Force of Law," (*Force de loi*), and "The Politics of Friendship" (*Politiques de l'amitié*), confirms. But this insight also preoccupies the earlier writings, whether they deal with it explicitly and directly—as in "Violence and Metaphysics"—or not.

If violence is everywhere and if, moreover, the concept, practice, and effects of violence are caught in a structure that the history of religion and philosophy has identified throughout as that of "sacrifice" (of the self and, more often than not, of others), then also all ethico-political decisions can be said to take place under the condition of some submission to—or at best some negotiation with— this general economy of "violence."[37]

In the remainder of this essay, I will analyze in what sense, precisely, "sacrifice" is read by Derrida as the very paradigm of every genuine decision. According to Derrida, this sacrifice—as the sacrifice of the identity of the self, and, in that sense, as *self*-sacrifice— becomes also a sacrifice of any self-sacrifice that is transformed into a norm, an ideology, or a religious demand. To explore this issue, let me first briefly return to the text that more than any other *seems* to challenge the Levinasian perspective, without therefore taking the position of Weil: namely, Kierkegaard's *Fear and Trembling*. In this reading of Genesis 22, Kierkegaard explores the disturbing fact that the divine command and the ruses of the demonic are intertwined. To my knowledge, no better interpretation of this uncanny resemblance has been given than the one proposed by Jean Wahl, one of the first commentators on Kierkegaard in France, who, in his introduction to the French translation of *Fear and Trembling*, points out that all its portraits of Abraham, Isaac, and Sarah are "haunted by the demon." Kierkegaard's writing incessantly borders upon and flirts with "the abysses of the demonic."[38] Wahl explains the necessity of this haunting as follows:

> Like the religious, the demonic is outside the general, above the general, in an absolute relation with the absolute. . . . Here Kierkegaard merely indicates that vast and somber region. "In general, one hardly hears people talking about the demonic even though in our days above all that domain demands to be explored." But he insists on the idea that one can only escape the demonic paradox by means of the divine paradox. Whoever has sinned has placed himself outside the general, but in a negative manner; he can no longer save himself unless, having lost all rapport with the general, he enters into rapport with the absolute. For ethics is insufficient to make one truly leave one's sin behind.[39]

In the hour of despair, Wahl notes, the knight of faith can only close his eyes: "Man says *adieu* to all understanding; he gives himself over to God [*à Dieu*] in all his weakness. At the same moment he recognizes the impossible and believes in the possibility; for everything is possible for God [*à Dieu*]."[40] The first gesture— that of the suspension of the ethical, the infinite resignation—is a movement by which our exposure to the absolute separates us "violently" (*violemment*) from the "real." The second gesture—that of the movement of faith—is the one which "violently" (*violemment*) leads us away again from this refuge and returns us to the real so as to "conquer and to transfigure" it. These two violences, however, do not occur after one another, as consecutive moments "in" time, but at one and the same time, that is to say, "with one breath [*d'un seul souffle*]."[41] What is more, these movements of faith are both indelibly temporal and historical, yet not of this world, eternal. As Wahl notes, faith both demands and suppresses time: for faith to be what it is, that is to say, to escape "immanence," it must be clear that "there has not always been faith." Faith annuls time or at least "transforms" its ordinary concept. It evokes a certain "contemporaneity," which allows us to be more than mere spectators of the "Christian drama," and in which we are no longer "spared" its anxieties. Faith marks the instant in which time, after having gone through a painful preparation, touches upon "eternity," "consecrates time," and "begins a new time."[42] Derrida says as much when he writes, in *The Gift of Death*, that the giving of death entails a temporality of its own: a temporality of the "instant," which, paradoxically, belongs to an "atemporal temporality," to an ungraspable "duration" incomprehensible for any work of negation and for any work of mourning.[43]

The two gestures correspond to two divine contradictions. By asking Abraham to sacrifice his son, God contradicts his promise that Isaac will be the first of an innumerable offspring. But, in a second instance, God also allows him to live, thereby contradicting the first contradiction. In speaking of these contradictions, *Fear and Trembling*, Wahl notes, analyzes the structure of a double will: a will to transgress and one of return and integration. Like the Nietzschean idea of a perpetual trespass and an eternal recurrence, Kierkegaard's doubling of the direction of the will constitutes a break with the more static "classical idea of the ideal."[44] Both Nietzsche and Kierkegaard seek to substitute for this notion, not so much some dialectical dynamism, guided by the mediation of the concept and its other and with a view to their ulterior and ultimate sublation, but rather the simultaneous affirmation of an irreducible "destruction" and "construction."[45] In the latter moment of reaffirmation—in which the repetition is given only to the one who has survived the test—the knight of faith not only rediscovers the commonality of the finite world, of morality and its generality, but also finds a "new heaven and a new earth."[46]

One of the most challenging features of Levinas's writing, one that keeps his work at an infinite distance from all forms of complacent moralism, is that, regardless of his incessant emphasis on the "peace of absolutes," he does not shy away from describing as violence the shock with which the infinite enters my consciousness and makes it responsible. Here, of course, violence is attributed—paradoxically—to the "welcoming of a being to which [consciousness] is inadequate."[47] This violence, therefore, is not of the same order as the violence that it comes to judge or call to a halt. For "good violence"—the violence with and as which "the good" appears—is not identical with the violations of identity attributed to

29

terror and war. And yet, in its very structure it seems to resemble "the worst."

Levinas thus invites us to consider an unsentimental and unsettling account of the intrigue and the drama of responsibility and the testimony it provokes. At its most disturbing, violence does not just aim at the face of another, at a face that is human; it also, as Jean-Luc Nancy stresses, "originates from a face, on which wickedness can, occasionally, be read as the devastation of this same face."[48] Even beyond this distinction between good and evil, another violence—the violence of another other—lurks.

The intrigue of inspiration, in which one no longer knows who speaks what to whom, or whether anything (ethical) is being said or given at all, entails an experience that is *catastrophic*, that disturbs and disrupts the paradoxical logic of desire, which, according to Levinas, is the very modality of responsibility. Not only does the apparent negativity of the infinite—of the *In* in *l'Infini*—in the drama of its divine comedy characterize the structure of a desire that deepens and exalts in the measure that it approaches the desirable, not only does the desirable call forth the immeasurable,[49] seemingly marked by a perverse, parabolic arithmetic that allows no calculation, no distributive justice, and no restitution, so that it must be said: "Plus je suis juste—plus je suis coupable."[50] The implications of this movement reach still further. Here, responsibility turns out to be a nonevent, inexplicable in terms of natural inclinations, social constructs, or cultural phantasms, which in its very taking place resembles a "devouring fire that devastates the place [*catastrophant le lieu, au sens étymologique du terme*]."[51] With an ironic displacement of Heideggerian topology or *Erörterung*, Levinas writes that the infinite "affects thought by devastating it and at the same time calls upon it; in a 'putting it back in its place' it puts thought in place. It awakens it."[52]

> To the idea of the infinite there corresponds only an extravagant response. What is imperative here is a 'thought' that hears/understands more than it hears/understands, more than its capacity and with which it cannot be contemporaneous, a 'thought' which, in that sense, can go beyond its death. . . .—To go beyond one's death, that is to sacrifice oneself.—The response to the being assigned by the sacrifice of the Enigma is the generosity of the sacrifice outside the known and the unknown, without calculation, since it goes toward the Infinite [*à l'Infini*]. . . . I approach the Infinite by sacrificing myself. The sacrifice is the norm and the criterion of the approach. And the truth of the

transcendence consists in establishing a harmony [*la mise en accord*] between one's discourses and one's acts.[53]

The ambiguity in "the sacrifice is the norm and the criterion of the approach" implies, not that Levinas subscribes to a religion of sacrifice, but that in the absolute relation to the absolute—which for Levinas, unlike Kierkegaard, is the ethical relation—every norm and criterion, in the strict and common sense of these terms (as *ethos* as much as abstract forms of morality), is sacrificed. This paradox is not contradicted by the fact that there should be some concordance or accord between words and deeds. But the tonal metaphorics (*la mise en accord*) that describes or evokes this performativity or, rather, performance is no accident.

According to Kierkegaard, the absolute command to which Abraham responds withdraws from the generality and universality that, in the intelligible realm of pure duty—in acting "out of duty" rather than merely "conforming to duty"—characterize the Kantian conception of the moral law, the categorical imperative.[54] Kant's conception lacks the qualities of and the qualifications for an absolute command. Absolute duty—in Derrida's words, in *The Gift of Death*: a duty "toward God and in the singularity of faith," substituting for the other without being able to expect or demand any substitution or restitution in turn—"implies a sort of gift or sacrifice that functions beyond both debt and duty, beyond duty as a form of debt. This is the dimension that provides for a 'gift of death' [*donner la mort*] which, beyond human responsibility, beyond the universal concept of duty, is a response to absolute duty."[55] The structure of the sacrifice or the gift, that is to say, of the giving of death, could be said to figure this structure of excess of a beyond of duty, in other words of "*over-duty.*"[56]

Abraham, Kierkegaard writes, "had faith that God would not demand Isaac of him, and yet he was willing to sacrifice him if it was demanded. He had faith by virtue of the absurd, for human calculation was out of the question; it was certainly absurd that God, who required it of him, should in the next moment rescind the requirement. He climbed the mountain, and even in the moment when the knife gleamed he had faith—that God would not require Isaac."[57] Abraham has faith "by virtue of the absurd, by virtue of the fact that for God all things are possible."[58] This absurdity, this "possible," Kierkegaard clarifies, "does not belong to the differences that lie within the proper domain of the understanding. It is not identical with the improbable, the unexpected, the unforeseen."[59] Indeed, it is precisely the impossible, the unthinkable, in the realm of the finite and the temporal on which mere understanding does not cease to reflect. And the "testimony"[60] of faith is only authentic, that is to say, only a testimony properly speaking, insofar as it acknowledges—at the very same instant—the necessity of this visible order, the legitimacy of its ethical claims, as well as the absolute command to transgress, to go beyond them, to leave them behind:

> The two duties must contradict one another, one must subordinate (incorporate, repress) the other. Abraham must assume absolute responsibility for sacrificing his son by sacrificing ethics, but in order for there to be a sacrifice, the ethical must retain all its value; the love for his son must remain intact, and the order of human duty must continue to insist on its rights [à faire valoir ses droits].
> The story [récit] of Isaac's sacrifice can be read as the narrative quintessence [portée] of the paradox constituting the concept of duty and absolute responsibility. This concept puts us into relation (but without relating to it, in a double secret) with the absolute other, with the absolute singularity of the other, whose name here is God.[61]

If the first recognition of this double affirmation or doubled binding were not as pertinent as the second, we could hardly speak of "resignation," let alone of "infinite resignation." Only where resignation forms the "antecedent," Kierkegaard writes, is faith more than a merely "aesthetic emotion," that is to say, "not the spontaneous inclination of the heart but the paradox of existence."[62] In order for faith to be what it is, it would thus have to "look the impossibility in the eye,"[63] risk the worst, and face the chance that in committing the crime—in the willingness to sacrifice, to give death—nothing would be given in return, everything would be taken away, and the whole episode would be less an "ordeal" than just a murder.[64] According to Kierkegaard, only the "paradox of faith" turns this possible murder into a possibly "holy and God-pleasing act"; only the paradox of faith, then, could give "Isaac back to Abraham again."[65] Abraham, Kierkegaard writes, was "the first to feel and bear witness to that prodigious passion that disdains the terrifying battle with the raging elements and the forces of creation in order to contend with God. . . . The first to know that supreme passion, the holy, pure, and humble expression for the divine madness that was admired by the pagans."[66]

In suspending the ethical in favor of a purportedly religious obligation, Abraham demonstrates what it takes to assume respon-

sibility for an absolute command. Abraham's passion when faced
with the sacrifice of his son, his anxiety at having to sacrifice his
love, is the example set for every decision—once and for all. It is the
example of all exemplarity. Every ethical decision that deserves the
name takes place as the similar pronunciation of a singular *shibboleth* and thus retains a certain idiosyncrasy or secrecy. As soon as it
enters language and becomes part of discourse or even the subject
of discussion, not to mention a *Diskurs*, an ethical decision loses
its distinctive character, its significance or, rather its *signifiance*, to
use the formulation Levinas employs to indicate how the ab-solute
relation with the ab-solute manifests itself without appearing, presenting, revealing or even being "itself."

Abraham shows that in every genuine decision, if it takes place,
the ethical *has* to be sacrificed. Morality *ought* to be suspended "in
the name of" an ab-solute duty or obligation that is always "singular" and for which the name—the proper name and, indeed, the
most proper name—would be "God." Strictly speaking, this name
is neither common nor proper. As the unpronounceable Tetragram-
maton, JHWH, it names the unnameable and therefore forces a
rupture in the typical grammatical function of the name, that of
capturing the multiple senses of Being. The trace that it leaves in
the face, in the face of the Other, facing his or her death, is also—
always already—*effaced*.[67] It is under this regime, then, that "God,"
in Derrida's reading, serves as the index or the "figure" not only
of the *wholly other—tout autre*—but also of every other, that is,
tout autre. Derrida's text plays here with the distinction between
"two homonyms, *tout* and *tout*, an indefinite pronominal adjective
(some, someone, someone other [*quelque, quelconque, un quelconque autre*]) and an adverb of quantity (totally, absolutely, radically, infinitely other)."[68]

On this reading, then, "God" is other than "Himself"; "He" (can
we be sure here that the *illeity* refers to "He"—that is, not to "Thou"
but to the third *person?*) is His own other. As the radically other,
God is everywhere, that is, wherever there is the other, whenever
there are others. And all that can be said about the anxious silence
of Abraham in his relation to God (*à Dieu*) could be applied to—
rather, reiterates itself in—our relation to everybody and perhaps,
Derrida adds, to everything else.[69]

The extraordinary, scandalous story of the sacrifice of Isaac, as
read by Kierkegaard, concludes Derrida, thus shows us "the structure of what occurs everyday [*du quotidien*],"[70] without allowing

33

any inference of a *proper* or *authentic* dimension implied by this ordinariness (as Heidegger would have it). Each little gesture of the other towards me obligates me to respond by sacrificing the other of the other, his or her (or its) other gesture, or the absence thereof, but also the other other and, finally, all the other others. The relation to the other demands that I sacrifice the ethical, that is to say, "whatever obligates me also to respond, in the same way, in the same instant, to all the others."[71]

To say *adieu*, if only for an instant, to the ethical order of universal laws and human rights by responding to a singular responsibility toward an ab-solute other—for example, the other par excellence, God—implies sacrificing the virtual totality of all innumerable others. And yet this singular dramatization and intensification of responsibility by no means lessens my equally absolute responsibility toward all other others, toward all that concerns them, directly and indirectly, whether they know it or not. Without ever being able to master *their* situation, I alone will have been obligated to step in, to substitute for these others and to be their hostage: "Ipseity, in its passivity without the *arche* of identity, is hostage. The word *I* means *here I am*, answering for everything and everybody [me voici, *répondant de tout et de tous*]."[72]

The so-called third person—*le tiers*—would therefore not mitigate my absolute obligation, but rather broaden and deepen it. This circumstance, precluding every *stasis* or stance, gives new meaning to the phrase that in (the) face of the other I am haunted by others. In the open-ended, permanent alternation of the *Saying* and the *Said*, of substitution and justice, of anarchy and economy, of the non-negotiable and of negotiation, the *différend* of conflicting responsibilities finds neither resolution nor rest.

In *The Gift of Death*, the thematization and problematization of the sacrificial structure takes a form that resembles the "double bind" that haunts so many of Derrida's earlier writings. It could be formalized as follows: *in being responsive and responsible, one must, at the same time, also be irresponsive and irresponsible,*[73] sacrificing one while respecting the other. Being responsible demands a double response or allegiance to the general and the singular, to repetition and to the unique, to the public sphere and to the secret, to discourse and silence, to giving reasons as well as to madness, each of which tempts the other. Indeed, Derrida writes, one does not have to raise a knife in order to slaughter one's own son to be caught in this logic of a given death which prescribes that one "can respond only to the one (or to the One), that is, to the other, by sacrificing that one to the other."[74] That sacrifice, that preference for one other over another, Derrida insists, is always *unjustifiable* for "*every other (one) is every (bit) other* [Tout autre est tout autre]."[75] Every other (that is to say everybody, everything) is other than every other other (i.e., other than everybody and everything else); put otherwise, every other (everybody, everything, e.g., God) is *totally* other, an other in an absolute sense of the word, another absolute. Of this, "God" would be both the "figure" and the "name": "what can be said about Abraham's relation to God [*à Dieu*] can be said about my relation without relation to *every other (one) as (every bit) other* [tout autre comme tout autre]."[76]

But are not some others more other than others, more other than ab-solutely other? Are not some others other otherwise? Is not God, as the tradition suggests, other—*the* Other—par excellence? Perhaps. Who knows? Precisely this uncertainty constitutes the other as other and—a fortiori—defines the Other, not in his, her, or its otherness, but as a singular Other. Otherwise, this Other would be an apodictic notion, not demanding to be believed but self-evident and ready at hand, in the open, out there, for all eyes. "God" is only given—indeed, only gives—in secret. His very name is a cryptogram, his very manifestation encrypted (and, according to at least one tradition, the Christian, tied to a crypt). The same could be said of the gesture with which one gives oneself to God or to every absolute other that takes his place. For if the response cannot measure up to the demand, if the former and the latter are inversely proportional to each other or, rather, are disproportionate, one can never know or calculate whether one has given enough or at all.[77]

Derrida acknowledges that his reading pushes the analysis of *Fear and Trembling* beyond commentary, let alone an interpretation *e mente auctoris*. If one claims there can be no ethical generality that is not always already subject to the Abrahamic paradox; if one infers, moreover, that with every genuine decision, insofar as it relates itself to the other—to everybody and everything as absolutely other [à tout autre comme tout autre]—every one else asks us at every moment to behave like a knight of faith; then this analysis, Derrida acknowledges, "displaces a certain *portée* of Kierkegaard's discourse." In particular, this analysis breaks away from the monotheistic doctrine of the oneness, the uniqueness, and the indivisibility or unsubstitutability of "God." Derrida says so explicitly: "the absolute uniqueness of Jahweh doesn't tolerate analogy; we are not all Abrahams, Isaacs, or Sarahs either. We are not Jahweh."[78]

As with "violence," the generalization, universalization or, for that matter, infinite substitution, of "God," of the infinitely other that is everywhere or everyone—*tout autre est tout autre*—promises to trivialize the quintessence of this notion as much as to intensify it. It begs the question of God, of the other, of their relation, of their relation to the same, and so on and so forth. It evades this question no less than it takes it for granted, as the *petitio principii* or, indeed, the tautology of all thought, all action, all judgment.

Yet the impossibility of ascribing or assigning an identifiable and responsible agent (God, Abraham, and those who follow their trace without ever being able to claim to follow *in* their trace) is precisely what is in question here. It is in this sense, then, that "we" could be said to "share" with Abraham "what cannot be shared, a secret we know nothing about, neither him nor us. . . . Such is the secret truth of faith as absolute responsibility and as absolute passion . . . ; it is a passion that, sworn to secrecy, cannot be transmitted from generation to generation. In this sense, it has no history. This untransmittability of the highest passion . . . , dictates to us nonetheless: we must [*il faut*] always start over [*recommencer*]. A secret can be transmitted, but in transmitting a secret as a secret that remains secret, has one transmitted at all? Does it amount to history, to a story? Yes and no."[79] It is for this reason, Derrida reminds us, that *Fear and Trembling* concludes by invoking the "nonhistory of absolute beginnings which are repeated, and the very historicity that presupposes a tradition to be reinvented each step [*pas*] of the way, in this incessant repetition of the absolute beginning."[80]

Paraphrased and varied, mimicked and parodied, the *à dieu* still retains something of its untranslatability. If "God," the invocation of "God"—speaking on the subject *of* or addressing oneself *to* God—is exemplary, does this exemplarity necessarily imply that God is the sole, or even the best, example, as if the name or term "God" stood for the highest or most elevated Being among beings? It means, rather, that "God" is the example par excellence, privileged not because of any quality that this name or entity can claim to possess in and of itself, but because of the act of our attribution. This act stands in relation to a powerful, inspiring, and terrifying history, which cannot be interpreted in terms of a metaphysical,

onto-theological epoch of *Seinsgeschichte* and *Seinsgeschick* or reduced to a mere enumeration of data.

Not only does every decision condemn itself to remain secret—
in the final analysis, there is nothing more to say about it ("il n'y a
rien plus à en dire")—ultimately, every genuine, that is, absolutely
singular, responsibility condemns itself to silence and demands a
sacrificium intellectus, if not more, and if only for an instant.[81] But
the more responsible (and, if one might say so, the more singular) it
is, the more guilty, the more responsible for others, it becomes. (*Plus
je suis juste—plus je suis coupable.*)[82] The mere facticity of my existence already incites (or should incite) bad conscience with respect
to, *vis-à-vis*, the Other, and thus the genuine fear of God given with
the "risk of occupying—beginning with the very *Da* of my *Dasein*—
the place of an Other and, thus, in the concrete, of exiling him,
dooming him to a miserable condition in some 'third' or 'fourth'
world, bringing him death."[83] This fear of God does not have the
modality of the *Befindlichkeit* (mood) described in *Being and Time*,
where "fear" (*Furcht*) comes to "double the intentionality of a feeling affected by a being in the world."[84] Nor does it correspond to
Angst of some sort. The fear and trembling revealed by the intrigue
of Genesis 22 has, Levinas suggests, an entirely different structure.

Abraham's decision, like any other genuine ethico-political act,
even or precisely where it passionately resists the realms of the
"ethical," the "political," and the common notion of "act," gives testimony. Abraham's decision does not testify in the sense of giving
a demonstration, a lesson or illustration for all eyes.[85] Instead, his
decision attests. Not unlike *Bezeugung*, which, according to *Being
and Time*, reveals death as "*Dasein's* most proper possibility," his attestation is "not a simple characteristic to be noted or described."[86]
Finally, any analysis that—rightly or wrongly—claims to describe
the conditions of possibility, indeed, the co-originary structures, of
all existence, of decision, of giving (oneself) death comes to be determined by a similar paradoxical attestation. The same holds for
any philosophical or literary interpretation of concrete, historical
and contemporary, examples of this attestation.

Thus, Derrida writes, if there is a "moral" to be found in the Biblical text of Genesis 22 as it is read by Kierkegaard and Levinas, we
should not too easily conclude that the narration (*récit*) is simply a
fable of responsibility. To take it for a fable would already (or still)
mean "that it loses the quality of a historic event [*événementia-*

lité]."[87] By the same token, the very act of interpreting the sacrifice of Isaac belongs, Derrida notes, to the same bloody scene that it seeks to depict, to translate, or to transcribe, if only by emphasizing some singular threads in its fabulous texture, while leaving out—that is to say, while sacrificing—others.[88] The history of the bloody conflicts between the so-called religions of the Book, Judaism, Christianity, and Islam, could be interpreted as the history of as many attempts to appropriate the secret fond of this narration of the *à dieu/adieu*, of the *unto-death*, of the *zum Tode* read as *à dieu/adieu*, and vice versa.

And yet, this history of sacrifice would forbid a reading of "death"—or, for that matter, "God"—in terms of some sort of ontological constancy, as a perennial figure or disfiguration operating from within a selfsame identity. Instead, Derrida conveys the insight that "the meaning of responsibility announces itself always as a *modality* of a 'giving oneself death.'"[89] The intricate "logic" of responsibility and irresponsibility, described *as* "the gift of death" could be regarded, Derrida suggests, as the common ground on which such different discourses as those written by Kierkegaard, Heidegger, Jan Patočka, Levinas, Jean-Luc Marion and perhaps Ricoeur stand.[90] The list could easily be expanded. The common feature among these writers is that this logic does not necessarily invoke *"the event of a revelation or the revelation of an event"*[91] to explain the paradox or, rather, the aporia of the ethical relation, its secret and its *mysterium tremendum*, its relation to the ab-solute other as well as the other of *this* other. The logic in question only needs to "think the possibility of such an event."[92] Although it can never immunize itself against reinscription in theology, it offers, strictly speaking, a "nondogmatic doublet of dogma, a philosophical and metaphysical doublet, in any case a *thinking* that 'repeats' the possibility of religion without religion."[93] Levinas's *à-dieu*, the to-God—more precisely still the *adieu*, the leavetaking, of every *à dieu*, haunted as it inevitably is by the specter of no-god or no-one's-god, *a-dieu* or *pas de dieu*—intersects with the ongoing project of a *neither theistic nor atheistic "doubling" of God* that lies at the source of all (responsible discourse on) responsibility and that does not allow itself to be reduced to the source or the resources of any one positive religion or worldview.

No phenomenology, then, to say nothing of metaphysics or philosophy, could ever hope to intuit, to construe, or to reconstruct analytically the givenness or the gift of this concept, of this concept without concept. No thought—not even the thought proposed here —could ever undo this indeterminacy, and the *"praxis"* for which it stands or that it calls into being and inspires.[94] Only its modality can be circumscribed with the help of the figure of the secret or mystery as it pervades the religions of the Book, and not them alone.

Precisely the question of attribution, of construing genealogies, of assigning a place of origination for responsibility, is at issue here. It would be difficult, even impossible, to decide whether the "knight of faith"—the figure of Abraham as he has been presented since the Genesis story was written down, including how he has been read by Kierkegaard and others—is, properly speaking, "Jewish, Christian, or Judeo-Christian-Islamic."[95] The sacrifice that he was prepared to risk should, rather, be seen as belonging to what might be called "the common treasure, the terrifying secret of the *mysterium tremendum* that is a property of all three so-called religions of the Book, the religions of the races of Abraham,"[96] and, one might add, haunts others.

The Gift of Death directly addresses the question raised by a certain place, Mount Moriah, which comes to stand for the site that situates and stages the real and symbolical sacrifices that mark history. Derrida reads Moriah as the hither side of Jerusalem, the place to which one does *not* turn one's face when one prays or otherwise contemplates one's next step. This place recalls the bloody primal scene—the *Urszene*—which founds, grounds, and (when remembered) uproots not only societies and religions, but also the most trivial decisions of our daily existence. We inhabit Moriah, writes Derrida, "every second of every day"[97]—in a nonfigural and nonrhetorical sense. Derrida recalls that according to the second book of Chronicles (chapters 3 and 8), this "so-called place of sacrifice" (*le lieu-dit du sacrifice*) is the site where God appeared to David and where Solomon decided to build the temple. But it is also the place where the Islamic holy places of the Dome of the Rock and the El Aksa are located, where we find, close by the Wall of Lamentation, the road Christ is said to have followed carrying the cross. Indeed, Derrida concludes, all the monotheisms, that is to say, all the religions of the Book, "make war with fire and blood, have always done so and all the more fiercely today, each claiming its particular perspective on this place and claiming an original historical and political interpretation of Messianism and of the sacrifice of Isaac. The reading, the interpretation, the tradition of the sacrifice of Isaac are themselves sites of bloody, holocaustic sacrifice. Isaac's sacrifice continues every day."[98]

Re-tracing the figure of *à dieu/adieu* as the silent echo of Genesis 22 and of all utter burnings, all sacrifices in which all (*holos*) is burned (*caustos*), is not to revive the Stoic doctrine of a universal conflagration in which the whole world returns to the primeval fire.[99] Nor would it be a tasteless theodicy of whatever divine or metaphysical agency allowed "Auschwitz" to happen: the murder in the camps cannot and ought not be thought in terms of a logic of sacrifice pure and simple, let alone be considered self-sacrifice.[100]

Rather, the *à dieu/adieu* names a "given death"—*la mort donnée*—given wherever and whenever responsibility comes to pass. That is to say, *everywhere* and *always*.[101] It comes as no surprise, therefore, that Derrida admits a certain resemblance or, rather, co-implication of this abyss (chaos, aporia, and antinomy) that opens up (in) every genuine decision and the open mouth (*bouche ouverte*) signaling speech (or the lack thereof) and hunger.[102]

Needless to say, it is tempting to shy away from so many uncanny and terrifying figures. What are we now to think of these lurid expressions, especially that of sacrifice? Are they really necessary—inevitable, helpful, responsible traces of mourning that cannot be removed without affirming the worst, the worst of the worst (*le pire du pire*), rather than its mere possibility? Would it not be more productive to de-transcendentalize and to de-figure the figure of death as and through sacrifice, whether symbolic or not, and to link it in a more concrete, and no less challenging, manner to the givens of the history of religion, of anthropology, of psychoanalysis, and the like?

Perhaps. But in so doing, one would lose sight of—indeed, would sacrifice—what enables Derrida's reading to unsettle confident assessments of this socio-historical material, as well as of the premises and methodologies that guide its reconstruction as data. Speaking of responsibility and of testimony in the violent language of sacrifice adds something decisive to analyses of these phenomena that would not have been possible in another—supposedly less violent and seemingly more responsible—language. Speaking of sacrifice, of the giving of death as an *à dieu/adieu* to be assumed or affirmed, reminds us of the quasi-theological overdeterminations of every genuine ethico-political decision, which are its inevitable risk. *The possibility of the worst is the condition—the limit and the de-limitation—of the best.* It is against this backdrop that Derrida can write in *The Other Heading* (*L'autre cap*): "Hope, *fear and trembling* are commensurate with the signs that are coming to us from everywhere in Europe, where, precisely, in the name of identity, be it cultural or not, the worst violences, those that we recognize all too well without yet having thought them through, the crimes of xenophobia, racism, anti-Semitism, religious or national fanaticism, are being unleashed, mixed up, mixed up with each other, but also, and there is nothing fortuitous in this, mixed in with the breath, with the respiration, with the very 'spirit' of the promise."[103]

To take our lead from the figure of the giving of death and the sacrifice it entails, to insist on its systematicity as much as on its historical singularity serves to remind us of the necessary "passage through the transcendental"[104] that problematizes any overly hasty or confident ascriptions of (divine) violence to empirical (psychological, sociological, historical, or, for that matter, linguistic and symbolic) constellations. This does not amount to justifying or calling forth horror. Instead, this logic of the sacrifice states: "only extreme horror keeps reason in a state of wakefulness [*en éveil*]. . . . the only wakefulness is wakefulness with respect to the horror."[105]

Indeed, evil may no longer be thinkable as the absence of the good, as a mere *privatio boni*. If that is so, evil must be circumscribed, if not as a presence, then at least as a certain "positivity." The word is Jean-Luc Nancy's. In his *The Experience of Freedom* (*L'expérience de la liberté*), Nancy relates the "modern *fascination* with evil" to the equally modern experience that there is "a proper 'positivity' of evil, not in the sense that it would come to contribute in one way or another to some *conversio in bonum* (which always rests on its negativity and on the negation of this negativity), but in the sense that evil, in its very negativity, without dialectical sublation, forms a positive possibility of existence."[106] This given of evil—indeed, this giving of death—by no means justifies death or legitimate violence, let alone evil. The ex-position of my always already being exposed to sacrifice or, for that matter, to Evil (*le Mal*), does not of necessity lead to an unintended justification of the unjustifiable, of violence and ultimately of war. Even though sacrifice is everywhere, there remains a striking difference between risking the worst, suspending the ethical for the sake of an absolute obligation in which the *il y a* resonates as a "modality" of transcendence, and committing a crime against humanity, deciding for the worst of the worst. As Kierkegaard says, "It is only by faith that one achieves any resemblance to Abraham, not by murder."[107]

War is everywhere, even in the heart of peace, even in peace of heart.[108] There is no way out, no interior refuge, no safe haven, here or elsewhere, which would be without terror or suffering. In a fascinating and troubling Talmudic reading, entitled "Damages Due to Fire" ("Les dommages causés par le feu"), Levinas pushes this analysis to an insupportable extreme:

> Here you have the ubiquity and the omnitemporality of the violence which exterminates: there is no radical difference between peace and war, between war and holocaust. Extermination has already begun during peacetime. . . . Everywhere war and murder lie concealed, assassination lurks in every corner. . . . There would be no radical difference between peace and Auschwitz. I do not think that pessimism can go much beyond this. Evil surpasses [dépasse] human responsibility and leaves not a corner intact where reason could collect itself [se recueillir].
>
> But perhaps this thesis is precisely a call to man's infinite responsibility, to an untiring wakefulness [éveil], to a total insomnia.[109]

We live in an age and a world—the twentieth century—which has lost its worldliness and become a place where there is no way out (le sans-issue), no localizable exterior, and which, therefore, no longer allows any proper space or dwelling where one could be (or be there): a sans-lieu and non-lieu of which the exile and the diaspora of Israel would be the universal example. And yet there will always be (and there will always have been) a chance to invent or institute a limit to limitless violence. There will always be (and there will always have been) a chance for innumerable and limitless responsibilities that would attest to the limitation of unlimited, illegitimate, or illicit violence. The claim, then, that violence is everywhere can never legitimate acquiescence in doing nothing at all.

Levinas exemplifies this paradox as follows: "Yes, there are war criminals!"[110] And they can and should be held accountable for their deeds. However, for this justice to be possible or to be done, the fires of destruction and revenge must be "transfigured" into a "protective" fire,[111] into a wall of defense. Here, the question of ethics in its necessary ex-position to the beyond-of-ethics—that is to say, to the infra-, super-, hyper-, and, in the precise sense, meta-ethical suspense of the sacrifice—transforms itself into a question of politics. This latter question is undeniably always the most urgent one. Politics, as the struggle for a lesser evil, for a mitigation, reduction, or even abolition of violence, the violence of the self as much as that of the other, should be considered an obligation no less than a necessity. Yet its pursuit of the better is always also shadowed and haunted by what — in itself or as politics' other — resembles or measures itself against the apparitions and specters of the worst.

Monastic Violence

M. B. PRANGER

This paper will confront a paradox: Can a human configuration that phrases its identity in terms of separation from physical violence be intrinsically violent? Generally speaking, we are inclined to think of civilization as a process in which physical violence is gradually banished. We should not, however, be so naive as to believe it could fully disappear. On the contrary, there are valid reasons to consider civilization a continuation of warfare by other means. The ability to recognize different layers of passions, conflicts, and scarcely controlled savagery under the smooth surface of civilized behavior is, all would agree, part and parcel of cultural sophistication. This mixed state of affairs notwithstanding, might safe havens in human society or even psychology, in however fragile and artificial a way, ever exist? Why should a book or, for that matter, the arts not qualify as such? Admittedly, books can and do cause violent reactions, though closed within their covers, they seem contained and innocent enough, however satanic their content. But what about real life? Do we not pay with a certain lifelessness· for the exclusion of physical violence from our works of art? How could we imagine our lives as a work of art, or, to put it in Robert Musil's terms, how could we begin to "live the way we read"?

Musil's terminology feeds the subject of this paper: monasticism. His *The Man Without Qualities* (*Der Mann ohne Eigenschaften*) contains notions such as remoteness and withdrawal, which we will come across in our analysis of monastic violence. Asceticism permeates the novel, as a means of understanding the breakdown of order in the beginning of this century, for *The Man Without Qualities* deals with the utopian problem of the book as a way of life. Situated in Vienna on the eve of the Great War, it evokes—retrospectively for the author and readers, by way of anticipation for the novel's protagonists—the brute violence which was to follow the seemingly idyllic prewar Viennese world of *Besitz und Bildung*. In it, the escapist culture of the ruling classes remarkably coincides with the almost mystical longing by the main character, the mathematician Ulrich, to "take a one year's sabbatical from life [*ein Jahr Urlaub des Lebens*]" to dream in a "utopia of exact life [*Utopie des exakten Lebens*]." Part of that effort is his "indulging in fanciful talk about the possibility of living the same way as one reads [*so zu leben wie man liest*]."

> And how do you do it [read a great deal]? I can give you the answer at once: your preconceptions leave out whatever doesn't suit you. The same thing has already been done by the author. In the same way you leave things out in dreams and in your imaginations. So I offer you my conclusion that beauty and excitement come into the world as a result of things having been left out. Obviously our behaviour in the midst of reality is a compromise, a medial condition in which the emotions prevent each other from developing to their full passionate intensity, blurring slightly into the grey. Children who have not yet acquired this attitude, are for that reason happier and also unhappier than adults. And I will at once add this: stupid people also leave things out. Stupidity is, after all, something that makes for happiness. I therefore suggest that we begin as follows—that we should try to love each other as though you and I were figures created by a poet and meeting in the pages of a book. In any case, however, let us leave out all the upholstery of fatty tissue that is what makes reality look round and plump.[1]

So the striving for the "utopia of exact life" is accompanied by a feeling of loss. Beauty and excitement turn out to be elusive moments in human life, whose very quality of extension guarantees a certain dullness and grayness. Ideally speaking, it should be possible to purge life of this tedium and deal with other persons as though one had met in the pages of a book. Yet for Musil, all efforts to realize this utopia are bound to succumb to the weight of reality. Alarmingly, Viennese (and Habsburg) society reveals its chaotic nature (its lack of *Ordnung*) when a military man, General Stumm von Bordwehr, tries vainly to detect a sense of order in the civil world ("General Stumms Bemühung, Ordnung in den Zivilverstand zu bringen"). But Ulrich's intellectual attempts to withdraw from society altogether in order to found a "Secretariat for Precision and Soul [*Sekretariat für die Genauigkeit und die Seele*]" are no more peaceful. Ultimately, the loss of a sense of order experienced in the quest for mystical precision is no less violent in its effect than the general's discovery of a basic emptiness in the civilian society his military apparatus is supposed to protect.

Medieval monasticism, in particular that of the twelfth century, was a literary model—or, to put it in Musil's terms, a spectacular attempt—to live by the book, to live the way one reads in order then to focus on the elements of violence implied in this attempt. Like Musil's Ulrich, the Benedictine monk—that is, a monk living according to the Rule of St. Benedict, this being the most common way of monastic life up to the twelfth century—had taken leave of life, whether permanently or just for one year.[2] Whether he had been offered to the monastery by his parents at an early age as an oblate or he had entered the monastery after a life lived to the full in the world, the monk had left behind the vicissitudes of the world. He had entered paradise. In the meantime, notions of space and time had changed. The uncertainties of the past and the future had changed into the uninterrupted rhythm of liturgical time, and space had been contracted into the narrow site of the monastery. Time had been deprived of its contingent nature, thus of its uniqueness, and space, of its extension. This transformation of temporal and spatial notions was succinctly expressed by the most eloquent spokesman of monastic life, Bernard of Clairvaux (1090–1253). After a British secular priest named Philip had made a stopover in Clairvaux on his way to Jerusalem and been so attracted by the monastic life that he decided to stay, the protest of his bishop was met by a cool reply from abbot Bernard:

> Your Philip has taken a short cut on his way to Jerusalem. Thus he arrived quickly at the place of his destination. In no time he crossed this vast and spacious sea, and sailing successfully, he has already landed on the shore of his destination and arrived in the harbour of salvation. . . . He is a devout inhabitant and a registered citizen of Jerusalem. . . . and if you insist on knowing, this is no other than Clairvaux. She herself is Jerusalem. . . . His promise to stay implies that it is here that his rest will be for evermore.[3]

This passage is more than metaphor—too much spiritual violence is in the air. In Bernard's phraseology, the Jerusalem in Palestine, whose importance in the history and the eschatology of Christian faith was universally accepted, is absorbed and transformed into the monastic site of Clairvaux. As a result, whatever metaphorical distance might exist between the two Jerusalems, for either a medieval or a modern reader, vanishes. This procedure is in accord with Bernard's hermeneutical adage: *non locus homines, sed homines locum sanctificant*:[4] things do not possess a pre-established meaning of their own, but receive their meaning from those who signify them. In terms of monastic literary theory, this means that the spiritual is in a sense prior to the literal.

Admittedly, the entire medieval system of exegesis is based on a distinction between the literal and the spiritual. Every schoolboy knew about the different layers of textual meaning, which had been taught to him through the example of the different meanings of the word "Jerusalem." According to the letter, Jerusalem meant the city of the Jews (in Palestine); according to the allegorical meaning, it meant the church of Christ; according to the mystical meaning, it meant the heavenly city; and in tropological/moral terms it meant the human soul. In monastic literature, however, this distinction was not applied in a simplistic and schematic manner.

For the monk, reading about Jerusalem—or about whatever holy theme, for that matter—was not an act of interpreting his source material, the Bible. For that, his life was too theatrical. The tropological/moral meaning of the text being of primordial importance, the monk identified with the text to so seamless a degree as to preclude whatever distance there might have been between him and its subject matter. Living in the monastery of Clairvaux did not remind him of a remote city in Palestine about which he had read in his holy book. Instead, this bare and empty place—which, by the way, did not resemble a city at all, since pictures and images were banished from Cistercian monasteries—provided his imagination with the opportunity to establish his readings on the spot, here and now, to materialize them and to contract them to the shape of his dwelling place. The rest of his life consisted in acting out his readings in prayer and song: playing the game of the angels, who, unhindered by the dimensions of space and time, are the lawful inhabitants of the heavenly Jerusalem.[5] I will return shortly to the different aspects of remembrance, forgetting, and violence implied in this monastic way of life and analyze exactly what it means to live by the book as identification and re-enactment rather than as interpretation.

At the outset, I would like to draw attention to some extramural events in the life of Bernard of Clairvaux, champion of the monastic Jerusalem, which accentuate the paradoxical nature of his Musil-like attempt to purge life of its gray dimensions and to live by the book. Once a Benedictine monk had withdrawn from the world and, like Philip, had laid down his soul to rest for evermore, he was supposed to stay put. Where better could he turn to after so decisive a move? This principle of the *stabilitas loci* was considered one of the pillars of monastic life. Bernard, who as an abbot was supposed to live an exemplary life and thus to uphold the principle of *stabilitas loci*, sinned blatantly time and again against this principle. Through a kind of double bluff he also turned his "involuntary" wanderings outside the monastery into an extra effort to purge life of its gray dimensions.

One of the main occasions on which Bernard left the monastery was to preach the Second Crusade in 1146.[6] At the request of the pope, he traveled all over Europe to incite people to take up the cross. Suddenly his lofty view of Clairvaux as the heavenly Jerusalem seems to have given way to crudely literal and violent language. The situation in the Holy Land, so his preaching voice fulminated, had become desperate because of the sacrilegious presence of the Saracens and their attacks on the Holy Places:

> "The waters have risen to the soul" of Christ and the pupil of his eye has been touched. Now both swords [i.e., the sword of the Church and the sword of the princes] should be drawn on the occasion of the suffering of the Lord: for once more the Lord suffers on the same spot where he suffered before. Who else should draw the sword but you [the pope]? . . . Now a voice is heard of him who cries out: I am coming to Jerusalem to be crucified once more [*Vox clamantis: Venio Ierosolymam iterum crucifigi*].[7]

In the argumentation that follows, it will be useful to keep the words "Now a voice is heard of him who cries out [*vox clamantis*]" in mind. The Second Crusade was an utter failure. In consequence, Bernard, who had been the *auctor intellectualis* of the whole enterprise, was accused of being a false and ineffectual prophet and preacher. Bernard countered this criticism in what I consider a spectacular example of the double bluff. In literary terms, Bernard, who as a monk and abbot officially and professionally was supposed to live by the book (that is, to live a life in which extramural vicissitudes and violence are to be absorbed in a peaceful and spiritual existence), suspends that life in order to deal with "real" violence and warfare, only once more to reduce the cruelties of history to the shape of his monastic, literary or bookish, existence.

To better grasp this complex move, we must examine the different stages of his argument. First, there is the priority of the metaphorical and spiritual: Clairvaux *is* Jerusalem, leaving little or no room for the original. Next comes into focus Jerusalem in Palestine, for whose liberation "two swords should be drawn," that is, for whom the forces of the Church and the world should be combined. The apocalyptic nature of this explosion of violence should be heeded. The idea that at the end of world history diabolical powers would manifest themselves, only to be combated by Christian forces in a final and inevitably triumphant campaign to convert the world to God, has always been part and parcel of the Christian view of history. We should not be surprised, then, that rumors of an attack on Jerusalem were seen as a signal of the end. Yet after the Crusade failed, Bernard returned to his monastery, leaving his critics bewildered and in doubt as to whether he had left it at all—as, we shall argue, he had not.

In his reply to his critics, Bernard shows himself unrepentant.[8] Admittedly, he is willing to accept the tragic nature of the event and to ponder, together with the other mourners, the cruel sight of the Crusaders lying slain in the desert and the even crueller absence of God, on whose orders the Crusade had been undertaken and whose failure to deliver success was bound to reflect negatively on his prophet. In the next passage, however, rather than console the bereaved relatives of the Crusaders by trying in one way or another to lend meaning to the horrors of history, Bernard turns attention on himself. Through a subtle process of identification with Old Testament heroes such as Moses rather than with the Israelites in the desert (alias the Crusaders), with God (in the book of Judges) as the supreme commander of the army of Israel rather than with the (twice unsuccessful) army itself (alias the Crusaders), and, eventually, with Christ, who wrought quite a few miracles but was not taken at his word, he highlights the lamentable and solitary fate of the prophet in both the past and the present.

Bernard's withdrawal from the cruel events of history bears the hallmark of bookishness. But the book to which Bernard refers, the Bible, is not about past matters and masters. Taking on the shape, the *figura*, of the biblical protagonists themselves (Moses, God, Christ), Bernard destroys the distance between the book as history and its present performance. His way of reading that book is to enact it on the spot. Ultimately, that spot is, again, the Jerusalem of Clairvaux, just as the past is nothing but the present of monastic life. Thus it becomes clear that Bernard's excursion into the world of cruelty and violence, in linguistic terms, his literalization of spiritual and metaphorical language, has remained monastic, and for that reason "bookish," all along. To illustrate this point, I return to the passage just quoted, in which Bernard writes to the pope about the horrors of the pagans' attack on Jerusalem. His call to meet (pagan) violence with (Christian) violence has a remarkably monastic ring about it, however: "A voice is heard of him who cries out: I am coming to Jerusalem to be crucified once more," the *vox clamantis*, is an allusion to the Song of Songs, where the voice of the bridegroom is heard in the fields. This allusion is further elaborated when in the following the pope is addressed as the *amicus sponsi*, the friend of the bridegroom. In other words, right in the middle of extramural business, Bernard evokes scenes from the Canticle and colors his call for violence with words from the biblical love song. From a literary point of view, he does just what he does when writing about lofty, spiritual matters. For him the basic *figura* of monastic life is the conversation, the acting out of the love game between the bride and groom in the Song of Songs. All the different figures he comes across both in his reading of the Bible and in his meetings with contemporaries are reduced to actors in that theater. Leaving that (monastic) theater only heightens the sense of drama. Is it not the apex of theatricality to see the uncertainties of history—such as the problems surrounding the preaching of the Second Crusade, which seem quite unrelated to the ritual and enclosed life of the monastery—be presented as pictures from a book? In that book, the Bible, which itself is reduced to the drama of the Song of Songs, the bridegroom has temporarily left the bedroom of the bride to rest in the fields, but his remote voice echoes battle and violence. Wrapped in that image is another one: the voice of the remote lover belongs to Christ returning to Jerusalem to be once more crucified.

Theater's effectivity can best be understood if one understands the parameters of the stage and the expectations of the audience. Similarly, Bernard's account of his wheeling and dealing outside the monastery makes fullest sense within the monastery's confines. There, where the dimensions of time and space, of Jerusalem condensed out of Palestine, have been contracted in a narrow spot, the *vox clamantis*, the remote voice of the suffering Christ, reveals its full dramatic impact, and Christ's distant and lonely fight comes to the fore. If we rephrase the foregoing analysis of Bernard's literary moves in terms of the wish of Musil's Ulrich to "live the way one reads," the following picture emerges. Bernard starts out from a bookish existence, the monastic life according to the Rule of St. Benedict. Next, he mixes his feelings with a little gray—namely, makes excursions into the extramural world of time and space, only to reduce that world once more to the shape of a bookish and theatrical existence: the Song of Songs. However clever, that procedure is not the same as Musil's "loving one another as if you and I were figures created by a poet and meeting in the pages of a book." Spatial and temporal extension is still suggested as a condition for the meaningfulness of monastic, mystical life. What are the mechanics, what is the intrinsic nature, of living by the book, what process of remembrance and forgetting, of love and violence, is being enacted in the monastic way of life?

Before discussing those questions in more detail, I should like to raise another, which might shed light on the nature of monastic language. Can the way Bernard manipulates monastic language to both reconstruct and destroy extramural language, as he apparently did in preaching the Second Crusade, be interpreted in terms of a mystical postulate? In modern debates about this issue, mystical language is often described as an elusive combination inside language of both presence and absence, affirmation and abnegation, although the two can no longer be seen as simple oppositions. One of the characteristics of this "mystical postulate" is that it reveals itself, as Michel de Certeau puts it,[9] as a fundamental *volo*, or, in Derrida's terms, as a *nombre des oui*.[10] However, this *volo* or *oui* should not be taken to express simple affirmation. Being absolute in the etymological sense of the word (I follow here Hent de Vries's summary of Certeau's argument[11]), it absolves itself from all objects and ends. Thus it is beyond the control of "normal" affirmation and negation. It is prepropositional. Therefore it manifests itself only in the modality of the future perfect. The "yes" has, in a way, already taken place. It has always already been given, although it never gives itself, as such.

> Instead of attempting to define its purported 'object,' to understand mysticism would therefore mean: to formalize the different aspects of its writings, of its 'style' or 'tracing,' of an infinitely reiterated (i.e., repeated, altered and even annihilated) invisible step (or *pas*). And it is only around this essential indeterminacy that all mystic speech would be centred and receive its peculiar *force*: a force, de Certeau claims, that is nothing else than the echo in language of the *divine anger* and *violence* that Jacob Böhme and others postulate at the origin of everything that exists, at the very beginning of history.[12]

De Vries's discussion of Derrida's reading of Certeau's *The Mystic Fable* takes this line of thought one step further.

Not only is the 'yes' strictly speaking never first—as if it were just another *primum intelligible* or *principium*—it also calls for another 'yes.' For, as a promise, no affirmation can stand alone: it envelops at least one more 'yes' that has to come in order to remember and re-confirm it. And it is precisely this reiteration which brings with it an inescapable menace or risk. As a consequence, the fabulous 'yes' is contaminated *a priori* by the possibility of forgetting that could also be signaled by its mere mechanical repetition or parody.[13]

Almost all these notions can be seen in one way or another to figure in Bernard's texts. Bernard's claim, for instance, that the Jerusalem of Clairvaux is the real one can be interpreted as a yes that goes beyond affirmation and negation, as a promise asking for both oblivion and reiteration. Precisely because the Jerusalem of Clairvaux, unlike its historical counterpart in Palestine, is a uto-pian place, a promise rather than "reality," in which one lives the way one reads, it offers the opportunity for endless reiteration in the shape of an unlimited number of configurations. That is what the ritual of endlessly repeated prayer and song is about. In that re-spect the monastery can be said to function as a mystical postulate, although it might rightly be questioned whether the ritual reitera-tion coincides with Derrida's interpretation of it.

There is one basic difference, however, between how Certeau and Derrida use the mystical postulate and how it is used in Clairvaux. This is how violence, or however one would describe Boehme's Ur-notion of divine anger, is or is not incorporated in the body of mystical language. In order to prevent their "yes" or *volo* from falling back into the realm of affirmation and negation, the later thinkers force themselves to maintain the notion of indeter-minacy to the bitter end.[14] Thus one ends up in a position in which either it becomes hard, if not impossible, to distinguish between the fabulous "yes" and its parody, between divine and Nietzschean space, or, as Certeau puts it, mystic speech becomes the celebration of madness, just as the early monks went to the Egyptian desert to be "the operators of the Spirit in the land and language of the Liar."[15]

In my view, a certain ambiguity can be detected in the use of "indeterminacy." On the one hand, it intends to guarantee the in-trinsic freedom, the ab-soluteness of the mystical postulate. On the other hand, it functions as an almost polemical concept, evoking, in a bipolar way, both the indeterminate aspects of mystical lan-guage and the rejected models of more objective speech. The second model of indeterminacy may explain the almost exclusive inter-

est of modern students of mysticism in the "other," mad side of it
(*folie: l'idiot, la femme, l'enfant, le sauvage*), or, more generally, in
negative theology as a means to speak, or not to speak, about God
(although Derrida's article "Comment ne pas parler" is a subtle exception to this rule). It is Eckhart's and Tauler's *Gelassenheit* and
Abgeschiedenheit, their desert/*Öde*, the madness of the possessed
of Loudun, rather than the sound articulateness of Bernard's monastic or Bonaventure's scholastic mysticism that capture the imagination of modern readers of mystical texts. Might it be that for Certeau *cum suis* other types of mysticism are of less interest because
they too much resemble the kind of models, the static codes (the
church, the state, doctrine) that modern mystics have intended to
open up?

What I criticize in Certeau is not that he links his mystical postulate (the *volo*) to divine violence, to madness, otherness, etc. What
I hold against him is that, flirting with notions such as violence and
madness, he secretly makes himself dependent on those models
of articulate language, of church and doctrine as historical bodies,
whose insufficient dynamics, in his view, have been brought to the
fore by the stranger, the wild man, the mystic. In other words, his
mystical postulate seems to be less indeterminate than he would
like it to be, associated as it is with very determinate historical developments. What is really indeterminate (in the sense of Certeau's
volo and Derrida's "yes," in its first, intrinsic sense) would indeed
be the language of the monks in the Egyptian desert: messengers of
the Spirit, yet indistinguishable from liars. But I know of no attempt
yet adequately to describe this simultaneous presence of truth and
lies in monastic literature. However, by focusing exclusively on the
"negative" aspects: the desert, withdrawal (*un lieu pour se perdre,
Gelassenheit*, etc.), Certeau does insufficient justice to his own
volo, to the "yes," however justified may be his fear of falling back
into "objective" language. I would like to illustrate this thesis with
an example. Talking about Boehme's concept of divine violence as
underlying everything that exists, Certeau remarks: "Thus the precondition of mystical discourse plants an act of will in the middle of
a desert [*La préalable du discours mystique plante ainsi un événe-
ment du vouloir au milieu d'un désert*]."[16] In my view, talking about
a desert rather than *the* desert is a contradiction in terms not only
for the mystic himself but also for the historian of mysticism. Here
a kind of indeterminacy (*a* rather than *the*) is suggested that we can
do without. Not unlike violence, "desert" does not allow for divi-

sion or multiplication, however diverse (and deceptive) its echoes may be. It is all-embracing and as such indeterminate, "ab-solved," in the way Certeau himself and Derrida would like it to be. That is the only way the desert can be a plantation for the "yes." The moment this "yes" in the desert sounds, it is unique and universal, just as there is only one Jerusalem (wherever that may be). That, so it seems to me, is the condition on which the "yes" and the *volo* can be repeated, forgotten, and betrayed.

On my way back to the theme of violence in twelfth-century monastic literature, I might rephrase my criticism of Certeau and others as follows. In my view, this focus on abnegation in past mystics shuns the power of images, as though images would be too solid a part of established corpora of language (such as doctrinal and devotional ones) to be taken seriously as performances of the mystical postulate. Admittedly, Eckhart's thought, and for that matter, that of other mystics between the fourteenth and eighteenth centuries, is marked by a greater degree of abstractness than that of their medieval predecessors. However, the power of Eckhart's language, for instance, is to be found in the way notions such as nothingness and *Abgeschiedenheit* electrify his subtle language about God and the adventures of the soul rather than in those notions themselves as manifestations of an almost nameless *volo*. As things are, though, I fail to see how, by focusing on madness, Certeau manages to get a grip on the intrinsic violence inherent to mystical language. Talking about the mystical postulate as *a* desert rather than about *the* desert tout court; in other words, ex- and abs-tracting an "absolute performative" from the linguistic structure of the texts under discussion, is, in my view, bound to reveal a conspicuous lack of performative power and lack of violence on the part of the interpreter.

Now let us entirely return to twelfth-century monastic literature. Bernard indeed makes a kind of mystical postulate: the Jerusalem of Clairvaux inside whose walls angelic language is being spoken. The angelic nature of that language is reminiscent of Ulrich's dream of living the way he reads. Purged of "the fatty tissue, the plumpness of life," there is room for "the emotions to develop their full passionate intensity" without running the risk of slightly blurring "into the grey." What I would like to analyze in this last section of my paper is the intrinsic violence implied in twelfth-century literary accounts of the monastic life of "full passionate intensity." As a result, we face the following paradox: monastic, angelic language,

54

which is supposedly innocent and peaceful, manifests itself in the shape of a heightened sense of violence and passion.

In the preceding pages, we have already come across the technique a monastic author like Bernard used to articulate this passion and violence. Touching extramural, violent affairs (the attack on Jerusalem, the tragic fate of the Crusaders) with the magic rod of his Canticle-language (the *vox clamantis*, the *figura* of the deserted lover etc.), he turned historical events into the literary drama of the Song of Songs. Extracting the plumpness from the physical suffering of history, he had left the nonmonastic protagonist of history cruelly behind. That in itself can, of course, be called an act of extreme violence. But, then, it may be asked, is this not the general problem of "bookishness"? Exactly what is the intrinsic nature of violence underlying so cruel a behavior toward the outside world? What does the inside, the book, of Bernard's monastic world look like? What happens in a community living according to Musil's adage: "Your preconceptions leave out whatever doesn't suit you. The same thing has already been done by the author. In the same way you leave things out in dreams and in your imaginations. So I offer you my conclusion that beauty and excitement comes into the world as a result of things having been left out"?

First of all, this world is built around a process of forgetting. The monk who has entered the monastery has left behind the plumpness of worldly existence and the uncertainties and vicissitudes of its passions, lust, and ambitions. In an endless process of reiteration the monk substitutes for the world of passion the ritual of praying and singing. Forgetting his murky past and its language, he gradually identifies with a new and better body of language, that of Scripture in its performative-ritual appearance. Doing so, he changes from man into angel. He no longer speaks with the tongue of worldly ambition and material gain. All he does is repeat the drama of Scripture, in terms of the Song of Songs, repeat the cry of the bride for the return of the bridegroom and the cry of the bridegroom that he is crucified once more.

For the monk, quite a number of things have been left out, but what about beauty and excitement? Further, what is the meaning of reiteration in this context? Does ritual repetition (of scriptural and liturgical language) allow for the "indeterminacy" caused by madness, the stranger coming in from the outside, parody, lies, and violence? Or does its enclosed and coded nature place it firmly and unmoveably on the side of "positive" language?

In an extremely interesting treatise, "About the Four Degrees of Violent Love,"[17] the monk Richard of St. Victor, a contemporary of Bernard, gives an extraordinary account of the stages of spiritual love. At the first stage one is wounded by love like the bride in the Song of Songs, so as not to be able to resist its fatal attraction. At the second stage one cannot escape it anymore. Being unable to think of anything else, one has become the prisoner of one's own desire. At the third stage, every other affection is banished as one focuses exclusively on the one and unique object of desire. The last stage is marked by immoderation and the impossibility of satisfying one's desire: *qui bibit adhuc sitiet*. Drunk with love, one suffers from the *furor* of an incurable disease, which may bring one to the brink of insanity: *insatiabilitas*/insatiability. As a result of this vehemence and this insatiability of desire, love may easily turn into hatred and vice versa. How often do we not see that lovers simultaneously love and hate one another, make life impossible for one another out of sheer passion, caught in a web in which "neither the fire of desire can melt down the ice of hatred nor the intensity of hatred can extinguish the fire of burning desire. It is beyond measure, beyond nature that this fire keeps burning in water because the fire of love gains more force from this mutual opposition than from the two living peacefully apart."[18]

Reading this passage without any knowledge about the religious status and aims of its author, one might be under the impression that Richard here is singing the praise of worldly passion. The opposite holds true. In a remarkable corollary to this passage, Richard warns the reader not to confuse worldly and spiritual love, thus bringing about a spectacular reversal. Violent love exclusively applies to the latter, that is, to the monk who has left the plumpness of worldly passion behind. For what would society look like if lovers were permanently absorbed by one another, so as to forget about their duty to keep society going? Further, how bitter love would turn out to be if it banished all other affections. Finally, could one think of anything worse than a love which would incessantly run hot and cold? To live life driven by a desire of "burning ice and ice-cold fire" would be but a foretaste of hell (*quaedam forma futurae damnationis*).[19] Violent love should be reserved, then, for an object proportionate to it, that is, an object without measure, which is really insatiable: God.

What Richard does here is quite unlike the mystic who claims a separate desert, a stranger, a madman, or violence in order to gain access to the mystical performative. He presents a picture of unbridled passion, desire, and ecstasy, which, at first sight, is indistinguishable from the general human experience. Then quite a number of things appear to have been left out. The plumpness of life is gone; the reduction of spiritual love enters. With one bold stroke—which recalls the force by which Bernard turned the cruelties of the Crusade into love poetry—the shape of the monastery is imposed on the insatiability of desire, not to close it off, but to open it up. In sum, the lovers appear to have met in the pages of a book. Really living out one's desire, that is, being so violently passionate outside the bookish existence of spiritual-monastic life, would be a foretaste of hell. Now it becomes clear that for the monastic author, only in the utopian place of the monastery can paradise and desert, heaven and hell, order and chaos, sanity and madness, fire and ice, love and hatred, lies and truth, peace and violence coalesce. In monastic literature, all those notions are telescoped into one another, and it is up to the reader to delight in the simultaneous experience of both their combined and separate occurrence. That is what monastic violence is about. To my mind, this "full passionate intensity" makes itself most powerfully felt in Bernard's mise-en-scène of Jacob's fight with the Angel, echoing the *vox clamantis* of the suffering Christ: "Fight with the angel lest you succumb (Genesis 32:24), for the kingdom of heaven suffers violence and the violent take it by force (Matthew 11:12). Or, is this not a fight: 'My beloved is mine, and I am his (Cant. 2:16)'?"[20]

Characteristic Violence; or, The Physiognomy of Style

MARIAN HOBSON

> To write naturally [is] to stray neither from the turn of phrase
> nor the character for which nature has given us a vocation; . . .
> in a word, to think naturally is to stay in the singularity of mind
> which has been allotted to us and in the same way as each face has
> its physiognomy, each mind also bears a difference proper to it.
> —Marivaux, *Journal et oeuvres diverses*

> Personal size and mental sorrow have certainly no necessary pro-
> portions. A large, bulky figure has as good a right to be in deep
> affliction, as the most graceful set of limbs in the world. But, fair
> or not fair, there are unbecoming conjunctions, which reason will
> patronize in vain—which taste cannot tolerate,—which ridicule
> will seize.   —Jane Austen, *Persuasion*

At the end of the eighteenth century and in the early nineteenth, a veritable mania for physiognomy swept western Europe.
Though Kant in 1798 described it as past, as lingering only in
the art of cultivating taste, and there not in matters of content,
but only in customs, manners, and usages,[1] it was taken seriously
much longer and more remained of it than we are perhaps aware.
Alphonse Berthillon, the founder of physical anthropometry as a
"new method of determining individual identity" in criminal investigation,[2] Cesare Lombroso, who sought to pick out "degener-
ates" with criminal tendencies before they had committed crimes,[3]
and, recently, work suggesting a correlation between narrowness
of the face and an inward-looking personality in infants,[4] all work
in the physiognomic tradition, as indeed do firms which use appli-
cants' handwriting (on grounds other than legibility) as a method
of selecting their personnel. Kant's implied distinction between
"social intercourse and knowledge of men," with which physiognomy can help, and science, a status he refuses it even in the future,
might serve here.[5] But, interestingly, science becomes a matter of
the chances of co-occurrence. Degrees of probability in the chances
of correlation between two examples of prose, or handwriting, or
body fluid make possible unique identifications of the individual

with a kind of scientific certainty. Thus "intercourse and knowl-edge of men"—or opinion and "idle chatter," as Hegel calls physi-ognomic judgments—attempt scientifically to predict future activi-ties or to predicate present qualities of an individual through the body, or handwriting, or style.

In the "diverse remarks" at the end of his discussion of physi-ognomy, Kant gives as the opinion of a "clever, traveling German doctor" that the inhabitants of Newgate in London, Bicêtre in Paris, and the Rasphuis in Amsterdam were "for the most part boney and convinced of their superiority." He condemns, however, the "violent" disappropriation made by the English actor Quin when he says of someone: "If this man is not a rascal, then the Creator does not write a legible hand."[6] The problem is that of character-izing. The title of the second part of Kant's *Anthropology* is "The Anthropological Characteristic"; its subtitle, "Of the Art of Recog-nizing the Inside of a Man from the Outside," is further glossed "from what one can recognize the particularity [*Eigentümlichkeit*] of each man."[7] Even though Kant refuses such violent appropria-tions and disappropriations in recognizing "particularity" (there are other, often stiffly humorous demurrals in the text), the pull exer-cised on Kant's anthropology by Lavater's physiognomy is apparent. Lavater (1741–1801), a Protestant pastor in Zurich and the main in-stigator and exponent of the physiognomical fashion at the end of the century, defines physiognomy thus: "the talent of discovering the interior of Man by his exterior—of perceiving by certain natu-ral signs what does not immediately strike the senses."[8] The char-acteristic is a "semiotics," a doctrine of signs, as it was in Leibniz's *characteristica universalis*. But it also points to the quality of your character, the way you are "signed," so to speak. Here the character-istic has a double function: it divides people into types or roles; it is of this or of that sort, whether by natural disposition or by tempera-ment. Throughout the century it has a link with the theater, with the development of a new kind of theater and new kinds of roles (as in Diderot and Goldoni). At the same time, "character" makes for individuality. In Kant's account, it is what you have (or don't have), in that your reason prescribes to you your principles, you are self-determining, you make yourself.[9] The first sense of "character" occurs in the realm of nature, the second in the realm of freedom. In Kant's divisions—"characteristic of the person; of the sex; of the people; of the species"—the realm of freedom appears only in "of the person" and "of the species," where the self-determination which was character in the second, absolute sense becomes also character in the first sense, the specific characteristic of man as against other species.[10]

For Lavater, a phenomenologically based semiotics determines the characteristic. For him, the physical, moral, and intellectual being

> never can become an object of observations and research to himself but as it is manifested in the body, by that which is visible, sensible, perceptible, in Man. There is not, in the whole extent of Nature, a single object whose properties and virtues are discoverable, in any other way than the external relations which fall under the examination of the Senses. These external indications determine the Characteristic of every Being; they are the foundation of all human knowledge. Man would be reduced to a state of total ignorance of himself and of the objects which surround him, unless, through universal Nature, every species of power and of life resided in a perceptible exterior; unless every object possessed a Character adapted to its nature and extent; announced at first sight what it was; and furnished a criterion to distinguish it from what it was not.[11]

Within this differentiated whole of Nature, man is distinguished from all other animals by his physiognomy: "the Head, especially the face; the figure of its bones compared to those of every other animal, discover to the more profound Observer, to the man who possesses a purer sentiment of truth, the pre-eminence and sublimity of the intellectual faculties."[12] By a kind of circle, the comparing observer discovers his own superlative in himself, in man.

Lavater insists on the difficulty of the enterprise; he also makes of it a kind of public concern. His publication of the first volume of *Physiognomial Fragments to Promote the Knowledge and Love of Mankind (Physiognomische Fragmente zur Beförderung der Menschenkenntnis und Menschenliebe)* in 1775 was followed annually by three others, which continued as well as expanded the matter of the first, and which compounded the textually composite nature of this collection of fragments and addenda by containing passages, sometimes unflagged, written by Herder and Goethe, among others, as well as excerpts from many of the earlier writers on physiognomy.[13] The work is also intellectually composite, with chapters on quite varied subjects (e.g., the humors, statues, natural history, moral qualities, and physiognomy as a science), their arguments illustrated by commentaries on engravings of a provenance every bit as heterogeneous. Friends and acquaintances were encouraged to send in engravings, which were used in addition to famous portraits, prints of statues, and pictures of ideal figures—the Laocoon or Christ, for instance. There is a gallery of Swiss notables. Fortunately, Lavater kept a copy with the names attached: some are his friends, others are from the Sturm and Drang coterie (Herder, Hamann, Goethe), still others appear to be portraits supplied from afar, whose originals Lavater did not know. This "promotion of the knowledge and love of mankind," to quote the subtitle of the book, joined with the method of composition, give a proselytizing air, a strangely speculative mixing of the personal and the public, which his enemies also found in the use he made of his vast network of correspondents.[14] The mode of composition gives the status of examples to the engravings: they bear a weight of moral commentary as well as an insistence on the need to keep up with the group enterprise. On three portraits of Admiral Anson, for example, Lavater comments: "He who remarks not the sensible difference of these three noses, most assuredly does not possess the Physiognomical Spirit of Observation."[15] The examples indeed function in the double sense Kant built into his account of character: they are arbitrarily chosen "details," cut out of a context standing out on the page as a member of their particular class, which, as examples in the commentary, they illustrate. ("Example" is derived from *eximere*, "to take out.") Yet they may also signify what is exemplary in the sense of being signal and significant, in some sense unique.[16]

Analogy and Proportion

For Lavater, exterior signs point to determinate or determinable characteristics: "These external indications determine the Characteristic of every Being: they are the foundation of all human knowledge"; the aim is "to pierce through all these coverings into his real character, to discover in these foreign and contingent determinations, solid and fixed principles by which to settle what the Man really is."[17] This is universal human practice, it is how you choose a soldier or a servant: "this tacit but universal acknowledgment, that the exterior, the visible, the surface of objects indicates their interior, their properties; that every external sign is an expression of internal qualities."[18] It is also a science, or will be.

Behind this phenomenology construed as semiotics lies a strange hinterland. In an earlier work, Lavater had claimed that the language of Heaven would be immediate, natural expression of the feelings, both successive and simultaneous, and that such a language would be "physiognomical, pantomime, musical."[19] He explains that as Christ is the true image of the invisible God, which can in a few moments awaken impressions that a continuous description by the highest archangel could not achieve, so each man is complete expression, beyond what any words could attain. Everything, not just eyes or lips, but each finger, each muscle, is a meaningful language, nothing but expression, nothing but physiognomy, and "visible presentation of the invisible, nothing but revelation and language of truth."[20] To this can be added the language of gesture and the language of tones, made of mixed and simultaneous sounds; each nerve and muscle, not just the tongue, can bring forth a component of the individual's sound. Ever since Goethe's review of Lavater's *Prospects of Eternity (Aussichten in die Ewigkeit)*, Swedenborg's influence on this text has been remarked: Swedenborg's angels do not speak in language; the inhabitants of Jupiter, for instance, speak via facial expression.[21] In the *Physiognomical Fragments*, however, for Lavater this immediacy of meaning in faces and bodies is both present and absent, present because subject to a "tacit but universal acknowledgement"[22] that faces express, absent because the expression has to be conceptualized by an effort of the physiognomist, who must discover the correlation between inside and outside:

> Physiognomy would be accordingly be, the Science of discovering the relation between the exterior and the interior—between the visible surface and the invisible spirit which it covers—between the animated, perceptible matter, and the imperceptible principle which impresses this character of life upon it—between the apparent effect, and the concealed cause which produces it.[23]

Lavater says many times in the *Fragments* that the correlation is between cause and effect; it is visible as the "characteristic signs."[24] Nature works only from the unique to the unique. It does not put together features as a printer does letters; the force which forms the eye forms the nose as well. There is a homogeneity of parts and of force in the workings of mind and body, an unarbitrary harmony of the visible and the invisible. If one does not assume *a priori* this irrefutable harmony of every single part of each organic body with its whole, then beyond doubt one can at least take it *a posteriori*, for certain outlines of the skull are only to be found with certain noses and certain jaws, and not with others. Both "natural" tones (tones of joy or sorrow) and "natural" lines are effects which presuppose certain efficient causes, and which spread throughout the organic universe. It is, for instance, a general law of nature that all perpendicularities of the face represent hardnesses of character, all curves weaknesses.[25] Such general laws highlight the essence of the characteristic, which is a sharpening of expression by classification: Lavater finds a universal, determining value in the perpendicular line. Yet every effect of nature is unique and uniquely bound up with the other effects produced in a face. Thus nature does appear to work with an alphabet like a printer, after all, throwing down the same letters in different combinations. This enables characterization. Yet nature also organizes a system of universal correspondence which is uniquely determining, a determination Lavater calls "cause and effect."

But the determining system, the physiognomic unity on which Lavater insists, is one of analogy between parts, not one of cause and effect. "Each part of an organic whole is of a piece with the combined whole, and bears the character of it." As with a plant, every part is interconnected. Analogy directs even the changes in a face—"these changes are still analogous to the face itself . . . . It can change only after its own manner, and every affected, borrowed, imitated or heterogeneous movement, still preserves its individuality, when determined by the nature of the combined whole, belongs only to that particular being."[26] And *ex ungue leonem*: "The smallest wrinkle of the forehead is analogous to the structure of the whole forehead, or, in other words, it is an effect of the whole."[27]

The English translation puffs Lavater's work as essentially designed for connoisseurs and artists. Certain social practices may have contributed to the vogue for physiognomy: the taking of silhouettes, exactly contemporary, and discussed by Lavater; the importance of drawing as a female "accomplishment"; the division between line and color.[28] The artist Fuseli, a longtime friend of Lavater, contributed engravings and a preface to the English translation. For him, Lavater's work was important because it develops techniques for expressing "unity of character" in a painting. It also teaches what only a little earlier was called "costume": "By consulting Physiognomy only can History [painting] hope to discriminate the forms of various climates, and to stamp its figures with national character."[29] This does not, however, imply the recommendation of a portrayal of the real world;[30] on the contrary, it liberates the artist from the need to follow an external model. It is the "mother of correctness," the science of "ascertaining from the measure of the solid parts [of man] the precise proportions of the moveable." This proportion is subject to a constraint: that of ancient art. "The whole of every proportionate object consists in the correspondence of singly imperceptible elements, and becomes a deformed man without it. On this process rests the still-unattained excellence of ancient art. . . . Let the twelfth part of an inch be added to, or taken from, the space between the nose and the upper lip of the Apollo, and the god is lost." Behind such a remark is the vast contemporary work of measuring ancient statues, of inquiring whether their effect was based on the use of proportion, on the repetition of a unit of measure throughout a work, or, on the contrary, on a fixed plan of relation according to predetermined character (for Antinous, Hercules, or Apollo), not toward use of the "model," not toward working from nature (which is the fault in Dürer's Adam or Caravaggio's Christ). Line, shape, and profile are stable, capable of being plotted on a grid or expressed as a proportion, unlike the fleshy parts of the face.

Comparison with Diderot is instructive here. Both Diderot and Lavater accept that "each individual differs from every other individual of the same species."[31] Each individual has a coherence within its difference from other individuals. Diderot implies that the unity at work within that difference is a projective one: it is one that nature sees, though we may not. An artist following nature and the model in all their detail might then be far more than the slavish imitator that many have called him. And yet any representation, even an "ideal" one, mangles nature. If nature developed the whole from a part of a work of art which "corrects" nature, the foot of the Medici Venus (the Venus de Milo), for example, she might construct a monster. "Received proportions" are perhaps rules of convention, based on our ignorance. Here the characteristic begins to be a justification for representing nature as she is, and not idealizing her, because we may project that unity into what we see, while still finding it ugly.[32] Moreover, in the great preamble to the Salon of 1767, Diderot claims that an artist works, not by conscious attention to proportion, but with "an underground, secret notion of analogy,"[33] built up by a long process of successive and forgotten observation. "Accurate" representation is a receding mirage; you would need the portrait of an arm, a hand, a nail.[34] The artist constructs an "ideal model of beauty," which is historically and geographically based, forming for a while the spirit, but never the embodiment, of the character, the taste, of a people, a century, a school. Analogy, then, is a process without term; within representation it reforms the human body in relation to an absent ideal "which existed nowhere but in the head of the Agasias, the Raphaels, the Poussins."[35] Neither the unity of nature nor the ideal line of art is available, and Diderot describes both in terms of formation: one is postulated through the different relations which are developing—in the face of the woman who has gone blind, for instance; the other is a continuing projection by genius from the givens of the culture. Rather than capping with a concept this sense of continuous development, limiting its scope, Diderot's prose and its rhythms create and sustain it.[36] He makes mobile and tentative what Lavater treats as determinate or determinable.

The Characteristics of the Species: Man as Species

In these passages, Diderot speaks of "the feet of the hunchback," "the neck, the shoulders, the breast of a woman who has lost her eyes in her youth."[37] The elements as they interconnect form the physiology of a physical type. Another, chronologically and thematically related work, his *Rameau's Nephew* (*Le Neveu de Rameau*), is full of lists of trades and professions, of moral characters, of characterizing gestures. The entomologist Reaumur "'distributes the class of flies into sewing, measuring, mowing, you [the "ME" of the dialogue] the species of men into carpenters, scaffolders, runners, dancers, singers.' . . . And then he begins to smile, to imitate the admiring man, the beseeching man, the obliging man."[38] The trades, the different varieties of flattering dependence, are so many species of man. Rameau can imitate their particularities: the mincing walk of the flirt; the society priest, lifting his long coat, breviary under his left arm, head on one side, eyes hypocritically lowered. The model for this is the classification of animal species. For Lavater and his friends, too:

> Every animal possesses an essential quality which distinguishes it from another. In the same way, one species differs from another, not by the structure only; the variety consists also in the difference of the leading character in each. This is manifested by a particular form, by the visible structure of the body. Every species has a character, as well as a form peculiar to itself.
> May it not be inferred now from analogy, that every one of the

principal qualities of the soul must have its expression in a particular form of body—just as every leading quality of animals is manifested in the combined form which is peculiar to them.[39]

The expressiveness of animals and their relation to human faces—the majesty of the lion, the superciliousness of the camel— had been explored by G. B. Della Porta in his famous *De humana physiognomonia* of 1603 and by the painter Charles Le Brun at the end of the seventeenth century. (It is hard not to believe that there is in this a tenuous but persistent trace of ancestral totemism.[40]) The fablelike linking of qualities to animal species—for Le Brun, pigs are "dirty, lubricious, greedy, and lazy"[41]—adds a character to a visible form, unique to the species. By analogy from animals, the leading characteristic of the human soul has its expression in a particular form of body. We have then Le Brun's "donkey-man" or the wonderful "cat-man." But already Le Brun, as he followed the ancient authorities (Pseudo-Aristotle, for instance) needed to consider whether a sign was "proper" to a species, and thus universally found in it, or whether it was also found among particular instances of another species. Common signs might be found across all species— the pig's lubricity, though especially found also in goats and donkeys, motivates other animals.[42] The question is whether the sign uniquely particularizes, uniquely specifies. Lavater's account of animals has references to such contemporary work on the classification of species as Buffon. Yet in his discussion of the bat, for example, there is an extraordinary conflation of a naturalist's view of its skeleton, whose aerodynamic qualities enable the bat to live in the way it does, and remarks about its expressive form: the tail and wing-tips characterize its malevolence; the eyes, ears, and teeth "have in my opinion the impress of a passion ardent, mean, malicious and concentrated."[43] The expression described is far more individual than that of Le Brun's pigs. Between engravings of the same species, heads are distinguished one from another and distinctively characterized. We are told of horse heads, for instance: "The three uppermost heads announce much more firmness, energy and courage than the two below."[44]

According to Lavater, animals, like humans, can be individuated by their character and by their visible forms, beyond any general characterization of their species. (Indeed, in the eighteenth century the body becomes the reference for individuation and identity.) Yet that individuation is limited by the species and by the lines expressing the strength and weakness of the species. Thus the system is at the same time strictly bounded and composed of ever more minute versions of itself:

> Endeavour then to find out in every organized body, the superiority and inferiority which belong to its species, which are inseparable from it, and cannot be taken away by the conventions of society. Fix exactly the boundaries which are contiguous to each other. Compare always the strong with the weak; characters firm and energetic, with characters soft and flexible. Extremes being once settled, you will easily discover intermediate relations. You will be able to determine, according to geometrical rules, the relations which are to be found between the forehead of a man formed for commanding and the forehead of one formed for obeying; between the nose of a monarch and the nose of a slave.[45]

The forehead will then act as "analogy" for the rest of the body. Although Lavater speaks of "every organized body," the model is man, and the most distinguishing feature of man is "his physiognomy, by which I mean the surface and the outline of his organisation," especially the face and the outline of its bones, because they reveal "the pre-eminence and sublimity of the intellectual faculties."[46] Lavater shows how to take silhouettes and illustrates a machine for measuring the exact shape of the skull. Through such measurement, the rest of the body can be deduced by analogy from the forehead. This reliance on analogy is also a reliance on proportion as exhibited by ancient art, and both are indicative of character. According to the physiologist Bell: "if we discover a broken portion of an antique, a nose or a chin, of marble, we can say, without deliberation, this must have belonged to a work of antiquity; which proves that the character is distinguishable in every part,—in each feature, as well as in the whole head."[47]

Particularity, Universality, and Beauty

The relation of the individual to the species is discussed in aesthetics, as is the relation between the individual and the *genre humain* (humankind, the human species) in politics. Rousseau argues in the first version of the *Social Contract* that the species cannot be treated as a more abstract version of the individual, as philosophers have been tempted to do, for that takes no account of the differentiations and hence divisions among men which result from personal interest.[48] Likewise, Diderot argues of the human form: "If there were a figure difficult to find, it would be that of a man of twenty-five, born suddenly from the clay of the earth, and who had done nothing; but this man is a chimaera."[49] Nothing in nature but is slightly out of kilter, no profile is the same each side on, no corner of a mouth but is slightly different from the other,[50] to which must be added the effects of class, work, health. Sir Joshua Reynolds, in his presidential lectures to the Royal Academy, would seem to agree; he might seem to agree that the investigation of the "idea of that central form . . . from which every deviation is deformity" is slow and hesitating.[51] But for Reynolds, a hierarchy of generalization underpins this and renders the man "born from the clay of the earth" the most general idea of man, that which takes the most central form. There can be particular figures which have their own perfection: Hercules, the Gladiator, Apollo.[52] This beauty is only that of a class, however; there is a further, most general beauty which is that of the species, "that form which is taken from them all. . . . The whole beauty and grandeur of the art consists, in my opinion, in being able to get above all singular forms, local customs, particularities, and details of every kind."[53] "These particularities cannot be nature: for how can that be the nature of man, in which no two individuals are the same?"[54] Art seeks to generalize; the artist will eschew minute discriminations and "like the philosopher will consider nature in the abstract, and represent in every one of his figures the character of its species."[55] He will thus idealize his figures, and avoid "peculiar marks" in his own style.[56]

Diderot pronounced this general aesthetic nature "a chimaera," as Rousseau declared the genre humain in political theory "a merely collective idea, supposing no real union between the individuals which constitute it." There are signs in Kant's work, too, of a tension between the individual and the universal, signs that their relation is changing.[57] In the group of texts around the Critique of Pure Reason (1781), Kant appears in some circumstances to correlate the universal judgment of quantity with the category of unity, in others, with that of totality. He appears to substitute the idea of what he calls plurative judgment (judgment about number) for judgment about species (the particular, the part, or, as German so graphically says, the be-sondere, the sundered, the cut out from). In other words, Kant moves from the particular, the species, as part of a whole and thus mediating between the single or individual and the universal, to the idea of the plural, which is not determined as part of a whole. He finally treats the particular as merely numerical, as several, more than one, without reference to its relation to any totality.[58] Instead of a hierarchy which subsumes the individual into the particular and then the universal, there is in the particular a plurality of finitely many singular judgments.

The same tension surfaces in the margins of Blake's copy of Reynolds's lectures when he annotates in irritation: "Every Class is individual."[59] Both the individual and the class to which he belongs are . . . individual. Diderot's theory of the characteristic seems designed to bring out what is disquieting in this logical loop;[60] the account of the characteristic in Aloysius Hirt, as expounded by Hegel, seems designed to resolve it through ideas of purpose. The perfect is "what corresponds with its aim, what nature or art intended to produce in the formation of the object within its genus and species."[61] This can be measured by characteristic marks, which are the beautiful in art: "by characteristic I understand that determinate individuality, through which forms, movement and gesture, mien and expression—local colour, light and shade, chiaroscuro and bearing are distinguished, and indeed as the previously envisaged object demands."[62] Only by observing this individuality can type in art be obtained, in which the particular [*eigentümlich*] reaches through all parts to the whole.[63] Hegel points out that "the principle of the characteristic involves as a fundamental feature an acceptance of the ugly and its presentation."[64] But the caricature—which to Hogarth and Kant seemed to exceed the characteristic, for the former because of its injection of chance into the perception of resemblance,[65] for the latter, because it breaks off the idea of purposiveness of the species[66]—is tellingly dismissed by Hegel as "a superfluity of the characteristic," one which makes the characteristic itself "unnatural."[67] A connection between the normalization of chance, purposiveness, and the characteristic comes to the surface here.

Normalization and the Characteristic of Self-determination

Marks, then, make up the determination of the individual, and this process is defined as the characteristic. This is to treat the individual as a character sui generis. In other words, the individual can be specified when it is defined as "of itself," "of its own genus." In *Rameau's Nephew*, Diderot explores (as, in a sense, does Hegel in his commentary on the text in the *Phenomenology*) the strange twists of this definition, in part through the notion of *idiotisme*. The "idiotisms" or features of a specific language are totally individual, yet, because they are linguistic, they are shared by the species. A "moral idiotism" is individual, but because many individuals have an individual morality, in that feature at least, it is shared by "most people." Hirt, writing after Kant, makes the idea of the genre or species part of the definition of perfection, as supplying a regulation through purpose. In the *Critique of Judgment*, Kant had earlier separated the "normal idea" of man as a thing belonging to a particular species of animal from the "rational idea." The "normal" idea is produced by a kind of analogy to the perceptual averaging process, which stabilizes what we see. What results is not a set of proportions but merely the preconditions for beauty, as Myron's cow was the model for an ancient sculptor sculpting a cow (or Polycletus's Doryphorus was for a man). It is never attained in any one individual; it merely gives correctness, and thus will differ culturally (the normal idea held by a Negro will differ from that of a Caucasian, or a Chinaman from that of an European, says Kant). Regularity of feature is a kind of average, it "says" nothing, it has nothing characteristic, it gives the idea of genus, not the specific of a person.[68] Kant is bringing together, in a way that runs counter to many of his immediate predecessors, such as Charles Batteux or Johann Joachim Winckelmann, the normal as empirical average, which was used to explain variations in the standard of taste, and the normal as regularity, but not as determinate rules. He has the aim, it would seem,[69] of freeing physiognomic expression from subjection to ideas of (academic) proportion, which is merely freedom from faults and cannot be an expression of genius.

The loosening of the vise of academic proportion is accompanied by a definition of the "rational idea," which enables human purposes which can't be portrayed nevertheless to be a principle of judgment through their effect on human form and its appearance. Physiognomic expression here becomes more than what can be taken from the experience of "the visible expression of the moral ideas which rule men inwardly," which is Lavater's definition.[70] It is an "ideal of beauty" which man alone is capable of judging, that is, of judging aesthetically the harmonization of his own purposes with essential and universal purposes. But the "ideal of beauty" is only available in the human form, which makes visible in bodily manifestation everything our reason brings together as morally good. In the same way, man alone, through his humanity, as intelligence, is capable of the ideal of perfection.

In a section of "Parergon," Derrida has explored the crux of physiognomic expression in the third *Critique*, the supposition that nature expresses in the outer person the proportions of the inner.[71] For Kant, man is deprived of "wandering beauty" because he has purposes against which he can be judged, and man goes beyond "dependent" beauty, the beauty of objects dependent on a definite purpose, because he is, precisely, independent, he has the purposes of his existence in himself. By expressing those purposes, man removes himself from the judgment of taste, which is pure of purposes, to make of the human form, his own form, the ideal of the beautiful.

In the *Anthropology*, though the anthropological characteristic allows one to recognize the inner man from the outer, Kant resists the opinion that, empirically, outward beauty is the effect of inner morality. By contrast, Lavater again and again affirms that opinion.[72] The participatory concept of analogy lying behind it is so thoroughgoing that Lavater claims the discriminating physiognomist needs beauty, too. He "must have the advantage of a good figure, a well proportioned body, a delicate organisation, senses capable of being easily moved, and of faithfully transmitting to the soul the impression of external objects; above all he must have a quick, penetrating and just eye."[73] This is based on an analogy between the human artist (the watchmaker, who will not put an expensive clock in a battered case) and God. But to the "unfathomable Creator of nature" such reasoning may not be attributed.[74] If, however, one characterizes not the individual but the human genus, there is a different problem with analogy: the *tertium comparationis* is missing, so that the distinction cannot be characterized, cannot be turned into a property. The highest concept of genus may be that of a rational earthly being, but we know nothing of a rational unearthly being. The only way to characterize man, to show him his rank in the system of living nature, is to allow him the character of creating himself;[75] he can make himself from a being capable of reason into a rational creature.[76] (This is glossed in the Rostock manuscript as recognizing *a priori* in himself the ideal of humanity, which becomes the *tertium comparationis*, his point of comparison for giving the pure character of his genus.) But what is then said to be characteristic of the human genus by comparison with the idea of possible rational earthly creatures is something more troubled than the pattern of the third *Critique*—it is, yes, self-creation, but this is the perfecting of man through progressing culture, "even if" bought at the cost of many of the joys of life.[77]

The communication between the concepts of autonomy and self-denial becomes clearer at the very end of the book. Nature wishes every creature to reach its determination by the purposeful development of all capacities in its species' nature, so that if her intention is not achieved by the individual, it will be achieved by the species. Man alone among the animals has this development not as actuality, but only as a purposeful tendency in his genus. This tendency is inscribed in the political development toward self-determination, which relates good and evil, individual and species. Some men, having evil inclinations but endowed with feelings and moral capabilities, see no way out of the evils they selfishly do to each other but to subject, although unwillingly, the private tendency of single men to the common discipline of the constraint of civil society (*des bürgerlichen Zwanges*). This discipline is that of the laws they give themselves, and they feel themselves ennobled through this consciousness, for they feel they belong to a species which is adequate to the determination of man, as reason presents it to him in the ideal.[78] The reference is to Rousseau's thought, to *Emile* and the *Social Contract*,[79] yet it is almost personalized here, as if with a glance at his *Confessions*. Those who move things forward are individuals, but nevertheless are described generally (*es sind Männer*), and the work ends with the statement that this progress through obstacles, which is that of the human genus, cannot be achieved through the free agreement of the individual, although his will may be good, but only through the species as a "system," that is, a geopolitical organization.[80] Both at the level of the individual (in morals) and at that of society (in the republic), character takes the form of self-determination. The individual with character creates himself; the republican society prescribes its own laws to itself. But for the individual, this is related to self-denial, because political self-determination must treat the human genus as a system. In this late Kantian text, societalization and normalization have been separated. The possibility of caricaturing the human race (undoing its normalization) is evidence of reason's demand to present the species of man as progressing against obstacles toward world peace.[81]

Analogy, Causality, and Style

The *Critique of Judgment* allows an argument about God as cause and the elements of the world as purposive products by analogy with man and his artificial works, but not the predication of characteristics to God, because he has no generic concept in common with man (except that of thing in general).[82] The argument in the Introduction makes the very possibility of connected experience an analogy—"empirical laws must be considered by us in accordance with such a unity as they would have if an understanding (although not our understanding) had furnished them to our cognitive faculties."[83] Our understanding puts things together in laws as if they had been designed on purpose for that, but actually gives laws not to nature, but only to itself.

In his insistence that "the external difference of face and figure must necessarily have a certain relation, a natural analogy to the internal difference of heart and mind," Lavater thinks he is insisting on cause and effect.[84] Chance cannot have been at work when Newton and Leibniz do not resemble "one born an idiot, who could not walk with a firm pace, nor fix his eyes, nor conceive nor express reasonably the plainest abstract proposition."[85] But in the very next sentence the intellectual qualities of the two scientists are attached to (imprecisely characterized) racial physiology. "What treatment would he deserve who presumed to add, that the one of these great men conceived the *Theodicea* in a brain like that of a Laplander," and, elsewhere, that the brain of a Newton could reside in the body of a black man? In these examples, Lavater confuses causality and representation (culturally determined mental association). Lichtenberg, in his attack "On Physiognomy," emphasizes the devious path of both.

By thinking of cause and effect as functioning like analogy, like a finely grained net of relations, Lavater normalizes chance. Lichtenberg argues, wonderfully, that he will not deny a relation between the different categories of beauty given by Lavater and spiritual beauty "so long as the present treatise has an influence on the American war."[86] In a world where everything is related by cause and effect, every part is indeed a mirror of the whole. He immediately brings together the small cause and great effect that others— Rousseau, for instance—were interested in:[87] a pea shot into the Mediterranean may have an effect on the China coast; the scratches on a plate tell of all the meals eaten on it. There is a connection, but we can't see it, though a sharper eye than ours could, as could the eye of He who sees all. The paths of causality are fraught and crooked to our eyes, that is, unseen and unforeseen. When the augur claimed to see the future of Rome in the sacrificed animal's entrails, he was right that it was there, but wrong that he could see it—there are too many jumps in the causal paths, too many indistinct relations for them to be discoverable.[88] Lichtenberg translates Lavater's idea of analogy as world correspondence into causality as statistical correlation (in "Against Physiognomy," he picks up the "often" and "very often" of Lavater's pronouncements on the relation between mental and physical) and, as will Kant, refuses the predication of characteristics to that correlation.

The mental association that shapes many of our representations is likewise quirky. In work that clearly influenced Freud, Lichtenberg speaks of the personal meaning that sounds acquire for us; he describes imagining the face and figure of a night watchman according to his calling of the hours and traces back the composite memories which led to his (totally misguided) mental image. Association can make a word into a face and a face into a word: he ascribes his imagination of what Robert E. Lee looked like to the double "ee" in his name and Lichtenberg's own unconscious reference to Michel Jean Sedaine's play *The Deserter*.[89] He relates this sort of mental activity to dreaming and to credulous belief: we all do it—"es geht uns allen so"—and there is no fixed boundary.[90] Thus the representations which accompany physiognomic observations are culturally, temporally, nationally, and, above all, individually determined.[91]

Chance and opportunity, which for Lichtenberg mark the individual in his bodily history as well as in his mental processes, mean that there are lacunae in our knowledge of these causal paths. The physicist makes explanation possible by manipulating time (through experiment, through bringing together phenomena widely spaced in nature, or through months of calculations, which become a quick, five-minutes-long read).[92] The physiognomist, by contrast, leaps from like to like via analogy—similar nose, similar mental capacity—and from outer deviations from the rule to analogical alterations of the soul.

Lavater, unlike Lichtenberg's account of him, assumes a continuity which allows his comparisons. Everything is continuous with everything else, and the hand of Raphael or Holbein is evident in every trace on their canvases. Physiognomy is a model for the interpretation of hand and style—in a letter to Christian Garve, he writes, "each product from me is an effect of my individuality."[93]

In his development of a "physiognomy of style,"[94] Hamann investigates the idiosyncrasy of style through the individuality of the

74

body. Indeed, in the early part of the eighteenth century, the body, individuated through its sense perceptions and tastes, seems to have been the model for individuality of style. Hamann considers such individuality in style, not in relation to the social pressures toward a common mode of expression, against which Marivaux protests in the epigraph to the present essay, but in relation to the nature of a particular language. The idea of "idiotisms," the "genius of a language," developed by the French grammarians in the eighteenth century allowed modes of expression which deviated from the universal structures of language, expressive of the particular "genius" of the people speaking it. Hamann writes:

> If our conceptions [*Vorstellungen*] dispose themselves according to the soul's viewpoint and if, as many believe, the latter is determined by the state of the body, then the same can be applied to the body of a whole people. The lineaments of its language will then correspond to the direction of its mentality, and each people will reveal its mentality through the nature, form, laws, and customs of its speech, just as through its outer civilization and through the theater of public transactions.[95]

and "As now nature makes unique to a people a certain color or cut of the eye; even so easily can she impart to their tongues and lips modifications which are not remarked by us."[96] But, unlike Lavater, his conception of the relation between individual style and the style of the language in which the individual writes is complex, allowing both the *a priori* arbitrariness of the word (it happens to belong to a particular natural language) and the *a posteriori* necessity of its expressiveness.[97] Hamann has reversed the usual relation between *a priori* and necessity, *a posteriori* and contingency. Language is both factitious and determining; the physiognomy of style is both arbitrary and revealing.[98]

Characterization and Violence in Language: Lavater, Levinas, Derrida

Lavater, like "Moi" in Rameau's nephew's accusation, sets the species of man into an array, with something of the same odd collocations—"learned men, thinkers, from the minds of collectors up to the highest genius."[99] The human species is presented as both endlessly differentiated and capable of being presented in degrees or grades. Of four profiles of "more and less foolish men," he says, "These four are all fools, but fools of the most different character. Foolishness has its classes, species, kinds, like wisdom."[100] In spite of that difference, the profiles have been classified: they are all of fools.

Lavater points out the difficulties of classification and of the language of physiognomy, but he makes of it a universal difficulty inherent in all language. Since every individual human is different—every face, every feature of a face, every nose, every eye—determination into classes might seem absurd. "Every judgement we form is, properly speaking, nothing but comparison, and classification; nothing more than the approximation of objects and the contrasting those we do not know, with those of which we have some knowledge."[101] All words save proper names generalize—a particular sign cannot be invented for every individual sensation or variation, yet all classification is defective and imperfect. Thus it merely approximates. The problem is one of language, but also of the mapping of different domains—the visual, the social, and the linguistic (in the listing of qualities)—onto each other. Animal species each have a leading characteristic; by analogy, the "principal qualities" of the soul have their expression in a particular form of body.[102] The implication is that the visual (the body) and the soul each have a repertoire of elements, and that these match. Moreover, they match because both can be itemized in language. The itemization inevitably involves sorting them into classes, but that is just what language is.[103]

To classify the physical appearance of noses is hard enough; to correlate such a characterization with an attribute appears peremptory and foolish, as Lavater admits when he calls some noses "judicious." Hegel attacks physiognomy as operating between two undifferentiated poles: external appearance as the expression of internal being. He nuances both: yes, facial traits are part of the body, but they comment on the individual's opinion of his action. They reveal consciousness of self, "the individual's speech with himself about the [external] action," in other words, how he looks at it, and what he meant. For Lavater, Hegel says, this, not the action itself, is the real nature, exteriorized in the face. The action can be characterized, but physiognomy lumps practical action with theory and looks for the capacity, not the act, with the result that physiognomic language cannot attain the individual either physically or mentally with regard to what might be, what is "meant." Physiognomic theory "mishandles" the doer of a deed; it is violent.[104]

In *Totality and Infinity*, Levinas constructs a relation to the

Other whose purpose is radically and fundamentally to protect the Other, not to agglomerate it into the same. The relation has to relate to the Other as infinite; the I does that, not by normalizing or characterizing the Other, nor by thinking of it as an object, but by folding into its own distance from the Other the distance between the idea we have of the infinite and the infinite itself. The Other can then be preserved as infinite, for our thinking of the infinite is just the gap between infinity and its idea—it is not the thinking of a determinate object. But this mismatch between the idea of infinity and that of which it is an idea, infinity, would leave us without hope if we were not able to communicate or to relate with the other. Levinas's construction of this relation, which is the ethical relation, and the possibility of communcation concerns the clash between singular and general, particular and class, with which we have been concerned throughout this essay. He insists that the Other presents itself as overflowing the representations I may have of it: this he calls the face.[105]

The other cannot be appropriated, and to allow oneself to be open to the other, to be called into question by the other, is to be vulnerable. But absolutely to lack proportion to the other, to lack analogy, is not to be part of a dialectic, but is to be radically independent and separate, to owe nothing to others. From this may come will and an interiority which cannot be subsumed, a radical individuation. There is no community of concept, no common genus: "Man as measure of all things, that is, measured by nothing, comparing all things but incomparable, is affirmed in the sensing of sensation."[106] As for Kant, or indeed Lavater, for Levinas man is the basis of proportion—but unlike for Lavater, his proportions cannot be surveyed. Man's sentience and sensation individuate, make fluid and heterogeneous, what philosophers have tried to normalize; they make being into becoming. This proportion in lack of proportion lets error in; but it also admits truth—it allows a kind of contact with the other which is not participation, not derivation of self from other.

Levinas calls this relation to the other, in which the other exceeds the idea of the other in me, the "face." This "face" is not a plastic image, for it overflows the image, which for Levinas is always adequate to my measure, a kind of bound form.[107] It is expression, "a coinciding of the expressed with him who expresses, which is the privileged manifestation of the Other, the manifestation of a face over and beyond form. . . . The manifestation of the face is already discourse."[108] In his discussion, Levinas tacitly contradicts Hegel's account of physiognomy: the dialectical mediation between poles integrates without respecting the other; Hegel ("the philosophical tradition")[109] calls "opinion" Lavater's taking of the irreducible Other into account, whereas one must seek a relation to the Other which is not imposed from without, which is not opinion. Contrary to Hegel, acts do not express—they are, in a sense, in the third person, removed from the other.[110]

This relation of the same to the other is said to be language. Yet it is not purely linguistic—for the revealer and the revealed coincide in the face, and the face is epiphany. "Meaning is the face of the Other, and all recourse to words takes place already within the primordial face to face of language."[111] The relation to the other keeps in play, keeps open. It is more than contact, for it is more than thematization, and goes beyond concepts. The naked face in its epiphany shifts the concepts of power. It is nonviolence; its defenselessness is its defense; it proposes a relation beyond power. The communication is not one of exchange, but of a one-sided gift. Expression is not self-determination through language, but a bearing of witness to oneself.[112]

In a sense, this is language without language. It does seem to descend, as do Frege's "thoughts," from accounts of the language of the angels. It might seem to be like Rousseau's *neume*,[113] wordless adoration or invocation. But Levinas refuses this "mysticism" as a playing of a role, begun outside. This language must be reason. Yet how can that be? Reason plays with concepts. Interpellation, the address to the other, says Levinas, even where it classifies, cannot place the other in a category.[114] And language cannot be reduced to representation.[115] Derrida, in his first discussion of Levinas, "Violence and Metaphysics," points out the connection with the absolute infinite: the face is expression and word, but in that it exceeds all representation, all categorization, all determination, it is beyond language. Then it cannot be other, for it cannot be said. "If one thinks, as Levinas does, that positive Infinity tolerates, or even requires, infinite alterity, then one must renounce all language, and first of all the words *infinite* and *other*."[116]

But Levinas does speak, even as he protests against the concept, even as he places the ethical relation beyond it. Derrida argues here, as he does in *Of Grammatology* and "Cogito and the History of Madness,"[117] that there is in language an originary violence, a violence not primarily of fact, but of a different order, inseparable from the process of phenomenonalization, the process of the appearing of the appearance. This violence is at the origin of sense. The face is not merely a glance; it is also speech, and in speech the cry becomes phrase and expression, and from expression moves to determination: "there is no phrase which is indeterminate, that is, which does not pass through the violence of the concept. Violence appears with *articulation*."[118] For Levinas, this violence of language is historical and secondary. For Derrida, who cannot accept thought as across or above history, even as he is wary of the very concept of history, this violence of language exists in syntax and articulation (not, as with Lavater, in categories and classes), in any making determinate because articulated against the hyperbolic, wordless excess. Derrida argues that this violence of language is not historical, in the sense that it is not localized as a moment of a scholarly class or priestly caste, as Lévi-Strauss appears to argue.[119] This violence is pre-ethical, it is what allows being to appear as difference, thereby making possible the defeat of indetermination, of "nihilist violence,"[120] that is, of the violence of inarticulation. Recognition that articulation is violent prevents our amalgamating it in our thought with determinate political violence or political classification,[121] which come after. The naturalization of the category, the normalization of specification, is thus disallowed. Articulation and syntax constitute a "violence," but this is an "anguish" (*angustiae*, "narrow pass") through which the indeterminate passes into concepts. It is the price of any discourse at all.

Wartime

SAMUEL WEBER

On the occasion of an international colloquium, it can hardly be superfluous to reflect for a moment on the question of language and its relation to our topic, or topics: violence, identity, self-determination. First of all, there is something both admirable and troublesome in the fact—or rather, in the *self-evidence with which this fact is accepted*—that a group composed of individuals from many different countries should come together to discuss in a language, English, that is "native" only to a few of them. It is admirable that all those for whom English is not their native language are willing and able to accept such a restriction to make possible a dialogue across national, linguistic, and cultural frontiers. In such readiness there seems a readiness to negotiate with alterity—with the idioms of others—that strikes me as not only admirable, but also profoundly related to the themes of our conference. The self-evidence with which such conditions are imposed—must be imposed—is troubling, however. As one of the organizers of this event, I too never questioned this rule, which imposed itself to such a degree, with such force, not to say violence, that there was never even any real discussion or debate about it: English was to be the lingua franca and that was that. This situation is obviously not new and, unless I am badly mistaken, it is becoming increasingly widespread, primarily in the sciences, but under their impetus in other domains as well. At the same time, the very spread of a single language, called upon to serve as a kind of "universal equivalent" in the domain of discourse, exposes that language and its claim to serve as a measure or medium of value to increasing scrutiny, to contestation, and, to a degree at least, also to alteration. The process is not univocal or transparent, but highly dynamic and complex.

It is *troubling* only when it is taken for granted—which is often enough. To do so here, where the term "identity" stands in the midst of our triad of topics, would be unconscionable for several reasons. First of all, it would signify that we are ready to accept without question that the language in which our discussions are to take place has itself no specificity worth mentioning or thinking about—that it is a neutral medium with regard to the issues we seek to address, *through* it, as it were, rather than *with* it. Taking English in particular, and language in general, for granted would be to assume that there is a universal essence of something that happens, in English, to be called "violence"—or "identity" or "self-determination"—but which possesses its constitutive properties independently of the specific medium in which it is articulated.

Nothing could be less self-evident than such a supposition. Part of the impetus for our discussion derives from the conviction that today it is no longer adequate, if indeed it ever was, to construe the resurgence of violence—political, economic, domestic, racial, gendered, intellectual—simply as a phenomenon to be examined, studied, analyzed, interpreted, and criticized. All this is necessary, indeed, more necessary than ever before. But to be adequate to the phenomenon as it is appearing today, it is imperative to go beyond— or rather, to take a step back from—the premises and presuppositions indispensable to critical analysis and interpretation in order to reopen the question of violence. To approach violence as something eminently *questionable*—in German, *fragwürdig*—is to take as little for granted with respect to it as possible.

We should not, for instance, take for granted that we always and indubitably know what violence is when we see it or think we see it. What we "see," perhaps even more significantly, the way in which we see it, is today more than ever before dependent upon the media, in particular, upon television. Once we go beyond the limited sphere of experience that is accessible to our unaided senses, television supplements our eyes and ears—indeed, it almost takes their place. Our images of violence, and the concepts that to a large extent depend upon those images, derive increasingly from the images presented to us on the television screen. It would be foolish to ignore the ways in which global television has opened up access to forms of violence that previously would have been largely ignored. At the same time, however, such extension of our sensibility to images of violence can only be selective, in a double sense. First, the images that are shown are, of course, selected from many possibilities, and those that are not selected tend to lose in value, if not in reality. Second, the question of the image as such, in its relation to violence, tends to be overshadowed if not fully eclipsed by the power of the TV images presented to us and by our increasing dependence upon them. There is a tendency to identify violence not simply with the content of the images presented by the media, forgetting their terrible and merciless partiality, but even more importantly, perhaps, to take for granted the relationship between image and violence: that is, to recognize violence only when and where it is "televisible," if not televisual. Forms of violence that are not "telegenic," that are not selected by the media for transmission, tend to be ignored and, in the process, forgotten or devalued.

But this entire discussion of the media and its power in imposing a certain view of violence still presupposes what I started out by trying to question: a certain concept of violence, if only one that could be used to evaluate, measure, and judge the relationship of the media to it. And yet, precisely such a concept of violence should, ultimately, be in question. And an essential part of that question has to do with the relation of violence to language.

One of the most exhilarating, astonishing, and thought-provoking experiences possible results from the discovery that most things —concepts, entities, issues—do not necessarily have direct verbal equivalents in different languages. Reflection upon the question of violence in recent years has been profoundly stimulated by an essay of Walter Benjamin which describes its object using a German word that has no direct equivalent in either English or French. That word is *Gewalt*, used by Benjamin to entitle his "Kritik der Gewalt," usually translated in English as "Critique of Violence." The German word *Gewalt*, however, by no means simply corresponds to "violence." Indeed, in part it almost contradicts it. The German word derives from the verb *walten*, "to rule or preside," while the English word is inseparable from the notion of violation. Etymologically, both words (as well as French *violence*) derive from the same Latin root, *uir* or *uis*, designating "strength" or "force." Yet the German *Gewalt* emphasizes the maintenance of rule, whereas in English the notion of external infringement, by force, is strongly implied. In both cases there is a more or less implicit reference to identity: in English "violence" suggests an incursion upon a sphere of self-containment or at least a sphere in which the self relates to itself. In German, *Gewalt* can entail such an incursion but it need not: it can designate quite the opposite, the self or institution maintaining itself, imposing its order upon others or against obstacles. In both cases, a conflictual relationship between self and other, identical and nonidentical, seems to be implied.

Out of the divergence between the German and English words, which overlap but by no means simply correspond to one another, emerges a question that can be formulated as follows: Just what is the relationship of violence to the self and its functions, above all, self-determination? What is difficult to think in English becomes somewhat easier to conceive in German: the possibility that violence may entail not just the imposition of a certain alterity upon the self, but also the imposition of the self upon others. Thus, in German one speaks of *staatliche Gewalt*, whereas in English one would rarely speak of "state violence," but rather of "state power."

Nevertheless, over and above the divergence of the semantic fields suggested by these two words, the problem of "legitimate" or "illegitimate" use of force—or is it "power"?—emerges as common to both languages. And what in turn seems to decide the legitimacy or illegitimacy of the exercise of power is not just existing laws, but, more fundamentally, the status of the self. What distinguishes English "violence" from German *Gewalt* is that in the former the exercise of force or power tends to exceed the norm—a norm that generally is determined in terms of the self, its prerogatives, and, above all, its property.

The comparison of "violence" and *Gewalt* thus leads us back to a determination that is as old as "Western" (i.e., European) thought. Book X of Plato's *Laws* begins:

> ATHENIAN: Now that we have dealt with assault, we may enunciate a single and comprehensive principle of law in respect of cases of violence, to the following effect. No man shall lift the goods and chattels of others, nor yet make use of a neighbor's property without the owner's permission, since such conduct is the beginning whence all the aforesaid mischiefs, past, present, or future, derive by consequence.[1]

Violence—at least in this English version of the Greek text—is, or is derived from, the infringement of property rights. From that is said to stem "all the aforesaid mischiefs, past, present, or future." Violence as the violation of the right to dispose over one's property is thus, according to Plato, the originary, founding violence. This of course presupposes that the question of property rights—and of the proper—can, in principle at least, be settled without violence. If this were not so, the definition of the Athenian in the *nomoi* would involve a *petitio principii*, for violence would then be necessary in order to define the condition whose violation is said to constitute violence.

If the interpretation of violence as the violation of property is as old as Western metaphysics, no less venerable is the gnawing doubt about the possibility of defining the self and its property in a way that would be anterior, in principle at least, to all violence. The Platonic *nomoi* are no exception: no sooner has the Athenian formulated the root cause of all violence as consisting in the violation of property, than he must acknowledge that his conception ultimately reposes not upon proof but upon belief, and that this belief is by no means shared by all. Those who mock the idea of the existence of the gods—and upon nothing less, according to the Athenian, does the belief in the proper depend—can draw support for their positions from "primitive stories" no less than from "our modern men of enlightenment."[2]

The effort to put violence in its proper place by subordinating it to the proper, and ultimately to the self, is so precarious and uncertain in its results, it would seem, that it itself easily turns violent: "When we see all this evidence [that the gods are not fictions, but the most certain of realities] treated with contempt by the persons who are forcing us into our present argument . . . how I ask is a man to find gentle language in which to combine reproof with instruction?"[3] In the modern epoch, as the secular self is called upon to assume in large part the theological function of the divine, such doubts are hardly put to rest. From Hobbes to Nietzsche, there is a growing conviction that what is proper to human existence is not only not beyond violence but somehow constituted through it. Such a conviction, however, does more than merely extend the scope of violence—it calls its very concept into question. For if violence is at work from the very beginning, then the notion of violence as violation or as abnormal, excessive, illegitimate force must be rethought. If violence is the law and the norm, how can it be defined as violation? And if it is not violation, in the sense of an external infringement or incursion upon the proper and property, how then is it to be thought? The remarks that follow seek to retrace one response to this question of violence.

Wartime: The Mobilization of Divisions

This response does not date from today, but it could have. One of the most striking aspects of Freud's essay translated in English as "Thoughts for the Times on War and Death" is its renewed timeliness. Were one to have read this text twenty years ago, or perhaps even ten, one might simply have read right over it. Twenty years ago, Freud's "Thoughts for the Times" seemed untimely indeed, as hopelessly out-of-date as the geopolitical names that situate his celebrated Signorelli dream at the beginning of *The Psychopathology of Everyday Life*: Bosnia, Herzegovina. The last decade, however, has reminded us of something that psychoanalysis should have made it more difficult to forget: that the past is never simply dead and gone but also, *in potentia* at least, the future.

In 1915, in the second year of what was soon to be known as The Great War, the editors of *Imago* appealed to Freud for an article to help fill the upcoming issue. Freud responded with the text in question, which was actually a combination of two relatively independent essays. In the first of the two parts, he addresses the enormous sense of "disappointment" that the war evoked, which he then seeks to explain in terms of psychoanalytical theory. That year, Freud was elaborating his metapsychology, above all, the theory of narcissism and its ramifications. The discrepancy between the "egoistic" tendencies of the individual and the "altruistic" needs of society provided Freud with a background against which to stress the intrinsically precarious nature of social relations and, in particular, the effects of the war.

After all his didactic explications are complete, Freud returns to the astonishment from which he departed. At the end of the first half of his essay—his thoughts on the topic of "war"—Freud finds himself, notwithstanding the entire battery of psychoanalytic theory that he has mobilized and the explanations it produces, more or less back where he started from:

> We had hoped, certainly, that the grandiose community of interests brought about through commerce and production would produce the beginnings of such a compulsion [to morality]; but it seems that nations [*Völker*] obey their passions far more readily these days than their interests. At best, they make use of their interests in order to *rationalize* their passions; they put forward their interests in order to justify satisfying their passions. Why collective individuals [*Völkerindividuen*] in fact despise, hate, and detest each other, even in peace-

time, each nation the others, remains, it is true, a mystery. I cannot say why this is [*Ich weiß es nicht zu sagen*]. In this case it is as though all the moral achievements of individuals were obliterated once many [*eine Mehrheit*] or indeed millions come together, and only the most primitive, most ancient, and crudest attitudes survive.[4]

One can rejoice, in reading these lines, at how much has changed since they were written: at how the "grandiose community of interests" has been able to establish relatively stable political and economic institutions. Or one can ponder how little has changed, with respect to the rationalization of passions, passions that have retained a largely destructive force. Freud's characterization of the aggressivity manifest in the war then underway could, alas, have been written today:

> Then the war in which we had refused to believe broke out, and it brought—disenchantment. Not only is it more bloody and more destructive than any war of other days, because of the enormously increased perfection of weapons of attack and defense; it is at least as cruel, as embittered, as implacable as any that has preceded it. The war exceeds all the limitations instituted in peacetime and known as International Law [*Völkerrecht*]; it ignores the prerogatives of the wounded and of the physician, the distinction between civil and military sections of the population, the claims of private property. It overwhelms, with blind rage, anything that stands in its way, as though there were to be no future and no peace afterwards. It tears up all bonds of community among the warring peoples and threatens to leave behind an embitterment that will make any renewal of these bonds impossible for a long time to come.[5]

These words not only speak for themselves, as though they were written not in 1915 but in 1994, they do something else, something even more uncanny. They resonate in the echo chamber we call history: the legacy of embitterment left behind by the First World War, the Treaty of Versailles and the draconian conditions it imposed upon the losers, which laid the groundwork for the even more terrible, more violent, more aggressive successor of that conflict. The violation of the rights, prerogatives, and, above all, of the private property of the adversary—the inimical other—defined, then as today, a violence that knows no bounds or boundaries except, apparently, the limitations of its own power. Such violence rages blindly, "as though there were to be no future," Freud writes, in a particularly gripping formulation. Gripping, because reading this text written at the beginning of this century from our vantage point, almost at its end, we are in the process of becoming that

86

future, but in a way that seems largely to confirm the violence of which Freud speaks, which has continued unabated until today. We read a text from a not so distant past that tells us that the future is put in jeopardy by the violence of the present. And since that violence continues to be present, what of the future: what of our time as the future Freud was describing? Are we the future of that past? Or merely the continuation of its present? And what of our present? Does *it* have a future?

Much has happened, and indeed, much has changed since 1915. But much of what has changed appears only to have intensified the situation described by Freud. On the one hand, the increase in "commerce and production" has, under the impact of the new electronic technologies of communication, assumed a qualitatively new dimension. Production has been reorganized on a worldwide basis as never before. With the advent and spread of global television networks and satellite transmissions, images and sounds have been made available with greater speed and to a larger part of the world's population than had ever before had access to such "information." Yet despite such accessibility—despite, or perhaps even because of it—what the First World War brought home to an astonished Freud rings no less true today: despite the enormously augmented means of communication, there persists "the barely comprehensible phenomenon that the civilized peoples [*die Kulturvölker*] know and understand each other so little that one can turn against the other with such hate and revulsion."[6]

Freud's reference here and elsewhere in this essay to *die Kulturvölker*—"civilized peoples"—indicates the ethnocentric bias that informs the "disenchantment" of which he writes: "We had expected the great, world-dominating peoples of the white race upon whom the leadership of the human species has fallen, who were known to have worldwide interests as their concern, to whose creative powers were due not only our technical advances toward the control of nature but the artistic and scientific standards of civilization—we had expected these peoples to succeed in discovering another way of settling misunderstandings and conflicts of interests."[7]

The imperialist and Eurocentric bias of such remarks would be more objectionable than it is were the role they are assigned within the economy of this essay not their own disavowal (albeit an implicit one). For the very expectations that Freud and his readers had placed in the "creative powers" of Western European culture and society are introduced in this text only to serve as the measure of the failure of "the white race" to live up to its own pretensions of world leadership. There can be little doubt that for Freud this failure is irreversible and definitive. To be sure, read closely, Freud's text reveals that the optimistic faith in the achievements of Western society ignored certain troubling signs in the historical behavior of those societies, long before the war broke out and brought its decisive lessons: "Observation showed, to be sure, that embedded in these civilized states there were remnants of certain other peoples, who were universally unpopular and had therefore been only reluctantly, and even so not fully, admitted to participation in the common work of civilization, for which they had shown themselves suitable enough."[8]

This indirect, but also unmistakable allusion to the fate of the Jews in Europe is itself equivocal, however: Freud criticizes the tendency of European societies to practice a kind of internal exclusion vis-à-vis "certain other peoples, who were universally unpopular," only by accepting without reserve the criterion of "civilization"—for which they (i.e., the Jews) had shown themselves suitable enough. Thus, one could infer from Freud's formulation, the exclusion of that other, "universally unpopular" people, the Sinti (gypsies), might be considered to be justifiable to the extent that such a people was deemed unfit or unwilling to participate "in the common work of civilization."

All the more reason, therefore, to examine just how that "common work" is defined and how Freud's remarks deal with it. As the formulation here suggests, whatever else civilization—read European civilization—is, it involves, precisely, *work*. European civilization defines itself as a civilization of work. An essential dimension of this work is constituted by the "commerce and production" already mentioned as well as the development of the technologies of communication that such trade requires.

Hence, the surprise, perplexity, and disenchantment that result from the discovery that, despite the advances in technologies of communication, the different peoples still appear "to know and understand each other so little that they turn against one another with hate and revulsion." This strikes at the very heart of Western civilization: its claims to universality and to world leadership are belied not just by its unconscionable comportment, but by the fact that its violence seems entirely compatible with the technologies that should, according to its own theories, have made such violence impossible.

Relatively few voices would be raised today to defend the "leadership" roles of the Western "white race"—although institutions such as the World Bank and the International Monetary Fund continue to impose a mode of development upon the world that has its model precisely in the history of nations in which the "white race" has dominated. But what holds today no less than at the time Freud wrote is the generalized belief in the "civilizing" function of the media, that is, of the technologies of communication by which the "work of civilization" is accomplishing itself today. The fact that a Bosnia or a Rwanda is possible in the glare of the TV screen is what renders Freud's psychoanalytic approach to the question of violence as pertinent today as it has ever been.

To get at what psychoanalysis can tell us about this situation, however, we must—as is often the case—be prepared to brush Freud's text against the grain of its explicit statements. The question that his essay raises, is not so much "how little the civilized peoples must know and understand each other" in order to treat one another with such violence and contempt, but rather, what it can mean to "know and understand" *the other*. His point of departure, here as elsewhere, is that knowing and understanding are anything but simply neutral, contemplative processes. We must never forget, he reminds his readers, that

> we are mistaken in regarding our intelligence as an independent power and in overlooking its dependence upon emotional life. Our intellect [we are told] can only work reliably when it is removed from the influences of strong emotional impulses; otherwise it behaves simply as an instrument in the hand of our will and provides the result demanded of it. Logical arguments are thus powerless against affective interests, and that is why disputes backed by reasons, which as Falstaff says, are "as plenty as blackberries," turn out to be so fruitless in the world of interests. Psychoanalytic experience has only further underscored this assertion.[9]

Freud thereby articulates a dilemma from which he, and psychoanalysis, by no means escape. The intellect can work reliably only when removed from strong emotional impulses. But, as both history and psychoanalysis suggest, the intellect is rarely if ever in such a position, and not just for fortuitous reasons. Cognitive interests and affective interests are profoundly intertwined, indeed overlap and converge. The implications of this convergence are enormous: they are apparent not just in the experience of individuals, but in the collective shock evoked by the outbreak of the war. Freud begins his essay with a description of that shock, one which merits attention to detail: "Caught up in the turmoil [*Wirbel*] of this wartime, one-sidedly informed, without distance from the great transformations that have already occurred or that are beginning to, and without a glimmer of the future taking shape, we ourselves are waylaid [*werden wir selbst irre*] by the significance of the impressions that overwhelm us and by the values of the judgments which we form."[10]

Note, in this breathless description of the confusion provoked by the war, the positioning of the grammatical subject in the sentence: introduced by clauses that define its situation as an object of history rather than as its subject ("Caught up in the turmoil . . . , one-sidedly informed, without distance . . . , without a glimmer of the future taking shape"), the "subject" emerges as that which is literally sub-jected to a series of impressions that it does not control, indeed that overwhelm it: "we ourselves are waylaid." In German this is even stronger: *werden wir selbst irre*. *Irre* means both "crazy," in common parlance, and more generally "to lose one's bearings, become disoriented." In German, this state is attributed to a reflexive subject: *wir selbst*. "We," the subjects, are not just disoriented by things that are going on outside us, these events make us lose our bearings with respect to ourselves as well. "We ourselves lose our grip," not just on things but on our selves, on our ability to form judgments, for instance. The effects of the war, which Freud in German designates as a *Wirbel*, a "whirlwind," allows for little or no "distance" and hence not even a "glimmer of the future taking shape." Will the future even have a "shape," a *Gestalt*? Or will it be like the whirlwind itself, a shape destroying all shape, a movement going nowhere, seizing and overwhelming everything in its wake? A figure of violence, if there ever was one, violating all property and all property relations not just from without, but also, simultaneously, from within.

What the violent whirlwind of "war time" does, among other things, is to disrupt all clear relations and distinctions, in what seems to be an unprecedented manner: "We cannot but feel that no event has ever destroyed so much that is precious in the common possessions [*Gemeingut*] of humanity, confused so many of the clearest intelligences, so thoroughly debased what is highest."[11] No longer able to distinguish between high and low, in all senses of those words, even "the clearest intelligences" lose their clarity, are led astray, *werden selbst irre*. This is the massive effect of what Freud, in a formulation that is more significant than it at first might appear, calls, in German, *die Kriegszeit*. The "event"—*Ereignis*— with which he is concerned is not simply war as such, or even simply the unexpectedness of its outbreak, but rather a more complex, more sustained process that he calls "wartime." Only when we examine this extremely peculiar time can we begin to take the measure of the violence and the shock with which Freud seeks to come to grips.

What is surprising, indeed shocking, about the time of war is that it is not time as it was heretofore known and expected to be. In this respect, Freud's essay spins out a strand of thought that goes back to an earlier text to which its title pays homage, although this relationship is effectively effaced in the English translation. However suggestive the English title—"Thoughts for the Times on War and Death"—reminding us that Freud's thoughts are relevant not just to his time but also to ours—it effaces the allusion to Nietzsche's *Untimely Observations*, a reference that resonates in the title of Freud's German text: "Zeitgemäßes über Krieg und Tod": "Timely Thoughts on War and Death." At the victorious conclusion of the Franco-Prussian war of 1870–71, Nietzsche wrote four *Untimely Observations* (*Unzeitgemäße Betrachtungen*). In the third of these, the "Use and Abuse of History," Nietzsche explained what he meant by his title: "This observation is also untimely, because what the time [*die Zeit*] is rightly proud of, its historical formation [*Bildung*], I try to understand as damage, breakage, and deficiency of the time [*der Zeit*]; indeed, I constantly believe that we suffer from an all-consuming historical fever, and that at the very least we ought to recognize that we are suffering."[12]

Nietzsche considered his meditation to be "untimely" because it flew in the face of the "historical fever" that followed the German victory in the Franco-Prussian war: the blind belief in history as progress and in the German nation as its driving force. Against this fervor, Nietzsche warned his countrymen that "a great victory" could also be "a great danger."[13]

Freud, by contrast, had to contend, not with the flush of victory, but with disenchantment: "When I speak of disenchantment, everyone knows immediately what that means." In this sense, Freud could label his essay a "timely" rather than an "untimely" reflection on war and death. He did not (yet) have to explore the reasons for a defeat but merely to discuss the surprise and disappointment produced by this war fought by the "civilized nations" against each other: surprise and disappointment at the outbreak of this civil war fought by European civilization against itself.

But the whirlwind of wartime is confusing, disorienting, not merely because it seals the split, apparently without appeal, between the European nations and peoples and thus condemns their claim to serve as a paradigm of human progress. In addition, wartime leads astray because it exposes belief in a universal history to be what Nietzsche called it: "an all-consuming fever." What that fever consumes is the possibility of historical orientation. To be oriented historically, history must have a discernible direction and goal. The whirlwind of war derails that direction and obscures that goal. Nothing can be discerned but a pure movement that sweeps everything up into its path and yet goes nowhere. As a movement, the whirlwind of war has a temporal dimension; but as a whirlwind it marks time, as it were, inscribing it in a destructive circularity that is both centripetal and centrifugal, wrenching things and people out of their accustomed places, displacing them and with them the places as well. What is high is now lowered, while the lowly is elevated. Wartime thus wreaks havoc with traditional conceptions of space and time and with the order they make possible. But that which it damages the most is what Freud, in this essay, calls the *individual*. This individuality has two forms: "It should come as no surprise that when individuals as a collectivity relax moral bonds, this should have repercussions upon their individual morality, for conscience is not the inflexible arbiter so dear to theoreticians of ethics: in its origins, it is nothing but social anxiety."[14]

Here, as elsewhere in this essay, the Nietzsche of the *Genealogy of Morals* is often echoed: morality depends upon the internalization of external constraint.[15] Strikingly, however, Freud's extension of the notion of the "individual" to cover not just single human beings but also their political and social institutions does not amount to a psychologization of politics. As Lacan rightly and frequently emphasized, psychoanalysis is not psychology, for the simple reason that its decisive concepts and categories are not based upon the notion of an individual, self-contained psyche. What separates Freud—and precisely at the point he discovered "narcissism"—from all such psychology is that the psyche, in the perspective of psychoanalysis, is anything but individual, especially if one takes that word at its word, that is, literally. The psyche of psychoanalysis is eminently *divisible*, and any element of unity that it may develop will always remain dependent upon its underlying divisibility. Only against the background of such divisibility does Freud's distinctive stress upon the priority of "external constraint" lose its semblance of pseudo-scientism. The "externality" upon which human being depends is not primarily that of an empirically or psychologically determinable social order or "conditions," but rather a domain of exteriority that cannot be attributed to any sort of "subject" as its unifying principle: not to "society," not to the nation, and above all, not to the "people." By speaking of "people-individuals," *Völker-individuen*, Freud in fact does something very different from what he might appear to be doing: he calls into question the identity of those *Völker* by determining them as singular "individuals" who themselves are, paradoxically, eminently divisible.

The processes that mark the "individual," as Freud uses this term, entail, curiously enough, an impulsive movement that is anything but indivisible. This is how Freud describes that movement:

> These primitive impulses undergo a lengthy process of development before they are allowed to become active in the adult. They are inhibited, directed towards other aims and fields, become commingled, change their objects, turn in part against one's own person [*gegen die eigene Person*]. Reaction-formations against certain drives assume the deceptive form of a change in their content, as though egoism had changed into altruism, or cruelty into pity. These reaction-formations are facilitated by the circumstance that some drive impulses appear almost from the first in pairs of opposites—a very remarkable state of affairs that is foreign to the popular mind [*populären Kenntnis*] and that has been called "ambivalence of feeling." The most easily observed and comprehensible instance of this is the fact that intense love and intense hatred are so often to be found together in the same object. Psychoanalysis adds to this that the two opposed feelings not infrequently also have the same person as object.[16]

The trajectory of the drives thus described does not exactly constitute a whirlwind, but it shares with it the characteristic of an overwhelming dynamics that is not going anywhere. Its force cannot be measured by its progress. Rather, what marks the dynamics of the drives is constant change: "They are inhibited, directed towards other aims and fields, become commingled, change their objects, turn in part against their own possessor." But the word "possessor" does not appear in Freud's German, and this for good reason. Instead, we find the drives turning against "one's own person"; this person, far from appearing as their proprietor, provides them rather with a stage. What plays itself out on and around this stage is a movement that excludes all possibility of durable possession and property.

This is undoubtedly the primary reason why the "remarkable state of affairs" known as ambivalence remains so foreign to the popular mind, even though it is frequently encountered and should have long since become quite familiar. For ambivalence marks the ineffaceable intrusion of the foreign, the alien, the other into the constitution of the self and the same. Ambivalence names the constitutive violence against which the constitution of the subject and the self retains the status of a persona, in the etymological sense of a mask. As ambivalence, the drives mark the heterogeneity and alterity of the person, who does not so much *possess* them as *make way* for them, giving them their space and their stage. No urge appears without its contrary, pulling in the opposite direction, counteracting the initial thrust. No drive remains simply self-identical. Each turns into another, away from its self, mingling with its contrary, deviating from its path.

Such ambivalent multiplication of divergent drives and trajectories resembles a war, but it resembles even more the effects that Freud attributes to wartime. Like the whirlwind, it seizes the subject and deprives it of all orientation by disrupting the binarism of frontal struggle and the calculations of strategy. At the same time, it reinstates the very binarism it has uprooted, above all in the polarity friend/enemy, and it makes strategic thinking unavoidable. What the reference to the ambivalence of the drives suggests, however, is that such a reinstatement has the status of a projective reaction-formation: the constitutive and irreducible conflict of desire—the fact that "drive impulses appear almost from the first in pairs of opposites"—is projected and in the process transformed into what appears as a series of mutually exclusive oppositions or polarities: inside *or* outside, us *or* them, friend *or* foe, victory *or* defeat. The results of this effort to reestablish the orientation shaken by the "whirlwind"—to find one's way out of the *Irre*—are the unspeakable and unprecedented violence and violations that characterize modern war. The individual strives to secure its indivisibility by mobilizing its constitutive divisions and directing them outward, against the other, now defined as the enemy.

But the process is intrinsically without limits, because inherently unstable and futile. Like all reactive formations, it reproduces what it seeks to overcome: the irreducible divisiveness of the

94

drives. Such reproduction takes place not merely spatially, in the geopolitical struggle to gain territory or to transform frontiers, but also temporally, an effect that is less visible but no less powerful. Wartime is a time that disrupts the notion of temporality as irreversible flow or linear progression. It is a time "out of joint,"[17] a time in which succession is subordinated to a quasi-simultaneity:

> We can deepen, however, our understanding of the transformation undergone by our former compatriots through the war at the same time that we receive a warning not to do them an injustice in the process. Psychic developments possess a peculiarity which can be found by no other developmental process. When a village grows up into a city, a child into a man, the village and child disappear into the city and into the man. Only memory can inscribe the old traits into the new image; in reality the old materials or forms have been done away with and replaced by new ones. A psychic development proceeds differently. This incomparable state of affairs can be described only by asserting that each earlier level of development remains preserved next to the later ones that emerged out of it. Succession here involves coexistence, although the entire sequence of transformations has, after all, operated upon the same materials . . . the primitive mental state [*seelische*] is in the fullest sense imperishable [*unvergänglich*].[18]

The response of the drives to their constitutive ambivalence is a strategy in which time, as temporal succession, is suspended and re-placed (in the most literal sense: turned into a place) by a "coexistence" which is anything but pacific, as the following lines, from "Drives and Their Vicissitudes" ("Triebe und Triebschicksale," published in 1915, the same year as the "Thoughts for the Times") unmistakably indicate:

> Perhaps yet another way of conceiving and representing the matter may be justified. We may split up the life of each drive into a series of thrusts [*Schübe*] that are temporally discrete and yet homogeneous within an (arbitrarily fixed) period, and which relate to one another roughly like successive lava eruptions. We can then perhaps imagine [*sich etwa vorstellen*: represent to ourselves] that the earliest and most primitive drive eruption continues without change and undergoes no development at all. The next thrust would then from the outset undergo a change, for instance, the turn toward passivity, and with this new characteristic it would add itself to the earlier one, and so on. If we then survey the drive impulse from its inception to a given stopping point, the succession of thrusts so described would present the picture of a definite development of the drive.[19]

The description of the drives and their history—their "destiny" [*Schicksal*]—as a series of lava eruptions condenses the two char-

95

acteristics of psychic life according to Freud: violent discontinuity and disjunction, on the one hand, and extreme persistence and tenacity, on the other. The lava erupts, breaking through all barriers and limits, but it also congeals, forming a series of extremely resistant layers. Effraction and congealment, transformation and persistence, dynamics and stasis all characterize the time of ambivalence and cause it to resemble a wartime.

This bellicose character of the "drives" suggests why one of Freud's key terms, used to describe the process by which the drive relates to a representation, has predominantly military connotations: the word *besetzen*, "occupy." The drive relates to its object, a representation, in the way an army "occupies" a territory. Nothing could better indicate the intrinsically violent and violating character of desire in Freud than the use of this term, which, perhaps not accidentally, is anaesthetized in its English translation as "cathexis."

But even the notion of "occupation"—*Besetzung*—and the mobilizing of divisions that it suggests falls short where the territory to be occupied defies definition and demarcation. The splitting of division in wartime reaches a point of no return in the question that haunts all discussion of war and of violence: the question of death and of our relation to it. Freud addresses this relation in the second part of this text, to which we now turn.

Tuer son Mandarin

Toward the conclusion of the section entitled "Our Relation to Death"—not, as translated in English, "Our Attitude Towards Death"—Freud recalls "the old saying *si vis pacem, para bellum* (if you want to preserve the peace, arm for war)" and suggests that it be updated: "It would be timely to change it: *si vis vitam, para mortem* (if you want to endure life, prepare yourself for death)."[20]

If war and its time involves the effort to mobilize divisions, what its reaction formations are seeking to control and master is, precisely, "our relation to death." The English translation of Freud's title is profoundly misleading because this relation is infinitely more complex—more performative—than the word "attitude," with its connotation of consciousness, would suggest. Freud's review of the modern relation to death will sound very familiar to readers of Heidegger and Levinas, and not only to them. This account, too, could have been written today instead of in 1915:

We showed an unmistakable tendency to push death aside, to eliminate it from life. We tried to silence it to death [*ihn totzuschweigen*];
we even have a saying [in German]: to think of something as though
of death [i.e., to think something unlikely or incredible]. As though it
were our own death, naturally. One's own death is of course unimaginable [*unvorstellbar*: unrepresentable], and whenever we make the
effort we can ascertain that we in fact continue to be there as spectators [*daß wir eigentlich als Zuschauer weiter dabei bleiben*]. Hence
the psychoanalytic school could venture the assertion that at bottom
no one believes in his own death or, what amounts to the same, that
in the unconscious each of us is convinced of his own immortality.[21]

The paradox here resides in that to think of death as one normally thinks of other things, namely, by representing it, is to transform it into a spectacle and ourselves into spectators and thereby to
miss precisely what is at stake in death: the cessation of our being
in the world. Imagining death thus becomes the opposite of what
it seems: a way of ostensibly overcoming the threat of nonbeing,
of no longer being there, in the world. To "think" of death in this
way, as representation, is to idealize it: to transform it into an appearance that preserves that from which it is abstracted. But the
problem and paradox—indeed, as Derrida has recently stressed, the
aporia of our relation to death, what makes it such an impossible
relation—is that such preservation precisely does not preserve the
relation to nonbeing that is inseparable from death.

Precisely this nonrepresentability of death leads Freud to "the
world of fiction," for in a certain sense, we are already living in
this world insofar as we relate to death through representational
thinking:

There we still find people who know how to die—who, indeed, even
manage to kill someone else. There alone too the condition can be fulfilled which makes it possible for us to reconcile ourselves with death:
namely, that behind all the vicissitudes of life we should still be able to
preserve a life intact. . . . In the realm of fiction we find the plurality of
lives which we need. We die with the hero with whom we have identified ourselves; yet we survive him, and are ready to die again just as
safely with another hero.

    It is evident that war is bound to sweep away this conventional
treatment of death. Death will no longer be denied; we are forced to
believe in it. People really die, and no longer one by one, but many,
often tens of thousands, in a single day. And death is no longer a
chance event.[22]

Freud thus pits the "realities" of war against the imaginative
surmounting of death through identification with fictional spec-

tacles (or representations, which may be verbal rather than visual). Once again we find the shock, indeed the trauma, of the wartime whirlwind: "I have said already that in my opinion the bewilderment and the paralysis of capacity from which we suffer are essentially determined by the circumstance, among others, that we are unable to maintain our former relation toward death and have not yet found a new one."[23]

Have we today, eighty years later, finally found a new relationship to death? War, poverty, and, more recently, AIDS have all brought home the ubiquity and necessity of death, challenging our traditional attempts to deal with death by relegating it to others. But has that challenge led toward another relation to death? What of the question of violence in all that? If identification with the other's mortality is a way to avoid confronting one's own, then the aporetic, or rather ambivalent relation to death is the germ of all violence, as Freud, with a reference to *Totem and Taboo*, strongly suggests:

> His own death was certainly just as unimaginable and unreal for primeval man as it is for any one of us today. But there was for him one case in which the two opposite attitudes towards death collided and came into conflict with each other; and this case became highly important and productive of far-reaching consequences. It occurred when primeval man saw someone who belonged to him die—his wife, his child, his friend—whom he undoubtedly loved. . . . Then, in his pain, he was forced to learn that one can die, too, oneself, and his whole being revolted against the admission. . . . Yet deaths such as these pleased him as well, since in each of the loved persons there was also something of the stranger. The law of ambivalence of feeling, which to this day governs our emotional relations with those whom we love most, certainly had a very much wider validity in primeval times. Thus these beloved dead had also been enemies and strangers who had aroused in him some degree of hostile feeling.[24]

Once again, ambivalence is at the bottom of our relation to death: we mourn the deaths of loved ones, which we feel as a loss and which as loss remind us of the impending loss of ourselves, the ultimate violation. But we also—and here Freud departs from all possible moralizing—we *also* rejoice in the death of loved ones, for they were in part still *others*, and as others, they appear to confirm by their disappearance the persistence and survival of the self.

Thus, we mourn and rejoice the death of loved ones at one and the same time. This splits that time, sundering irrevocably its sameness. There is every indication that the trace of this split is what we call guilt: guilt of the survivor with respect to the dead. "The fear of death," Freud remarks, "which dominates us more often than we know, is . . . usually the outcome of a sense of guilt."[25]

In any case, according to Freud the ambivalence arising from the death of loved ones, of others who are not simply foreign or alien, compels human beings to approach the aporetic possibility of the impossible and yet ineluctable relation to death: "Man could no longer keep death at a distance, for he had tasted it in his pain about the dead; but he was nevertheless unwilling to acknowledge it, for he could not conceive of himself as dead. So he devised a compromise: he conceded the fact of his own death, but denied it the significance of annihilation—a significance which he had no motive for denying where the death of his enemy was concerned."[26] All at once we see both the function of wartime and its limitations. Its function is to institutionalize the other as enemy and thus to hold death at bay. Violence is thereby given the form of an act performed by one subject upon another. Death is presented as a state that can be inflicted upon another, upon the enemy, the result of intentional, strategic planning, a means of establishing control and acquiring power. War makes death into a spectacle that can be observed by spectators who can, for the time of their inspection, forget that it is also an endemic condition that resists all representation and calculation. In this sense, there is a profound complicity between art and war: both turn death into a spectator sport.

The advent of the electronic media, and in particular of television, have, however, given this age-old sport a new twist. Once again, Freud provides the scheme in which such twists and turns can be approached:

> It was beside the dead body of someone he loved that (primitive man) invented spirits, and his sense of guilt at the satisfaction mingled with his sorrow turned these newborn spirits into evil demons that had to be dreaded. The [physical] changes brought about by death suggested to him the division of the individual into a body and a soul—originally several souls. In this way his train of thought ran parallel with the process of disintegration which sets in with death. His persisting memory of the dead became the basis for assuming other forms of existence and gave him the conception of a life continuing after apparent death.[27]

We are close here to the spectral logic, the "hauntology," elaborated by Derrida in *Specters of Marx*. A certain experience of the body—of the disintegrating body—gives rise, says Freud, to the spiritualization and idealization that seek to impose the division of body and soul upon the subject and thus to represent the unrepresentable. The disintegrating body gives rise to the idea of the soul, and with it to a "persisting memory of the dead" which opens the way to assuming "other forms of existence" and the "conception of a life continuing after . . . death."

This ghostly, spectral life—or at least one aspect of it—is precisely what the electronic media has contributed to the spectator sport of death. If technology in general has always been defined as a kind of prosthesis, a substitute for the finitude and deficiencies of the body, television carries this relation to a qualitatively new degree. Television suspends the attachment of visual and auditory perception, the power to see and to hear, to individual bodily organs—which is to say, to entities that exist in a particular place at a particular time and whose situation thereby supposes a certain proximity to what they perceive. With television, that supposition is rendered problematic: television is there and here at one and the same time, or almost.

But if television seems to separate the power of seeing and hearing from its attachment to the individual body, this attachment is only displaced: from the place of perception to that of reception. More isolated, dependent, and vulnerable than ever, the television viewer nevertheless inhabits a new type of space in which the denial of death can go hand and hand with the representation of lethal violence.

For the denial of death—through its attribution to an other that is definitively separated from the self—is, like all denial, first and foremost the denial of a relationship:

> Denial [*Verneinung*] is a way of acknowledging [*zur Kenntnis zu nehmen*] the repressed, indeed, it is actually even a surmounting of repression, but certainly not an assumption or acceptance [*Annahme*] of the repressed. We see here how the intellectual function separates from the affective process. With the help of denial only a single consequence of the process of repression is undone: that of keeping its representational contents from reaching consciousness. What results is a kind of intellectual acceptance of the repressed while at the same time what is essential in repression is retained [*bei Fortbestand des Wesentlichen an der Verdrängung*].[28]

This passage is revelatory because it indicates that what is essential in repression is not so much the keeping of a certain content from consciousness as the task of limiting its ramifications. What is dangerous to consciousness and what must therefore be kept from it is not a particular *Vorstellungsinhalt* as such—not the particular contents of a representation—but the implications that such a representation can have—in other words, the network of associations it can spawn.

This is why the paradigmatic instance of the defense mechanisms of the ego is not so much repression, as commonly assumed —also by Freud—but rather what he calls isolating. In isolating— which resembles, Freud notes, the common activity of concentrating, and which therefore is so difficult to separate from the processes of "normal thought"—in isolation "an event or idea is not repressed, but rather separated from its affect and from its associative relation . . . so that it stands as though isolated."[29] What is separated in this way involves above all "things that once belonged together," albeit in an ambivalent relationship, which have therefore "been torn apart in the course of [one's] development." What most belongs together and has been torn apart is the inseparability of self and other, and such sundering opens the space in which the semblance of a clear-cut opposition between self and other can be deployed. If this self is the conceptual (and psychological) premise of nonviolence, then such nonviolence is itself a product and function of violence: the violence that isolates and tears apart what belonged together, albeit in a conflictual unity.

The advent of the media heightens this process of isolation. The separability of image from context, of vision and audition from the organs of an individual body, of perception from reception—all this is intensified with the media in general, and with television in particular. At the same time, the ramifications of such separability are also rendered more apparent: the reception of TV images depends increasingly upon a global network that is the condition of all representation even though it itself is not directly representable. The two extremes of the chain are determined, first as the network, eluding perception as such (except allegorically, as, for instance, the multiple monitors that constitute the backdrop of certain news programs), and second as the television *set*, set and sitting *there* in *front* of the viewer, as firmly positioned in its singularity as the network is elusive in its ubiquity. The spectral reality of the image on the television screen allows both the illusion of the spectator sport and the gnawing suspicion that the isolation of the viewer is a prelude to an even greater and more lasting "isolation."

Against this constitutive ambivalence—of the medium "television" no less than of the Freudian drives—the spectacle of war and of violence appears to interrupt, provisionally, the ambivalent synchronicity of (our relation to) desire and death with a more familiar, more reassuring *story*: the "events" reported on television are generally presented as parts of a linear narrative, often involving catastrophic violence, anticipated and yet unpredictable, a situation in which teleological thinking finds temporary refuge and the viewer can, once again, have the illusion of taking it all in—and surviving. But since the violence overturns the isolation of the viewer less often than it underscores it, it does not, per se, remove its mortal shadow.

Here, perhaps, is a function of war, particularly as spectator sport. For "war," like sports, creates the semblance of mobilization: of a community coming together, of an "us" against "them," a "home team" against "visitors," who are also "invaders." The spectacle of war, filtered through the television screen, allows for the kind of collective identification that scenes of individual or civil violence rarely permit. Through such collective identification guilt is not overcome, but at least it is shifted to others, separated—by birth or race or conviction—from "us."

The spectacle of war is increasingly supplemented by that of "terrorism"—which, as its name indicates, defines itself less through institutional acts than through emotional effects: the production of terror. The efficacy of terrorism depends upon the affect it provokes: it addresses a world inhabited by isolated individuals, each alone with his or her fear, seeking aid and comfort from the televisual representation of violence as act. The isolated act of terrorism becomes the pretext for a war against it, in which cause and perpetrator tend to converge in the shadowy figure of the elusive enemy.

Freud's "Timely Thoughts on War and Death" allows us to glimpse something of the interconnections that have been forged between the representation of violence, the media, and the ambivalent structure of desire and anguish. But those thoughts also allow us to envisage an alternative to simple identification with the hero, the star, the individual—in short, with the immortals—and against the enemy, the foreigner, the mass, that being the form in which our divisions are most violently and destructively mobilized. That alternative would involve remembering not just the mortality of our bodies, of our bodily situatedness, which in turns means our relations to others, however ambivalent. With the loss of the beloved other by death, Freud writes, "a part of our own beloved ego is also lost." Only a part, to be true—which can, as we have seen, be occasion for rejoicing. But an ego that consists of such parts is a composite. Perhaps this is one of the implications of Freud's enigmatic remark that the ego resembles the projection of a surface—the surface of the body—upon a screen. If the ego is understood first and foremost as a "body-ego," this surface projection demonstrates that the "body" is construed not as a container, separating self from other, inside from outside, but as itself a screen, where outside and inside, other and self touch each other. The ego would be the result not of the narrative fiction that in Freud's text bears the equivocal title "Castration," but rather of a non-narrative friction through which a certain surface collects itself into body-ego. This would also give new significance to Freud's insistence on the affective character of ambivalence—*Gefühlsambivalenz*, in German. As feeling, ambivalence would consist not in the interiority of a sentiment but in the constitutive contact with the other that marks the body as divided support of erogenous zones—or, more precisely perhaps, of heterogeneous zones.

The new, electronic media appeal to this medial situation of the body, and of the ego that depends upon it. With their dislocations, reducing the usual parameters of space and time to an inauthentic simultaneity, the electronic media make way for representations that are theatrical insofar as they address the other not simply as beholder but as frictional surfaces, otherwise known as "bodies": as any-body and as no-body. Through their appeal, the body reveals itself as that which it perhaps has always been: not simply the dispensable container of the soul, but a war zone: a riven site that disrupts the very organizations and mobilizations it calls forth. The body as war zone is no longer the material condition of the "proper" and of property, but rather a stage prop that bears witness to a situation that is irreducibly theatrical. From this theater, violence can never be eliminated. It might, however, be theatricalized with less destructive effects.

Toward the end of his discussion of our relation to death, Freud cites a fictional example of that relation, drawn from Balzac's *Père Goriot*. In that passage, one of the characters asks the other—Freud transforms this fictional relationship into one between author and reader—what he would do "if—without leaving Paris and of course without being discovered—he could kill, with great profit to himself, an old Mandarin in Peking by a mere act of will. Rousseau implies that he would not give much for the life of that dignitary. *Tuer son Mandarin* has become a proverbial phrase for this secret readiness, present even in modern man."[30] The anecdote is attributed by Freud, following Balzac, to Rousseau. But subsequent scholarship has been unable to find any such anecdote in Rousseau's writing.[31] The obscurity of the reference, however, can perhaps serve to point us toward the crux of the story, which is no longer a story or a narrative but the result of a dislocated and "disembodied" phrase: *Tuer son Mandarin*. To be sure, the proverbial phrase (Freud refers to it as *sprichwörtlich*) also entails a story, which in turn articulates a desire, or rather a fantasy as old as modernity itself: that of freeing oneself from the burden of the past, from the traditions of forefathers and fathers, in order to reign without restriction. To do away with the past, by remote control, as it were, and "with great profit to (one)self"—in order to acquire the wherewithal to be oneself, before and above all others.

But perhaps what is most significant about this "proverb" is the way this story, whose origins are difficult to assign to a single author, is transformed through its circulation. In the Balzacian text referred to by Freud, as in that of Chateaubriand which precedes it, the "Mandarin" is a stranger, a "foreigner," and as such the noun takes the definite article: *le*, "the." But in Freud's recitation of the "proverbial" phrase, "the" has metamorphosed into "his": the "stranger/foreigner" is no longer simply alien; he has been refigured into the title of a story, one which can be circulated at will. *Tuer* son *Mandarin* thus designates not just, as Freud remarks, the "secret readiness" of "modern man" to appropriate the wealth of the other, despite all the restraints that civilization places upon individual aggressivity, but also how the institution of narrative can serve to efface the alterity of the other by pro-verbalizing it. The story puts "the" Mandarin in place as "his" Mandarin. It foregrounds the Mandarin and, in so doing, appropriates him. Out there in front, the positioning of the Mandarin is the condition of the fantasy: he can be done away with only if he can first be located. Not in Peking, to be sure, but in front of the desiring, speaking subject. Such positioning, pro-verbally, enables the Mandarin to become the support of a fantasy, whose meaning is the desire to keep death at a distance by assigning it to another: to the member(s) of another group, nation, culture, world. This fantasy thus entails not so much the desire of an object, but the desire of power: the power to distance death by controlling its representations. The scope of this fantasy is global, for only through the fantasy of an all-encompassing power of representation can the *singularity* of death appear to be brought under control. It is a fantasy in which the will triumphs over the world, transcending all distances, all obstacles; it is the triumph of mind over body, but perhaps even more, of media over matter. Only thus can death appear as something capable of being inflicted upon others at profit to oneself.

But there is another side to the story. The proverbial expression *Tuer son Mandarin* is not just directed at a distant other; it is also directed at the self. Reminiscent of the conflicted mechanism of autoimmunization identified by Derrida as constituting a driving force of "religion,"[32] it reveals that the "secret readiness" of the self to kill the other also turns out to be a threat to its own property. *Tuer son Mandarin* can be read as designating not just the fantasy of enriching oneself by doing away with the other, but also that of doing away with one's own property and provenance. To kill *one's* Mandarin would then be to do away with everything required for the one to be a proper and property-owning subject.

The "upshot" of the story would be inseparable from the ambiguous movement of the proverbial phrase itself: instead of moving directly toward its goal, like a properly formed pro-position, this pro-verb would turn in mid-flight, as it were, suspending and redoubling itself in order to become citable, repeatable, circulatable. This is, perhaps, what always happens when a *Wort* becomes *sprichwörtlich*.

About such an event—not so much a speech act as a verbal gesture becoming citable—one can never be entirely certain that it has ever taken place once and for all. Perhaps it is precisely the problem of the "once and for all" that is at stake here: the impossibility of reconciling *once* with *all*, except, perhaps, *all at once.* Perhaps that is the time of the Mandarin—of *our* Mandarin: a time neither of origin nor of conclusion. A time of precipitation into a proverbiality whose anonymity no proper name can ever fully appropriate. If there must be a last word, it is not to "Rousseau," "Balzac," "Chateaubriand," or "Freud" that it falls, but to a "Mandarin," whose fate, in being proverbial, may also have become prophetic.

The Camp as the *Nomos*
of the Modern

GIORGIO AGAMBEN

What happened in the camps so exceeds the juridical concept of crime that the specific juridico-political structure in which those events took place is often simply omitted from consideration. The camp is merely the place in which the most absolute *conditio inhumana* that has ever existed on earth was realized: this is what counts in the last analysis, for the victims as for those who come after. Here we will deliberately follow an inverse line of inquiry. Instead of deducing the definition of the camp from the events that took place there, we will ask: What is a camp, what is its juridico-political structure that such events could take place there? This will lead us to regard the camp, not as an historical fact and an anomaly belonging to the past (even if still verifiable), but in some way as the hidden matrix and *nomos* of the political space in which we are still living.

Historians debate whether the first appearance of the camps is to be found in the *campos de concentraciones* created by the Spanish in Cuba in 1896 to suppress the popular insurrection of the colony, or in the "concentration camps"[1] into which the English herded the Boers toward the start of the century. What matters here is that in both cases a state of emergency linked to a colonial war is extended to an entire civil population. The camps are thus born not out of ordinary law (even less, as one might have supposed, from a transformation and development of criminal law), but out of a state of exception and martial law. This is even clearer in the Nazi *Lager*, concerning whose origin and juridical regime we are well informed. The juridical basis for internment was not common

---

Translated by Daniel Heller-Roazen

law, but *Schutzhaft* (literally, protective custody), a juridical institution of Prussian origin which the Nazi jurors sometimes classified as a preventative police measure insofar as it allowed individuals to be "taken into custody" independent of any criminally relevant behavior, solely to avoid danger to the security of the state. The origin of *Schutzhaft* lies in the Prussian law of June 4, 1851, on the state of emergency, which was extended to all of Germany (with the exception of Bavaria) in 1871. Even earlier, *Schutzhaft*'s origin can be located in the Prussian laws on the "protection of personal liberty" (*Schutz der persönlichen Freiheit*) of February 12, 1850, which were widely applied during the First World War and in the disorder in Germany that followed the signing of the peace treaty. It is important not to forget that the first concentration camps in Germany were the work not of the Nazi regime, but of the Social-Democratic governments, which interned thousands of communist militants in 1923 on the basis of *Schutzhaft* and also created the *Konzentrationslager für Ausländer* at Cottbus-Sielow, which housed mainly Eastern European refugees and which may, therefore, be considered the first camp for Jews in this century (even if it was, obviously, not an extermination camp).

The juridical foundation for *Schutzhaft* was the proclamation of a state of siege or of exception and a corresponding suspension of the articles of the German constitution that guaranteed personal liberties. Article 48 of the Weimar constitution read as follows: "The president of the Reich may, in the case of a grave disturbance or threat to public security and order, make the decisions necessary to re-establish public security, if necessary with the aid of the armed forces. To this end he may provisionally suspend [*ausser Kraft setzen*] the fundamental rights contained in articles 114, 115, 117, 118, 123, 124 and 153." From 1919 to 1924, the Weimar governments declared a state of exception many times, sometimes prolonging it for up to five months (for example, from September 1923 to February 1924). In this sense, when the Nazis took power and proclaimed the *Verordnung zum Schutz von Volk und Staat* on February 28, 1933, indefinitely suspending the articles of the constitution concerning personal liberty, the freedom of expression and of assembly, the inviolability of the home, and postal and telephone privacy, they merely followed a practice consolidated by previous governments.

Yet there was an important novelty. No mention at all was made of the expression *Ausnahmezustand* ("state of exception") in the text of the decree, which was, from the juridical point of view, implicitly grounded in article 48 of the constitution then in force, and which without a doubt amounted to a declaration of a state of exception ("the articles 114, 115, 117, 118, 123, 124, and 153 of the constitution of the German Reich," the first paragraph read, "are suspended until further order"). The decree remained de facto in force until the end of the Third Reich, which has in this sense been aptly defined as a "Night of St. Bartholomew that lasted twelve years."[2] *The state of exception thus ceases to be referred to an external and provisional state of factual danger and comes to be confused with juridical rule itself.* The National Socialist jurists were so aware of the particularity of the situation that they defined it by the paradoxical expression "state of willed exception" (*einen gewollten Ausnahmezustand*). "Through the suspension of fundamental rights," writes Werner Spohr, a jurist close to the regime, "the decree brings a state of willed exception into being in view of the establishment of the National Socialist State."[3]

The importance of this constitutive nexus between the state of exception and the concentration camp cannot be overestimated for a correct understanding of the nature of the camp. The "protection" of freedom which is at issue in *Schutzhaft* is, ironically, protection against the suspension of law that characterizes the emergency. The novelty is that *Schutzhaft* is now separated from the state of exception on which it had been based and is left in force in a normal situation. *The camp is the space which is opened when the state of exception begins to become the rule.* In the camp, the state of exception, which was essentially a temporary suspension of order on the basis of a factual state of danger, is now given a permanent spatial arrangement, which as such nevertheless remains outside the normal order.[4] When Himmler decided to create a "concentration camp for political prisoners" in Dachau at the time of Hitler's election as Chancellor of the Reich in March 1933, the camp was immediately entrusted to the SS and—thanks to *Schutzhaft*—placed outside the rules of penal and prison law, which both then and subsequently never had any bearing on it. Despite the multiplication of the often contradictory communiqués, instructions, and telegrams through which the authorities both of the Reich and of the individual *Länder* took care to keep the workings of *Schutzhaft* as vague as possible after the decree of February 28, the camp's absolute independence from every judicial control and every reference to the normal juridical order was constantly reaffirmed. According to the new notions of the National Socialist jurists (among whom Carl Schmitt was in the front lines), which located the primary and immediate source of law in the *Führer*'s command, *Schutzhaft* had, moreover, no need whatsoever of a juridical foundation in existing institutions and laws, being "an immediate effect of the National Socialist revolution."[5] It is because of this—which is to say, insofar as the camps were located in such a peculiar space of exception— that Diels, the head of the Gestapo, could declare that "neither an order nor an instruction exists for the origin of the camps: they were not instituted; one day they were there [*sie waren nicht gegründet, sie waren eines Tages da*]."[6]

Dachau and the other camps which were immediately added to it (Sachsenhausen, Buchenwald, Lichtenberg) remained virtually always in operation—what varied was the consistency of their population (which in certain periods, in particular between 1935 and 1937, before the Jews began to be deported, diminished to 7,500 people). But in Germany the camp as such had become a permanent reality.

The camp as a space of exception is a paradox. The camp is a piece of land which is placed outside the normal juridical order, but it is nevertheless not simply an external space. What is excluded in the camp is, according to the etymological sense of the term "exception" (*ex-capere*), *taken outside*, included through its own exclusion. But, above all, the state of exception is itself taken into the juridical order. In so far as the state of exception is "willed," it inaugurates a new juridico-political paradigm in which the norm becomes indistinguishable from the exception. The camp is thus the structure in which the state of exception—on whose possible decision sovereign power is founded—is realized *normally*. The sovereign no longer limits himself, as he did in the spirit of the Weimar constitution, to deciding on the exception on the basis of recognizing a given and factual situation (danger to public safety): laying bare the inner structure of the ban which characterizes his power, he now de facto produces the situation as a consequence of the decision on the exception. This is why in the camp the *quaestio iuris* is, if we look carefully, no longer strictly distinguishable from the *quaestio facti*, and in this sense every question concerning the legality or illegality of what happened there simply makes no sense. *The camp is a hybrid of law and fact in which the two terms have become indistinguishable.*

Hannah Arendt once observed that in the camps, the principle that supports totalitarian rule and that common sense obstinately refuses to admit comes fully to light: this is the principle according to which "everything is possible." Only because the camps constitute a space of exception in the sense we have examined—in which not only is law completely suspended but fact and law are completely confused—is everything in the camps truly possible. If this particular juridico-political structure of the camps—whose task is precisely to create a stable exception—is not understood, the incredible things that happened there remain completely unintelligible. Whoever entered the camp moved in a zone of indistinction between outside and inside, exception and rule, licit and illicit, in which the very concepts of subjective right and juridical protection no longer made any sense. What is more, if the person entering the camp was a Jew, he had already been deprived of his rights as a citizen by the Nuremberg laws and was subsequently completely denationalized at the time of the "Final Solution." Insofar as its inhabitants were stripped of every political status and wholly reduced to bare life, the camp is also the most absolute biopolitical space ever to have been realized, in which power confronts nothing but pure life, without any mediation. This is why the camp is the very paradigm of political space at the point at which politics becomes biopolitics and *homo sacer* is virtually confused with the citizen.[7] The correct question to pose concerning the horrors committed in the camps is, therefore, not hypocritically to ask how crimes of such atrocity could be committed against human beings. It would be more honest and, above all, more useful carefully to investigate the juridical procedures and deployments of power by which human beings could be so completely deprived of their rights and prerogatives that no act committed against them could appear any longer as a crime. (At this point, in fact, everything had truly become possible.)

The bare life into which the camp's inhabitants were transformed is not, however, an extra-political, natural fact which law must limit itself to confirming or recognizing. It is, rather, a threshold in which law constantly passes over into fact and fact into law, and in which the two planes become indistinguishable. It is impossible to grasp the specificity of the National Socialist concept of race—and, with it, the peculiar vagueness and inconsistency that characterize it—if one forgets that the *biopolitical body* which constitutes the new fundamental political subject is neither a *quaestio facti* (for example, the identification of a certain biological body) nor a *quaestio iuris* (the identification of a certain juridical rule to be applied), but rather the site of a sovereign political decision that operates in the absolute indifference of fact and law.

No one expressed this peculiar nature of the new fundamental biopolitical categories more clearly than Schmitt, who, in the essay "State, Movement, People," approximates the concept of race, without which "the National Socialist state could not exist, nor could its juridical life be possible," to the "general and indeterminate clauses" which had penetrated ever more deeply into German and European legislation in the twentieth century. In penetrating invasively into the rule, concepts such as "good morals," Schmitt observes, "proper initiative," "important motive," "public security and order," "state of danger," "case of necessity," which refer not to a rule but to a situation, by now rendered obsolete the illusion of a law which would *a priori* be able to regulate all cases and all situations and which judges would have to limit themselves simply to applying. Moving certainty and calculability outside the rule, these clauses render all juridical concepts indeterminate. "In this sense," Schmitt writes, with unwittingly Kafkaesque accents, "today there are now only 'indeterminate' juridical concepts. . . . The entire application of law thus lies between Scylla and Charybdis. The way forward seems to condemn us to a shoreless sea and to move us ever farther from the firm ground of juridical certainty and adherence to the law, which at the same time is still the ground of the judges' independence. Yet the way backward, which leads toward the formalistic superstition of law which was recognized as senseless and superceded long ago, is not worthy of consideration."[8]

A concept such as the National Socialist notion of race (or, in the words of Schmitt, of "equality of stock") functions as a general clause (analogous to "state of danger" or to "good morals") which does not refer to any situation of external fact, but instead realizes an immediate coincidence of fact and law. The judge, the civil servant, or whoever else has to reckon with such a notion no longer orients himself according to a rule or a situation of fact. Binding himself solely with his own community of race with the German people and the *Führer*, such a person moves in a zone in which the distinction between life and politics, between questions of fact and questions of law, has literally no more meaning.

Only from this perspective does the National Socialist theory that posits the immediate and intrinsically perfect source of law in the word of the *Führer* acquire its full significance. Just as the word of the *Führer* is not a factual situation which is then transformed into a rule, but is rather itself—in so far as it is living voice—rule, so the biopolitical body (in its twofold appearance as Jewish body and German body, as life unworthy of being lived and as full life) is not an inert biological presupposition to which the rule refers, but at once rule and criterion of its own application, *a juridical rule that decides the fact that decides on its application.*

The radical novelty implicit in this conception has not been sufficiently noticed by historians of law. Not only is the law issued by the *Führer* definable neither as rule nor as exception and neither as law nor as fact. There is more: in this law (as Benjamin understood, projecting the Schmittian theory of sovereignty onto the baroque monarch, in whom "the gesture of execution" becomes constitutive and who, having to decide on the exception, is caught in the impossibility of making a decision),[9] the formation of the rule (*normazione*) and the execution of the rule—the production of law and its application—are no longer distinguishable moments. The *Führer* is truly, according to the Pythagorian definition of the sovereign, a *nomos empsukhon*, a living law.[10] (This is why, even if it remains formally in effect, the separation of powers which characterizes the liberal-democratic State loses its meaning here. Hence the difficulty of judging according to normal juridical criteria when judging those officials who, like Eichmann, did nothing other than execute the word of the *Führer* as law.)

This is the ultimate meaning of the Schmittian thesis according to which the principle of *Führung* is "a concept of the immediate present and of real presence."[11] And this is why Schmitt can affirm, without any contradiction, that "it is general knowledge among the contemporary German political generation that precisely the decision concerning whether a fact or a kind of thing is apolitical is a specifically political decision."[12] Politics is now literally the decision concerning the unpolitical (that is, concerning bare life).

The camp is the space of this absolute impossibility of deciding between fact and law, rule and application, exception and rule, which nevertheless incessantly decides between them. What confronts the guard or the camp official is not an extra-juridical fact (an individual biologically belonging to the Jewish race) to which he must apply the discrimination of the National Socialist rule. On the contrary, every gesture, every event in the camp, from the most ordinary to the most exceptional, enacts the decision on bare life by which the German biopolitical body is made actual. The separation of the Jewish body is the immediate production of the specifically German body, just as the application of the rule is its production.

If this is true, if the essence of the camp consists in the materialization of the state of exception and in the subsequent creation of a space in which bare life and the rule enter into a threshold of indistinction, then we must admit that we find ourselves virtually in the presence of a camp every time such a structure is created, independent of the kinds of crime that are committed there and whatever its denomination and specific topography. The stadium in Bari into which the Italian police in 1991 provisionally herded all illegal Albanian immigrants before sending them back to their country, the winter cycle-racing track in which the Vichy authorities gathered the Jews before consigning them to the Germans, the *Konzentrationslager für Ausländer* in Cottbus-Sielow in which the Weimar government gathered Jewish refugees from the East, or the *zones d'attente* in French international airports in which foreigners asking for refugee status are detained will then all equally be camps. In all these cases, an apparently innocuous space (for example, the Hôtel Arcades in Roissy) actually delimits a space in which the normal order is de facto suspended and in which whether or not atrocities are committed depends not on law, but on the civility and ethical sense of the police who temporarily act as sovereign (for example, in the four days during which foreigners can be held in the *zone d'attente* before the intervention of the judicial authority).

In this light, the birth of the camp in our time appears as an event which decisively signals the political space of modernity itself. It is produced at the point at which the political system of the modern nation-state, which was founded on the functional nexus between a determinate localization (land) and a determinate order (the State) and mediated by automatic rules for the inscription of life (birth or the nation), enters into a lasting crisis, and the State decides to assume directly the care of the nation's biological life as one of its proper tasks. If the structure of the nation-state is, in other words, defined by the three elements *land*, *order*, *birth*, the rupture of the old *nomos* is produced not in the two aspects which constituted it according to Schmitt (localization, *Ortung*, and order, *Ordnung*), but rather in the point marking the inscription of bare life (the *birth* which thus becomes *nation*) within the two of them. Something can no longer function within the traditional mechanisms that regulated this inscription, and the camp is the new, hidden regulator of the inscription of life in the order—or, rather, the sign of the system's inability to function without being transformed into a lethal machine. It is significant that the camps appear together with new laws on citizenship and the denationalization of citizens (not only the Nuremberg laws on citizenship in the Reich, but also the laws on denationalization promulgated by almost all European states, including France, between 1915 and 1933). The state of exception, which was essentially a temporary suspension of order, now becomes a new and stable spatial arrangement inhabited by the bare life that more and more can no longer be inscribed in that order. The growing dissociation of birth (bare life) and the nation-state is the new fact of politics in our day, and what we call *camp* is this disjunction. To an order without localization (the state of exception, in which law is suspended) there now corresponds a localization without order (the camp as permanent space of exception). The political system no longer orders forms of life and juridical rules in a determinate space, but instead contains at its very center a *dislocating localization* which exceeds it and into which every form of life and every rule can be virtually taken. The camp as dislocating localization is the hidden matrix of the politics in which we are still living, and it is this structure of the camp which we must learn to recognize in all its metamorphoses into the *zones d'attentes* of our airports and certain outskirts of our cities. The camp is the fourth, inseparable element which has now added itself to—and so broken—the old trinity composed of the state, the nation (birth), and land.

In a certain sense, the camps have reappeared in an even more extreme form in the territories of the former Yugoslavia. What is happening there is by no means, as interested observers have been quick to declare, a redefinition of the old political system according to new ethnic and territorial arrangements, which is to say, a simple repetition of processes that led to the constitution of the European nation-states. At issue in the former Yugoslavia is, rather, an incurable rupture of the old *nomos* and a dislocation of populations and human lives along entirely new lines of flight. Hence the decisive importance of ethnic rape camps. If the Nazis never thought of effecting the "Final Solution" by making Jewish women pregnant, it is because the principle of birth which assured the inscription of life in the order of the nation-state was still—if in a profoundly transformed sense—in operation. This principle has now entered into a process of decay and dislocation. It is becoming more and more impossible for it to function, and we must expect not only new camps, but also always new and more lunatic regulative definitions of the inscription of life in the City. The camp, which is now securely lodged within the City's interior, is the new biopolitical *nomos* of the planet.

א Every interpretation of the political meaning of the term "people" must begin with the singular fact that in modern European languages, "people" always also indicates the poor, the disinherited, and the excluded. One term thus names both the constitutive political subject and the class which is, de facto if not de jure, excluded from politics.

In common speech as in political parlance, Italian *popolo*, French *peuple*, Spanish *pueblo* (like the corresponding adjectives *popolare, populaire, popolar*, and late Latin *populus* and *popularis*, from which they derive) designate both the complex of citizens as a unitary political body (as in "the Italian people" or "the people's judge") and the members of the lower classes (as in *homme du peuple, rione popolare, front populaire*). Even the English word "people," which has a less differentiated meaning, still conserves the sense of "ordinary people" in contrast to the rich and the nobility. In the American Constitution one thus reads, without any distinction, "We the people of the United States." Yet when Lincoln invokes a "Government of the people, by the people, for the people" in the Gettysburg Address, the repetition implicitly opposes the first "people" to another "people." Just how essential this ambiguity was even during the French Revolution (that is, at precisely the point at which claims are made for the principle of popular sovereignty) is shown by the decisive role played by compassion for the people understood as an excluded class. Hannah Arendt noted that "the very definition of the word was born out of compassion, and the term became the equivalent for misfortune and unhappiness—*le peuple, les malheureux m'applaudissent*, as Robespierre was wont to say; *le peuple toujours malhereux*, as even Sieyès, one of the least sentimental and most sober figures of the Revolution, would put it."[13] But in the chapter of Bodin's *République* in which Democracy or the *Etat populaire* is defined, the concept is already double: as the titular holder of sovereignty, the *peuple en corps* is contrasted with the *menu peuple*, whom wisdom councils excluding from political power.

Such a diffuse and constant semantic ambiguity cannot be accidental: it must reflect an amphiboly inherent in the nature and function of the concept "people" in Western politics. It is as if that which we call "people" were in reality not a unitary subject, but a dialectical oscillation between two opposite poles: on the one hand, the set of the People as a whole political body, on the other, the subset of the people as a fragmentary multiplicity of needy and excluded bodies; on the one hand, an inclusion which claims to be total, on the other, an exclusion which is clearly hopeless; at one extreme, the total state of integrated and sovereign citizens, at the other, the preserve—court of miracles or camp—of the wretched, the oppressed, and the defeated. In this sense, a single and compact referent for the term "people" simply does not exist anywhere: like many fundamental political concepts (similar, in this respect, to the *Urworte* of Karl Abel and Freud or Dumont's hierarchical relations), "people" is a polar concept that indicates a double movement and a complex relation between two extremes. But this also means that the constitution of the human species in a political body passes through a fundamental division and that in the concept "people" we can easily recognize the categorial pairs which we have seen to define the original political structure: bare life (people) and political existence (People), exclusion and inclusion, *zoē* and *bios*. The "people" thus always already carries the fundamental biopolitical fracture within itself. It is that which cannot be included in the whole of which it is a part and which cannot belong to the set in which it is always already included. Hence the contradictions and aporias to which it gives rise every time that it is evoked and put into play on the political scene. It is that which always already is and yet which must, nevertheless, be realized; it is the pure source of every identity but must, however, continually be redefined and purified through exclusion, language, blood, and land. Or, at the opposite pole, it is that which is by essence lacking to itself and whose realization therefore coincides with its own abolition; it is that which must, together with its opposite, negate itself in order to be (hence the specific aporias of the workers' movement, turned toward the people and, at the same time, toward its abolition). At times the bloody flag of reaction and the uncertain insignia of revolutions and popular fronts, the people always contains a division more originary than that of friend-enemy, an incessant civil war that divides it more radically than every conflict and, at the same time, keeps it united and constitutes it more securely than any identity. When one looks closely, even what Marx called "class conflict," which occupies such a central place in his thought—though it remains substantially undefined—is nothing other than the civil war which divides every people and which will come to an end only when, in the classless society or the messianic kingdom, People and people will coincide and there will no longer be, strictly speaking, any people.

If this is true, if the people necessarily contains the fundamental biopolitical fracture within itself, then it will be possible to read certain decisive pages of the history of our century in a new way. For if the struggle between the two "peoples" was certainly always underway, in our time it has experienced a final, paroxysmal acceleration. In Rome, the internal division of the people was juridically sanctioned by the clear division between *populus* and *plebs*, each of which had its own institutions and magistrates, just as in the middle ages the distinction between the *popolo minuto* and the *popolo grasso*[14] corresponded to a precise ordering of various arts and trades. But starting with the French Revolution, when it becomes the sole depository of sovereignty, the people is transformed into an embarrassing presence, and misery and exclusion appear for the first time as an altogether intolerable scandal. In the modern era, misery and exclusion are not only economic or social concepts, but eminently political categories (all the economism and "socialism" that seem to dominate modern politics actually have a political—and even a biopolitical—significance).

In this sense, our age is nothing but the implacable and methodical attempt to overcome the division dividing the people, thereby radically eliminating the people that is excluded. This attempt brings together, according to different modalities and horizons, right and left, capitalist countries and socialist countries, which are united in the project—which is in the last analysis futile, but which has been partially realized in all industrialized countries—of producing a single and undivided people. The obsession with development is as effective as it is in our time because it coincides with the biopolitical project to produce an undivided people.

The extermination of the Jews in Nazi Germany acquires a radically new significance in this light. As the people that refuses to be integrated into the national political body (it is assumed that every assimilation is actually only simulated), the Jews are the representatives par excellence and almost the living symbol of the people and the bare life that modernity necessarily creates within itself, but whose presence it can no longer tolerate in any way. And we must see the extreme phase of the internal struggle that divides People and people in the lucid fury with which the German *Volk*—representative par excellence of the people as a whole political body—seeks to eliminate the Jews forever. With the Final Solution (which does not by chance involve gypsies and others who cannot be integrated), Nazism darkly and futilely seeks to liberate the political scene of the West from this intolerable shadow in order to produce the German *Volk* as the people that has finally overcome the original biopolitical fracture. (This is why the Nazi leaders so obstinately repeat that in eliminating Jews and gypsies, they are actually also working for the other European peoples.)

Paraphrasing the Freudian postulate on the relation between *Es* and *Ich*, one could say that modern biopolitics is supported by the principle according to which "where there is bare life, there will have to be a People"—on the condition that one immediately adds that the principle also holds in its inverse formulation, which has it that "where there is a People, *there* there will be bare life." The fracture that was believed to have been overcome by eliminating the people (the Jews who are its symbol) thus reproduces itself anew, transforming the entire German people into a sacred life consecrated to death and a biological body that must be infinitely purified (through the elimination of the mentally ill and the bearers of hereditary diseases). And in a different, yet analogous way, today's democratico-capitalist project of eliminating the poor classes through development not only reproduces the people that is excluded within itself, but also trans-forms the entire population of the Third World into bare life. Only a politics that will have learned to take the fundamental biopolitical fracture of the West into account will be able to stop this oscillation and to put an end to the civil war that divides the peoples and the cities of the earth.

Enlightenment and *Paranomia*

STATHIS GOURGOURIS

Not long ago the President of the United States, in a tone that suggested presiding over the closing ceremonies of the twentieth century, publicly admitted that the country he was chosen to lead is the world's most violent society. He offered this insight as he would announce any other self-evident fact, such as the country's ever-accumulating debt or its inviolable entrepreneurial spirit. With matching equanimity, an HBO Special recently boasted of "Violence, a National Pastime." Even when voicing concern, the general nonchalance is indeed striking. No doubt, violence in the United States is perfectly self-evident, but what does this mean exactly? Where does this evidence reside? Where is it directed—meaning, how does it become perceptible and for whom? Is the matter domestic or geopolitical, and what is the difference, if any, where American society is concerned? And what might lie behind this self-evidence? a permanence? an immanence? a history?

Simply enough, there is a general historical marking to this condition. It is what marks our culture as modern, which isn't a matter of pinpointing its precise origin in history and in geography but of distinguishing the moment when historical praxis lends itself to the demands of a different process of social symbolization. Whether one cares specifically for the American condition or not, it is not enough to trace the genealogy of violence in modern society. Rather, one must understand what lends the relationship between violence and our contemporary world an almost natural quality. Surely, to examine a social phenomenon that achieves the status of nature means facing the work of society's imaginary. Which is to say, we must be prepared to address society's mythic domain, the interminable flux of the self-representations out of which and by which society alters itself. For this reason, my interrogation is directed toward the significance and function of the institution of law as the organizing matrix of modern society's production of meaning (which is, in another sense, the performance of its foundational fantasy).

Incidentally, to say "our" culture is to risk attributing a restrictive pronoun to a substantive whose historical "substance" cannot be clearly determined, a risk that becomes necessary if one is not to eschew one's complicity as a historical being in the making of culture, indeed in the making of historical time itself. Assuming this risk, I will address what is often called "Western culture" (with all the catachrestic aspects of the term) and the contemporary instance in the course of this cultural tradition, whose idiomatic condition is that it recognizes no geographical core, that it enjoys a continuous geographical mutation. This geographical mutability, characteristic of a tradition that believes itself to be founded on an exclusive sense of modernity, is linked to the shift in social symbolization I mentioned above, a shift in the parameters of historical praxis. Broadly speaking, I would place this shift at the point when law was instituted as the primary agent of social organization, as an almost "autonomous" agency, perhaps the representation of *archē* itself (in the Greek sense: both as point of departure and as point of governance). In historical terms, this concerns the advent of Enlightenment thought as a new signifying framework in which the question of society is posited as a worldly affair, as a secular sphere that casts some doubt on the impermeable boundaries of the divine.

Two sorts of objections could be raised to this claim. First, if we take as a reference point Harold Berman's monumental work, the split within the Western legal tradition that gave rise to a body of law outside the Church was due neither to the great revolutions of the eighteenth century, nor to the English Revolution before them, nor even to the Reformation or Renaissance humanism that preceded it all; it was rather due to what Berman calls the Papal Revolution of 1075–1122.[1] Here, in a series of radical decisions by the leadership of the Catholic Church, Berman sees the first institution of legal pluralism, "the differentiation of the ecclesiastical polity from secular politics." For Berman, this moment signifies the *Ursprung* of Western legal history (despite the long tradition that goes back to Justinian and the Romans): a revolutionary event that institutes Western history as a characteristic trajectory of revolutionary practices within the domain of the law. The American and French revolutions, in this respect, are predicated on an already revolutionary legal imagination that subscribes to a notion of law which "contains within itself a legal science, a meta-law, by which it can be both analyzed and evaluated."[2]

However, without doubting the basic framework of Berman's argument (whose eccentricity and erudition I particularly value), there is something that takes place in the era we call the Age of Enlightenment or the Age of Revolution that sets it apart from previous incarnations of the revolutionary imaginary in the history of the Western legal tradition. Simply put, this is the conceptualization of autonomy as a social and political project: the notion that legislation is potentially within the capacity of every rational individual. The articulation of this project—from the epistemological tenets of Locke and the Scottish Enlightenment (and their influence on Thomas Jefferson) to the moral metaphysics of Kant—hinges on an altogether different conceptualization of subjective agency. In fact, anticipating the argument below, I would go so far as to say that the project of autonomy inaugurates the modern subject as we now understand it, that is, as a primarily legal entity whose external (social) boundaries are sanctioned by a set of "inalienable" rights and whose internal imagination adheres to the belief that these rights are indeed inalienable (that they represent one's irrevocable independence before the law, the safeguard of self-determination).

Even if we grant the historical origins of secular law to the High Middle Ages, we cannot speak of a secularization of one's relation to the law until the eighteenth century, in other words, until society institutes an internalized conviction of one's right to determine what is right. This conviction is internalized at the level of the individual imaginary—indeed, seen from the reverse angle, it is tantamount to the imaginary institution of the individual.[3] But this is not to say—and here we come to the second possible objection to my genealogy—that the advent of Enlightenment law managed to clear the board of religious conceptions, not even at the level of social and political institutions. Quite the contrary, in fact—which is precisely where the problem begins and precisely why the problem begins there. The point is that the Enlightenment reconfigured the notion of law on a radically different foundation (by altering the terms of one's relation to the law), despite the persistence of the monotheistic imaginary that permeates the history of the Western legal tradition. To put it bluntly, the American and French Constitutions overwrote the social-imaginary network of the Holy Scriptures, despite the fact that, for example, the dollar bill still banks its symbolic credibility in the motto "In God we trust."

To speak of the Enlightenment, of course, is always to speak tentatively, both because the Enlightenment involves a fundamental duplicity (a secular metaphysics, an ethnocentric universality, a mythological rationality, etc.) and because the idiom of the Enlightenment is profoundly plural (the French *les Lumières* is hardly an unfortunate designation). The scholarship on this matter, starting with Horkheimer and Adorno's groundbreaking attempt to delineate its dialectic, is enormous and cannot occupy us here. What this argument is particularly concerned with is the genealogy of violence within the domain of the law in modern societies, a matter that involves a discussion of the Enlightenment, if nothing else, on the ground that the Enlightenment's notion of law (the project of autonomy) was instituted with acts of inordinate social violence.

The argument's progression is somewhat circuitous, a journey that starts with the examination of Enlightenment as rule (meaning both the institution of a set of rules of social behavior as well as the invention of rule—of power—as an exclusive domain of the law) and extends to a discussion of law's monopoly of violence/force and law's intrinsic outlaw nature, its *paranomia*. Several figures serve as the journey's guides, always partial and mutually contentious. They remain intertwined because they make each other possible, because together they point to the complicity between law and violence and to the mythic parameters that preserve such complicity to this day. If the traditional perception of what has already been accomplished at the start of this journey can be summed up in the notion of "progress from *mythos* to *logos*," then my impetus here is to unravel instead the transition from *nomos* to *mythos*, the transition from law to myth.[4] This is not a retrospective transition, a case of history looking over its shoulder—unless it is the history personified by Walter Benjamin's angel who, were he to dare look over his shoulder as he is being blown backward into the future, would face myth in its moment of self-generation out of the void. Myth is not the exclusive privilege of archaic societies. It is always contemporary, for it is linked to society's imaginary, its capacity to make and alter history. In this respect, myth is precisely what presides over the Enlightenment's so-called disenchantment of the world.[5]

Enlightenment as Rule

In response to the question *Was ist Aufklärung?*, Kant proposes that Enlightenment hinges on the unfettered exercise of thought in the public sphere. Although he is quick to pay deference to the State's instrumental authority that sanctions this public sphere, the proposition inaugurates a rupture in the way that both thought and rule shall henceforth be exercised: "Enlightenment is man's release from his self-incurred tutelage [*selbstverschuldeten Unmündigkeit*]. Tutelage is man's inability to use his understanding without direction from another."[6] The gist of Kant's argument points to Enlightenment as the exercise of free thought conducted against a self-incurred unfreedom, a self-limitation in the private sphere that I would translate as *self-generated heteronomy*.[7] The significance of this heteronomy, this "enchanting" paradox, is often blurred because what is accentuated is the recognition that it is "self-incurred." Thus, even when Kant proposes Enlightenment as a sort of ethical self-interdiction (presumed to be the primary gesture of self-determination), he is taken to affirm the Enlightenment as the realization of the human will, as society's awakening to the capacity of human will. In formal terms at least, Enlightenment thought is figured literally as a project of autonomy. Human freedom becomes possible precisely because the fetters of humanity are self-made and thus can be unmade.

Putting aside for a moment this debilitating contradiction in Kant's Enlightenment horizon, we might find it difficult to dispute the unraveling in the domain of self-conception and constitution of European societies generated by this mode of thought. If the Enlightenment project is at all useful as a social/cultural entity, it is useful insofar as it establishes—or claims the attributes of—a new set of rules, or even more, a new mode of ruling. What lies at the foundation of Enlightenment thought as social rule is the tacit institution of law as the cauldron of society's imaginary significations. Henceforth, the argument goes, society will no longer be linked by allegory to a divine universe but will become exclusively a worldly affair, guaranteed by a series of sentences that hand society the gift of acting as a subject. This is the source and purpose of such documents as The Declaration of Independence, The Bill of Rights, The Declaration of the Rights of Man and the Citizen, and so on.

Etienne Balibar identifies this rupture as the transition from *subjectus*—the medieval sense of being a subject, being subjected (to a lord, a king, etc.)—to *subjectum*: the individual agent and political subject, the citizen.[8] In other words, he recognizes in "the citizen" an extraordinary double subjectification. Suddenly (for this is a revolutionary matter), a given community considers itself the *archē* of the law: the limit of law's justification (what lends law its claims to governance), as well as law's limitless beginning. This becomes possible because suddenly each member of this community—each and every one who imagines this community his/hers, who imagines himself or herself as an entity of this community—assumes the burden of the law. What enables this paradoxical simultaneity, where the singular and plural are retained untainted, is the co-articulation of two incompatible projects, as they are put forth in the Declaration of the Rights of Man and the Citizen: equality and liberty. Balibar employs an avowedly impossible and baroque phrase ("the proposition of equaliberty") to open up the contemplation of the fundamentally contradictory terms of the Enlightenment's revolutionary idiom.[9] As he goes on to argue, the task of determining within which limits equality and liberty become identical is the paradoxical task of this idiom, whose modality constitutes a rupture because it is determined to unify opposites, and whose resistance to resolution testifies to its intrinsically differential and contested character.

Balibar argues convincingly for the break of revolutionary law from the long history of natural law, including those proponents of natural law (Locke, Rousseau) who facilitated the emergence of revolution. He is particularly successful in dispelling the traditional hang-ups on the exclusivity of class rule (or class ideology) that allegedly permeated the new Constitutional statutes. His whole argument serves to unveil this document as a site of class struggle—indeed, as an ideologically heterogeneous and antagonistic document. He underplays, however, the extent to which haunting shadows of the past are animated precisely by the fundamental contradictions that drive this new relation to law (implementation of equal recognition or equal distribution of wealth vs. indiscriminate freedom of assertion; universal aspiration vs. diversity of social relations; permanent revolution vs. permanent institution of power). Particularly in the sense that the Declaration of the Rights of Man and the Citizen is de facto an institution of the national imaginary, the task of assuming the burden of the law becomes abstracted to an invocation of the "national will" ("the will of the people"), which assumes in turn a transcendental authority of enormous, enchanting powers.[10]

There is no reason to believe that the American case is any different in this respect. The famous opening of the American Constitution establishes the people as the undisputed subject of the law of the land: the utterance "We, the people" enacts a supreme subjectification of power behind which there is no backdrop, no justification. The law entails an irreducible subject whose plurality is deceiving. The heterogeneity and even relative autonomy of the thirteen States, gained and affirmed by the revolutionary schism from royal singularity, is subsumed in the new imaginary singularity created and legally bound by the Constitutional utterance. Constitutional law is always an act of nationalization, no matter what might be its claim to the universality of rights.[11]

But the American case is particularly intriguing because this nationalizing utterance was performed twice. The Declaration of Independence should not be seen as the historical and philosophical precedent of the Constitution, but part of the same multifocal flash at the origin of national imaginary institution whose time frame is a kind of simultaneity in suspension. (This is why it is irrelevant, for our purposes, that the Declaration of Independence is not, strictly speaking, a legal document.) Garry Wills has elegantly demonstrated the multiple moments of (re)generation of American national foundation between 1776 and 1789, despite his insistent focus on the resistance to union by the signator states.[12] The most elementary claim of the Declaration of Independence is the demand for self-rule posed against the singularity of a ruler who is thereby displaced to an unbridgeable elsewhere:

> When in the course of human events, it becomes necessary for one people to dissolve the political bands which have connected them with another, and to assume, among the powers of the earth, the separate and equal station to which the laws of nature and of nature's God entitle them, a decent respect to the opinions of mankind requires that they should declare the causes which impel them to the separation.

In other words, despite the strong social and cultural affinity of the states with the community of British society, the Declaration of Independence begins with an announcement of the necessity of a new imagined community. Only if British society was prepared to adopt the framework and principles of this new imagined community could we consider this cultural affinity stronger than the imagination that rose against it.

What we have in this opening paragraph, enclosed in the boundaries of a highly refined and grammatically precise single sentence, is an epigrammatic totality of the conceptual universe that enables and justifies this revolutionary act of writing. It is here, in this introductory phrase, more than in the declarative part that follows (or the declarative parts of Constitutional texts that must spell out the nature of rights), that the decisive power of Enlightenment as rule registers unchallenged. What comes across is the calm certainty of a scientific treatise which, in pure Enlightenment form, recognizes the force of natural necessity, the duty of demonstrable causality, and the imperative of justifying historical action before the court of worldly law. In other words, we are dealing with an act of political dissolution, an erasure of historical boundaries, which is simultaneously an act of radical institution, an assumption of new epistemological boundaries. How else are we to account for the extraordinary statement that follows: "We hold these truths to be self-evident"?

Wills argues that the traditional interpretation that wants Jefferson to have copied Locke's maxims on self-evidence is misguided. Rather, the influence at work here is Thomas Reid, one of the major figures of the Scottish Enlightenment, whose notion of self-evidence is much closer to the cognitive qualities of so-called common sense. While for Locke, self-evident truth is a matter of uncontestable and irreducible identity ("the same is the same"), from which it is impossible to deduce anything, for Reid (and, according to Wills, for Jefferson), self-evident truth is a kind of direct apprehension of reality, a proto-cognitive level upon which a complexity of ideas can be built.[13] Reid's humble empiricism certainly suits Jefferson's philosophical designs behind the formulation of the Declaration of Independence. It does not, however, dispel the transcendental overtones of this phrase, which in the context of a revolutionary act assumes almost magical qualities.

"We hold these truths to be self-evident" is itself in many ways the casting of a spell. It is a double gesture. On the one hand, it cements the supreme authority of the subject *We*: we, the undersigned, the ones who exercise our "understanding without direction from another" (to remember Kant), the ones who come together because we recognize and share (have a share in) the power of the self-evident truth. On the other hand, "We" are also "All"—insofar as the reiteration of this phrase is "We, the people"—all who declare our independence, which is all those to whom the Declaration finds an addressee, all who will then be the subject of the law (but also *subject to* the law). The self-evidence of truth allows us to subjectify the general will, which is none other than to unify the plurality of particular desires toward a shared object. This object is the law, literally the constitutional element, the utterance that instantly appears as the focal point from which emanates all meaning, the source from which collective identity is conferred (and in which it is also confirmed). The law, therefore, comes to name its subject(s) by an act in which the subject that makes the law ("We, the people") occludes itself. It is a disappearing act, an act of magic, in which the legislative will of a community (indeed, the nation) simulates the divine authority to name, to found the law, and then lays itself as the recipient, the addressee before this authority, before the law.[14] But in the last instance this is a substantive act: a subject acts through speech and becomes a subject by means of this act. More than a simulation, this is a replacement of the divine decree; it is essentially a matter of taking the place of divine naming and therefore a reiteration of its power. By the time of the French National Assembly's official Declaration of the Rights of Man and the Citizen, this reiteration is explicit ("in the presence of the Supreme Being and with the hope of his blessing and favor") and the law is literally pronounced "sacred."[15]

The people thus institutes itself as a sort of ventriloquist divine power, certain as to its worldly domain but also desirous of transcendental authority.[16] The unfathomable assertion "We hold these truths to be self-evident" is therefore simultaneously a confession and a call to faith—in the transparency of Reason that makes all myth, as social force, obsolete. This failed demystification in practice is concealed by being presented as a theory of demythification (hence the disastrous conflation of the two notions still prevalent today). But since this imposture of divine knowledge is inevitably a "conscious" imposture (to the degree that this text's explicit desire is to supplant divine authority), then it is a socially psychotic posture, a social contract with the void. Herein lies the seduction and violence of Enlightenment rule: its fascination with the abyss as generative trope and its uncompromising self-occultation of this abyss in the guise of a textualized rationality.

Trying to come to terms with the conditions of real violence that made it possible, the new scripture of the law sought therefore to institute and safeguard a rationality of violence—literally, to rationalize violence. It did so by representing the terms of society's rationality, by holding a monopoly over the means of definition (of what is rational and what is not). Incidentally, this is why the interpretation of the law (and the vast armies it commands at its service) is so crucial to its foundation. From this standpoint, it is not odd to say that the Declaration of the Rights of Man and the Citizen found its legendary expression in the Reign of Terror, while the American Declaration of Independence served as the totemic alibi for the extermination of the Plains Indians. But we need not go so far back. As we shall see, this particular mythology of rational violence defines the contemporary action of the law, a contradictory condition that finally orchestrates the Enlightenment's own remythification of society. What needs to be explored then is in what sense the contradictory terms of this remythification both make possible an insight into the foundational co-incidence of law and violence and also perhaps afford us the capacity to envision its undoing.

Law and the Monopoly of Violence

In making law the primary social institution, the Enlightenment brought forth a fundamental contradiction. It exposed what had always been implicit in the very makeup of law but had never been acted upon, since the ultimate referent of medieval law lay in the distant realm of "divine justice." The Enlightenment made it possible to see that law is always authorized force, that law cannot be dissociated from the matter of its applicability (and thus enforcement).[17] This means two things: first, that force is immanent to law, since the notion of law without its application and enforcement becomes nonsensical; second, that the question of justice in relation to the law can no longer be avoided. It must be posed, and what allows it to be posed is the inevitability of law enforcement. If the law could exist as an institution without ever having to face the possibility of its enforcement, then the question of its being just or unjust would be irrelevant. Force thus becomes primary to the whole discussion; it is what accounts for the law's authority, what grants it authorization.

This new co-incidence between force and justice in a context that allegedly grounds social autonomy also accounts for the characteristic complicity between law and violence in modern societies. Here, Benjamin's insight into the intertwined nature of a "law-making force" (*die rechtsetzende Gewalt*) and a "law-preserving force" (*die rechtserhaltende Gewalt*)—a nature supposed to ensure that the two moments of the same do not collapse into each other—is paramount.[18] It is important to keep in mind that the word *Gewalt* carries not only the coincident meanings of force and violence, but also the notion of sovereign rule, legitimate power (which is precisely what Derrida seizes upon to underline that law is authorized force). In this respect, Benjamin's text is just as much an attempt to establish the criteria for approaching the nature of power, for moving toward a critique of what lends legitimacy/sovereignty to power. The evident answer is violence, but the real question is what sort of violence (whose implicit extension would be what sort of legitimacy). Therefore, the issue at once posited is what constitutes the rule of law "behind" power, which is also to say, what is the position of law in the very constitution of rule, particularly Enlightenment rule.

In post-Enlightenment societies law-preserving agents (the agents of law enforcement, the police force) participate in the legitimation of power by actually assuming a law-making role. Of course, the converse is also true, and Benjamin knows it well, although he does not address it here: law-making bodies (parliaments, legislators) often introduce or modify laws, and sometimes in summary fashion—as "states of exception"—for the singular purpose of preserving order. The blurring of limits is hardly surprising. Law is by necessity involved in a discourse of limits, of boundaries. Its nominal purpose, if nothing else, is to set limits and discipline society to respect those limits. But we know that the discourse of limits is by definition ambiguous. Whatever force draws as the limit also opens itself to contamination from what is being (de)limited. Thus, the means of law's social discipline can be said to exist in a constant see-saw struggle with the power exerted by the notion of limits. Violence may be perhaps the most dramatic expression of law's encounter with its limit. Violence is what makes the performance of this encounter visible, what makes the blurring of the limit visible (keeping in mind that the blur is the proper condition of the limit).

Consider, for a moment, a much discussed contemporary example that brought about a dissolution of the social fabric, even if just for a few days: the beating of Rodney King by the Los Angeles police and its ramifications. This beating was not an isolated incident, but in fact an example of the habitual relationship between the Los Angeles police department and the city's black population. My contention is that in this relationship police action is hardly engaged in simple law enforcement. On the contrary, the police is meant to lay down the law in the streets, to impose the parameters of proper behavior for both "law-enforcing" and "law-abiding" subjects, for both itself (subject *of* the law) and those irrevocably other to it (subject *to* the law). What becomes painfully visible here is that the didactic method of the law, the means of enlightenment, is unabashed violence.

Yet when law's violence becomes visible is precisely when differences are registered: the difference between the law's institution and preservation, but also the difference between those who speak the law and those addressed by the law. Curiously, when the police express the violence of the law (which is, at the limit, the foundation of their legitimacy/sovereignty) their status as the law's addressees (since, as citizens, in principle they can never evade the law) seems to drop out of sight. That the police are above the law—or more precisely, that they are *with the law* and not necessarily *within the law*—was aptly demonstrated in this case by the elaborate orchestration of the accused policemen's trial and the triumphant (if latently frantic) style with which the legal apparatus (which included the city's entire governing mechanism) arrived at their acquittal. The way that the policemen's trial was conducted revealed, with no ambiguity whatsoever, that such hard evidence of "law-making violence" is something that the liberal social institution must repress at any cost (considering that a possible outbreak of violence by the enraged black community was a matter that the city's officials had discussed openly and had even weighted as a cost).

If the experience of social upheaval in the 1960's taught us anything about the limits of liberalism's alleged capacity for self-regulation, it would be that when police violence reaches uncontrolled heights in "democratic" societies, the institution is undergoing a crisis. What causes the crisis is not merely that society's law-making has been turned over to the police, but that it registers as an event on a mass scale. This does not mean mere extension of witness testimony beyond the particularity of an event's circumstances, beyond the present tense of all those implicated in the scene of violence. In a media age, the scene of violence already includes not merely those individuals who literally give and take the beating, but the entire mechanism of spectatorship that surrounds them. Official media coverage succeeds in generalizing the event's singularity by virtue of suspending its actual time frame and reconstructing it on the basis of mass dissemination of the image. This sort of mass visibility leads to a certain streamlining of the field of vision, a condition where history becomes a blur. Although we must not underestimate the historical importance of social violence being brought into everyone's livingroom in the 1960's (the effects were quite real and verifiable), we also cannot dispute the fact that this orchestrated visibility of violence did more for the launching of televisual culture than for the actual problems in the social arena. In the Rodney King case, however, the mass dissemination of witness testimony had a stunning impact. The answer as to why should be rather obvious: it was random videotaping, a chance witness, an amateur, unscheduled act. The fact that it was immediately absorbed into the mass media apparatus did not compromise its impact because the event of its random witnessing could not be effaced. It was structurally guaranteed to be unerasable precisely because it was not orchestrated, precisely because it registered, at its core, a locus outside the scene, thereby making an indelible print of its historical singularity. Suddenly, the fact that police violence against black men was habitual practice (and rather widely known in the hearts and minds of the American urban population, even if extensively repressed) came through in its totality, in the brutal totality of its randomness, condensed like so much gravitational matter on the surface of a single, random, black body. The full force of the law making its mark on the body, blow by blow, was visually de-scribed in a way that rivals Kafka's descriptions of the Apparatus in the Penal Colony—which is to say, that the violence of the law was suddenly seen in its originary, mythical state.

Benjamin recognizes that police violence in such moments is emancipated from the instrumental promise that links the legal decree to its proposed results. It breaks the promise by eliminating the distance between instrument and purpose, means and ends: "the 'law' of the police really marks the point at which the state, whether from impotence or because of the immanent connection within any legal order [*Rechtsordnung*], can no longer guarantee through the legal order the empirical ends that it desires at any price to attain."[19] In other words, police violence is literally the conjunction of law and order as an end in itself. It is also the conjunction between law's contemplation of violence and the violent deed, to use Robert Cover's terms, and therefore the elimination of the chasm that keeps the two phases distinct. Under "ordinary" circumstances distinction is made between the psychological violence that ensures obedience to the law and the experience of socialization that

131

makes physical violence unnecessary. This distinction is subjected to a ceaseless negotiation that tends toward its abolition, which is what characterizes the limit-space of law's existence: "Were the inhibition perfect, law would be unnecessary; were it not capable of being overcome through social signals law would not be possible."[20] We return, then, to the originary co-incidence of law and violence, a co-incidence that is structurally essential and unavoidable. In fact, Cover argues with considerable authority that violence, as a general principle in Constitutional law, is not explicitly stated because it is understood in the very idea of government. Violence exists at the core of Constitutional power, in the sense that the Constitution grants power to the State (in the name of the People) to practice violence over the people, while the office of the judge includes a fully sanctioned and absolved "homicidal quality."[21]

Yet it seems in the nature of law and order to occlude its origins in violence, to occlude the fact that law and force are intertwined, in plain view of the historical legacy of modern Constitutional law which testifies to its violent generation. This condition of self-concealment is so widely (though not categorically) practiced in the history of human societies that one is tempted to engage it in psychological terms. Society's self-occultation seems paradigmatic of its heteronomy. Or rather, the heteronomy of society is merely the effect of self-occultation, an effect, however, that has taken on the attributes of a cause.[22] One represses precisely what is constitutively traumatic: the originary event that encumbers one with the burden of self-determination. This event is constitutive because it continuously exercises an enchanting allure, a dominating desire, and simultaneously (by virtue of this domination) a catastrophic threat. A condition of unalloyed self-determination both serves as the foundation of subjectivity and poses the threat of annihilating it under its unbearable weight of responsibility. In this sense, every system of law and order is not only predicated on but also maintained by a violence that at any time could dissolve it. This is precisely why law has an "interest in a monopoly of violence"; it *knows* at some deep structural level that the violence it unleashes as its foundation will eventually lead to its demise.

This notion, which Benjamin liberally uses, is known primarily through its Weberian variant, "the monopoly of legitimate violence"—itself probably a legalistic modification of a notion championed by Friedrich Engels. But the insertion of legitimacy makes for a superfluous distinction because law's monopoly of violence consists precisely in its delimiting/dictating what is legitimate. The very act of naming and representing the legitimate is a monopoly act, a monopoly of authorizing (and thus enforcing) the boundaries or limits of the law. Whatever exists outside these boundaries is always, potentially, under elimination. This object of the annihilating violence of the law is simultaneously declared, in the eyes of the law, to be the personification of violence: the outlaw, whatever dares exist outside the economy of the law, outside the borders of the legitimate. Therefore, because bourgeois law and order is always on the brink of (self-)destruction, it becomes imperative to build a society that remains in control of its self-generated violence, a task that requires ever greater violence and so on *ad absurdum*. On this untenable condition Benjamin rests his critique of bourgeois order, his critique of violence, which is in effect a critique of Enlightenment law.

He also reads this paradox, however, as the source that makes violence in a revolutionary situation credible, for it provides the conditions of possibility for the foundation of some new law in some indeterminate future, which can be envisioned only once the projected image—the facade—of its foundation is launched: a kind of justice that occurs in a future anterior. This absurd and utopian moment is the constitutive, temporal condition of law in general as a social-imaginary institution. Consider Robert Cover's explicit statement: "Law is the projection of an imagined future upon reality." Cover frames his argument by an analysis of the phenomenon of martyrdom, an extreme case of resistance to established law in the name of an envisioned other source of law. Martyrs are literally (in the Greek sense of the term) *witnesses* to this imaginary kernel of the law. For although every society's law aspires to an organization of social reality, it simultaneously provides a window on its imaginary reality: not what society (or reality) *is* but what it *ought to be*. Martyrdom partakes of the same revolutionary defiance that Benjamin mentions, as certain members of society willingly sacrifice themselves for a different (not yet instituted) *ought*, just as some others might be willing to kill for a different (not yet instituted) *ought*.[23]

The Lawlessness of Law

The police, as the vanguard of the entire court apparatus, exemplifies the contradictions of law as a social institution. Embody-

ing both law-enforcing and law-making capacities, the police becomes the spirit of the law: in Benjamin's terms, its *Geist*, which,
of course, also means its ghost. The police thus embodies law's
phantasm, what constantly haunts the imaginary institution of the
law by animating, by offering a body to law's phantom condition.
The police force, as the ghost of the law that must return to enforce (and, by dialectical extension, undermine) the law, must do so
explicitly: it must be made visible in its *uniform(ity)*—its formless-
ness, its blue/black, gunslinging phantom nature—in order to exist
and, more importantly, in order to make law exist. This radical uniformity, the categorical nature of the uniform, lends the police a
singularity that effaces the reality of each individual policeman, in
the same way that police violence temporarily exempts the policeman from his position of citizen before the law. The uniform is how
the police acquires a proper name, a name that effaces the plurality
of citizen names and yet, paradoxically, assigns the police a ubiquitous nature. Like Balzac's image of the peasantry as the one-headed
beast with twenty million arms (*Les Paysans*, 1844), the police is
both radically singular and ubiquitous, uniform and formless, full-
fledged body and full-fledged ghost. In this categorical formless-
ness, which is also foundation, the police exemplifies law's pure
aesthetics of violence.[24]

We should note the gravity of this contradiction: a pure aesthetics of violence in a social context founded on the institution of an
ethics of freedom sanctioned by law. Benjamin rightly points out
that the police is a radical disruption of democratic logic—indeed,
that in a democracy the police cannot but act illegitimately, for it
must exercise an order of despotic violence that a truly democratic
polity ought to have dissolved: "[Police] power is formless, like its
nowhere tangible, all-pervasive, ghostly apparition [*Erscheinung*] in
the life of civilized states. And though the police may, in particulars,
everywhere appear the same, it cannot finally be denied that their
spirit is less devastating where they represent, in absolute monar-
chy, the power of a ruler in which legislative and executive power
are united in a totality [*Machtvollkommenheit vereinigt*], than in
democracies where their constitution [*Bestehen*], elevated by no
such relation, bears witness to the greatest conceivable degenera-
tion of violence."[25] In other words, police violence in a monarchical (or theocratic) order is perfectly "legitimate" regardless of its
excesses (or rather, its excesses are perfectly legitimate), since the
nondemocratic state has no need to render invisible its predication

on (divine) violence. In a democracy, the police violates society's foundational principles by definition, for a democratic society is predicated on law and order being every citizen's domain as part of his/her political *prattein*, not the task of an other, a designated specialist. In occupying this position of the designated enforcer, the police also bears out the equally foundational fact of democracy's voluntary oblivion of the violence at its origins, the violence of law itself.[26]

Thus, police violence both exposes modern society's self-occultation and safeguards it. It is both society's repressive mechanism and its mechanism of memory, both society's ego and its bad dream. All this contributes to the general mystification of law and order that we observe particularly in American society: the American Revolution's radical and violent mystification of the nation as the quintessential form of legality founded on the radical demystification of monarchical law. This foundational mystification of law and order—of law *as* order (and indeed, as rational order)—grows more and more as American society becomes more and more violent. Hence, the specialization of American mass culture in the production of cop shows, a genre that has refined and finally become independent of the crime mystery that prevails in popular nineteenth-century and early-twentieth-century literature.

This fascination with the business of law and order, which is also a celebration of violence, cannot be disentangled from the fascination with law and order's underside: the violence of criminality. It, too, has a long tradition in post-Enlightenment fiction, particularly in the nineteenth century. From William Godwin's novel *Caleb Williams*, to Balzac's ultimate master-criminal, Vautrin, to Sherlock Holmes's great Other, Moriarty, nineteenth-century literature is rife with such instances. But in the American imaginary the great criminal, the outlaw, is a figure of great distinction, so much so as to embody American society's general cultural distinctions. If American society is paradigmatically founded on the primacy of law (the Bill of Rights), it is also *co-incidentally* founded on the phantasmatic allure of the outlaw—the Wild West, the frontier, and so on: the errant loner who forges his own rights, in some improvisational fashion, as he goes along. Obviously, this co-incidence is only recognized retrospectively. From the standpoint of ongoing American history, the time lag between the Puritan ethos whose Enlightenment variation led to the Bill of Rights and the frontier ethos that commanded the great territorial expansion in the name of such rights is retroactively erased. The inevitable and nonnegotiable conflict between law and outlaw exercises intense fascination in the popular imagination (from John Ford's Westerns to *Blade Runner*, from Civil War lore to *Taxi Driver*). Interestingly enough, in the classic popular narratives, the notoriety of the name—what makes this conflict memorable—seems to lie on the side of the outlaw. The outlaws have names: Jesse James, Al Capone, Charles Manson. The law is ultimately nameless, uniform. Or, to put it from the reverse point of view (but in essence the same), the law has come to occupy (*besetzen*) the territory of the Name in its full-fledged metaphysical void. The law remains nameless but also commands the very territory of naming. Let us not forget that, although outlaws may achieve legendary status by virtue of their lawless actions, it is the act of being declared outlaws that seals the notoriety of their name. There is nothing gratuitous or folkloric about the *Wanted!* sign in the history of the Western. What is wanted is the name (much as the wanted man is officially named an outlaw as a result).[27]

The fanatical obsession of law and order with what is other to it goes beyond mere dialectical antagonism. By its constitutive nature, law enforcement imagines criminals everywhere; the J. Edgar Hoover character is merely a symptom. To interpret this symptom as paranoid would be a mistake. On the contrary, it testifies to an obsessive-compulsive condition that demonstrates the law's own entrapment in the allure of the criminal. In this respect, the law is not exempt from the popular fascination with the great outlaw. Derrida is right to point out that "the people's shudder of admiration before 'the great criminal' is addressed to the individual who takes upon himself, as in primitive times, the stigma of the lawmaker or the prophet."[28] No doubt, there is something primitive about outlaw behavior, especially at levels of great excess. Within the domain of an Enlightenment imagination, particularly, the outlaw returns us to a prerational condition, a condition that refuses to recognize the new covenant of rights and in so doing unveils the covenant's foundational void, the fact that its truth is neither arguable nor demonstrable but self-evident. In other words, the sublime allure of, say, the Bonnie and Clyde figures springs from the fact that their outlaw excess reaches deep into the mythical power of the law, the violence of its foundation. This power registers itself at the level of flesh and blood, which is why the great criminal also seems to exercise enormous sexual power. In the legendary film about Bonnie and Clyde, sexual explosiveness should be engaged beyond its obvious dimension of Hollywood fashion, and it was Arthur Penn's scenographic brilliance to stage the last scene, where the now mythical outlaws meet their death at the hands of the law, in such a self-consciously sexualized crescendo.

The law thus desires the outlaw's death with a drive that is itself a life-and-death matter. But this is because there is something in the outlaw endemic to the law. *Paranomos* is the one who is simultaneously beside the law and on the other side of the law—one who is, in this respect, against the law but also with the law, proximate to the law's domain. There is, in other words, a similar functioning of the Greek preposition *para* as in the cornerstone notion of metaphysics: *par(a)ousia*, a presence with(in) the essence, the essence as presence. Lawmaking violence in "primitive times" showed no mechanism for veiling its lawless foundation, because the presence of the law in the majority of cases belonged to an irretrievable Outside: the presence of the divine. The Enlightenment imaginary sought to eliminate the violent memory of this lawless lawmaking figure by textualizing a constitutional law whose origin was its own rationality, which was, moreover, thought to be inalienable and self-evidently true. Anyone who did not accede to this self-evidence was necessarily either insane or self-consciously alien.

But precisely because the outlaw (*paranomos*) makes the paradoxical remainder of the violent *archē* of the law emerge in its repressed plenitude, he produces an uncanny mirroring effect. Risking a generalization, I would argue that mirroring is always a heteronomous activity, if only because an alien and ultimately unreachable other presides over one's constitution of identity. If this is true, then the identity of Enlightenment law hinges necessarily on the law of an other. And if this other is no longer God—because this is no longer historically possible, given that the Citizen has taken over the *rights* of God—then the other of the law cannot but be literally the other side of the law: lawlessness. The outlaw figure in modern society exercises enchanting fascination and yet produces the desire for its just elimination because it stands witness, not only to the originary violence of the law, but to its constitutively lawless nature. At the same time, the police (which, as we saw, shares the same imaginary configuration) completes the mirroring by being the outlaw of the law, the exemplary expression of the law's own *paranomia*. This perfect co-incidence of mutually reflective images might help illustrate better the paradoxes of the institution of law in modern society and the violence it seems increasingly to incur instead of abating. The master lesson, however, is to be found in Franz Kafka's representations of the legal apparatus in his mythical renditions of modern society, which might explain why we continue to refer to our social experience as Kafkaesque.

From Law to Myth

Kafka, a brilliant ethnographer of modern society, wrote unhesitantly about the body as the terrain of history, as the most palpable location of society's otherwise imaginary and intangible investment/occupation (*Besetzung*) of the law. Kafka's mythographic imagination exposes the underside of the capitalist social imaginary—an imaginary that explicitly posits the values of free choice in the market place, the sanctioned right to act freely in a free market of rights (to action, to opinion). What this positing effectively silences in its infinite desire for expansion is the fact that it exists as mechanism, as a self-engendering machine of significations and identity formations in brutal repetition.[29] Everything in Kafka's world points to an undeconstructible aspiration for a disembodied autonomy, whose cost (depicted with stunning fidelity to its intrinsic violence) is the inscription of the law on one's actual body. What Kafka invites us to contend with is the infinite capacity of self-engendering law to veil its radical disengagement from the realm of human action and reign by means of the delusion, the self-occultation, that it is in fact engageable, proximate. In Kafka, all depictions of autonomy are heteronomously derived, and any real autonomous desire is dragged through the most insufferable process of degradation.

Certainly, the predicament of being "before the law" (*Vom der Gesetz*) is a perfect illustration of the heteronomous mirroring that feeds the violence of the law. The citizen lies powerless before the law—in that devastating phrase, "there he sits for days and years"—because he seeks (and constructs) his identity in relation to the invisible, even inconceivable, alien entity that he imagines to represent society's justice: his own rights. But in doing so, he abdicates his rights, he consents to live without rights—without even gaining access to his rights—and thus he dies. He constructs his identity by choosing as a mirror the void; he tries to mirror himself on the abyss behind the gate, the abyss upon which the law institutes its mystique. The monstrous realization upon his death that the gate to the law was his and his only—*his inalienable right*—demonstrates the fundamental duplicity that lies at the abyssal origin of the law: the fact that the law must act in order to preserve itself. Hence, the citizen's violation—his intimidation by violence—and the law's lawlessness. "In Kafka's universe, law is *lawless* in a formal sense."[30] But Kafka's universe is merely a mythified expression of our own historical condition, and I would go so far as to say that by virtue of this mythification the historical registers more dramatically, the pain of history is actually made palpable.

The preposition's stunning ambivalence in the famous parable "Before the Law" announces, at the very instance of the title (before a narrative takes place, before the story of the law is posited), the disembodied autonomy of the law. The two notions of "before" (in advance of and in the presence of) cancel each other out. The law is a radical boundary, a chasm that separates and unites simultaneously, which means that nothing can enter its space; it contains everything and is self-contained. Thus, neither the man nor the doorkeeper is ever in the presence of the law, and neither, of course, precedes the law, for there is no *archē* (no beginning but also no authority) outside the domain of the law. Jacques Derrida's well-known theorization of this paradoxical topography is one of his most skillful moments and rivals the theoretical richness of Kafka's original. His conclusion that both the man and the doorkeeper stand before the law without being capable of facing the law (because the law demands that they stand in opposition to each other, that they stand before each other) is essential to understanding that the law operates by means of self-interdiction, which leads to the paradoxical condition of law fostering a self-generated interdiction in all those named as subjects of/to the law: "The law is forbidden. But this contradictory self-prohibiting leaves man 'free' in the matter of self-determination, although his freedom lapses in that, through self-interdiction, he cannot enter."[31] This description is striking in its accuracy; it might well serve as the ultimate *précis* of the narrative. The crucial notion here is that the law is not forbidding but forbidden—meaning, it is forbidding to itself. There lies the possibility of humanity's self-determination, a possibility that ends, however, the moment one comes in contact with the law, when self-determination becomes self-interdiction. The law is forbidden precisely in terms of this contact with its *archē* (origin and authority), which is why it infinitely postpones—postpones by means of containing infinity—one's entrance into its domain.

Derrida recognizes here that the problematic of the law in Kafka is the problematic of literature itself: "the play of framing and the paradoxical logic of boundaries, which somehow upsets the 'normal' system of reference, while *revealing* an essential structure of referentiality."[32] Literature becomes an event the moment the particular intersects with the general, hence it is an event inconceivable outside the *archē* of Enlightenment. The co-incidence of law and literature occurs as a result of the institution of the right of the particular (right of property, the individual, the signature, etc.) intertwined with the absolute sovereignty of the general (the Rights of Man). Thus, Derrida argues, in modern society literature legislates, and it legislates subversively, against the law that protects it and preserves it. I would add that the subversion resides in the performative aspect, the theatricality of the mythistorical, where the performance entails the takeover of *logos* by *mythos*, the placing of myth on the stage for it to be theorized.

Kafka's mythistorical writing works against the grain of society's self-occultation, society's need to turn the mythical into the mystical. His mythification of the law might be the critique that Benjamin so urgently seeks. For Benjamin reads the mythical through the divine—or perhaps more accurately, by inserting the divine in the middle, in between the mythical and the legal (nomic). A contradiction arises here between Benjamin's gesture and the language it evokes, a contradiction that may be interpreted as the characteristic ambivalence that distinguishes Benjamin's entire oeuvre and is at the core of his desire: the antagonism between revolution and redemption (and the constant failure to turn one into another). In locating the divine at (or as) the middle, Benjamin seeks to outperform the *archic*, to render the divine disruptive or *anarchic*. Yet, in occupying the middle, the divine cannot but also become a medium, a means (*mittel, meson*) that mediates the discrepancy between the mythic and the legal (nomic) by sublating this discrepancy to an always already unsignifiable location of future redemption. In this sense, middle/*mittel*/*meson* is messianic. It is a middle that contains the beginning, not simply as divine *archē*, the origin of the law, but as the *means* to the law's promise.[33] The promise of redemption is certainly the significance of Benjamin's famous phrase near the conclusion of his essay: "Mythical violence is bloody power over mere life for its own sake, divine violence pure power over all life for the sake of the living. The first demands sacrifice, the second accepts it."[34] The statement follows the assertion that divine violence is bloodless expiation ("lethal without spilling blood"), while mythic violence (which equals "lawmaking violence") is a bloody affair, where "blood is the symbol of mere life." What makes this syllogism possible is a monotheistic conception of myth. When Benjamin speaks of divine violence occurring "for the sake of the living," he evokes the incarnation of the logos and its salvational hold predicated on the annihilation of elemental life. That is, salvation (of the living) is possible precisely because and insofar as their life is not their own *to begin with* (*kat' archēn*, meaning also "as a rule"). Only if we assume pure unmitigated identification with the divine—which is the paradigmatic condition of a monotheistic conception of mere life—could we talk about an (other's) act "for the sake of the living."

In a particularly deft reading of Benjamin's essay, Tom McCall contends that Benjamin never quite succeeds in "purifying" violence as he wishes, both because "the mythic shades imperceptibly into the messianic" but also because divine violence itself partakes of the mythic the moment it is articulated: "it performs as a mythical text Benjamin's own philosopheme of the pure."[35] What enables this blurring is the constitutively ambiguous (*zweideutig*) nature of violence, which in Benjamin's description does not differ from the limit-logic of law itself, which we just saw in Kafka's parable. One cannot help but pose the question in brutal literalness: What is violence without blood? From the standpoint of the instituting imagination (humanity's psychic abyss), there is only one answer: guilt. In this respect, a divine violence—but also the sovereignty of the divine (*göttliche Gewalt*)—becomes traceable in the human realm only as the resignation of sovereignty, which is to say, a heteronomous bliss sustained by guilt. (I cannot but emphasize here the double nature of the action: to resign is also to re-sign, to abandon one for an other.)

The greatest shadow over Benjamin's conception of the mythic in this text, however, is cast by the terms of Georges Sorel's passionate anarchism in his *Reflexions sur la violence* (1906), a text that presupposes Benjamin's own reflections not so much as avowed influence but as foundational framework. As is well known, Sorel conceives the general strike as the exemplary instance of violence that undoes the violent logic of the State precisely because it is propelled by the catalytic power of mythic imagination. Sorel's revolutionary figuring of the mythical, which is catalytic as much as it is constitutive in its radical projection of an undecidable future, is transformed in Benjamin's essay into the pure redemptive violence of the divine against the mythical. On this striking (re)naming, where the terms of the One come to bear the content of its Other, hinges the entire bet of whether the lawlessness of law can in fact become *deconstructive*.

A few words on this peculiar argument, particularly because of its deep significance for Benjamin, justifies a slight digression. Sorel speaks of the general strike as a figure, as an entity whose importance lies more in its potentiality and less in its eventuality, since even in the strictest historical terms the general strike never quite occupies the status of event. The general strike, he argues, exists in the domain of myth, and precisely this insight makes Sorel's contribution invaluable. He claims from the very beginning that "proletarian violence entirely changes the aspect of all the conflicts in which it intervenes."[36] In the context of bourgeois history, proletarian violence is not of the same epistemic order because it exposes the so-called primordial rights of man as a historical construct; it demonstrates that the rights of man possess class content. The general strike promises nothing short of paralyzing society. It disregards bourgeois society's foundational right: the free right to produce, to develop. The catastrophic promise of the general strike thus operates at society's mythic level, at the level of social-imaginary signification, with a sense of certainty irreducible to its parts, impervious to analytic technique: the intuitive knowledge of myth.

Anticipating the usual objections, Sorel quickly clarifies that myths are neither illusions nor facts.[37] Myths are incommensurable to facts because they may exceed facts, much like revolutionary desire (or utopian vision) can never be exhausted in the fact/event of revolution. But also, myths are not illusions because myths are demonstrably historical forces: imagined alterities of society that make historical action possible. Here, the question of whether the result of a given historical action may or may not correspond with the imagined content is irrelevant. From the standpoint of revolutionary desire/vision, it is certainly irrelevant that the imaginary of the October Revolution led itself to suicide in Kronstad a few years later. As we know from history, this did not mean the death of the fact of worker's councils (their historical existence, potential and actual), nor did it mean the abolition of their intrinsic revolutionary content.

The main characteristic of myth, according to Sorel, is infinity, which is also said to include a sense of indefiniteness. Socialism, as theory only, is ultimately reducible to its words, indeed to its *word* (of promise, of definition, etc.). But praxis, exemplified for the anarcho-syndicalist Sorel in the act of the general strike, "puts forward no definite project of future social organization"[38] and is thus irreducible: indefinite and infinite both because it is irreducible to its parts (that is, singular) but also because it is interminably reproducible each time anew. What enables Sorel to make this argument is Henri Bergson's philosophy of singularity within duration: "To act freely is to recover possession of oneself and to get back into pure duration," which is to say, "[to] carry ourselves back in thought to those moments of our life when we made some serious decisions, moments unique of their kind, which will never be repeated—any more than the past phases in the history of a nation will ever come back."[39] Sorel believes that in society this idea is exemplified in those moments when we create new imaginary forms to replace existing ones. It should be made clear that this replacement has nothing instrumental about it. The general strike is itself a creation of a new social imaginary, whether it will actually succeed or not. In the same way that its instrumental failure (the fact that it won't lead to a takeover of power) does not preclude its reoccurrence with an equally radical transformative potential each time, its actuality is always singular and exhausted in its own historical moment.[40]

There is in this respect "a heterogeneity between the ends in view and the ends actually realized,"[41] which is Sorel's way of describing the relation between theory and praxis. It is praxis, more than theory, that "takes place" in the domain of myth, and it is the very unspeculative sway that praxis holds over theory—an irrevocable present whose potential future as analytical plan is irrelevant —that registers the mythic nature of proletarian violence. The general strike is "the myth in which Socialism is wholly comprised, a body of images capable of evoking instinctively all the sentiments which correspond to the different manifestations of the war undertaken against modern society. . . . We thus obtain that intuition of Socialism which language cannot give us with perfect clearness— and we obtain it as a whole, perceived instantaneously."[42] This is what Bergson calls alternatively "global knowledge" or "integral experience," and it is also, I might say, the principle that encapsulates literature's intrinsic theoretical capacity (of which Kafka is an exemplary instance).

Sorel is right to point out that the mythic dimension of proletarian violence has nothing to do with utopian yearning. In the

sense that myth is an irreducible expression of collective conviction (not attained by rational analysis but intuited as integral experience), it is a radical language of the moment which does not
bear dissection and classification at the level of historical description. Let us keep in mind that the social imaginary of the general
strike is by definition catalytic of social order; its very conceptualization enacts an abolition of that order. In contrast, utopia is a
projected model, which invites discussion "like any other social
institution." Utopias, according to Sorel, are concrete projections,
which are therefore definite and linked to the present by analogy.
Myths are not projections. They are always present and yet, insofar as they don't belong to the order of fact, they are indefinite and
indeterminate, hence beyond analogy. The radical present of the
general strike enacts a "framing of a future in some indeterminate
time,"[43] but it is not utopian because it lacks teleology, whether
conceptual or actual. Sorel's terms suggest that violence performs
myth, not the reverse. And proletarian violence is a sort of antinomic condition to the paranomia of bourgeois law.

The distinction between myth and utopia is crucial in trying
to disentangle what accounts for the impossible proximity to this
law, as we encounter it in both Kafka's lawless universe and Kant's
categorical ethical universal. But whereas in Kafka the law exists
in a suspended mythical present, in Kant the law is always elsewhere, either to be remembered or to be imagined. It is placeless
(utopic) by design, because one cannot encounter the law other
than by pretending to be it, to act *as if* one's personal ethics is universal law. Kant's example is famous: the legitimacy of unbinding
oneself from an intentionally deceitful promise made under duress
collapses the moment it is imagined as universal law.[44] No ethical
decision, no matter how warranted on a personal level, can achieve
the status of ethics, if it does not submit to the regime of figurative pretense (*hypokrisis*) of being universal law. The *as if* universal
is, of course, another sort of promise, a performative promise (for
after all, to pretend is always to stage) which is also the projected
institution of utopia in Sorel's terms. Kant's law occurs in a time of
precedent (*pro-mis*): a future set before us by an act in the present,
but also a present that follows a universal that has been set before
us in time. Obeying the same ambiguous logic, to find ourselves in
Kant's staged moment of the law is to find ourselves before the gate
of the law like the poor man from the country in Kafka's parable.

There is thus a heteronomy at the heart of Kant's prescription

144

of autonomy, indeed a perverse identification between the two. The formal law of personhood—the ethical positing that makes one a subject, a political subject in Enlightenment terms—turns out to be completely alien to our being. It exists because it will have come to bear—the verb tense of promise—a universal validity. For Kant, this impossible passage from the personal to the universal is to be achieved by the mysterious ways of practical reason, although, as J. Hillis Miller has pointed out, this mystery is none other than the performative moment of narrative (the narrative of law but also of literature).[45] The moment of the *as if* universal is a moment of the subject fictionalizing itself as a legal entity in the full Enlightenment sense: as lawgiver and citizen of the law, subject of and subject to the law. This is a moment of fiction indeed: a story, a legend, a narrative that mediates the utopia of the law, a guaranteed passage to utopia that veils utopia, that acts *as if* there is a topos of fulfillment—the universe of rights. Miller recognizes that Kant's rule, his force of law, involves a performative teleology that is tantamount to a self-occultation of the abyssal realm of decision. But unlike Miller's attribution of a necessity to this self-occultation, based on the inherent failure of language itself to perform the promise (true of the legislator as much as the prophet), I would insist on the historical dimension of this self-occultation, particular to Kant as an exemplary instance of the Enlightenment legal imaginary. The promise of reason is ultimately based on faith in the other's reason, not based on the exercise of critical reflection over the abyssal, nonrational terrain of law's violence.

Our relationship to this violence is always singular, much as our relation to the law is singular. But this hardly means individual—autonomous in Kant's sense of the term. Any notion of individual autonomy is not only the epitome of identitary logic but for all practical purposes impossible. Autonomy means freedom only as a social entity/act, always differential and antagonistic, plural and polemical. It is always social autonomy: society—as the aggregate of political subjects, as *koinonia politōn*—giving itself the law. This aggregate is never achieved by a pluralization of the personal (*as if* universal) that a notion of straight narrative implies. What takes place is rather an "allegorical transference of a non-sequitur" which, since it is allegorical, keeps the non sequitur intact.[46] Although modern society's imaginary relation to the law is as a rule occluded, Enlightenment law institutes a plurality at the legislative *archē* ("We, the people"), whose real power hinges on its existing in a radical present that keeps the law perpetually in a state of being made and unmade. The quintessentially duplicitous nature of this law and its violent rule (*Gewalt*) conceals law's mythic ambiguity at the same time that it also forbids the moment of decisive pure violence. To fall prey to such duplicity is to close once and for all the gate of the law. The law remains open only insofar as it can be made and unmade, which is to say that it keeps open, unconcealed, its historical being. To know that the law can be made and unmade is to know that being subject of/to the law is a historical matter; it is to bare our complicity to the violence of the law, a violence which is never redemptive and never pure.

This knowledge requires an uncategorizable sense of self-limitation at the core of political subjectivity, a self-limitation that recognizes no categorical principle because it has nothing to do with an a priori principle of (moral) action that disguises the necessity of obedience, nor an a priori taming of desire that begs repression. Self-limitation does not mean self-interdiction, a sort of Odyssean mastery of the Sirens by self-binding. It is a historical condition peculiar to the democratic imagination, based on the paradoxical desire not to desire absolute power, whose other side is the desire not to desire the transcendental security of absolute law.[47] It is therefore a self-limitation without limit, which is also to say (obeying the paradoxical notion of the limit) that it occupies (*besetzen*) the limit, the domain that both interrupts and diffuses: it is an exercise *at* the limit of morality that orchestrates in turn the limitless act of politics. Self-limitation may be the process of mediation involved in autonomy, insofar as autonomy presupposes a self-generated process of othering, a continuous self-alteration. In this respect, self-limitation is a poetic act—properly speaking, an *askesis* that knows no fear before the other, which is why it can hardly be called ascetic. (Whatever notion of limit is invoked in a social imaginary as the property of an other, even if this other be termed Reason or Liberty or the iron laws of history or what have you, it defines a heteronomous politics which, strictly speaking, is no politics at all.) Kant himself exemplifies an ascetic perversion of autonomy in the face of the unlimited capacity of the human imagination, whose autonomous command of the limit looms before him like a terrifying chimerical object. His understanding of self-limitation is one of self-interdiction, so that his own fundamental insight—"understanding without direction from another"—is subsumed into the ground of something that will always precede it:

the law as such. This is Enlightenment's state of madness, a mode of being that suffers from experiencing itself as the refraction of divine will—neither its agent, nor its flock. Lost and abandoned before the terror of autonomy, the terror of facing society as one's own responsibility, Kant's practical reason offers the guarantee, the legal cover, for society's automatism.

Kant philosophically foreshadows Kafka's world: the dialectic of Enlightenment. Yet, Kafka's sense of the law's formal lawlessness stages, by a kind of Brechtian negative didactics, the entire predicament of living in Kant's heteronomous world. In this world, when the gate of the law is shut forever, an abyss is opened before us, the chasm that carries as a sign the letter K. What does it mean to occupy the position of K.? This may be the most undecidable question in the twentieth century. If it is possible to name the site, it should be *Antigone*—not the figure, the woman, but the staging of the figure, the social predicament that the woman helps stage before us (for she also faces once and for all the foreboding gate of the law as it is shut before her, as she is shut inside it).

Antigone has nothing to do with kinship's resistance to State rule, nor is it the tale of some brave and defiant revolutionary heroine, nor is it, moreover, the paradigmatic idiom of *Dasein*. Modern philosophy's need for Antigone testifies to the interminable power of staging myth before the polis. It signifies no less than the "mythic foundation of thought," which means traversing the phantasm, the screen projection, of God and leaving God far behind.[48] In this trajectory, one looks out from the position of the abyss to see that both *nomos* and *anomia*, *archē* and anarchy, can never be sublated, that they are always in crisis: objects of *krinein*. And how is *krinein* ever to be presented, to be (self-)taught? By placing myth on the stage, by performing myth in all its undecidability, a performance that cannot but be political by definition, just as its pedagogy cannot but be a pedagogy of undecidability in order to make possible the emergence of decision (*krisis*) in each one of us. For the Athenians, both Antigone and Creon are tragic in their transgressive monomaniac decisions—one for not respecting the law, the other for not respecting the myth. The play as a whole demonstrates this undecidable relation between these two elements, which once read from our contemporary vantage point might suggest a transition from law to myth. Antigone opts for myth against the law, and this is what makes her the great, if socially insane, outlaw.

The moment of Antigone in Kafka's world, our world, is the

revolutionary moment that Benjamin seeks in a pure elsewhere. It demonstrates without a doubt that the mythic is not embodied in the legal (nomic). On the contrary, the legal has devoured the mythic. But it is easy to forget this cannibalization, for, still unable to overthrow the weight of Judeo-Christian monotheism from our secular shoulders, we forget that the mythic means nothing outside a pagan imaginary (while the legal/nomic is perfectly suited to the transition from the monotheistic to an atheistic imaginary). In a polytheistic context, mythic thought does not signify a law-preserving *Gewalt*, as Benjamin is led to argue, for the simple reason that polytheism entails a society of imaginary dispersal at the core, a society where truth and falsehood co-exist, not as antagonistic partners but as mutually negotiable possibilities without guarantee. In a plurality of modalities of belief—where belief itself is by definition never devoid of interest, never disinterested—there is no law to be preserved, but only the daring of the social community to institute itself and yet always recall (in the sense of both *remind* and *repeal*) its own institutions.[49]

We are now, as a world nurtured in the Enlightenment, at a peculiar juncture: at the fin de siècle that trembles before its end, for it is the Enlightenment's first confrontation with the end of a millennium (the millennium being a characteristically messianic configuration of time)—and thus, its first-ever confrontation with the end of time since it dared abolish divine time (the Christian calendar) with a mere social decree. This is a historical juncture consumed in an array of apocalyptic fantasies, dark desires that bear the tremendous anxiety at the prospect of the final failure of the project of so-called autonomy. The allure of such fantasies confirms that the Enlightenment (as condensed in Kant's paradigm of autonomy—freedom of contention in the public sphere, ethical order in the private sphere) not only failed at the "disenchantment of the world," but instead fed an explosive core of repressed violence that returned to swallow liberal institutions with a vengeance. In what were resolutely ancient times, *Antigone* issued a warning against the propensity of *anthropos* to play god alone—*monos phronein*. The advent of a monotheistic God, a human invention, came as a vengeance on all those who left the theater without thinking. The explosion of repressed violence against this God (the decapitation of the King, the daring erasure of the calendar) was in turn duped by its own antithetical force, and monotheistic desire was further strengthened by the radical imaginary institution of an atheist law. Kafka merely let this institution resound in its annihilating silence through the enigmatic idiom of a literature he thought better burned.

At the end of the twentieth century, Kafka teaches us that this is hardly the end of modernity, but rather the time when modernity's abyssal nature passes from project to experience. If the foundations of modernity are legal—predicated on foundations of authority presumed mystical—then we might want to traverse the terrain of the legal and its mystical guilt (the complicity with violence) and embrace, with an ineffable sense of mortality (which is nothing but the most sensuous devotion to life), the order of the mythical. Let us not forget, however, that before the eyes of Enlightenment law myth is constitutively criminal; it belongs to the order of the outlaw. In modern society, where law *as* order rules unencumbered, myth is dangerous because it accedes to the most forbidden (*l'interdit*: the interdicted, but also the interstitial),[50] because it opens up the horizon between the necessary and the contingent and therefore demands acrobatic alertness to the slippery mysteries of life.

To make the transition from law to myth is to abolish the order of the sacred. Myth exists when nothing sacred exists. This is actually the moment of ethical decision, the moment of *krisis*. The moment of ethical decision—which is always a political decision (a decision open to contention) and is always a social act in its full singularity (the instance of social autonomy)—is just that instance, not *before the law*, but *beside the law*, the moment of *paranomia*, when myth is staged (as *l'inter-dit*) in an ever-transitional theater of history.

Cannibals All: The Grave Wit of Kant's Perpetual Peace

SUSAN M. SHELL

The insight that individuals and nations perpetuate them-selves by violence is at least as old as Machiavelli, who argues, in defiance of "imaginary republics," that one must conquer in order to survive. "Violence," after all, derives from *vis*, which means, as Peter Fenves has reminded us,[1] both vitality and destructive force. Things live, as every gardener knows, at the expense of other living things.

If such Machiavellian wisdom strikes us today with novel force, it is perhaps in part because of an intervening modern tradition (itself born of an effort to reconcile the realism of Machiavelli with the idealism of Plato), a tradition in which Kant plays a particularly important and instructive role. The crux of that role, I will argue, is an equivocal conjunction of biology and politics, an assimilation of embodiment, individual and collective, that lends revitalized rigor to the ancient comparison of city and soul.

Empirically speaking, Kant suggests, every existing common-wealth—every coalition of private wills into a people (*Volk*) origi-nates in force or lacks the means of proving otherwise. But every commonwealth also presupposes the rational idea of an origi-nal contract, an idea that has, Kant insists (in partial defiance of Machiavelli's derision of the imaginary republics of the philoso-phers, meaning, above all, Plato), "undoubted" practical reality.[2] Every political body, for Kant, originates in an "unexplorable" junc-ture of the phenomenal and the noumenal, of matter and intellect, that resembles, if it is not identical to, life itself. This underlies Kant's allusion to the state organization that makes accessible (as nothing else does) the causality peculiar to a product of nature.[3] Hence, he characterizes the formal execution of a monarch as "civic suicide"[4] and revolutions—at least of the Cromwellian sort—as abortive monstrosities.[5] Organisms, natural and civic, are a peculiar amalgam of force and reason, and Kant's views of them are as much sanguinary as they are sanguine, as witness his repeated and notorious comparison of the generative act by which the human species is sustained to cannibalism, since there is no difference in principle, as he puts it, between being consumed by sexual exhaustion or in childbirth, and being consumed by the teeth and maw of a hungry savage.[6]

Let me turn, then, to *Toward Perpetual Peace* (*Zum ewigen Frieden*), a work often taken as a brief for "national self-determination," though that phrase does not appear in Kant, who speaks of "self-determination" in the sense, then common, of freedom of the will. (The term "national self-determination" seems to have been brought into popular usage by Kerensky, the leader of the Mensheviks.) *Perpetual Peace* was written in 1795, around the time of the Treaty of Basel, and it takes as its point of departure the satirical title (*Überschrift*) of the same name on a Dutch innkeeper's sign or shield (*Schild*), which portrayed a churchyard.[7] Kant writes:

> Of whom the innkeeper's sign is valid—mankind in general, heads of state who are never sated with war, or philosophers' sweet dreams—may here be ignored. But the author of the present [signpost?] stipulates the following as a condition [as in a legal contract]: namely that since the practical politician deems himself independent of the theoretical politician, whom he looks down on with great contempt as [merely] school wise, and as one whose empty [literally, "empty of things," *sachleer*] ideas bring no danger to the state, which must be guided by empirical principles, and as one who may therefore be allowed to throw all eleven pins without the worldly wise statesman turning in his direction; this being the case, if a conflict [*Streit*] should arise with the above, the statesman, insofar as he must proceed consequently, must not scent out danger to the state in the theoretical politician's opinions, which are uttered publicly and with daring on an off chance.[8]

Kant's philosophic sketch, then, is formally equivalent to the shield painting of a churchyard—equivalent, at least, in the sense of sharing (almost) the same *Überschrift*, or title. (A *Schildbürger*, it may be useful to recall, is a proverbial term for Abderite, or citizen of Gotham.) Does this reduce Kant's vaunted "world citizenship" to mere abderitism or folly?

The nub of the innkeeper's satire amounts to this: what men yearn for (permanent deliverance from death at one another's hands) is identical, in the last analysis, to death itself. The sweet dreams of philosophers turn literally to ashes—unless perpetual peace can be given nonsatiric meaning. The central question is thus the following: Can human aspiration rise above the grave? The issue is not merely whether manipulative techniques, based on experience (as the practical politician believes) can do so, but whether something not based on experience (or nature)—something that has its source in reason alone (and hence in human freedom)— has worldly effect. Without some assurance on this score, Kant is, seems, no different from the *Schwärmer*—the philosophical dreamers—whom he professes to despise.

What, then, does Kant's essay "sketch" (or "throw out" [*werfen*], as in a game of pins, or bowling)? Not perpetual peace, which cannot be represented, but its progressive approximation: the essay aspires *Zum ewigen Frieden, toward* perpetual peace. Literally speaking, we cannot see what the goal we are enjoined or forced perpetually to approach would look like. "Perpetual Peace," Kant's "philosophic *Entwurf,*" schematizes, so to speak, a rational idea whose immediate actualization is, for human purposes, self-canceling. A universally lawful condition (force and freedom perfectly combined) cannot, literally speaking, be imagined. The idea is, as it were, invisible. Yet it remains real as an object of approximation, the limit of our progressive striving. As we shall see later, one most readily approaches the goal not by aiming at it directly, but by laying down and consistently adhering to its form or formalizing condition. The main meaning of *Entwurf* is "sketch" or "plan." Kant uses the term in an early work to designate God's and his own respective sketches of creation. On a humbler note, *entwerfen* also means "to throw back or abort." Is Kant's *Entwurf* a mere wind egg or *Luftmensch*, like Hyperion, Faust's evaporating child?[9]

Before throwing his eleven pins, Kant puts in a "little saving clause" (or *clausula salvatoria*), "expressly guarding" (*verwahren*) in the "best form" against all "evil/malicious/harmful" interpretation.[10] Kant's own protective device (or shield) is roughly as follows: if you believe me to be morally naïve, you cannot consequentially or consistently suspect me of deception. Kant is, to this extent, a *Schildbürger* after all, but one whose shield dispels ambiguity rather than creating it. Kant stipulates how his document is to be read by appealing to the same contempt for theory that calls forth his effort in the first place, no small point, since it is connected with Kant's later insistence on the law's complete determinacy—its ability to furnish an unambiguous criterion for its own application.

For all that, Kant's argument is not altogether convincing, given the existence of mystifying conspirators—practitioners of what he elsewhere calls *Adeptensprache*—of whom rulers are understandably wary. In other words, it is not initially obvious why the practical politician cannot (without contradiction) find philosophic ideas at once naïve and underhanded (hence the need to stipulate a "consequence" for which reason alone might otherwise be deemed sufficient). This need points to a larger issue: that of avoiding any gap between the letter of the law and its intention, not only as a lawyerly convenience, but also (as Kant suggests in a later footnote) as a necessary requirement of the law-based ethic Kant insists on, a law which is in principle self-sufficient (as distinguished, say, from the tradition of Aristotelian prudence). To give a final note on Kant's eleven pins (nine articles, two supplements), "throwing pins [*Kegel*]" is proverbial for making the impossible possible. It also calls to mind a certain sort of savage game: proverbial wild men or gods who play at skittles with human bones, a tie-in with rulers whose insatiable appetite for war Kant here and elsewhere likens to consuming human flesh.[11] Still, unlike the innkeeper's sign, Kant's essay is not even potentially an advertisement for cannibals.

In sum, Kant's essay blends earnestness and irony—it moralizes, if you will, without illusions. His humorous wit is both melancholy and adventurous, combining morality and cleverness (the dove and the serpent) in what he later calls the only imaginable way, that is to say: by striving to actualize the idea, while "not acting with precipitous violence, but as occasions present themselves" (VIII 378; 122).

Let me, then, briefly summarize Kant's articles (articles not *of* a treaty of peace but *toward* peace), for it is not at all self-evident what sort of thing Kant's essay is—what genre, if any, it belongs to. First come the "preliminary articles," which prohibit: secret treaty reservations containing pretexts for a future war; acquisition of one state by another through their rulers' marriage; standing armies; war debts; forcible interference in the internal affairs of foreign states; and conduct of hostilities—for example, the use of spies and assassins—so as to make mutual trust impossible in a future time of peace. Second are the "definitive articles," which demand that the constitution of every state be republican, that the right of nations be based on a federation of free states, and that cosmopolitan right (or the right of world citizenship) be limited to that of hospitality—a right consistent with the exclusionary policies of China and Japan toward an expansionist Europe, policies that Kant applauds.

The most striking thing about these articles is the extent to which the future Kant projects has actually arrived. (I draw here on the remarkable calculations of my colleague Michael Doyle, in an article published in the mid-eighties; today the figures would be even more impressive.)[12] Consider the following criteria of "republicanism" in a roughly Kantian sense:

1. free-market economy
2. juridical rights (equality before the law)
3. external sovereignty
4. republican government (meaning a separation of legislative and executive powers, with an effectually elective legislative body based on suffrage for at least thirty percent of all males—e.g., the government of Britain after the Reform Bill of 1833).

If one accepts these as criteria of republicanism, the number of republics in the world has increased from a qualified three at the time Kant's essay was published, to eight by 1850, thirteen by 1900, twenty-nine by 1945, and more than fifty today. Even more remarkably, in the same two-hundred-year period, not once has a republic gone to war with another republic (taking that term in its special Kantian sense). I leave aside the violent manner in which republics have frequently conducted themselves—contrary, it seems, to Kant's expectations—toward nonrepublics. There is, however, some recent indication that republics will interfere in the internal affairs of other states that do not pose a direct military threat only when explicitly invited or during times of civil war. Bosnia and Rwanda come immediately to mind.

My object is not to defend Kant's notion of justice (with which many will disagree), nor to claim that the process in question has made world devastation and the self-destruction of the human race less likely. It is, however, to lend some credibility to Kant's sketch: a gradually evolving organism, a federation of republics as surrogate (his word) for the world republic whose idea is practically real, but whose complete actualization as true world government would be "soulless" and hence self-canceling. The fulfillment of the law is its annulment (in a non-Christian sense), a contradiction overcome only by an image of constant progress constantly exposed, as Kant admits, to breakdown. The vital force of the cosmopolitan system (whose "perhaps most reliable means" is the "spirit" of commerce— the *Handelsgeist*) is "produced and maintained" not (as the analogy with individual republics would suggest) in a universal state, but through the liveliest competition (*lebhaftesten Wetteifer*; VIII 367–68; 114). This pacific condition can only arise among nations that have been seized or overpowered (*bemächtigt*) by the *Handelsgeist*, a spirit that, Kant insists—and his words are, I think, chosen carefully—cannot coexist with war. This great organism, which counts as nature's highest end, requires from humans only something well within their capabilities: namely, creating a good state organization. Kant can thus claim that the problem of politics is soluble even for a nation of devils, if only they are intelligent. Yet this organism remains ghostlike (in ways Jacques Derrida's *Specters of Marx* helps explain to us). It is not yet nor will it ever be born. For all that, it is no hybrid monster or chimera:

> Because of all powers [*Mächten*] or means [*Mitteln*] at the disposal of the power of state [*Staatsmacht*], the power of money [*Geldmacht*] may well be the most trustworthy, states see themselves compelled (and not exactly from motives of morality) to promote noble peace, and wherever in the world war threatens to break out they will try to prevent it by mediation [*Vermittlung*], just as if they had stood in permanent league for this very purpose. (VIII 368; 114)

The community of commerce, which assures that violations of right anywhere are "felt" everywhere, creates, then, only the surrogate or simulacrum of a true world-whole. A genuinely lively whole would, he indicates, be nature personified, Greece's *Konx Ompax* by way, thanks to the same spirit of commerce, of the ancient holies of the East: nature, in other words, as the supreme being diffused (*verbreitete*) throughout the world.[13] Kant, by contrast, keeps matter and reason properly distinct; his own personification of nature (whose figure is the "great artist" of Lucretius) is therefore veiled, if only in borrowed irony: Lucretius invoked "Nature the great artist" to convince us that a world as harsh as ours cannot be the work of gods, and that we therefore have nothing to fear beyond the grave— a reminder that philosophy has long been identified, not only via Plato, with learning how to die.

Kant, however, does not aim (like Lucretius, his favorite Latin poet) to reconcile us to the grave by proving that the gods do not exist, but rather to evade the despairing conclusion that a stamp

(*Schlag*) of beings as doomed or corrupted (*verderbt*) as ourselves should never have been born, a conclusion to which we are "inevitably driven" if we lack hope that mankind will someday be put in better order (*besser bestellt sein werde noch könne*). For the sake of that hope, it must be possible to support the juncture of matter and reason (for that is what perpetual peace amounts to) without abolishing their difference, even though it is as contradictory to yoke such disparates together as it is to mate griffins with horses (VIII 361n.; 109n.).

In this equivocal juncture of matter and reason,[14] the "moral politician" is the designated go-between, reconciling morality and politics in the only manner, as Kant puts it, that can be "imagined" (VIII 372; 118), namely, by uniting in a "single commandment" politics' "be ye therefore as clever as serpents" and morality's command to be "as without falsity [*ohne Falsche*] as doves" (VIII 370; 116), a Biblical reference that likens Kant's message to the Gospels. In effecting this marriage, there is no possible resort to bisection or compromise—*halbieren* or *Mittelding* (VIII 380; 125)—though medium, *Mittel*, is just what the power of money was earlier called. Rather, the "art" of politics must serve or pay homage to morality by utilizing the mechanism of nature to construct peace from the antagonism of men's hostile attitudes. Without that (invisible) homage, politics (as the art of using nature's mechanism to govern men) would be the whole of practical wisdom bereft of freedom, and the concept of right would be an idea empty of content or things (*sachleer*). What makes progress impossible is the perverse inversion of the moral politician—namely, the political moralist—who "prettifies" or "tricks out" (*beschönigt*) principles contrary to right under the pretext that human nature is incapable of attaining the good which reason prescribes as an idea. Such a politics without consolation, such a self-fulfilling prophecy of doom, dispossesses us of good-humored hope by "eternalizing" the violation of right (VIII 373; 119). Kant thus rests everything, linguistically speaking, on the difference between moralized politics and political moralism, that is, on a verbal usage that subordinates the substantive noun to a conditioning, or limit-setting, adjective, a usage, in other words, that evades the copula and its presumptive indifference (on which Hegel's logic will later insist). In any case, politics, the art whose forceful element is man's disposition or *Gesinnung*, is also the only art that requires a rational (rather than merely sensible) idea (hence the need to disavow all dispossessing or *absprechende*

Beschönigung—so much for the aestheticization of the political), at least if the hope of perpetual peace is to perpetuate itself.

How, then, is one to evade the serpentine trails (*Schlangenwendungen*), the tricks and artifices of mere cleverness? Or, which amounts to the same thing, how is one to imagine the conjunction of nature and reason in the figure of a spirit—man as species being—that refuses, or is unable, to appear to itself? How, in short, can one think the "matter" of an idea without emptying it of rational substance, without rendering it *sachleer*, as do moralizing politicians, who put their end before their principle? Precisely, Kant says, by not trying to look to, or be guided by, that end directly, but instead by dissolving prettifying deceptions (by politicians who dare not expose the merely violent basis of their claims), uncovering thereby the ultimate principle from which the aim [*Absicht*] of perpetual peace derives (VIII 376; 121).

Subordinating the material principle, or goal, of perpetual peace to the formal principle "act in such a way that you can wish your maxim to become a universal law (irrespective of the end you have in view)" unites form and matter and illuminates in the only way humanly conceivable the otherwise mysteriously providential juncture of formal and final cause. Where the union of politics and morals is concerned, the less conduct depends upon the end in view, as Kant goes on to state, the more conduct in general will harmonize with that end—indeed, the more (so long as one proceeds "consequentially") the end will be furthered by the very mechanism of nature. Hence the appropriateness of the title of the first supplement: "on the disagreement of morality and politics with regard to [*in Absicht auf*] perpetual peace," for perpetual peace is precisely what we cannot make our *Absicht*, at least not directly, if this disagreement is to be overcome.

The problem of combining morality and politics, then, so long as one keeps in mind the subordination of matter to form, thus solves itself, the solution, as Kant puts it, leading directly to its goal, so long as we prudently remember that it cannot be realized precipitously by violence (*Gewalt*), but must be steadily approached as favorable opportunities present themselves (VIII 378; 122). At the same time, he adds, the crooked paths of violence and cunning are entirely "cut off" by a common saying that, though it rings somewhat braggingly (*etwas renommistisch klingende*), is true: "Fiat justicia, pereat mundus!" Kant translates this (*das heisst zu deutsch*) as: "Let justice be master, though all the tricksters

[*Schelme*] in the world go under" (VIII 378–79; 123).[15] Still, if, as Kant puts it in a roughly contemporaneous work, deceit is the one defect that cannot be expunged from our species,[16] the image conveyed by this translation of the injunction to perpetual peace is once again, without remission, one vast graveyard. Kant's paean to peace threatens to become a gallows song, or *Schelmenlied*. That a decline in the number of bad men will not destroy the world, that moral evil is self-contradictory in its aims and therefore in the long run self-destructive, does not relieve the picture—or it would not, were there no difference between honesty (whose absence is our "racially" defining mark),[17] and the requirement of publicity or public openness, by which agreement between morality and politics (as Kant now goes on, in a second and final supplement, to claim) is transcendentally accomplished.

Accordingly, "If, in considering public right . . . I abstract from all its matter, . . . there still remains the form of publicness [*Publicität*], the possibility of which every juridical claim intrinsically contains, because without it there would be [given] no justice (which can only be thought as publicly notable [*kundbar*])" (VIII 381; 125). Kant therefore proposes the following negative test: any maxim that I cannot openly declare without frustrating its intention, that must remain hidden (*verheimlich*) to succeed, is ipso facto unjust—a test by which Kant summarily dispatches maxims of political expediency (including, but not limited to, the putative right to revolution).

Maxims that cannot in principle be publicized if they are to succeed in their purpose may not be so in fact. Unjust force, if sufficiently powerful, may guilelessly succeed. Transcendental claims and real world conditions must align. But how is one to proceed, when moral politics aims at precisely this alignment? How can one separate perpetual peace as the condition of moral politics from perpetual peace envisioned as its goal? Kant's answer is the federative association of republics, whose sole intention is to eliminate war: a federation that, as the "only lawful arrangement of states that can be reconciled with their freedom," is also the only condition in which the union of politics and morality is fully operative. The rightful basis of all political prudence (*Klugheit*) is thus the founding of a state federation in its greatest possible extent (*Umfang*), "for without this end [*Zweck*], all [prudential] reasonings are unwisdom and disguised injustice" (VIII, 385; 129).

Such a false or backside politics (*Afterpolitik*), whose lack of goals is the flip side of putting goals first, finds its ultimate resource in a certain "duplicity" (*Zweizüngigkeit*), by virtue of which false politics refuses to acknowledge the priority of justice to ethics, preferring to deny the reality of rights by construing all duties as mere benevolence. Philosophy "would easily defeat this ultimate subterfuge or bottom trick [*Hinterlist*] of a politics bashful of light [*lichtscheuen*], would politics but dare to allow philosophy to publicize its own transcendental maxims" (VIII 386; 130), that is, if political moralists would but take up Kant's own daring challenge, and thus set in motion the vital competition (*Wetteifer*) to which Kant earlier alluded.[18]

With this intention (*Absicht*), Kant stamps out (*schlägt*) a second transcendental principle, this time affirmative: all maxims reconciling right and politics require publicity in order to succeed. This transcendental *Schlag* replaces, it seems, the human *Schlag* that earlier threatened a concluding despair, the dooming thought that it would have been better had humans never existed on the earth. This final principle, whose further export or discussion Kant here inexplicably defers, extends distrust in order to remove it by putting people on guard (if only for the sake of their own happiness) against the ruling maxim—fatal to all right—of deceptive benevolence or benevolent deception.

Philosophy could easily defeat the contrivances of a light-shunning politics (which reduces morality to benevolence, thus denying the rights of the people), says Kant, by publicizing the maxims of such a politics, if only that politics dared allow philosophy to publicize maxims of its own. The very publication of the essay *Perpetual Peace* (which Kant has dared, and the head of state has dared allow), is thus itself a ground of the hoped-for hope with which the essay concludes: "If it is a duty to make real (if only through approximation in endless progress) a state of public right, and if there is well-grounded hope that this can actually be done, then perpetual peace is not . . . an empty idea . . . but a task that, gradually resolved, constantly draws nearer to its goal . . . as the periods in which equal progress are made hopefully grow shorter" (VIII 386; 130).

The very publication of Kant's essay—itself an exercise in serpentine innocence, in spiraling upward flight—grounds hope, and thereby brings nature and reason, force and right, into alignment. Through Kant's courage—as in his motto of enlightenment (*sapere aude!*)—(and the reciprocal daring, or indifference, of rulers) the cosmo-political organism is at once enlightened and enlivened.

There is, however, one dark region that remains off limits to the public, namely, the point when civic life begins. For "to pursue the trace of the political mechanism's historical notice [*Geschichts-urkunde*] is futile [*vergeblich*]," and indeed "punishable" if undertaken "with the intention of changing the standing constitution by violence" (or so Kant puts it on a later occasion).

The notoriety, or *Kundbarkeit*, without which public right cannot be thought seemingly exempts its own inaugurating moment, whose necessarily violent character may be gathered (*abnehmen*) in advance from the nature of humanity in the raw (*aus der Natur roher Menschen*).[19] One is, withal, left with a certain disturbing asymmetry—a breakdown in the analogy between individual and civic persons, since only the former can be rightfully coerced by a higher, albeit in principle collective, power. On the one hand, the natural separateness of human bodies in the raw assures that civic members will retain their individual identities so long as they are not consumed against their will (e.g., as cannon fodder). The unification of incorporated nations, on the other hand, would conflate (*verschmeltzen*) humans into an undifferentiated (soulless) mass, exterminating the germs of goodness (whose indestructibility one might have thought to be assured). Within the community of nations, articulated boundaries must be historically established and preserved; they remain intrinsically contestable (however discreetly we avert our eyes from their conception) in a way that bodily boundaries are not.[20]

Hence derives the peculiarly knowing character of a work that is generally taken (as Kant anticipated) to be naïve and whose effectiveness loses nothing, is indeed enhanced, by this very (mis)reading. Hence, too, Kant's entirely permissible duplicity. *Perpetual Peace* is itself a kind of *Geschichtsurkunde*, or documentary warrant, of the truly cosmopolitan regime—hence itself a true treaty of peace. Unlike the merely political treaties Kant dismisses as mere "truces," Kant's *Perpetual Peace* is a deal struck upon publication, in defiance of the otherwise unsurmountable incompatibility (*Un-verträglichkeit*) between right and politics, an incompatibility that lies, in Kant's words, in the refusal of politics to enter into any contract at all (*sich gar nicht auf Vertrag einzulassen*).

Kant ventured, on the occasion of the Treaty of Basel, which followed Napoleon's early victories, to make the impossible possible: to sketch out a plan for the worldly actualization of what he elsewhere treats as the Platonic Idea—the maximum freedom of each, compatible with the maximum freedom of all others. Whether the world today is better or worse for Kant's conjuring enterprise—his raising of the "republican spirit"—is perhaps less evident than its eerie prescience or extraordinary efficacy. To an extent that a few years ago would have seemed almost unimaginable, the world today is as Kant made it out to be. A few years ago, most thoughtful students of politics found Kant laughably naïve. Today, fewer are laughing, and this despite (or because) later thinkers—otherwise inspired—have taken *Perpetual Peace* more and less literally than he intended.

Otherwise than Self-Determination: The Mortal Freedom of *Oedipus Asphaleos*

MICHAEL DILLON

Modern politics is the politics of subjectivity. Self-determination becomes the violent determination of the self when it assumes—takes on, or presupposes—the subjectivism of modern politics. The violence of the determination to secure self-determination, and the paradox (if that is what it is) that the upshot of this project is often the violent determination of the self, puts in question the way in which human freedom and identity are understood and pursued politically. I want to suggest, through a reading of Sophocles' *Oedipus Rex*, that the tragic offers a way of interpreting both freedom and identity radically superior to the subject/object thinking which so radically determines modern political thought, with its allied aspiration to self-determination, because the tragic's sensibility to human being surpasses that of subject/object thinking. My reading of *Oedipus Rex* is, therefore, an explicitly political reading; I read the play for what I think the poet might be said to be saying about the problematic of the political.

This reading is also, in a certain sense, an explicitly Heideggerian one. I read the play politically—amplifying what I think it can be said to say about the problematic of the political—after Heidegger's understanding of Being and being. Being is not an element, a substance, or a medium for Heidegger, but a mode. It is a verb and not a noun—a disclosing. That disclosing is disclosed in how human being poses the question of Being, thus disclosing that the very character of human being is disclosing. As a disclosing mode of being, human being is responsible. Its responsive responsibility arises when it poses the question of Being. By asking the question of Being, human being discloses that it is a responsible kind of being. By responding to the being that it undergoes, human being becomes individualized—becomes a specific human being. The question of Being is ultimately my own, one I must answer for myself. That is how the possibility of justice arises, for in responsiveness I give being, my own and that of others, its due or not.

Because it is a disclosing mode of being in the disclosing of Being, this mode of being that we enjoy is exposed. It stands out, exists in the open. In short, it is free. Only because human being is free—that is to say, itself a disclosing in the opening of disclosing—can the possibility of justice, of giving things their due, arise. But precisely because it is free, human being must give an account of its being if it is to be one thing or another at all. In giving an account, it owns up to the being granted to it and to others. Freedom, therefore, is inseparable from indebtedness. It comes neither before nor after justice, but arrives as the project of justice. Moreover, because human being is free there is no determination of what justice is or any guarantee of how to dispense it. How to do justice to being is the very venture of human freedom. That is the risk of freedom, the risk that freedom is, what is at stake in, for, and as it.

Given the character of Heidegger's thought, however, any such reading is also a reading of Heidegger. It operates at a certain limit of Heidegger—in this instance, that concerning human freedom and the entire question of the political. Consequently, it is not quite Heideggerian. Clearly, it seeks to dilate something disclosed in and by Heidegger—his account of Being and of the ontological difference between Being and being—in order to say something else, something more, about this being of freedom and responsibility which human being is. It does this by taking self-determination's preoccupation with determining the self to be another instance of the impulse to secure a ground for all being which distinguishes "Western" thought, especially that of the political. Third and finally, therefore, my reading of *Oedipus Rex* interprets how the play deconstructs security and in the process expresses a different understanding of freedom and politics. The clue to this is the Greek word for security, *asphaleia*. *Asphaleia* is the privative of *sphallo*, which means to trip up, fall down, fail, or err. *Asphaleia*, then, is not to trip up, fall down, fail, or err. It is to be able to stand in the truth of Being.[1]

Oedipus' Standing

Dawn. Silence. The royal palace of Thebes. Many years after its deliverance from the scourge of the Sphinx, the city is now assailed by a mortal plague. Double doors to the palace dominate the facade. Before and below them stands the altar of Apollo. Seated there are supplicants of all ages. At their head is a priest of Zeus. Through the doors enters Oedipus, the king. Regal, he limps. The priest kneels. The king bids the supplicants to say why they have come to sacrifice to the god and solicit his aid. Unsteady on his own feet, Oedipus solicitously assists the priest to his, and invites him to speak for the rest. A speech follows in which Sophocles anticipates and encapsulates the entire problematic of the play (as Heidegger notes he does also in *Antigone*). Oedipus spends the rest of the drama catching up with himself.[2]

The priest replies that the *polis* is foundering in the bloody waves of a deadly blight that has afflicted all procreation. Oedipus is no god, but he is first among men. An interface between men and gods, his godlike or god-inspired knowledge—his *techne*—once saved them from the Sphinx. The Greek here is especially revealing. The priest literally says that then he lifted up their lives (*th'emin orthosai bion*[3]), a phrase which directly invokes the connection between securing, standing, and truth.[4] In bidding him do the same again—*anorthoson polin* (line 46), raise or lift up the polis—the priest appeals directly to Oedipus' concern for his name and reputation. Praying that his reign should not have to be recorded as one which elevated Thebes only to see it fall and fail again, and reminding Oedipus that his own survival is at stake in that of the city, the priest asks the king to use the same knowledge to rescue it again now and secure it upon a rock: "stanthes t'es orthon kai pesontes husteron. All 'asphaleia tend' anorthoson polin" (lines 50–51).

Because the plague threatens to empty the city of all life, the priest identifies the essence of *asphaleia*—that is, the problem of rule for the *polis* (*krateis*, to grasp, hold firm, or support something; lines 54 and 55) that Oedipus now confronts—not with *techne* or the provision of the engines of defense (battlements and warships), but with the challenge of being-in-common, living together, *xunoikounton esso* (line 57). This is the challenge Oedipus must face if he is to put the city back on its feet and secure it there. The expression of the challenge in this formula discloses the central theme of the play—the understanding of what political life is about and of how the polis realizes it, for the polis is fundamentally allied to the disclosive truth of Being and replicates the *polemos,* or agonal bonding, which characterizes Being and the ontological difference between Being and beings. It concerns, then, the tragic freedom of insecurity which Oedipus—the figure of mortal human being—is destined to bear.

Oedipus' response, emphasizing as he did in his opening address that he knows what problem has brought them there (the irony that he does and he does not is inescapable), dedicates himself to the task by identifying himself with his people. He bears the sickness they bear—the divided being of mortal being—but in him it attains a magnitude and intensity that outstrips its presence in them: "noseite pantes, kai nosountes, os ego ouk estin humon ostis ex' isou nosei" (lines 60–61). All he lacks to root out the problem is the return of Creon from an embassy (*theoria*) to Delphi, on which Oedipus has already dispatched him, to bring news of what the oracle says.

Creon, the brother of Oedipus' consort and his co-ruler in Thebes, has a significantly different political temper from the king's. When he arrives, he quickly demurs announcing the oracle's message publicly: "If thou wouldst hear my message publicly, I'll tell thee straight, or with thee pass within" (lines 91–92). Oedipus commands a public declaration: "speak before all" (lines 93–94).[5] The oracle reveals that the man who murdered the previous king (Laius) is responsible for the pollution and that he is still living in Thebes. If Thebes is to be saved, he must be driven from the city. By means of Oedipus' urgent cross-examination of Creon, the first account of Laius' murder is given. Oedipus, doubting that it was a random killing and suspecting some greater political motive behind the crime, is horrified to hear that a king's murderer or murderers (a deliberate ambiguity is inserted at this point) was not pursued then and there. Creon explains that the city was preoccupied with meeting the demands of the Sphinx. Oedipus then commits himself, with his renowned investigative skill and resource, to reopening the inquiry and hunting down the killer, to exposing the truth, bringing everything to light, ridding the city of its plague, and saving himself as well . . . for, as the limit, all these things are gathered together in Oedipus.

The opening closes with the same emphasis upon lifting and standing with which it began. Oedipus' confidence-inspiring commitment is a deliberately stirring response to the supplications of the priest and people sitting and kneeling before him. He knows how to save them—literally, how to put them back on their feet— and is confident he has the courage and skill required. Stand up, he tells them, or we fall/fail. With that, mobilizing the supplicants, he calls for the mobilization of the whole city. And he exits, limping, into the palace. The priest echoes his words ("let us stand up," *isto-mestha*; line 147), announces that Oedipus has volunteered what they came for, and prays that the god who sent the oracle will save them from the plague. The scene closes with representatives of the city rising to their feet and leaving the stage.

Oedipus' Fall

We already know the outcome of this story. Oedipus is himself the pollution which threatens the city, and its salvation from that threat is his own banishment, which he effects, after blinding himself, when he realizes the terrible truth of his being.

The time of the play is, therefore, the untimely. That is to say, it concerns action in time counter to its time. It is about action acting on its time for the benefit of a time to come.[6] At the end of the play, the downed King yet "stands"—neither revengeful against the "it was" nor seeking flight into some calculable future. Oedipus does not simply fall. No fall is simple. First, he falls back upon the polis—returns to its public space—and discloses himself there again. Second, and uncannily, by doing so he somehow arrests his fall. Arresting, the fall also secures the attention of the polis (and ours). Held up, it elevates Oedipus while serving to sustain the polis and its members, who are all implicated in, and threatened by, this downfall. Precipitated by Oedipus' self-blinding, this crisis is the limit as a moment of judgment and resolution. Here Oedipus is decided. The scission between his being and Being is withstood as— open, disclosed, and disclosing toward beings—he withstands his response-ability as a human being.

He is responsible. He takes up what he undergoes—the freedom of his mortal being—in his new-found respect for the polis and for the fate which he bears amongst them, for having his being be in, and in virtue of, the ontological difference in which he and they stand revealed together. He chooses himself through his self-mutilation. But in making that choice, he is choosing for them also. Always already thrown into the midst of them, his relationship to them is ultimately not one of fear, or the anticipation of violent death at their hands and the imperatives and calculations concerning security that provokes. It is in respect of, and so also exhibits a respect for, them. That is to say, he *marks* himself ("anything which bears the mark of their experience also bears the mark of an *ordeal*"⁷). Henceforth he not only determines his own existence, but also contributes directly to determining the polis's existence from out of that choice, which is his insistence upon standing up, choosing his own end. Yet that end is for the freedom of others. He stands up before and for them.

However mutilating and bloody his actions may be, Oedipus therefore comes across as an individual mortal being. But in this, as we shall see, he can only come across, and we only come across him, when he comes across with others in the space of the polis. He literally comes across for the sake of others when he stands again as a fallen king. In a sense, he has only ever come across for the sake of others. The whole play is about how this figure—the figure of mortal being—comes across by taking up responsibility for the sake of others. In the early part of the play, Oedipus shoulders that responsibility by attempting insistently to stand in for the polis and its members. In effect, he seeks to substitute for them—Creon struggles in the middle of the play to remind Oedipus that he is not the only Theban—and fails/falls. He is also a stand-in for himself, of course, because he does not know who he is.

So, how are we to understand this creature who was fated to mistake himself from the very beginning? What is Oedipus' share or part of life, since the "self" that he is is clearly neither antecedent nor determined but somehow given only in his choosing? Strictly speaking, of course, Oedipus is not, or does not possess, a "self" in the sense that we have come to understand it—in terms of subject, subjectivity, subjectification, and will. His share or part of life is, in Greek terms, his *daimon*. That is his lot—his part, his wager, or his share of fortune.

Moreover, the responsibility of choice is the responsibility of self-disclosure, and self-disclosure is necessarily public. It is for the sake of others. But Oedipus' for-the-sake-of-others undergoes a crucial shift at the end of the play. Throughout the body of the play, Oedipus has tried to exorcise doubt about himself, and in himself—simultaneously trying to exorcise doubt about the polis in the polis—by resort to his cognition, his *techne*. All he achieves, however, is the intensification and ultimate exposure of the uncertainty, or insecurity, he is trying to overcome. Seeking to indemnify the polis, he systematically inflates the premiums he exacts from himself and the polis in order to secure both, until the cost outstrips what he was trying to indemnify himself and the polis against: namely, the very freedom of mortal being. No longer capable of securing certainty either of himself or for the polis, he nonetheless now exercises a commitment to himself and the polis in the public reappearance he makes at the end of the play, through which he takes up his being again.

Where there is commitment, of course, certainty is absent, and so inevitably there is also doubt: doubt as to what now happens to him; doubt as to the future of his issue; and doubt as to the future of the polis. In nonetheless thus standing up for himself and the polis, its people, and his family—by insisting that his fate is his own, by possessing it through the act of self-mutilation, and, finally, by removing their responsibility for it by insisting upon his own responsibility and banishment—Oedipus assumes the risk of living within doubt and lets himself, and all of them, be.

Oedipus is, therefore, free: free not as an autonomous sovereign will antecedently given, but as thrown into a space wherein he has the capacity to act with and be-fore others. Moreover, they all share in this freedom. It is their being-in-common, because what they share is that they are a share of being. Specifically, then, his capacity for choice, his capacity to realize himself, is his capacity to choose for the sake of the others' freedom: that of the otherness in himself as a differentially constituted being; that of the others in the polis; and that, specifically, of the daughters he is about to leave behind there. Here, at the end of the play, Oedipus acts and discloses himself so as to make the polis's free potentiality for being transparent to it. His last words to his daughters enjoin them to pray for their own lives, similarly making transparent to them their own free potentiality for being. This cripple takes a certain stand— and so discloses himself as he is—to preserve their possibility and not to fashion them into a final, determinate reality.

Recall that at the beginning of the play the priest begged the crippled Oedipus to secure the polis, to lift them up and found them upon a rock. The priest appeared to be asking Oedipus to stand in for them, and that is what the king tried to do throughout what followed, employing his securing *techne*—his calculative knowledge—as a substitute for both them and himself. Oedipus has an eye for commensurability. That was how he solved the riddle of the Sphinx, the very riddle of representation, which concerns the riddle of humankind. Was it not because of this commensurability that Oedipus was able to take the measure of things? And did not Thebes come to count upon the king precisely because he seemed able to take account of everything which threatened the fate of the polis? So it did, and so it came to pass. But the message of the play is clear. Such a hubristic and tyrannical project is vain and impossible. This human being, the figure of all human beings, ultimately did not have the legs for it.

But this is by no means the ultimate message of the play. At its end, Oedipus discovers a way of serving them all better. By the painstaking (he blinds himself), care-ridden act of taking responsibility for his own original contamination (born of a caesura, and bearing that duplication within his own being as a differentially constituted being, a stranger to himself fated always to mistake himself, the very model of duality), he stands up both for himself and for them. No longer a stand-in, either for himself (his *techne* stood in for himself while he did not know himself) or for the others, he lets himself and them finally be. So much for the thought that letting-be (*gelassenheit*) might amount to a careless, benign neglect.[8] At the cost of his vision and his old standing, Oedipus eschews the project of securing himself and them—standing in for himself and them—for that of redisclosing their freedom. Standing up as a fallible, fallen creature, he withstands his fate in his recognition of the truth of which Teiresias the prophet speaks in the play. Sophocles' brilliance is nowhere more brilliant than in the end he contrives here, for in this very act of letting them be, Oedipus leaves them all standing.

That, then, is why they have nothing to fear in encountering his "pollution." They are all human beings, all mortals. This is an account of that freedom. Being human is not something anybody or anything else can do for you. It is not something the play insists on, for which you can ultimately find a substitute. Equally, being human is not a contagion; you cannot catch it. Rather, it is a gratuitous gift which, as you take it up and persevere with it, individualizes. While you enjoy it, there is, therefore, no escaping the responsibility (openness to and within the ontological difference, not only to the mutually disclosive relationship of Being and your being, but also to other beings with whom you share this being-in-common) that is conferred upon you by this donating, and in which you yourself participate in the living that you do. All mortals bear their own responsibility, therefore, for how they discharge the life into which they have been thrown, and ultimately no one can bear that of another. Bearing in mind that this mortal life is a being-in-common, however, the responsibility it invokes nonetheless involves the Otherness that integrally comprises it. You cannot live another's life, and others cannot live yours. Yet the life that you have necessarily involves you in a responsibility for and with others without living their lives for them, precisely because this responsibility is not an identification with them or an assimilation of them to what you may think you may be, but a commitment continuously to remain open and responsive to them as they present themselves to you, because you yourself are such an open being, by virtue of your own openly granted differential constitution in openness. It is a responsibility, from out of your own openness, to allow them to be rather than to substitute for them. To do that you must yourself stand up, for when you do stand up, you do it simultaneously for yourself and for others. You present yourself to them, and them to you. This, too, for the tragic sensibility, defines the project which is the public space of the polis.

Even at the end Oedipus is free to act and does so in a very special way. This action is not an extension of the past, another imitation of it, and it is not an exercise of the will—the idea of the freedom of the will was, of course, unknown to the Greeks. It is not teleologically driven, either. It is not a means to an end, and it does not aim at progress toward a positive future in whose name the present may be sacrificed. Neither, finally, is it merely a private and individual act.

Oedipus does not seek to retreat back into the supposed automaticity of "tradition" (the time of the before), and he does not flee forward and outward into the making of "history" (the calculated future). He falls back once more upon public appearance, and returns to the time and the place of this event—the here and now—as it is provided for through the polis. He thereby takes up his political responsibilities as he lays down his power, or rather, he takes up his political responsibilities *by* laying down his power. His public response to the historical possibilities he shares with other mortals, here at the play's end, frees the historical space of destining to be something different from what it has been hitherto. That is the whole point of his disclosing himself again publically, and in doing so he both affirms the public space of the polis—through his continuing courage to exercise the freedom for action which mortal life bestows upon human being—and takes up, though now differently, what he is undergoing (his very being), while freeing others to do the same. Here he is again, then, seen in action in the space whose purpose is to allow such action, thus confirming its central significance in ensuring mortality's freedom of action, the freedom and action that together comprise the possibility of a free political life.

Oedipus' response to repeatable historical possibilities, the conjunction of traditions, discourses, practices, happenings, and events in which we are always already immersed in a destined way—and thus to repetition itself—ultimately disavows any notion of slavish continuity or identity with the past even as it freely acknowledges its indebtedness to the past. His actions, however destined by how he is inescapably thrown into a world he did not make and cannot master, no matter how fully he has responded to the way in which he is challenged technologically to do so, disrupt identity and continuity. In his destiny, any simple routinization of life was pre-empted from the outset, and in the living out of that destiny, his action in coming before the polis (self-blinded, and so newly sighted and newly sited) disrupts the routine of life once more. This free and critical response to the occurrence and to the recurrent repetition of the specific and unique is itself specific and unique.[9] It leads, by realizing the possibility of something else unexpected and unpredictable, not only to the repetition of the polis but also to that of Oedipus himself: his release from the destiny bequeathed to him towards another, Thebes' release from the irruption of that destiny, and its projection into another.

This action does not ultimately rely upon and does not appeal to any authorization of repeatable historical possibilities founded upon myth (the oracle is not a myth but a prophecy), nor upon the projection of a past into a future as the extension of automatic processes and of repeatable occurrences—a succession of nows—that come to pass as if human beings did not act, as if nothing unexpected occurred in virtue of the fact that they do act, and in virtue of the fact that even as they act other things happen which are unaccountable in terms of those actions. Just as tragedy is itself more than mere mimicry, so the action it enacts is more than mere repetition and identification with past practices.[10] In thus "cultivating and sustaining the strife between what is assigned to him as a task and what has been given him as his endowment,"[11] Oedipus' act re-enacts the agonism of the polis and the freeing act of political responsibility. It seems a perfect expression of Heidegger's understanding of resoluteness: "Here, then, it is a matter of decision—and of incision—in our lives, a matter of cutting away what has prevailed hitherto, what has by now run its course, from what still 'remains.' Obviously, the cut is made by the thought of return, which transforms everything."[12] And, yet. Oedipus' resoluteness, this point at which he gathers himself together by gathering together all the trammeled strands of his history, is also a new dispensation, a redispersal and redistribution of himself, of the beings he has been with, and of the place in which they have shared the being-in-common that has been shared out amongst them there in that place.

Because there is an ontological difference, and not a sovereign point of departure, a multiplying process of duplication and reduplication ("which animates and inspires all human activities and is the hidden source of production of all great and beautiful things"[13]), there is renewal in and through the human freedom to act. Whatever impels the chain of infinite improbabilities which produces human being also animates human being. However improbable it may seem, particularly in the depths of a nemesis such as this, the play affirms that things can begin again. But so long as this "source" does not appear, is not manifested, "freedom is not a worldly, tangible reality."[14] It requires a space and a place where it can make its appearance. First evident in human being itself, it nonetheless requires the confirmation, amplification, celebration, and perspective provided by the public space of the polis—the space in which human being can show itself and where "freedom can manifest itself and become a [mundane] reality."[15] (Remember that if people cannot appear, they cannot fully be. Visibility, individuating responsibility, and equality are intimately related here in the phenomenological symmetry and asymmetry of human being.) It does so because freedom ultimately concerns not merely the capacity of being-in-common to act but also the "I can," not the "I will," of being-in-common. It necessarily entails the public action required of the "I can" with respect to otherness with others, wherein lies the prospect of calling something new into being, rather than the mere solipsistic dreaming of the "I will."[16]

Here Oedipus' struggle—his striving—is the struggle of the polis as well. It is not a willing, a struggle that is representational in that it is always thought to be related to that for which it strives; rather, it is a striving to reach beyond himself, because as a mortal human being—simultaneously living and dying, bearing difference within himself and on his way to death, as we all are—he is always already beyond himself. And so ultimately he strives toward himself. In this striving, like the striving of the polis of which the chorus sang earlier in the play, he not only gathers himself together but also initiates a new dispersal of freedom and responsibility amongst them. It is not a matter of asking why he should do this. He does it because that is what it is to be mortal, that is what he is as a mortal. Here is the human being, then. Fully extended at its extremity, gathered together in its extremity by its extremity, it is nonetheless also redistributed through that extremity. Here it repeats itself through the capacity for repetition which originally frees the being that it enjoys, because—like it or not—it bears the indelible trace of that mortal freedom in its very corporeality.

This act of judgment, this judgment on himself so publicly disclosed, is based upon no political standard or model. Creon forcefully objects to it. Neither does it re-present an external standard or *eidos* according to which Oedipus is finally compelled to judge himself: he insists that the gods did not require it; he did it himself. Incest is an abomination in the eyes of mortals and gods, of course, but Oedipus is not compelled to this judgment and this disclosure here in virtue of the operation of some universal law which tells him what must be done. Incest is his inheritance, his very own hermeneuticity. He has had to read it, to interpret and interrogate it, because it was never transparent to him or to anyone else. Even here, at the end, it retains its fundamentally enigmatic and opaque character. Through it he has not only been decided, he has also had to decide. This radically ambiguous and fluid condition—of simultaneously being decided and of having to decide so as to keep the possibility of the future open—he withstands now as the play approaches its climax. The choice, in which he tears himself away, effects another rent or opening. Law, then, is missing and must be engendered.[17] That is what Oedipus' final acts do. In so doing they establish another ineradicable difference or dissension, serving notice of a further terrible severance, Oedipus' banishment, which acknowledges the excessiveness of the indeterminate (witness Oedipus' new-found reverence, for example) that sustains the openness of the play, because it engenders a new accord between the determinate world of mortals and the indeterminate Being of their world.

Oedipus' judgment upon himself is not, finally, a private thing, either. It cannot be. Rather, because the ability to judge one's situation depends upon the radical excess of judgment, it must be given perspective. It must, therefore, "free itself from the private and idio-syncratic view and engage in the 'enlarged mentality,' which always finds itself in and among the perspectives of others."[18] Hence, because Oedipus is being-in-common, his self-judgment must be public.

The freedom he enacts, which integrally involves the polis be-cause that is where it is exercised and amplified, is the capacity for the repetition which initiates a new beginning. Oedipus' action is glorious, if bloody, because this freely chosen public display of his terrible condition reaffirms the publicness of the public world, re-engenders the polis, and restores the freedom to begin again. The political life of the polis is not therefore merely given—it is not present and presentable. Rather, mortals are drawn toward it in their resolute public and responsible actions. What is not given has therefore, in this way and with this kind of effort, to be con-tinuously engendered. Ultimately, Oedipus' destiny is not to kill his father and marry his mother. His destiny—remember that it is the destiny of all mortal beings—is to engender and re-engender the freedom of the political in moments of dread. Incorporating the terrible discordance of the ontological difference within his own mortal corporeality—as witness his bad foot, of which he is the embodied site—Oedipus is challenged to exercise the resoluteness to judge himself with and in response to others. From being the body which threatens difference, Oedipus becomes the body in which and through which difference is redistributed, meted out. His actions at the play's end are an example of that resoluteness, a resoluteness which "must esteem what is of worth and signifi-cance, . . . must judge what is of worth in its historical possibilities from within the terrible discordance between the determinate and the indeterminate which characterizes the very moment of reso-luteness itself."[19]

In effect, Oedipus' final act does this by dispersing a last politi-cal will and testament. In doing so, while still exhibiting much of his earlier practice, he now exhibits a significantly different under-standing of the political than the urge to secure calculability which largely impelled him hitherto. Once more he demands his banish-ment—the city must be rid of him—though Creon demurs until the gods have been consulted again and have clarified what ought to be done. He commands, then corrects himself and begs Creon to bury Jocasta properly. His sons will be of no concern to Creon. Being already men, they will be able to fend for themselves.[20] His two younger daughters will, however, require Creon's wardship, for which he pleads. Creon, out of mercy and pity, knowing Oedipus' deep love for them and anticipating his wish, has already had them brought out to say their last goodbyes.

Hear Oedipus' goodbye to them:

> You little ones, if you were old enough
> to understand, there is much I'd tell you.
> Now, as it is, I'd have you say a prayer.
> Pray for life my children,
> live where you are free to grow and season.
> Pray god you find a better life than mine,
> the father who begot you.[21]

Oedipus, whose life from first to last has been daunted and diminished by life, nonetheless speaks a loving father's last words to the daughters he cherishes, in an astonishing affirmation of life. Pray for life and live a life in which your being can flourish. Even at the end he enacts his life in letting life be for them. What can this life be that, despite the life which he has had, he wants with all his being for them? Not the particular life that he or any of them has led thus far, of course, but the very donation—giving, receiving, gathering, and sending on—of life that life itself is and of which they are an instance, a measure of whose mysterious unfulfillment they must live for themselves. He asks them to pray for the infinite improbability of givenness—the potentiality for being—of which they are an instance. In loving the mystery of life which they themselves are—native and strangers to himself, as he has been to Thebes— Oedipus can do no other than express his love of the existence of life itself: "The will of love takes precedence over the will of the ground, and this precedence and eternal decidedness—that is, the love of being for being—this decidedness is the innermost core of absolute freedom."[22] Because his love desires them to explore and celebrate their participation in it, it must affirm life.

Here, then, love breaks the surface of the play and intrudes into the polis (his daughters are effectively being made wards of "state"), with Oedipus teaching us more, once more, about the motions and e-motions of our freed being-in-common. This brings us to the relationship between love, the freedom of mortal life, and the idea of politics which the tragedy of the polis presents, though to address them in detail is beyond the scope of this essay. Suffice it to repeat that love of his daughters enjoins Oedipus to affirm life, because if he did not affirm life he could not love them. He must affirm life if he loves them, for how could he love them—the living which they are—if he did not love living itself? If he loves them, how can he not love living? And love he does. In doing so he re-engenders the law of the inviolability of the possible, allowing their death to be their uttermost possibility and displacing all attempts to make this unpresentable present, so that they can be free to exist in their potentiality for being this side of death, until death ultimately claims them, too. His love strives to let the possibilities of their Otherness be. He directs an unconditional yes to them. He wants them to be what they are in their essence: a specific, unique, radically open potentiality for being, engendered by him yet also stranger to him and free of him, sharing his exile without nostalgia as other human beings. His final words, I suggest, say this to them in this his own dread moment of resolute judgment: "I love you, I want you to be."[23]

Addressed so far through the play's preoccupation with knowledge and power, standing and seeing, grounds and heights, the mystery of life here assumes a different mask as the face of the play metamorphoses into a visage of love: love not as an explanation, causation, or justification—a reason—as if it stood outside the life it affirms, love not as a goal, but love as the struggle of life for life, with life and the nothing: "According to the old saying of Heraclitus, struggle is the basic principle and moving force of being. But the greatest struggle is love—which provokes the deepest contest precisely in order to be and display itself in its reconciliation."[24] Love, then, is integral to the movement of the free being that human being is, itself another expression of its struggle to be. Love is another name for being-in-common as it articulates its desire for the difference of which it is comprised and that it shares with others, exulting in the prospect which its differential constitution in a world of openness excites. Love, coming in many tempers and guises, finds one form of exemplification in the love of one's child, that uncanny, infinite improbability of yet another singular instance of identity/difference.[25]

But do not mistake this love for a peaceful reconciliation, a reconciliation which brings peace, or a release that brings tranquility. There is a force in this "I love you, I want you to be." Do not be fooled into thinking that the only violence of any consequence is the violence which elides, effaces, and defaces the other, as if, by facing up to rather than effacing the other, we might put an end to violence. In this releasing love also lies the power and latent violence of an injunction—"an injunction that is itself disjointed."[26] Issuing from someone who is himself out of joint, this injunction effects another disjunction. Oedipus, with love and through love, releases his daughters to their inheritance of life. That injunction insists, albeit lovingly, that the other can be no other than other, come what may, and exhorts it to remain so. Ultimately, he says, you can (must) be no other than other because that is what you are and I love you for it. Smitten as he is with love, Oedipus smites back in the same currency:

> Pray for life my children,
> live where you are free to grow and season.
> Pray god you find a better life than mine,
> the father who begot you.

In being loved and finding love, these lines suggest, you do not find peace. Instead, the struggle of your being is refreshed.

This, therefore, is not the struggle-free love of a happy ending. Love does not gather everything together in unison and unicity here. An expression of their being-in-common, of their belonging together in virtue of difference, this love also effects a new scission or severance in which the possibility of the being of these other beings, his daughters, takes place. It consequently splits asunder, severs, and divides, allowing for a further duplication of difference. Only in division does the possibility of possibilities and their multiplication occur. There is violence in it precisely because it accepts this mortal freedom. Moreover, it is not a freedom which is paternally, or patriarchically, granted by Oedipus. His offspring are being wrenched from his grasp, and, in any event, this freedom is not within his gift. Instead, it is the antecedent freedom of ek-sistence which, in extremity, he now recognizes that he shares in common with them. This "I love you, I want you to be" therefore says: stand up—for yourself and before others—take up the burden of freedom afresh and live it out more fully.

Just as Oedipus tries to give what he does not have, so his love amounts to an impossible command. He cannot free his daughters of himself, nor can he efface what he is and what has happened. He cannot withdraw what has already been given, and nothing can free them of the inheritance into which they have come.[27] In short, they cannot be delivered of their life. But can it be delivered over to them, freely to assume as best they might, in a freeing way? Perhaps this is what Oedipus is trying to do. They alone can bear their inheritance. But in how he comports himself in handing it on—saying something like "grieve for me, therefore; keep me enough to lose me as you must"[28]—Oedipus tries to contribute to their free reception and assumption of it. Ultimately, however, that is impossible because (irrespective of the awful inheritance he leaves them) there is nothing he or they can do to secure compliance with a command to find a better life. And yet that is precisely the forceful, insistent desire of love.

"At the extreme limit of distress," Hölderlin noted about *Oedipus*, "there is in fact nothing left but the conditions of time and space."[29] It seems as though nothing much is destined for this derelict mortal being any more. If there is a motivating fear in the play (and I think, on the contrary, that the entire disposition of the play amounts to an astonishing exploration and affirmation of human being's free capacity to undertake what it undergoes, in the irresponsible clearing of space and time), I would say it is the fear of losing destiny. This echoes what I said at the beginning about the tragic: the supreme danger to which the tragic alerts us is the loss of destiny or limits. Destiny is the liminal freedom which happens within limits because of limits; between the limits of birth and death. And so I somewhat demur from the poets reading.

Precisely because of his responsible actions, Oedipus' fate at the close of the play is on the way to being accomplished rather than lost. Of course, he is cast down. Of course, he is cast out. But in the process Oedipus assumes a spirituality which elevates him. As he finally passes out of life and is buried at Colonnus, the body of *Oedipus Rex* is bequeathed as a treasure not only to Athens but also to us. After all, the play is a play, though we are haunted by it.[30] It is the play of the play which bears repeating, that is to say, which transports the message of repeatability itself. Millennia later, repeating the accomplishment of Oedipus' fate, we are recalled to the burden of human freedom. Thus Oedipus' destiny is never, in fact, brought to a close.

Directing the audience to look upon this spectacle, the chorus reminds them of the envy they once felt at Oedipus' ability to hold on to the truth and master the world through the *techne* of his knowledge and urges them to reflect now upon the downfall this has wrought. But that is not its conclusion. Rather, its final message is that there is no conclusion. There is no simple moral, no final accounting, no summary last look of ultimate understanding. You cannot hold on securely to the last *scène/sens* played here either.

oste thneton onta keinen ten taileu thaian idein
emerau episkopounta meden' olvizein, prin an
terma tou biou perase meden algeinon pathou. (lines 1526–30)

Wait. Keep watching. What you see now is not the end of things. It is also another beginning, for there is a liminal belonging together of beginning and ends.

Heidegger's inconspicuous law of the possible, which demands that one act so that the possibility of the impossible not be made actual, is operating here.[31] In a world radically endangered by a politics of security concerned with securing the self of self-determination and now ultimately capable of making the impossible happen, human being must learn politically how to follow this inconspicuous law of the possible or finally realize its own impossibility. That is the challenge which, successfully met, might inaugurate a new *mise en forme* (*mise en scène/mise en sens*) of the political. Failed, it is now capable of accomplishing the end of our world, the closure which it is Oedipus' destiny both to threaten and yet ultimately also to forestall.

The Burden of Mortal Freedom

We must remember, therefore, not only that Oedipus is the figure of mortal human being—which, though deathbound like a beast and creative like a god, is neither beast nor god and therefore free, thus capable of its own particular kind of greatness—but also that his parricidal and incestuous pollution is a complex sign of the mortal condition of a divided being whose very condition of life is the capacity for duplication and reduplication which it bears within itself. Incest represents the immanence and imminence of the endless cycle of reciprocal violence which threatens to overwhelm being by effacing the difference that constitutes it, and which is so much in evidence in the modern political world.

Mortal being lives in duplication and reduplication, directly participating in its own begetting in the caesura, replicated throughout its being, in which its being arises. As with Oedipus, so with all human being: "the sower is not only the sower," but is sown and is "also the seed."[32] Incest draws attention to the inherent duality of the human condition, however, by signifying a perversity which threatens the composition of our being-in-common. One of the features which distinguishes human being from other beings and from Being is the way human being is freed to take re-

179

sponsibility for regulating the self-producing procreative power of which it is a manifestation by remaining open to, preserving and respecting, its own freeing duality. That way mortal being seeks to respect the immanent alterity within its own singularity, and so ensures its possibility of "repetition" or new-found composition. That, I think, is what Heidegger means when he says that *Dasein* has its being to be. But this freedom also entails an aversion to itself, to the burden it bestows upon being human. Thus, while Oedipus is the paradigmatic figure of the immanence of alterity in every human being, he is also a progenitor, as René Girard says, of "formless duplications, sinister repetitions, a dark mixture of unnameable things."[33] He threatens the differential composition of the "unstable arithmetic"[34] of the self, because his own example of scandalous equivalence—as "a slayer of distinctions"[35]—threatens the difference within the self. Oedipus violates the boundaries of self and other in his own self: husband and son, son and parricide, native and stranger. He "collapses what should be distinct and plural [even in the self itself] into a perverse singularity."[36]

Incest does more than signify, as Peter Euben notes, "a political disease as much as a familial one."[37] Because it effaces the viable system of differential relations necessary for a being which bears freeing difference within itself, because it threatens to obliterate all distinctions, including those co-joined within that self, it subverts the very possibility of such a being. It therefore signifies, in the strongest and most immediate way possible, the fundamental link between the loss of distinction and the violent chain of reciprocal violence which conducts a general offensive against the freedom, and hence the kind of being, that human being undergoes and is challenged to assume.

Incest, then, is a paradigmatic representation of the nondifference of self-determination (the determination of the self) which Oedipus threatens in all his relationships, including those with other members of the polis. The fusion of singularity in incest is a cardinal offense against being-in-common, because the sovereign oneness which it symbolizes fatally abuses the immanent alterity which is integral to the freeing differential constitution of mortal life. A fatal corruption of the intrinsic corruption (duality) of origination, incest subverts the entire social order because it assails the very condition of being-in-common.

We must remember that a limit is a multi-valent thing. It both allows something to be what it is and marks the point beyond which it cannot be. Moreover, the limit always points beyond what is limited to the excess upon which anything relies, even though that supplement cannot be contained within the thing which is delimited. Herein lies the obligation to the stranger, the debt which all identity, all dwelling, and all place acquires with its very inception. The limit makes politics both possible and impossible. It signifies that there is always something beyond politics—beyond the political self, especially the political self of self-determination—with which the understanding and practice of politics must continuously come to terms.

Free to be either destructive or capable of politics, human being also signifies through its own existence—its ontological difference—something beyond that existence, something with which it remains inextricably, if mysteriously, involved and to which it remains indebted. In the play, of course, that beyond is figured through what were live political issues in fifth-century Athens: prophecy, the oracle, and the gods.[38]

Oedipus, then, is quite literally the limit. He is exasperating. He is violent and tempestuous. He rules and remakes Thebes. He both gathers it together in its time of extremity and threatens its utter destruction. It cannot contain him. Yet he is the limit most of all in that his effacement of limits signals the limit beyond which mortal life, which is demarcated life if it is anything, cannot be. In *Oedipus*, the limit seems to be figured most obviously in relation to death. Oedipus was to be killed. Oedipus is a multiple killer. His wife/mother commits suicide. The Sphinx demanded human sacrifice. The plague, consequent upon Oedipus' own beingness, pollutes procreation.[39]

Yet the play's profound exploration of the limit does not stall at what seems most apparently limiting. Instead of the Hobbesian fear of violent death at the hands of other men—the violent imperative to security which fuels so much of the aspiration to self-determination and of its declension into murderous determination of the self—Sophocles teaches us to fear the loss of distinction and to reflect upon the vital connection between the possibility of political life and the maintenance of difference. Murder is the proximate instrument, but the ultimate threat to being-in-common is the obliteration of its own inherent Otherness. Sophocles surpasses the sophisticated Hobbesian, as well as the naively realist, reading of the limit. Instead, our sensitivity to limits is enhanced by this Oedipal figuration of the limitless.

Thus the polity's creative medium—mortal human being—is a threat to it. That is the sickness afflicting the Thebans. The plague does not demand tribute like the Sphinx.[40] Instead, it both is integral to human being's procreative power yet fatally afflicts the human capacity for reproduction and repetition.[41] It is not confined to Oedipus, the figure in whom ontological difference is most forcefully inscribed. (He knows neither whence he came nor where he is headed.) Though amplified and intensified within him until it threatens his life, this sickness, the free capacity for being-in-common, is what Oedipus shares with the other members of the polis. There must be freedom for there to be tragedy, hence Oedipus' fate is partially predicted, not totally determined.[42] Although it is the condition for political life, being-in-common also inevitably entails the potential for self-destruction.[43]

In *Oedipus Rex*, then, we are presented with an exemplar of the limit engaged in the violent dissolution of limits who is, in turn, an exemplar of (political) human being. As the chorus says, Oedipus is a paradigm (*paradeigma*). He is neither political nor apolitical, but a double. Simultaneously political and apolitical, Oedipus is the threshold over which the political comes and goes as a possibility for human being. Oedipus' self-haunting reminds us that the political always already haunts the apolitical within the self. A paradigm of human being—"of all mankind, and of the city which is man's greatest creation"[44]—Oedipus' greatness is signaled not only by his capacity for the political but also by the limits of that capacity, in that he continuously oversteps the political. This apoliticality cannot be escaped because mortal being must realize the possibility of a political life in action that constitutes and sustains a political community. Capable of political life, of "statute and limit," mortal being must create the statutes and limits of political life, which means that it must also always already be "without statute and limit."[45] Hence its integral struggle.

Thebes is a polity newly formed around the (a)political power—a form of political intelligence derived from the forensically calculative expertise Oedipus employed to resolve the puzzle and remove the Sphinx—of its savior and protector. When they find themselves not merely threatened but on the point of total dissolution (the plague appears to present a quite different order and magnitude of threat from that offered by the Sphinx) the Thebans appeal once more to that expertise. However understandable, the appeal is bound to be frustrated because the soteriological credentials of any being-in-common are inherently compromised. But that does not mean that all is lost from the very beginning. Oedipus the saved is Oedipus the savior and Oedipus the fell pollutant, but also, finally, Oedipus the transformed. What saves threatens, what threatens saves, though in the sense of preserving itself in its openness, not in that of succeeding in some final solution to the human condition. Crucially for those who know Heidegger, this occurs in human action.[46] Preserved for this fate, human being (being-in-common) is elevated by its freedom to act in such a fate and, by recognizing and taking responsibility for it, retains the capability of always responding to it.

The play, then, is about the extremity which both creates and threatens the possibility of *politeia*. But it is equally concerned with how what lies beyond the polis yet is displayed in the mortal life of human being limits the political. Thus both the city and Oedipus are sanctified rather than deified. Moreover, the threatening Otherness which Oedipus represents is not merely banished from the city, but spiritualized in Oedipus' transformation from king to exile and his interment at Colonnus. The fate of the king demarcates the liminal limit of the political and emphasizes that, despite the intricate complicity of knowledge and politics, the question of the political is not exhausted by the question of the calculative knowledge of making. The political is threatened by its reduction to *techne* because it originally concerns the question of the creativity entailed by limits. Even as he comes to learn that he has been ignorant all along, Oedipus learns something new, acquires a different form of understanding and composure.[47] Moreover, the (political) duality of Oedipus' (a)politicality is fundamentally played out in terms of security—specifically, in terms of the play on words which the Greek word for security (*asphaleia*) allows.

The strength of the play, read politically, is not that "man" is a political animal. Neither is it that "man" is an apolitical animal (much less that he is an *animal rationale*). The point is that he is both at once and, moreover, that there is always already something "beyond" the polis that *politeia* must continuously respect. The inherently liminal character of the political, and of the challenges to it, continuously arises in that ambiguity. To see it is to recognize both the possibility and the impossibility of the polis,[48] in virtue of the identity and difference that inhere in human being and *logos*, explored through the character of knowing and being, and of the way that each (being, knowing, and their relationship) is integrally involved in the constitution and maintenance of a political community. It is not so much a masterpiece of political analysis as it is a masterly analysis of the ambiguous inner problematic of the political as it liminally arises at the limit with respect to the dissolution of limits—an analysis which surpasses in subtlety and range (while being concerned with many of the same essential questions of truth, appearance, prudence, machination, ground, and calculation) even that provided, for example, by Machiavelli.

While Oedipus' life and career describe a constant political passage, a journeying to and fro which revolves around the polis, his talent for solving puzzles indicates the political intelligence which brought him to power by once securing the polis, through which he continues to rule. Oedipus the champion hermeneut is, however, an irresolvable hermeneutical puzzle to himself: "an expert at decoding difficult messages, the hero cannot decode the meaning of his own name."[49] The resolution of that puzzle precipitates a self-blinding which signifies the advent for him of a different kind of self-recognition. Language, knowledge, and power—the complexities and mysteries of identity, appearance, and misrecognition—are all intermeshed in this account of the rise, fall, and transformation of the one seeking self-determination who also secures the polis. Oedipus' self-recognition accepts the riddle of human being, a being-in-common that is both friend and enemy to itself, united in its division and diversity, yet in receipt of its being by virtue of something in itself beyond itself.

Oedipus' will to know trips him up. Though he cannot forbear trying to master himself through the calculus of his knowing, the play does not simply insist that the will to know must be denied. Oedipus cannot escape his destiny by ceasing to question, as he is advised to do on no fewer than four occasions.[50] The failure to question, like the failure of questions, leads to a new understanding and to transformation of the knower. Ignorance, despised by rationalism but actually the liminal limit of knowing, must be learned and understood in its own, and for its own, unfixed liminality.

His fall remains, however, essentially ambiguous and marginal: "when the hero, revealed as homeless, most desires exile and homelessness, he is made to feel most fully his responsibilities to and his protection by an *oikos*."[51] Indeed, his full acceptance of them is brutally signaled. He is down but actually not (quite) out. Indeed he remains what he has always been, both within and without, hence outwith, the polis.[52] Even at the end he continues to be a question for it, and tragedy forte is to pose the question more deeply still. Because it does so, we gain a greater understanding of the kind of issue that Oedipus represents to the polis: the question of the political, of its relation to limits and to all the cognates of limits (including, for example, those of tolerance) that are so involved in accepting responsibility.[53]

Here, then, political human being is explored at the limit in order to examine not only the violent dynamics that arise in the pursuit of self-determination, and not only the violence and fragility of its liminality, but also the play of Otherness within it which initiates that liminality as the source of the freedom which comprises the being of human being. The question of the political is thereby posed and addressed, not in terms of how human being can be ordered and domesticated, nor in terms of mere self-determination, but in terms of what is required of a civilizing movement through which human beings can accept and accommodate the freed, uncanny thing that human being is without betraying the uncanniness of that freedom. Because it insists on posing that question *in extremis* as a question of limits, the tragic enlarges our political and ethical sensibility beyond the moralistic boundaries within which a politics confined to the representational-calculative thought which infuses so much of our contemporary politics of self-determination would secure it. This is why it remains so desperately pertinent to the extremity of our current world.

The Victim's Tale:
Memory and Forgetting
in the Story of Violence

PETER VAN DER VEER

The Preamble to the Indian Constitution, the foundational text of the Indian nation-state, reads as follows: "We, The People of India, having solemnly resolved to constitute India into a Sovereign, Socialist, Secular Democratic Republic and to secure to all its citizens: Justice, social, economic and political; Liberty of thought, expression, belief, faith and worship." The Indian historian Gyanendra Pandey reports that he heard these lines read out on national television on the eve of India's Republic Day, January 25, 1990, when he visited Bhagalpur, a small town in Northern India.[1] Just a month before his visit a massacre had taken place in Bhagalpur, in which as many as a thousand people, most of them Muslims, had been killed and some forty thousand people had to leave their homes for relief camps. Pandey had come to record the victim's story, to get a full picture of the massacre, but was made to reflect on the story of the nation, on national history, when he watched national television in Bhagalpur.

Simultaneously hearing the victim's story and watching the pomposity of the nation's self-celebration lends itself to black laughter, to ironic distance from the official discourse of the nation-state. But these are only moments of escape from the fetishization of state power, fragments which are soon domesticated into national history. Maurice Halbwachs and recently Pierre Nora make a sharp distinction between history and collective memory. Nora argues that history wishes to suppress memory and that only "Lieux de Memoire," fragmented, archival remains, are allowed to stay within the historical narrative.[2] What does national history do with the victim's tale? Such history is the grand narrative of the modern nation-state. In it, the stories different groups

186

have about their past, about inner differences within the nation, are incorporated, reinterpreted, framed into History. "History" as sign of the modern is central to the idea of "progress" or "development" and thus to both colonialism and the liberal nation-state.[3] The eighteenth-century idea of progress combined Christian salvational expectation with social disciplines of rational prediction. And the schematization of evolutionary stages by the Utilitarians, the ideologues of British colonialism, inserted the people without history into the story of progress.[4] Liberation of People in the West and colonization of the People in the Rest are thus much more closely connected than one might gather from critiques of post-Enlightenment thought.[5] Let us invoke the "specter" of Marx: in Marx's view, "history," through the agency of British colonialism, had by necessity and however cruelly to wake the Indian nation from its oriental slumber. Indeed, the history of colonialism is the history of the nation-state, both in England and in India. The modern state is a nation-state, the hyphen indicating that the modern state requires a nation and vice versa. Although Britain and India are now both nation-states, in the colonial period only Britain was a nation-state, while India was a colony. This, at least, seems to indicate a time lag, in which colonizing Britain was an established nation-state and colonized India became one—perhaps as a result of colonization. However, one must remember that the nation is a nineteenth-century historical formation, so that the time lag is a relatively minor one. Another way of putting this is to say that while Britain was colonizing India, England was colonizing Greater Britain, trying to unify what was not yet (and would only partially be) the united kingdom. We can see the historical outcome of the latter process even today in Northern Ireland and Scotland. I do not want to make too much of this, but would simply like to point out that a notion of time lag, in which blueprints of a finished nation-state are exported to less-evolved societies via colonialism, may lead us to miss the processual and differential nature of nation-state formation, and to miss as well that this process involved Britain and India simultaneously, within the same historical time.

Often the question of what comes first in this hyphenated phenomenon, nation or state, is raised. Does the state produce the people or the people the state? I agree with Marcel Mauss, who in his unfinished work on "the nation" argues that the idea of the nation combines the idea of the "fatherland" (*patrie*) and the idea of the citizen:

these two notions, fatherland and citizen, are ultimately a single institution, one and the same rule of practical and ideal morals and, in reality, one and the same central fact, which gives the modern republic all its originality, all its novelty and its incomparable moral dignity. . . . The individual—every individual—is born into political life. . . . A society in its entirety has to some extent become the State, the sovereign political body; it is the totality of citizens.[6]

Through "history," as the story of liberation from oppression, the individual citizen learns to identify with the nation-state. History is therefore a necessary social discipline to produce the modern subject, but, again, what is done with the victim's tale?

Ernest Renan argues in a famous lecture on the idea of the nation, delivered at the Sorbonne in March 1882, that memories of the past are connected with the collective will to live together in the nation of today.[7] Renan saw serious historical scholarship as a danger to nationalism, since it forces us to look at the violent origins of the nation-state. In his view, "forgetting and even historical error are essential factors in the formation of the nation." In another passage in his lecture, Renan claims nationalism implies "that every French citizen should already have forgotten Saint Bartholomew's Day and the massacres of the Midi in the thirteenth century." Recalling these historical events in his lecture, Renan both assumes that his audience knows them and suggests that they "should have been forgotten already." Benedict Anderson argues that this is precisely how "the lessons of history" work, namely, through the remembering/forgetting of historical experience within the national narrative.[8]

Thus dark stories of terror and bloodshed are memorized only to be remembered/forgotten. They are reinterpreted as either necessary steps toward liberation or "incidents" of no consequence to the unfolding of the main plot. The official history of Indian nationalism, as told in Indian education, is the progressive story of the liberation of the people from foreign domination and thus the narration of patriotic love, but within that general frame there is the story of partition, of hatred and violence between Hindus and Muslims. The subtext is that of events or incidents which are called "communal" in order not to let them disturb the text of the "national": the emergence of freedom, of a normal, liberated nation-state. They have to be given meaning within the narrative frame of the emergence of a liberal nation-state. And when they do not fit, they are signs of "backwardness," of "a revolution not only against a tyrant, but against history," to quote Salman Rushdie's *The Satanic Verses* on the Iranian revolution.[9]

I think it is wrong to say that a unitary, homogeneous history obliterates the memory of pogroms and massacres, although in some cases and to some extent there are attempts to do just that. Textualizations of violent events are open to a variety of interpretations, and while there are often many versions of what happened, only one version gets an official status, becomes part of the state's archive. That version is often plotted along the lines of a master narrative. If one has read one account, one has read them all. The official version is sometimes not established by marginalizing other accounts, but by the systematic destruction of evidence, as Gyanendra Pandey saw during his visit to Bhagalpur. Not only do the police records (the historian's favorite source for violence) often ignore massacres in which the police have been involved, but the destruction of evidence is itself an element of violence. In communal riots, fire is a favorite instrument for destroying the bodies of the victims and the houses in which they lived, so that the story of the victimized community can the more easily be disputed. The fetishization of numbers in debates about what actually happened is often striking. It is impossible to deny totally that something happened, but numbers can be used to contest how "serious" the events were. Ironically, the politics of numbers in deciding modern elections is sometimes a motivating force in these massacres to begin with.[10]

Nevertheless, more often than not the memory of violent events is not obliterated or suppressed; rather, such events are remembered as fragments of a story whose unitary, rational subject is the liberal nation-state. History is a teleology leading to "India," to the liberated Indian nation-state. Suffering and pain acquire meaning from the larger story of progress; otherwise they would be "senseless," incoherent, without any meaning for the larger story. This narrative strategy can deal with the present as well as the past. The suppression of civil riots by the state—which often claims more victims than the riots themselves—is thus generally called a "return to normalcy." Civil riots are illegitimate and worrisome incidents which are "senseless" because they threaten not only the state's monopoly of physical force but also its narration of its own legitimacy, based on the collective will to live together. The state uses "government," not "violence," to describe its own use of physical force.

Liberal government allows for debates in the *Öffentlichkeit*, the public sphere, and for the expression of the people's will in elections. According to its own theory, however, it must monopolize violence by suppressing violence between individuals and groups in society. In this way the theory presupposes a distinction between the free expression of opinion and the use of violence, between speech acts and other acts. But words can hurt, and the role of insults, slander, rumors, and propaganda is quite important in the dynamics of physical violence. Slogans like "Babar ki santan, jao Pakistan ya kabristan" ("Babar's offspring [i.e., the Muslim community], go to Pakistan or to the graveyard"), when uttered freely in the streets, are forms of personal violence. When college and university teachers teach their students a history of Hindu oppression by Muslims, the discursive premises of violent acts have been laid. And words are often the main objects available for study. Even when visual material is also used to "tell the story," words are what we have to interpret in examining the narrativization of violence in victims' accounts, police reports, and media representations.

There is a strong urge in recent historiography and anthropology to go beyond the story of the state, to get "history from below," from the people.[11] The idea is to disrupt and decenter the singularity of statist and elitist narrative. In the history and anthropology of violence, one would thus go straight for the victim's tale. One of the challenges here is not to slip into an essentialist humanism, which would construct the authenticity of a victimized subject. Derrida's work has alerted us to this kind of problem. Let us look briefly at a fairly typical argument which derives its interpretive authority from the victims' point of view. I take as a rather random example the account Mark Tully, former BBC correspondent in India, gives of the Ahmedabad riots between Hindus and Muslims in 1990.[12] On April 3, 1990, a Muslim was stabbed to death in the old city of Ahmedabad. Within an hour of that murder, four Hindus were stabbed in separate incidents. A curfew was imposed in the immediate vicinity. Over the next three days trouble built up, with police opening fire to disperse groups who were throwing stones at each other. On the fourth day of the riots, April 6, twenty-three people were killed and seventy injured. Curfew was extended to other areas of the city that had a record of communal violence. Then, on April 7, a rumor swept through the city that the priest of the Jagannath temple had been killed. That sparked another round of violence, which was stopped by the army on April 14.

The Indian press interpreted the violence as caused by religious fundamentalism. Tully, however, spoke to poor Muslims in the city, who blamed politics, not religion. In his view, most editorial writers don't speak to poor Muslims and so are easily carried away by the fashionable fear of fundamentalism. He ends his discussion of the Ahmedabad riots by writing: "the politicians and the press continue to blame the riots on religious fundamentalism. This may be convenient for the politicians and fashionable for the press, but according to the victims—who ought to know best—it's just not true. The victims of the riots don't even know the meaning of the word 'fundamentalism,' but they do know that it is not religion that divides them."[13] If religion does not divide Hindus and Muslims, what does? In the view of the poor Muslims interviewed by Tully, the economy and politics divide people into rich and poor, and the poor get killed. Tully elaborates this view by arguing that politicians make use of the underworld (which is heavily involved in bootlegging) to create riots between Hindus and Muslims whenever it suits them politically. Moreover, the police and the underworld are hand in glove. Besides the political reasons for Hindu-Muslim riots, Tully looks at economic causes, such as large-scale unemployment due to a crisis in the textile mills.

It is a bit disingenuous of Tully to say that the Indian press has overlooked the explanation of communal violence by political economy, since they do not speak to the victims of riots, whereas he does. In fact, this explanation is perhaps the most generally accepted in at least the English-language Indian press, and it cannot have escaped anyone in India. What is interesting, rather, is that the victim's tale agrees with nationalist historiography that the state is the subject of history. The state is not represented as an instrument of the people, however, but as an evil, autonomous force outside of society, which causes disharmony. The people are represented here as essentially tolerant, peace-loving, and not given to religious strife. The victims' stories say that what appears to be religious is not religious at all, that violence does not come from the people, but from the state. Tully privileges the victims' narrative. The victims ought to know best, he says.

The discursive strategy of the victims is to externalize the state and, in that way, to exorcize violence. This externalization can be interpreted as a sign that the victimized community wants to stay on in the neighborhood and attempts to recreate the imaginary neighborhood community by saying that an external force, the state, was the perpetrator of violence, not the neighbors. More profoundly, however, the victim's tale draws attention to the ambiguous hyphen in "nation-state" and to the insecure location of religion in modernity. Let us explore the hyphenated nation-state somewhat further. Not only in the victim's tale, but also in much radical historiography about violence the state is its perpetrator. In the colonial period the divide-and-rule politics of the colonial state first created religious communities and then pitted them against each other. The state had a perfect raison d'etre for dividing Indian civil society along religious lines: to ensure order. As that function increasingly failed, the single state was replaced by two nation-states, India and Pakistan, in which the rulers derived their legitimacy from "the people." The postcolonial state, however, inherited the divisions in civil society which had been created by the British. The colonial census operations had a tremendous effect of mobilizing people through caste associations. The colonial project consisted largely in a politics of statistics, of numbers, essential to the later democratic process. It thus brought about caste alliances which became the basis of social movements that went far beyond the spatial boundaries within which particular castes had meaning in terms of marriage and hierarchical arrangements.

One of the ironies of history is that the political attempt to do away with India's hierarchical caste system has given caste a growing political and economic importance. I have no room here for the details of this history, but let me just mention a few things. In 1932 the National Congress Party decided that all the social disabilities imposed by custom upon the so-called untouchable castes had to be removed and that in the Constitution provisions had to be made to accomplish this by reserving jobs and seats in educational institutions. To these provisions for untouchables a larger, more embracing policy of reservation was added after Independence, intended for what were described in the Constitution as "socially and educationally backward classes."

The Indian state has increasingly turned to policies of reservation to change access to education and government employment. Thus the modernizing state increasingly penetrates civil society, in what Ashis Nandy sees as a disruption of the social fabric and thus a cause of violence.[14] In themselves, policies of reservation should not affect Hindu-Muslim relations, but in the Ahmedabad riots discussed by Tully, the discomfort of the higher castes about such policies was rapidly transformed into anti-Muslim rioting, since these policies were regarded as a threat to Hindu unity.

One problem of this account of social engineering by the state is that it depends on "scientifically" drawing a boundary between state and society. This is a general theoretical problem, which applies to all empirical cases, not only to India. The state is conceived as an autonomous entity, outside of society. It is seen, voluntaristically, as a structure of intentions, plans, and policy making which has effects on an external society. Timothy Mitchell has recently argued that this topological metaphor is misleading for any state, since it tends to reify both state and society. He suggests that "the state should be addressed as an effect of spatial organization, temporal arrangement, functional specification, and supervision and surveillance, which create the appearance of a world fundamentally divided into state and society. The essence of modern politics is not the formation of policies on one side of this division and their application to or shaping by the other, but the producing and reproducing of this line of difference."[15] He argues that the distinction between state and society is not just an analytical tool which enables one to look at the centralizing role of powerful institutions that claim monopoly of legitimate force. More importantly, "methods of organization and control internal to the processes they govern create the effect of a state structure external to those processes."[16] At the same time that power relations become internal as disciplines, they appear to take the form of external structures. To go one step further, the methods of organization and arrangement that produce the new effects of structure also generate the modern experience of meaning as a form of representation. As Derrida seems to argue, the metaphysics of modernity creates the experience of an ontological distinction between physical reality and its representation.

In the Indian discussion, the problems with drawing the boundary between state and society often emerge in criticism of the role of the state. Seemingly opposite positions about whether the state is too strong (authoritarian and centralizing) or too weak (fragile and ineffective) are often taken by the same writer in discussing the Indian state. For example, Rajni Kothari, a leading political scientist in India, has recently argued that "even the repressive character arises out of the fragility of the modern state rather than its power, especially in post-colonial societies. The more fragile and ineffective and powerless a given state, the more repressive it becomes."[17] One would imagine that in order to be effectively repressive the state needs power. What Kothari perhaps wants to say is that the state does not effect social change in the direction he thinks desirable. One of the main reasons it falls short of expectation is the erosion of the autonomy of the state vis-à-vis "dominant interests, be they the monied interests in the form of the private sector and its international purveyors trying to influence economic decisions, be they the communal and caste interests seeking to hoodwink the state for sectarian ends, or be they the more professional mafia interests that have spread themselves through criminalization of the polity at the grassroots."[18] Again, the externality of the state becomes problematic as soon as interest groups to which the writer does not belong become dominant.

Kothari (like many others) brings the international context into the discussion of the state. This larger context reinforces the trope of externality, since the Indian state is part of a global system, which is often understood as even more external—indeed, as "foreign." Kothari argues that there is an "erosion of self-reliant statehood and a growing hold over the state by transnational interests and their technocratic agents."[19] Again, interest groups are taking hold of the state, but now they are located mainly outside of Indian society, with, as collaborators within Indian society, the much-maligned middle class. This feeling that the middle class, with its economic ideology of privatization, sells a formerly self-reliant society out to world capitalism makes the Indian state seem as foreign as its predecessor, the colonial state. The connection is made with some rhetorical overkill by Jan Breman in his analysis of the causes of recent anti-Muslim riots in Surat, West India: "For the flourishing condition of her informalized economy, so praised by the overseas lords of the global syndicate with its headquarters in Washington, the late-twentieth-century version of the former East India and other foreign Companies, Surat has paid a high price in recent months."[20] We seem to have come full circle: communalism has been caused by the colonial state, and independence has not liberated Indian society from this problem, imposed on it, as it were, from outside. Instead, it is perpetuated under the neo-colonial conditions of late capitalism. The metaphor of "the foreign hand" is routinely used in India to summarize this and other kinds of externalizations of communal troubles. Here the state to some extent dissolves in larger economic processes, although it is still the agent of privatization because it gives subsidies and tax exemptions and regulates labor and capital inputs.

Modern political ideas hold that the state should be the instrument of the political will of the people. The modern state grounds its legitimacy in regular election of the people's representatives. There is a certain circularity here, however, for a variety of social disciplines sponsored by the state produce not only the modern individual as a disciplined social subject, but also the community as a political entity. Indeed, the state is not an external, essentialized agent, but a series of often violently conflicting disciplines for ordering society. This it does by means of classification, of which the census was one of the main examples in the colonial period. The modern Indian state has an elaborate system of communal representation and entitlements, which determines what counts as a person or a community. The political process incessantly redraws the boundaries between state and society and between individual citizen and member of a community, giving these fraught distinctions a constant potential for contestation. Thus one might say that the state, by using these distinctions as operators, produces violence.

I do not mean to reject the concept of the state. To quote Michel Foucault, "Maybe what is really important for our modernity—that is, for our present—is not so much the etatization of society, as the 'governmentalization' of the state."[21] By "governmentality," Foucault refers to the new relations of power under modernity, which are not simply the product of the expanded capacity of the state apparatus, of "the etatization of society." A new, self-regulating field of the social for articulating effects of power—public opinion, private property, the market, the judiciary—emerges to produce the nation-state. But what does Foucault mean by "our modernity"? I would argue that a singular, universal history of modernity does not exist, although Western history since the nineteenth century has unquestionably had considerable importance in the making of the modern world. The post-Enlightenment teleology of the modern nation-state, of "our modernity," demands that both state and nation be secular.[22] In consequence, religious difference has become a site for contesting Western modernity in some parts of the colonial world.[23] In that struggle new religious discourses and practices have emerged, which have—complexly and problematically—been categorized as "fundamentalism," a term derived from American Protestantism, precisely because they are different from the dominant secularized, privatized religious forms of the late-twentieth-century West. "Religious nationalism" would be a better name for at least some of these new discourses, since they articulate discourse on the religious community with discourse on the nation.

It is a fundamental Enlightenment tenet that nationalism must be secular before it can be truly "modern." "Politicized religions" threaten both reason and liberty. The post-Enlightenment urge to define religion as an autonomous sphere, separate from politics and the economy, is, of course, also a liberal political demand that religion *should* be separate from politics.[24] The flip side of the normalizing and disciplining project of secular modernity, however, is that religion becomes so important a source of resistance. Theories of nationalism often forget that the very forces of centralization and homogenization which are integral to nationalism always create centrifugal forces and resistances based on assumed difference.[25]

Whatever the success of the political demand that religion should be apolitical in Western societies, it is unwise to try to understand religious nationalism as a flawed and hybrid modernity. Rather, one should try to understand it, as one does the nationalisms of Europe, as a product of a particular history of at least one century. Here, that particular history is one of Western colonial domination. To say this is not to blame colonialism for producing a flawed religious nationalism, since there is nothing flawed here, but to say that the postcolonial predicament can only be understood in relation to the colonial transformation of these societies. What is regarded there as religion might be quite different from what modern Christians or modern liberals regard as religion. Surely the question is how religious power—institutions, movements—produces religious selves and religious models for correct behavior. Part of this is the socialization of religious identity and difference. As Talal Asad has observed, it is not mere symbols that implant true religious dispositions, but power ranging from laws and other sanctions to the disciplinary activities of social institutions. The mind does not move spontaneously to religious truth, but power creates the conditions for experiencing that truth. Augustine catches this in one word: *disciplina*. Power works not only positively to inculcate certain truths, but also negatively by systematically excluding, forbidding, and denouncing.[26]

Again, the "politicization" and "depoliticization" of a separate sphere called "religion" results from the Enlightenment discourse of modernity, which assigns religious faith to the private domain as a matter of personal beliefs without political consequences in the public sphere. In the contemporary West, religious discourse and practice in the political arena have come to be seen as a transgression of what religion is supposed to be,[27] and there is a strong feeling that violent conflict between religious communities is a violation of the "original intent" of the founders of the religions involved or of God himself. "Real" religion produces harmony and tolerance and can thus be sharply distinguished from "politicized religion," politics in religious disguise. In important ways, this entire mode of thinking is a response to the European religious wars of the sixteenth and seventeenth centuries.

These interpretations of "religion" cannot account for the central role of power and violence in many forms of religious discourse, not to mention, over the centuries, the forcible imposition of some religions on their "converts." This is much more evident in the analysis of Islam, given the exclusionary beliefs it shares with Christianity, than in that of Hinduism. Tolerance is a prevailing theme in discourse about Hinduism, and in that of the modern Hindu as well. This consensus along the political spectrum in India is ultimately founded on a nineteenth-century construction of "Hindu spirituality," in what I consider to be the product of a collusion between orientalism and Hindu nationalism.[28] Modern Hindus have come to interpret hierarchical relativism in Hindu discourse—there are many paths leading to god, but some are better than others—as "tolerance." This, universalized, leads to including all religions in the Vedanta, the spiritual "essence" of Hinduism in its philosophical form, as in the philosopher-president Sarvepalli Radhakrishnan's famous formula: "The Vedanta is not a religion, but religion itself in its most universal and deepest significance."[29] In a concrete, political context, such an interpretation, with its stress on tolerance, can operate to exclude religions that "come from the outside" and are evangelically bent on converting Hindus.

Power and violence are as crucial to Hindu discourse and practice as they are to Islam, or to Christianity. Religions are not pleasant, and theology is a cruel calling. They deal with evil, with the dark forces of the night, with demons. They are about violence, both sacrifices and slaughter. Hinduism is strongly interested in blood sacrifice, in the killing of large numbers of goats and buffaloes, and the frenzy of the participants grows palpably with the progress of the ritual. While Robertson Smith and Durkheim may want to stress the creation of social bonds through sacrifice, it is striking how disruptive these things really are.[30] Georges Bataille is at least partly right when he argues in his comment on Michelet's *La Sorcière* (*The Witch*) that sacrifice is performed to increase the intensity of life by the contradictory act of killing the other.[31] Moments of intensity are moments of excess.

Hinduism abounds in gory stories about the slaying of the demons who threaten the order of things. The god Rama, for example, fights with the demon Ravana, who has four heads. Whenever he cuts off one head, a new set of heads pops up to replace it. This obsession with numbers, of threatening fertility, is also one of the deepest emotions in relation to the Muslim other.[32] The fertility of Muslims is seen as overwhelming; since the colonial census operations of the nineteenth century there has been a fear that soon Muslims will outnumber Hindus and take over the country. There is also a strong element of sexual jealousy in this myth of fertility, which harps on the notion that Muslims, as licentious as the oversexed demons, may marry four wives. The holy foreskin (or rather the absence thereof) is fetishized as a sign of difference. The pants of suspect males are pulled down during riots to see whether they are Muslims. If they are, they are killed. The equation of Muslims and demons is quite explicit also in the popular belief that only Muslim saints can deal with the powers of darkness, since they are so close to them.[33] From the logic of Hindu beliefs and ritual practices, it follows that Muslims, who do not know their place in the hierarchy and want to usurp the higher place of the Hindus, are like demons who want to take over the place of the gods. The only way to sustain the *dharma*, "the order of things," is to kill the demons, that is the Muslim other.

Particularly important is the articulation of Hindu ideas of sacred space and modern ideas of national territory. This expresses itself most clearly in a politics of space which constitutes the context of much communal violence in India. Riots and rituals have come to be linked in the construction of communal identities in public arenas.[34] Ritual processions through sensitive areas often end in full-scale riots. Often one is confronted here with "rituals of provocation." A symbolic repertoire, derived from the ritual realm of animal sacrifice, is often used to start a riot: a slaughtered cow in a Hindu sacred space or a slaughtered pig in a Muslim sacred space. Riots often contest boundaries between communities whose notions of public space are related to personhood and community. Irving Goffman speaks of "territories of the self," which can be invaded by specific rituals of violation. Therefore, the form of killings, the mutilation of bodies, the murder of adult men in front of their wives and children is so important not only in the creation of maximum terror, but also in violating the physical and moral integrity of the victimized community. In the anti-Muslim riots in Surat and

Bombay after December 6, 1992, the victims were forced to utter "Jaya Sri Ram" ("Hail to Lord Rama") before they were killed or raped.[35] Public space itself is, to an important extent, constructed through ritual and rioting: one ends up having Muslim areas, Hindu areas, and mixed areas.

Violence is in my view a "total" social phenomenon. As Marcel Mauss explains in *The Gift*, "these phenomena are at once legal, economic, religious, aesthetic, morphological and so on."[36] It is interesting to note, however, that in modern society this total fact is discursively cut up in different pieces. The economic and political pieces are considered "real" elements, while the religious is relegated to the "unreal." This depends to a significant degree on a discursive construction of Western modernity in which a modern construction of public and private makes religion a private matter of the individual. Something similar is also true for the way modern power results in the drawing of a boundary between state and society. Unlike religion, however, the state comes to be seen as a very real, but external agent whose actions impinge on society.

The trope of externality is also used by victims of violence, but in a very functional manner, namely to pacify communal relations on the local level. Community members externalize violence by blaming it on the changing economy or the changing maneuvers of politicians or the changing tactics of the police. It seems to be difficult to regard religion, however, as an external, historical force like the state, because religion makes itself appear as a habit of the heart, the hard core of a community's identity, as a thing that cannot change and is non-negotiable. To say that violence is religiously motivated makes it seem inescapable, although we know that religion does change, that religious institutions lose functions over time and sometimes disappear. But religious discourse tries to deny historical change and to an important degree derives its power from its success in doing so. Indeed, in that sense, religion is ideology, but it does not hide class dominance, it hides its own history, its rootedness in society.

There is no true story of violence. Violence is a total phenomenon, but it comes to us totally as a fragment. Sometimes, when the *Traumarbeit* of the nationalist imagination or the externalizations and *verschiebungen* of the victims have not done their work (as yet), fragments are just that. Something terrible has happened, and there is no plot, no narrative, only leads that go nowhere. Gyanendra Pandey, with whose visit to Bhagalpur I began my talk, argues that the fragment shows the limits of historical knowledge. He cites poems of a Muslim teacher in Bhagalpur, Manazir Aashiq Harganvi, and I will end with one of them:

In search of yourself you have now reached	Khud apne aap ko dhoondte hue
that shore	Ab tum us kinare par khare ho
From where no one has returned	Jahan se koi nahi lauta
No one ever returns, my friend	Koi nahin lautta dost
Now you too are lost forever:	Ab to tum bhi nahin laut pauge
There remains but one condition of memory	Yaad ki sirf ek shart rah jayegi ki jab bhi
that whenever, wherever	kahi
A riot occurs	Fasad hoga
I shall remember you.	Tum bahut yaad aoge.
(Pandey's translation)[37]	

Eroticism, Colonialism, and Violence

ALI BEHDAD

The question of European colonialism has often been articulated by its theoreticians in terms of political and cultural mastery. Edward Said, for example, has defined "imperialism" as "the practice, the theory, and the attitudes of a dominating metropolitan center ruling a distant territory."[1] The relation between the colonizer and the colonized has thus been read as a "Manichean allegory" in which racial or cultural difference is transformed into "moral and even metaphysical difference,"[2] investing the former with the power of an infallible master and reducing the latter to an exploited slave. In what follows, I wish to shift the focus of colonial studies from such a binary and repressive model to an understanding of colonialism as a violent ritual of erotic dissolution. My aim here is not to undermine the exploitative structure of European colonialism but to underscore the crucial role of the colonizer's erotic desires in the construction of political domination and unequal relations of power. In particular, using J. M. Coetzee's 1980 novel *Waiting for the Barbarians* as the focus of my fragmentary reflections,[3] I would like to address the ways in which violence functions as a necessary component of eroticizing the colonized's body and how such a notion of eroticism is crucial to the production of colonial rule.

In *Waiting for the Barbarians*, Coetzee carefully charts out the violent topography of what one might call "colonial eroticism." Narrated by a magistrate in an outpost of an unnamed Empire and set in an indeterminate geographical and historical location, the novel begins with the arrival of Colonel Joll, an officer from the Third Bureau, who comes to investigate the rumored attack of bar-

barians, an investigation that involves the violent torture and killing of some prisoners considered barbarians. As representative of
imperial rule, Joll posits himself as the powerful sacrificer invested
with the right to immolate the "feminized" other to establish political sovereignty.

When Joll leaves, the magistrate, a humanist servant of the Empire, engages in a more benevolent form of colonial eroticism by
taking a crippled and half-blinded barbarian girl into his house.
With her, he develops a sexual relationship that consists for the
most part in the ritual of washing her body and discussing her torture at the hands of Joll and his soldiers. Later, he makes an ardu-
ous and transgressive journey to the barbarian territory in order to
return the girl to her people, during which he also consummates
his relationship with her. Upon his return, he is himself subjected
to colonial violence when he is arrested, imprisoned, and tortured
for his transgression. The colonial army, after a couple of setbacks,
abandons the village and leaves the magistrate and the villagers
awaiting the arrival of barbarians, who, given the novel's intertex-
tual reference to Constantin Cavafy's poem, we know will never
arrive.[4] As I will argue in the remainder of this essay, for both Joll
and the magistrate, the aim of colonial eroticism is to create a sense
of political continuity by subjecting the colonized to a violent process of dissolution in which he or she is subsumed in the hege-
monic power of the Empire.

If we agree with Bataille and Freud that "violence is what the
world of work excludes with its taboos," then the project of colonialism offers a disturbing attempt to reconcile the opposing poles
of this binary.[5] Colonialism works through violence and violation.
Eric Weil, in *Logics of Philosophy* (*Logique de la philosophie*), argues that in Western consciousness the idea of violence has always
been opposed to reason.[6] But colonialism provides a site where the
banishment of violence through taboo, its opposition to reason, can
be subverted. In the colonial project, violence is not opposed to reason; rather, it completes the colonialist logic.

Like war, colonialism is the "collective organization of aggressive urges, and it is organized by the community."[7] The will to
power in the colonial context demonstrates Bataille's claim that the
opposition between reason and violence in Western consciousness
is itself based upon violence, for "if some violent negative emotion
did not make violence horrible for everyone, reason alone could
not define those shifting limits authoritatively enough."[8] Thus the

colonizer is able to rationalize an otherwise treacherous and violent practice as a "civilizing mission."

Colonial violence is about an erotics of dissolution. Imperialism is ultimately a disturbing attempt to produce a sense of continuity between the discontinuous identities of the colonizer and the colonized. The aim is to achieve a state of dissolution that produces continuity between the two, at the cost of robbing the colonized of his or her difference. The colonizer views himself as the "active" agent and forces the colonized into the "passive" role, which must be dissolved as a separate entity to create the sense of colonial continuity. Dissolution can be achieved either through a cold-blooded militarism—discipline, torture, and pain—or through a benevolence and humanism that embodies pleasure, desire, sexuality. These positions can be ultimately continuous, for, as the magistrate discovers painfully, one is "the lie that Empire tells itself when times are easy," and the other is "the truth that Empire tells when harsh winds blow" (135). Both sides of imperial rule involve a violent binarism between the colonizer, who assumes the active role of sacrificing, and the colonized, who is forced into the position of passivity, as the sacrificed.

In the case of cold-blooded militarism, the colonizer occupies the position of the torturer who destroys the self-contained and yet discontinuous body of the colonized. Colonial torture is an attempt to penetrate the body of the other so that a sense of continuity is achieved between the master and the victim:

> "What did they do to him?" I whisper to the guard, the same young man as last night.
> "A knife," he whispers back. "Just a little knife, like this." He spreads thumb and forefinger. Gripping his little knife of air he makes a curt thrust into the sleeping boy's body and turns the knife delicately, like a key, first left, then right. Then he withdraws it, his hand returns to his side, he stands waiting. (10)

The "érotisme des corps"[9] is a violent and deleterious sacrificial rite, extravagantly cruel and sinister, because dissolution is here achieved by destroying the discontinuous other. But paradoxically, corporal eroticism, as Bataille tells us, "holds on to the separateness of the individual in a rather selfish and cynical fashion," thus engendering a mode of violation bordering on death, on murder.[10] Colonialist logic is contradictory because "the contour of difference [in colonialist ideology] is agnostic, shifting, [and] splitting."[11] Placed at the border of discipline and desire, the body of the colonized is at once the sign of incommensurable difference and utterly dissolvable through colonial appropriation. Difference, in other words, is the precondition for colonial dissolution.

The erotics of dissolution in this instance is not merely corporal but also discursive, since it aims to extract what the colonizer calls "truth" from the other's body. Colonial "truth" is derived from corporeality and produced by inflicting pain on the body of the colonized; the surface of the other's body must be violated to the point of achieving the inner experience of "truth," which would ultimately confer upon the colonizer a sense of continuity with his victim. The sacrificer is above all an interrogator who can hear the "tone of truth" in the material voice of his victims. Consider how Colonel Joll describes the discovery of "truth" through pain: "First I get lies, you see—this is what happens—first lies, then pressure, then more lies, then more pressure, then the break, then more pressure, then the truth. That is how you get the truth" (5).

Joll's interrogatory technique relies, above all, on violence, for as Debra Castillo cogently remarks, "violence provides the only copula the Empire knows between the featureless savage and the knowledge she hides, the knowledge the torturer desires her to possess."[12] In the process of interrogation corporeality and discursivity converge: the extraction of truth from the body of the colonized dissolves him or her as a separate entity; to confess is to acknowledge what the colonizer posits as the "truth." "The whole business of eroticism," Bataille reminds us, "is to strike to the inmost core of the living being."[13] At the inmost core of the colonized's body lies the "truth" of empire, a truth embedded in a violent lie.

The benevolent colonizer, by contrast, assumes the position of the healer, trying to erase the marks of violence his militarist counterpart has left on the colonized. Here the ritual of ablution replaces the ritual of torture, but this ritual is no less violent. They are both rituals of sacrifice in which the colonizer is the active agent and the colonized is the passive recipient:

> First comes the ritual of the washing, for which she is now naked. I wash her feet, as before, her legs, her buttocks. My soapy hand travels between her thighs, injuriously, I find. She raises her arms while I wash her armpits. I wash her belly, her breasts. I push her hair aside and wash her neck, her throat. She is patient. I rinse and dry her. I close my eyes and lose myself in the rhythm of the rubbing, while the fire, piled high, roars in the grate.
> . . . in the very act of caressing her I am overcome with sleep as if poleaxed, fall into oblivion sprawled upon her body, and wake an hour

or two later dizzy, confused, thirsty. These dreamless spells are like death to me, or enchantment, blank, outside time. (30–31)

The magistrate performs the ritual of washing the girl's body in pursuit of secrets she is believed to withhold. But the washing of the tortured body is thematized as erotic, as the magistrate becomes engulfed in the pleasure of ablution. The body of the colonized provides the benevolent colonizer with the erotic vehicle for achieving the state of dissolution his counterpart achieves through torture. This is a kind of "érotisme des coeurs," which is less constrained than the "érotisme des corps," but no less sinister or violent. The need for continuity demands in both cases a ritual of sacrifice in which penetration or piercing the body of the other forms a privileged moment:

> I have just come from the bed of a woman for whom, in the year I have known her, I haven't for a moment had to interrogate my desire: to desire her has meant to unfold her and enter her, to pierce her surface and stir the quiet of her interior into an ecstatic storm; then to retreat, to subside, to wait for desire to reconstitute itself. But with this woman it is as if there is no interior, only a surface across which I hunt back and forth seeking entry. Is this how her torturers felt hunting their secret, whatever they thought it was? . . . I behave in some ways like a lover—I undress her, I bathe her, I stroke her, I sleep beside her—but I might equally well tie her to a chair and beat her, it would be no less intimate. (43)

Even though the magistrate claims elsewhere that "There is nothing to link me with torturers," he is ultimately forced to acknowledge how his erotic relationships with colonized women implicate him in colonial violence (44). The domain of colonial eroticism, to borrow Bataille's definition, is always the domain of violence and violation—the latter to be understood here in the French sense of "rape." The colonizer must always assume the position of the sacrificer, forcing his victim into an erotics of dissolution that involves ultimately the violation of her self-containment, her discontinuity —always by piercing.

This form of emotional eroticism is also invested in the power of "truth," which implicates it once again in the discipline of interrogation. Like Joll, the benevolent colonizer is equally obsessed with obtaining the "truth."

The opaqueness of the colonized's body, her inaccessibility, does not thwart the colonizer's will to truth; on the contrary, it invigorates it with a vengeance. It is a veil that arouses the violent desire to tear, to unmask, to penetrate. One of the most decisive aspects of eroticism, Bataille argues, is unveiling, the *mis à nu* of a concealed state. This is why, even though the magistrate has been seeing the barbarian's tortured body, he insists on verbal acknowledgment of her torture at the hands of the interrogators: " 'Tell me,' I want to say, 'don't make a mystery of it, pain is only pain' " (32). The benevolent colonizer, like his cold-blooded militarist counterpart, works within a teleological framework in which the unmasking of the truth is necessary to his final goal of achieving the state of dissolution, of the violence of colonial continuity.

We must go beyond the binary logic of the colonizer as the sacrificer and the colonized as the sacrificed to account for the complexities of colonial violence. New distinctions can impose themselves on the map of violence, because, in the erotics of dissolution, the colonizer can transgress, can attempt to pass over to the other's side. The mutilated body of the other is a reservoir of knowledge which moves the colonizer to the limits of colonial law; the benevolent colonizer cannot remain indifferent to this map of violence and violation on the colonized's body. In fact, he actively seeks the traces of a history her body tells: "It has been growing more and more clear to me that until the marks on this girl's body are deciphered and understood I cannot let go of her" (31). The violated body of the colonized is the material locus of what Benjamin calls "the tradition of the oppressed,"[14] and as such it forms a depository of historical knowledge that propels the benevolent colonizer to transgress the limits of Empire to embrace the barbarians, a ritual that completes the erotics of dissolution: "The barbarians stand outlined against the sky above us. There is the beating of my heart, the heaving of the horses, the moan of the wind, and no other sound. We have crossed the limits of Empire. It is not a moment to take lightly" (70).

We should not take this moment of transgression lightly. Through "illegal" crossing of the Empire's borders and geographical "penetration" into barbarian territory, the colonial taboo transcended and completed. By such a geographical immersion in the other the colonizer can finally penetrate the other's body in a climax to the "érotisme des coeurs": "In the snowbound warmth of the tent I make love to her again. She is passive, accommodating herself to me. When we begin I am sure the time is right; I embrace her in the most intense pleasure and pride of life" (66).

The colonizer is finally able to enter the other's body when he transgresses the limits of the Empire and arrives in barbarian territory. The transgression of the taboo, however, is only temporarily possible. There is, in other words, a momentary point of opposition to the binary logic of the colonial order: a "bond is broken." He is a free man, but only for a short moment. The price of "treasonously consorting with the enemy" is high, high enough to transform his position as the sacrificer into that of the sacrificed (77).

The magistrate's attempt to overcome the binaries of colonizer/colonized, sacrificer/sacrificed is illusory, however, because his identity is always already inscribed in such a hierarchical relation. As the magistrate himself acknowledges at a self-reflexive moment, his wish to cross the border of identity leads only to confusion: "Thus I seduced myself, taking one of many wrong turnings I have taken on a road that looks true but has delivered me into the heart of a labyrinth" (136). And yet, it is precisely this illusion of a transcendence that would be made accessible through his own torture that implicates him even more profoundly in the discourse of humanism. Such an illusion is possible because of the impact of the process of torture, its overwhelming excess over "ordinary" experience.

Torture, according to the benevolent colonizer, is ultimately a useful lesson about a rudimentary aspect of our humanity, that is, the very physicality of our bodies:

> In my suffering there is nothing ennobling. Little of what I call suffering is even pain. What I am made to undergo is subjection to the most rudimentary needs of my body: to drink, to relieve itself, to find the posture in which it is least sore . . . [my torturers] were interested only in demonstrating to me what it meant to live in a body, as a body which can entertain notions of justice only as long as it is whole and well, which very soon forgets them when its head is gripped and a pipe is pushed down its gullet and pints of salt water are poured into it till it coughs and retches and fails and voids itself. . . . [my torturers] came to my cell to show me the meaning of humanity, and in the space of an hour they showed me a great deal. (115)

The magistrate's experience of pain through torture teaches him that his humanity does not reside in his principles, nor in his intellectual existence; rather, it is his body that defines his humanity. This is a crucial lesson for the magistrate, whose humanism has made him blind to the corporal aspect of colonialism's technology of power—that the body is ultimately the site where the desire to dominate is articulated.

Traumatic Awakenings

CATHY CARUTH

Les désirs entretiennent les rêves. Mais la
mort, elle, est du coté du réveil.
—Jacques Lacan

Ever since its emergence at the turn of the century in the
work of Freud and Pierre Janet, the notion of trauma has confronted
us not only with a simple pathology but also with a fundamental
enigma concerning the psyche's relation to reality. In its general
definition, trauma is described as the response to an unexpected
or overwhelming violent event or events that are not fully grasped
as they occur, but return later in repeated flashbacks, nightmares,
and other repetitive phenomena. Traumatic experience, beyond the
psychological dimension of suffering it involves, suggests a certain
paradox: that the most direct seeing of a violent event may occur
as an absolute inability to know it, that immediacy, paradoxically,
may take the form of belatedness. The repetitions of the traumatic
event—which remain unavailable to consciousness but intrude repeatedly on sight—thus suggest a larger relation to the event, which
extends beyond what can simply be seen or what can be known
and is inextricably tied up with the belatedness and incomprehen-
sibility that remain at the heart of this repetitive seeing.

In the present essay I will study the problem of seeing and
knowing as it appears in a dream told by Freud—the dream of a
father who has lost his child and who dreams about this child in
the night following the child's death—and in the reinterpretation
of this dream by Jacques Lacan in his seminar "Tuché and Automaton."[1] While Freud introduces the dream in *The Interpretation
of Dreams* as an exemplary (if enigmatic) explanation of why we

208

sleep—how we don't adequately face the death outside of us—Lacan suggests that already at the heart of this example is the core of what would later become, in *Beyond the Pleasure Principle*, Freud's notion of traumatic repetition, and especially the traumatic nightmares that, as Freud says, "wake the dreamer up in another fright." In Lacan's analysis, Freud's dream is no longer about a father sleeping in the face of an external death, but about the way in which, in his traumatic awakening, the very identity of the father, as subject, is bound up with, or founded in, the death that he survives. What the father cannot grasp in the death of his child, that is, becomes the foundation of his identity as father. In thus relating trauma to the identity of the self and to one's relation to another, Lacan's reading shows us, I will suggest, that the shock of traumatic sight reveals at the heart of human subjectivity not so much an epistemological, but rather what can be defined as an *ethical* relation to the real.

The Story of a Dream

At the beginning of the seventh chapter of *The Interpretation of Dreams*, Freud introduces a surprising dream that links his theory of dreams and wish fulfillment to the question of external reality, and specifically to a reality of violent loss. Freud narrates the dream as follows:

> A father had been watching beside his child's sick-bed for days and nights on end. After the child had died, he went into the next room to lie down, but left the door open so that he could see from his bedroom into the room in which his child's body was laid out, with tall candles standing round it. An old man had been engaged to keep watch over it, and sat beside the body murmuring prayers. After a few hours' sleep, the father had a dream *that his child was standing beside his bed, caught him by the arm and whispered to him reproachfully: "Father, don't you see I'm burning?"* He woke up, noticed a bright glare of light from the next room, hurried into it and found that the old watchman had dropped off to sleep and that the wrappings and one of the arms of his beloved child's dead body had been burned by a lighted candle that had fallen on them.
>
> The explanation of this moving dream is simple enough. . . . The glare of light shone through the open door into the sleeping man's eyes and led him to the conclusion which he would have arrived at if he had been awake, namely that a candle had fallen over and set something alight in the neighbourhood of the body. It is even possible that he had felt some concern when he went to sleep as to whether the old man might not be incompetent to carry out his task.

> . . . the words spoken by the child must have been made up of
> words which he had actually spoken in his lifetime and which were
> connected with important events in the father's mind. For instance,
> *'I'm burning'* may have been spoken during the fever of the child's last
> illness, and *'Father, don't you see?'* may have been derived from some
> other highly emotional situation of which we are in ignorance.
>   But, having recognized that the dream was a process with a mean-
> ing, and that it can be inserted into the chain of the dreamer's psychi-
> cal experiences, we may still wonder why it was that a dream occurred
> at all in such circumstances, when the most rapid possible awakening
> was called for.[2]

Unlike other dreams, Freud remarks, this dream is striking,
not in its relation to inner wishes, but in its direct relation to a
catastrophic reality outside: the dream takes its "moving" power,
it would seem, from the very simplicity and directness of its reference, the burning of his child's body that the father sees through
his sleep. Seeing the light through his closed eyes, the father comes
to the conclusion he would have arrived at if he were awake: that
the candle has fallen on the body of his child. Yet the very directness of this dream, Freud remarks, does not, surprisingly, wake the
father and permit him to rush to save the burning corpse, but precisely delays his response to the waking reality. If the meaning and
reference of the dream are indeed clear, Freud suggests, then it is
not apparent why they should appear *in a dream*, that is, in a form
that delays the father's response—a response that is urgently called
for—to the reality to which it points. Precisely because the dream
is so direct, and because the reality it refers to is so urgent in its demand for attention, this dream poses the question: In the context
of a violent reality, *Why dream rather than wake up?*

Freud first attempts to answer this question by referring the
dream to the theory of wish fulfillment, in spite of its direct representation of the child's unwished-for death. While the dream points
to the horrible reality of the child's burning, it does so, Freud points
out, precisely by transforming the dead child into a living one.
The dream fulfills, therefore, the father's wish that the child be
still alive:

> Here we shall observe that this dream, too, contained the fulfilment
> of a wish. The dead child behaved in the dream like a living one; he
> himself warned his father, came to his bed, and caught him by the
> arm, just as he had probably done on the occasion from the memory of
> which the first part of the child's words in the dream were derived. For
> the sake of the fulfilment of this wish the father prolonged his sleep

by one moment. The dream was preferred to a waking reflection because it was able to show the child as once more alive. If the father had woken up first and then made the inference that led him to go into the next room, he would, as it were, have shortened his child's life by that moment of time.[3]

While the dream seems to show the reality of the burning outside, it in fact hides, Freud suggests, the reality of the child's death. The dream thus transforms death into life and does this, paradoxically, with the very words that refer to the reality of the burning. It is in order to fulfill the wish to see the child alive, in other words, that the knowledge of the child's burning is turned into a dream. If the father dreams rather than wakes up, it is because he cannot face the knowledge of the child's death while he is awake. It is thus not that the father simply "doesn't see" the burning corpse ("Father, don't you see?")—he does see it—but rather that he cannot see it and be awake at the same time. For the father, Freud seems to imply, the knowledge of the death of his child can perhaps only appear in the form of a fiction or a dream.[4] The dream thus tells the story of a father's grief as the very relation of the psyche to reality: the dream, as a delay, reveals the ineradicable gap between the reality of a death and the desire that cannot overcome it except in the fiction of a dream.

After completing his original analysis, however, Freud remains unsatisfied with the explanation and returns to the dream again at a later point in the chapter, where the problem of the dream's delay of awakening comes back to take on new meaning. For the interpretation of the dream as the fulfillment of the father's wish leads to a deeper question, which concerns not only this singular instance but the way in which the father may represent the very nature of consciousness itself:

> Let me recall the dream dreamt by the man who was led to infer from the glare of light coming out of the next room that his child's body might be on fire. The father drew this inference in a dream instead of allowing himself to be woken up by the glare; and we have suggested that one of the psychical forces responsible for this result was a wish which prolonged by that one moment the life of the child whom he pictured in the dream . . . we may assume that a further motive force in the production of the dream was the father's sleep; his sleep, like the child's life, was prolonged by one moment by the dream. "Let the dream go on"—such was his motive—"or I shall have to wake up." In every other dream, just as in this one, the wish to sleep lends its support to the unconscious wish.[5]

The wish in the father's dream to keep the child alive—the first reason Freud gives for the father's dream—is inextricably bound up, it turns out, with a more profound and enigmatic wish, the father's wish to sleep. This wish is enigmatic because, Freud suggests, it comes not only from the body but from consciousness itself, which desires somehow its own suspension. And this wish, moreover, is not limited to this single father, exhausted by his task of watching over the child, but refers to a desire common to all sleepers. The dream of the burning child does not simply represent, therefore, the wish fulfillment of a single father, tired and wishing to see his child alive once again, but more profoundly and more enigmatically, the wish fulfillment *of consciousness itself*:

> All dreams . . . serve the purpose of prolonging sleep instead of waking up. *The dream is the GUARDIAN of sleep and not its disturber. . . . Thus the wish to sleep (which the conscious ego is concentrated upon . . .) must in every case be reckoned as one of the motivations for the formation of dreams, and every successful dream is a fulfilment of that wish.*[6]

The specific wish behind the dream of the burning child, the wish to see the child again, Freud suggests, like the wish behind any dream, is tied to a more basic desire, the desire of consciousness as such *not to wake up*. It is not the father alone who dreams to avoid his child's death, but consciousness itself that—even at the expense of a burning reality—motivates the dream. The dream is thus no longer simply linked to a wish within the unconscious fantasy world of the psyche; it is rather, Freud seems to suggest, *something in reality itself that makes us sleep*. The question concerning the father—*Why dream rather than wake up?*—thus ultimately becomes, in Freud's analysis, a more profound and mysterious question concerning consciousness itself: *What does it mean to sleep? And what does it mean to wish to sleep?*

The Story of an Awakening

Freud's analysis of the dream and the implicit question it raises in *The Interpretation of Dreams* seem to leave us with the sense of a consciousness not only tied up with but also blinded to a violent reality outside. But when Lacan turns to the dream in his seminar, he suggests that the question of sleep and Freud's analysis of it contain within them, implicitly, another question, a question discovered not through the story of the father's sleep but rather through the story of how and why the father wakes up:

> You will remember the unfortunate father who went to rest in the room next to the one in which his dead child lay—leaving the child in the care, we are told, of another old man—and who is awoken by something. By what? It is not only the reality, the shock, the knocking, a noise made to recall him to the real, but this expresses, in his dream, the quasi-identity of what is happening, the very reality of an overturned candle setting light to the bed in which his child lies.
>
> Such an example hardly seems to confirm Freud's thesis in the *Traumdeutung*—that the dream is the realization of a desire.
>
> What we see emerging here, almost for the first time, in the *Traumdeutung*, is a function of the dream of an apparently secondary kind—in this case, the dream satisfies only the need to prolong sleep. What, then, does Freud mean by placing, at this point, this particular dream, stressing that it is in itself full confirmation of his thesis regarding dreams?
>
> If the function of the dream is to prolong sleep, if the dream, after all, may come so near to the reality that causes it, can we not say that it might correspond to this reality without emerging from sleep? After all, there is such a thing as somnambulistic activity. The question that arises, and which indeed all Freud's previous indications allow us here to produce, is—*What is it that wakes the sleeper?* Is it not, *in* the dream, another reality?—the reality that Freud describes thus—*Dass das Kind an seinem Bette steht*, that the child is near his bed, *ihn am Arme fasst*, takes him by the arm and whispers to him reproachfully, *und ihm vorwurfsvoll zuraunt: Vater, siehst du denn nicht*, Father don't you see, *dass ich verbrenne*, that I am burning?
>
> Is there not more reality in this message than in the noise by which the father also identifies the strange reality of what is happening in the room next door?[7]

By explaining the dream as fulfilling the wish to sleep, Lacan suggests, Freud implicitly points toward the fact that this wish is enigmatically defied in waking up, for if consciousness is what desires as such not to wake up, the waking is in conflict with the conscious wish. But what is particularly striking for Lacan is that this contradiction of the wish to sleep does not simply come from the outside, from the noise or light of the falling candle, but from the way in which the words of the child, themselves, bear precisely upon sleeping and waking. In Lacan's analysis, indeed, the words of the child—"Don't you see I'm burning?"—do not simply represent the burning without, but rather *address* the father from within and appeal to him as a complaint about the very fact of his own sleep. It is *the dream itself*, that is, *that wakes the sleeper*, and it is in this paradoxical awakening—an awakening not to, but against the very wishes of consciousness—that the dreamer finally confronts the reality of a death from which he can no longer turn away. If Freud, in other words, suggests that the dream keeps the father asleep, Lacan suggests that it is because the father dreams, paradoxically enough, that he precisely wakes up. The dream thus becomes, in Lacan's analysis, no longer a function of sleep, but rather a function of awakening. If Freud asks, *what does it mean to sleep*? Lacan discovers at the heart of this question another one, perhaps even more urgent: *What does it mean to awaken?*

It might seem that Lacan, in his focus on awakening, moves from the fictional dream world of Freud—the fictional world of the child once again alive—to the simple reality of the external world, the accident of the candle falling on the body, which reduplicates and underscores the reality of the child's death. But what can Lacan mean by saying that the father is awakened, not simply by the sound of the candle's fall, but rather by the words of the child *within* the dream? What does it mean, in other words, that the dream achieves, not the desired resuscitation of the child, but the dreamer's awakening to the child's death? Indeed, to the extent that the father is awakened by the dream itself, his awakening to death, Lacan seems to suggest, is not a simple movement of knowledge or perception, but rather a paradoxical attempt *to respond, in awakening, to a call that can only be heard within sleep*.

I would propose that it is in this paradoxical awakening by the dream itself that Lacan discovers and extends the specific meaning of the confrontation with death that is contained within Freud's notion of trauma.[8] If the dreamer's awakening can be seen as a response to the words, the address, of the child within the dream, then the awakening represents a paradox concerning the necessity and impossibility of confronting death. As a response to the child's request, the plea to be seen, the father's awakening represents not only a responding, that is, but also a missing, a bond to the child that is built upon the impossibility of a proper response. Waking up in order to see, the father discovers that he has once again *seen too late* to prevent the burning. The relation between the burning within and the burning without is thus neither a fiction (as in Freud's interpretation) nor a direct representation, but a *repetition* that reveals, in its temporal contradiction, how the very bond of the father to the child—his responsiveness to the child's words—

is linked to the missing of the child's death. To awaken is thus to awaken only to one's repetition of a previous failure to see in time. The force of the trauma is not the death alone, that is, but the fact that, in his attachment to the child, the father was unable to witness the child's dying as it occurred. *Awakening*, in Lacan's reading of the dream, *is itself the site of a trauma*, the trauma of the necessity and impossibility of responding to another's death.[9]

From this perspective, the trauma that the dream, as an awakening, reenacts is not only the missed encounter with the child's death but also the way in which that missing also constitutes the very survival of the father. His survival must no longer be understood, in other words, merely as an accidental living beyond the child, but rather as a mode of existence determined by the impossible structure of the response. By shifting the cause of the awakening from the accident of the candle falling outside the dream to the words of the child inside the dream, that is, Lacan suggests that the awakening itself is not a simple accident, but engages a larger question of responsibility.

In rethinking the meaning of the accident and in linking it to this profound question about the nature of survival, Lacan is drawing here, I would like to propose, on Freud's late work on trauma, and specifically, on Freud's emphasis on the traumatic accident nightmare in *Beyond the Pleasure Principle* and on the example of the train accident in Freud's last major work, *Moses and Monotheism*.[10] Freud shows how the traumatic accident—the confrontation with death—takes place too soon, too suddenly, too unexpectedly, to be fully grasped by consciousness. In Lacan's text, this peculiar accidentality at the heart of Freud's notion of trauma is linked to the larger philosophical significance of traumatic repetition:

> Is it not remarkable that, at the origin of the analytic experience, the real should have presented itself in the form of that which is unassimilable in it—in the form of the trauma, determining all that follows, and imposing on it an apparently accidental origin?[11]

Likewise, in the awakening of the father from the dream, the gap between the accident of the burning outside and the words of the child in the dream produces a significance greater than any chance awakening out of a particular night's sleep, a significance that must be read in the relation between the chance event and the words this chance event calls up:

> Between what occurs as if by chance, when everybody is asleep—the candle that overturns and the sheets that catch fire, the meaningless event, the accident, the piece of bad luck—and the poignancy, however veiled, in the words, *Father, don't you see I'm burning*—there is the same relation to what we were dealing with in repetition. It is what, for us, is represented in the term neurosis of destiny or neurosis of failure.[12]

If the awakening reenacts the father's survival of his son's death, then it is no longer simply the effect of an accident but carries within it, and is defined by, its response to the words of the dead child.

It is this determining link between the child's death and the father's survival that constitutes, I would propose, Lacan's central discovery in the dream and his profound insight into its analysis by Freud: whereas Freud reads in the dream of the burning child the story of a sleeping consciousness figured by a father unable to face the accidental death of his child, Lacan reads in the awakening the peculiar narrative of the way father and child are inextricably bound together through the story of a trauma.[13] Lacan, in other words, reads the story of the father as a survival inherently and constitutively bound up with the address of a dead child.

The father's story of survival is, therefore, no longer simply his own, but tells, as a mode of response, the story of the dead child. This story has a double dimension: depending on whether the child's words are read as referring to the burning within or to the burning without, the father's survival can be understood, as we shall see, in terms of two inextricably bound, though incompatible, responses to the child's address. In thus implicitly exploring consciousness as figured by the survivor whose life is inextricably linked to the death he witnesses, Lacan resituates the psyche's relation to the real not as a simple matter of seeing or of knowing the true nature of empirical events, not as what can be known or what cannot be known about reality, but as the story of an urgent responsibility, or what Lacan defines, in this conjuction, as an *ethical* relation to the real.[14]

A Failed Address

If the words of the child—*Father, don't you see I'm burning?*—can be read, in this light, as a plea by the child to see the burning *within* the dream, the response of the father in this awakening dramatizes

the story of a repeated *failure* to respond adequately, a failure to
see the child in its death. To see the child's living vulnerability as
it dies, the father has to go on dreaming. In awakening, he sees the
child's death too late, and thus cannot truly or adequately respond.

From this perspective, the dream reveals a reality beyond the
accident of a single empirical event, the chance death of a child by
fever. Showing, in its repetition, the failure of the father to see even
when he tries to see, the dream reveals how the consciousness of
the father as father, as the one who wishes to see his child alive
again so much that he sleeps in spite of the burning corpse, is inextricably linked to the impossibility of adequately responding to
the plea of the child in its death. The bond to the child, the sense
of responsibility, is in its essence tied to the impossibility of recognizing the child in its potential death. And it is this bond that the
dream reveals, exemplarily, as the real, as an encounter with a real
established around an inherent impossibility:

> What encounter can there be henceforth with that forever inert being
> —even now being devoured by the flames—if not the encounter that
> occurs precisely at the moment when, by accident, as if by chance,
> the flames come to meet him? Where is the reality in this accident, if
> not that it repeats something actually more fatal *by means of* reality, a
> reality in which the person who was supposed to be watching over the
> body still remains asleep, even when the father reemerges after having
> woken up?[15]

In awakening, the father's response repeats in one act a double failure of seeing: a failure to see adequately inside and a failure to see
adequately outside.

Indeed, Lacan's interpretive movement from the accident of the
candle falling to the dream as what repeats something "more fatal"
by means of reality could be said to represent a parable about the
notions of reality and trauma in Freud's late work, and specifically
a parable about the movement implied by the transition from chapter 4 to chapter 5 of *Beyond the Pleasure Principle*. In this work,
Freud moves from a speculation on consciousness that explains
trauma as an interruption of consciousness by a violent event, such
as an accident, that comes too soon to be expected, to an explanation of the origins of life itself as an "awakening" from death
that establishes the foundations of the drive and of consciousness
alike.[16] This peculiar movement therefore traces a significant itinerary in Freud's thought from trauma as an exception, an accident

that takes consciousness by surprise and thus disrupts it, to trauma as the origin of consciousness and all of life itself. This global theoretical itinerary is revisited in Lacan's interpretation and rethinking of the dream of the burning child, in his suggestion that the accidental in trauma reveals a basic ethical dilemma at the heart of consciousness insofar as it is essentially related to death, and particularly to the death of others.[17] Ultimately, then, the story of father and child is, for Lacan, the story of an impossible responsibility of consciousness in its originating relation to others, and specifically to the deaths of others. As an awakening, the ethical relation to the real is the revelation of this impossible demand at the heart of human consciousness.[18]

An Unavoidable Imperative

But the words of the child, *Father, don't you see I'm burning?*, can be read another way as well, not only as the plea to see the child burning in the dream, but also as the command to see the child burning without—as the imperative, that is, to awaken. While Lacan does not explicitly articulate this reading, he does suggest that the missing of the trauma is also an encounter: "For what we have in the discovery of psycho-analysis is an encounter, an essential encounter— an appointment to which we are always called with a real that eludes us."[19] From this perspective, the awakening embodies an appointment with the real. The awakening, in other words, occurs not merely as a failure to respond but as an enactment of the inevitability of responding: the inevitability of awakening to the survival of the child that is now only a corpse. The pathos and significance of this awakening derive not simply from the repeated loss of the child, in the father's attempt to see, but rather from the fact that the child itself—the child whom the father has not seen in time, the child he has let die unwitnessed, the child whom the dream (in the father's desperation to make the child live again) shows as once again alive—it is this very child who, from within the failure of the father's seeing, commands the father to awaken and to live, and to live precisely as the seeing of another, a different burning. The father, who would have stayed inside the dream to see his child alive once more, is commanded by this child to see not from the inside—the inside of the dream, and the inside of the death, which is the only place the child could now be truly seen—but from the outside, to leave the child in the dream so as to awaken elsewhere. It is precisely the dead child, the child in its irreducible inaccessibility and otherness, who says to the father: *Wake up, leave me, survive; survive to tell the story of my burning.*

To awaken is thus to bear the imperative to survive: to survive no longer simply as the father of a child, but as the one who must tell *what it means not to see*, which is also what it means to hear the unthinkable words of the dying child:

> Is not the dream essentially, one might say, an act of homage to the missed reality—the reality that can no longer produce itself except by repeating itself endlessly, in some never attained awakening?
>
> Only a rite, an endlessly repeated act, can commemorate this not very memorable encounter—for no one can say what the death of a child is, except the father *qua* father, that is to say, no conscious being.[20]

The father must receive the dead child's words. But the only way truly to hear is now by listening, not as a living father listens to a living child, but as the one who receives the gap between the other's death and his own life, the one who, in awakening, does not see but enacts the impact of the difference between death and life. The awakening, in its very inability to see, is thus the true *reception of an address* that, precisely in its crossing from the burning within to the burning without, changes and reforms the nature of the addressee around the blindness of the imperative itself. In awakening, in responding to the address of the dead child—*Father, don't you see I'm burning?*—the father is no longer the father of a living child but the father as *the one who can say* what the death of a child is. The father's response to the address is not a knowing, that is, but an awakening, an awakening that, like the performance of a speaking, precisely carries with it and transmits the child's otherness, the father's encounter with the otherness of the dead child.

Such an awakening, if it is in some sense still a repetition of the trauma (a reenactment of the child's dying), is not, however, a simple repetition of the *same* failure and loss—of the story of the father alone—but a new act that repeats a departure and a difference: the departure of the father at the command of his burning child, and the difference to which he awakens, the intolerable difference between the burning within and the burning without.

As an act, the awakening is thus not an understanding but a transmission, the performance of an act of awakening that contains within it its own difference—"repetition," Lacan says, "demands the new."[21] This newness is enacted in the fact that the words are no longer mastered or possessed by the one who says them—by the child who has died and for whom it is eternally too late to speak, or by the father who receives the words as coming from the place of the child, the self that was asleep. Neither the possession of the father nor the possession of the child, the words are *passed on* as an act that does not precisely awaken the self but rather *passes the awakening on to others*.

The accident is thus not a reality that can simply be known once and for all, but an encounter with the real that must take place each time anew in the accident of where the words happen to fall:

> But what, then, was this accident? When everybody is asleep, including the person who wished to take a little rest, the person who was unable to maintain his vigil and the person of whom some well intentioned individual, standing at his bedside, must have said, *He looks just as if he is asleep*, when we know only one thing about him, and that is that, in this entirely sleeping world, only the voice is heard, *Father, don't you see I'm burning?* This sentence is itself a firebrand—of itself it brings fire where it falls—and one cannot see what is burning, for the flames blind us to the fact that the fire bears on the *Unterlegt*, on the *Untertragen*, on the real.[22]

The accident, the force of the falling of the candle, cannot be confined to a real that consists in the empirical fact of burning or the fever, the accident by which the child caught fever or by which the candle fell and set the body of the child on fire while the father slept. The force of the fall lies precisely in the accident of the way in which the child's words transmit a burning that turns between the death of the child and the imperative of the father's survival, a burning that, like the candle, falls to awaken, anew, those who hear the words.

The implications of such a transmission will only be fully grasped, I think, when we come to understand how, through the act of survival, the repeated failure to have seen in time—in itself a pure repetition compulsion, a repeated nightmare—can be transformed into the imperative of a speaking that awakens others. For now, however, I will simply point to the imperative of awakening that underlies Lacan's own text, the theoretical text of psychoanalysis. It is in the language of theory itself, Lacan suggests, that psychoanalysis transmits, as he puts it, the "fever" of Freud, the burning of Freud's driving question, "What is the first encounter, the real, that lies behind the fantasy?"[23] And it is to this burning question, and to this fever that he senses in Freud's text, that Lacan's own text precisely responds:

> The function of . . . the real as encounter—the encounter in so far as it may be missed, in so far as it is essentially the missed encounter—first presented itself in the history of psychoanalysis in a form that was in itself already enough to awaken our attention, that of the trauma.[24]

Lacan suggests that the inspiration of his own text is awakened by the theory of trauma at the center of Freud's text, and that the Freudian theory of trauma speaks already (in this story of the burning dream and of the burning child) from within the very theory of wish fulfillment. The passing on of psychoanalytic theory, Lacan suggests, is an imperative to awaken that turns between a traumatic repetition and the ethical burden of a survival.[25] It is, indeed, not simply Freud's perception and analysis of a reality outside or inside (a reality of empirical events or of internal "fantasies") that Lacan transmits in his reading of the Freudian text and in his concept of "the real," but rather, most importantly, what Lacan refers to as the "ethical witness" of Freud.[26] The transmission of the psychoanalytic theory of trauma, the story of dreams and of dying children, cannot be reduced, therefore, to a simple mastery of facts and cannot be located in a simple knowledge or cognition.

Indeed, the event of the trauma of the dream and the story of the child's death in the texts of Freud and Lacan resonates uncannily with the unexpected stories of their own losses: Freud's text is inadvertently shadowed by the death of his daughter Sophie from a fever, and Lacan's text gains prophetic resonance from the death of his daughter Caroline in a car accident a few years after the delivery of the seminar on the dream of the burning child.[27]

In Lacan's text, as in Freud's, it is rather the words of the child that are ultimately passed on, passed on not in the meaning of the words alone, but in their repeated utterance, in their performance: a performance that, in Lacan's text, takes place in the movement of the repetition and the gap between the German from which these words address the future and the French in which they are heard and received, and in which they are endlessly echoed:

> *Qu'est-ce qui réveille?* N'est-ce pas, *dans* le rêve, une autre réalité?— cette réalité que Freud nous décrit ainsi—*Dass das Kind an seinem Bette steht*, que l'enfant est près de son lit, *ihn am Arme fasst*, le prend par le bras, et lui murmure sur un ton de reproche, *und ihm vor-*

wurfsvoll zuraunt: Vater, siehst du denn nicht, Père, ne voit-tu pas, *dass ich verbrenne?* que je brûle?[28]

The passing on of the child's words does not simply refer to a reality that can be grasped in these words' representation, but transmits the ethical imperative of an awakening that has yet to occur.

Habeas Corpus: The Law's Desire to Have the Body

ANSELM HAVERKAMP AND

CORNELIA VISMANN

> But mercy is above this scept'red sway;
> It is enthronèd in the hearts of kings;
> It is an attribute to God himself.
> —*The Merchant of Venice*, 4.1.193–95

The point has been made more than once, and runs through the debate on violence like a leitmotif, that the progress of legal procedures is embarrassed by the shadow of violence that attaches itself to the law and cannot be shrugged off. The pathos of law's shadow haunts analytical descriptions by Benjamin and Heidegger, by Foucault and Lyotard, by Luhmann and Robert Cover.[1] It reminds us of something that is wrong, "something rotten," as Benjamin has put it, in law's rule and empire.[2] Something has been overlooked in the various histories of progress, whose pride and prejudice law invariably is, in which it was to have overcome the cruelty of darker ages. By contrast, Robert Cover ended his famous article "Violence and the Word" with "the overwhelming reality of the pain and fear that is suffered," again and again, by those subjected to the law's procedures, now as ever. He concludes his analysis of "what all would agree is an unredeemed reality" with law's inescapable shadow: "Between the idea and the reality of common meaning . . . falls the shadow of the violence of law, itself."[3] Whose shadow, then, is it? The law's "itself"?

Cover's observation that, in "an unredeemed reality," the shadow of violence belongs to the law itself—that, in other words, this shadow is not the detachable aftereffect of legal acts, whose pure words would be overshadowed by the circumstances of their execution, but rather part of the law's ways of coming into being and being real (its "phenomenology," so to speak)—contradicts any faith in the law's possible purification, or any final epiphany of justice as such. It may not completely contradict the notion of progress in the domestication of violence. But it first poses the question of how to account for the violence implied by, and administered through, legal acts. Where, actually, does the performative force of a sentence reside, and what is its extension? How, literally, does a judge act in sentencing, and how, figuratively, if the sentence is indeed to be taken literally, is the act to be taken? (For a "sentence" to be literal, the act that produces it would have to be metaphorical in the first place.[4])

We shall leave open the answer to this rather complicated technical question (technical in the sense of the rhetorical *techne* to be applied), while pursuing the issue in a different register, on the descriptive level of history. What is the law's part in violence? Is it the law's "itself"? If violence is bound to come with the law, as part of the law's own performance rather than with the social or representational functioning of this performance, what part of the "illocutionary force" of sentencing would violence play with respect to the "perlocutionary effect" of execution? Is it possible to conceive of the legal sphere apart from the violence inflicted as the mere result or outcome of the law's force (or "illocutionary potential")?[5] Must we go beyond the law, do we leave the legal sphere behind, in order to avoid the violence involved both in the making of law and in its administration?

To answer these questions, we must face the contingencies of a particular legal history, for example, the set of procedures, devices, and circumstances that well into the nineteenth century amount to the "legal fiction" that is English Common Law. It "permeates," according to Owen Barfield, "the whole of our jurisprudence, which most certainly is law, and not merely procedural."[6] Though full of inconsistencies, the history of habeas corpus provides us with a starting point: the topology of where the law takes place. Moreover, *Habeas corpus*, the writ and the act, exemplify the technical, procedural "interaction" of sentence and execution; in the transfer of "due process" (qua metaphor), it also exposes the displacement (metonymy) of its taking place, the sentence's taking place *in* the execution, and the execution's taking the place *of* the sentence: the topology, in short, of the process due.

There is no act, it seems, without the presence of the body in question, and no process without an act. As we shall see, habeas corpus the writ guarantees habeas corpus the act in that it produces the body, if only to interrupt and delay the process by the very same token. Or, to put it in the idiom of speech-act philosophy, the exemplary instance of the act performed *in saying,* the juridical act, participates silently in the writing of an underlying, fundamental writ.[7] It is this essential participation more than any other, moral obligation that carries the institutional pathos of the habeas corpus act. The primordial act of jurisdiction depends on this transfer, and it asks for further translation, displacement, and delay rather than speedy execution.

After exile—the local solution which made trial superfluous— had become impossible, the temporal solution of delay and such substitutes as bail became imperative. Do we read this problematic correctly, that is, do we do justice to the underlying legal crux, if we take the measures of displacement and delay as merely practical responses to otherwise unmanageable situations and take the means of speedy execution as the logic and the rule of the law "itself"? Or is the law first of all an institution of citation rather than execution, the sentence a means of interruption rather than implementation? It all depends, we submit, on the law's desire to have the body cited rather than executed.

I

The coincidence of body and law begins with a command, the king's command addressed to a sheriff: "Have, [or produce,] the body of the defendant on a given day before the court."[8] The beginning of the order—"Have the body"—lends its initials to the fact of *actually having it,* of how to have and, that is, produce it. The habeas corpus writ, later *Habeas Corpus Act* of 1679, names what is at stake and owes no small part of its notoriety to the intricacy of the named, the law's desire for the body. It is an institutional desire, a desire produced by an institution and manifest in writing, a desire whose reference, or extension, is re-enforced through the institutionalization of what became notorious at the time as "the rule of law."[9] It is the institutionalization of the warrant that "the writ," the written request for the body, bring the body before the law, produces it, seizes it for the law. Capias captures the body in order to secure the defendant's appearance in court and enable the trial literally to take place.

It follows thus almost by definition, that is, by locating the trial in time and space, that body and law are to coincide in court and not in prison. Remarkably enough, every body involved in a trial must gather there, in the courtroom, since the habeas corpus served as a summons for the jurors as well as the defendant. They all were equally commanded by a single writ. At first they were simply summoned by a call, a crier's voice or a bell comparable to the *vocatio* in Roman law.[10] The scene invoked, however, was the king's; it is the theater of his sovereignty, where jurors and defendant are called upon as dramatis personae. For the instant of the trial they belong to one *corpus juris*, which embodies the king's power over his subjects—or so it seems until the "rule of law" came to contest the king's jurisdictional power and to limit his involvement. Most notoriously, in 1608 Chief Justice Edward Coke went so far as to tell James I that he had no authority to participate in the judicial decisions of his own courts. Habeas corpus clearly belongs to the "steady stream of medieval statutes from Magna Charta onwards" that insist on "due process of law" against royal prerogatives, as in arbitrary deprivation of life, liberty or property.[11]

Beginning in the thirteenth century, the trial-body, including jurors and defendant, embodied the king's power, his power to produce and dispose of bodies; it incorporated that power. After the trial, the ad hoc body produced by the "interlocutory mandate" of a habeas corpus was released into bodylessness. The decisive function of the habeas, it seems, was to secure the scene, not to secure or enforce the punishment. The desire for the body in question was satisfied by the scene, satisfied by the performance itself. Afterward, the corporate body of the trial fell apart; outside the topos of the court, it could not be located or defined. It could be neither fixed nor defined within the coordinates of writing or geography. Naturally, because the body is fugitive, the defendant could evade trial by either escaping from the king's realm or throwing him or herself on the king's mercy. These two options entailed different types of risks.

Evading the trial was easy so long as the sheriff summoned without searching. A summons, though hardly distinguishable from a warrant of arrest, was altogether unlike the elaborate apparatus of a police search nowadays. But evading trial and escaping liability meant becoming an outlaw, whereas to go for the king's mercy was the opposite of recognizing the law. Exception through mercy resembled evasion in that both suspended the law. Precisely for that reason, the law was eager to have the body before the court, with the principle rationale of securing the trial scene. Its most impressive mise-en-scène was in the court of Frederick the Second, who became notorious for a stupendous display of "law-centered-kingship," as Ernst Kantorowicz has shown.[12] Whether we speak of

Iustitia mediatrix or *lex animata* (in Frederick's own terms), the motif of clemency, traditionally taken from Seneca's *De clementia*, added to the intricacies of these concepts of mediation an indispensable ingredient easily overlooked and systematically forgotten.[13] Clemency made manifest the king's position *above* the law, but *with respect* to it. Both aspects are decisive for this moment of representation. That the king is bound to a law never to be applied against his will is not a simple but a double bind; it cannot be dissolved by the logic of due execution.

Thus the trial opened a space for the ceremony of clemency; it exposed the king's power over life and death. Mercy was the king's prerogative despite and beyond the law, a monopoly with respect to the law's formal existence as well as its fulfillment, justice— of "that within which passes show," in Hamlet's words (we have to twist them just slightly). The king needed the convicted body in order to perform, above the law, the law's innermost self. The historically far-reaching formula "Master over Life and Death"— Fredrick's maxim from Seneca—establishes the power to pardon as the power to produce and dismiss bodies through judgment and mercy. As a warrant of arrest, habeas corpus demands and remands bodies according to the *voluntas regis*; that is, it demonstrates the king's power over the law by producing an interlocutory body. It performs, creates, and annihilates, in the double act of summoning and discharging, calling and pardoning.[14]

English law distinguishes pardon *de cursu* and *de gratia*; only the latter is due to the king's sovereignty. Whereas the first is jurisdictional, that is, concerned with questions of excuse, the second depends entirely upon the king's grace. Obviously, those summoned often bought themselves off.[15] Pardon was granted in the majority of cases recorded from the thirteenth century onward, which may have led to the later perception that pardon was a symptom of weakness. The royal prerogative as such, however, in its function of balancing rather than executing, attested to a different "economics" of the law. The merely procedural economy was able to absorb, to a certain extent, the *gratia* part and to neutralize the instrument that was to produce the body with respect to the law; the king's superior exercise of mercy turned into the very act which, in turn, individuated the body wanted into a bearer of rights. Clemency declined, and the rule of mercy came to seem mere favor. Not by accident, then, did the execution of Charles I precede the celebrated *Habeas Corpus Act* of 1679.

Foucault's juxtaposition of the monarchical body politic and "the least body of the condemned man" presupposes this decline of pardon and tries to make sense of it.[16] But against the grain of Foucault's homage to Kantorowicz in this point, the same king's body politic is constituted by the king's court and claimed by the law's rule. Thus Chief Justice Coke's (rather unlucky) successor Mountagu was still able to take a middle position and explain habeas corpus as "a prerogative writ, which concerns the king's justice to be administered to his subjects; for the king ought to have an account why any of his subjects are imprisoned."[17] The formulation is telling, because it manages, if only for the moment, to reformulate the king's position above the law in terms of a responsibility for his subjects.

The decline of pardon thus coincides with a functional change of habeas corpus into the crucial device for determining the lawfulness of detention. Earlier, habeas had been used to contest the validity of imprisonment, but the bearer of rights—of human rights, after all—produced and invested by the act of 1679 was no longer the body produced by the older writ as subject to the king's grace. Edward Jenks, the most thorough historiographer of habeas corpus at the beginning of this century, argues that this shift, rather than constituting progress, "created no new remedy, but merely strengthened and perfected an engine which had been used with effect in the great struggle between Crown and Parliament."[18] The king's clemency, in other words, became superfluous because the law found a parliamentary device, not against the king's arbitrary execution of mercy, but against its own jurisdictional errors.

The tedious system of control instituted in 1679 bound legal agencies up to the Lord-Chancellor, to whom the sheriff was to "bring or cause to be brought the body of the party so committed or restrained," in order to "certify the true causes of his detainer or imprisonment."[19] To guarantee such certification, money could be substituted for the body in question, as explained by the same introductory section of the *Habeas Corpus Act*: "many of the king's subjects have been and hereafter may be long detained in prison, in such cases where by law they are bailable, to their great charges and vexation." Since detention in the seventeenth century had the purpose of custody and was not yet a means of punishment, bail was a placeholder for the time before the trial took place and before "the true causes" could be certified. Or, as F. M. Maitland, in his classical work, puts it: "When a person is said to be bailed this means that he and some sureties have entered into recognizance, have been bound over, for his appearance at the trial."[20] Not the physical presence of the body, not the body of tortures, emerges, but the body's freedom of movement. From now on, imprisonment, the deprivation of personal liberty, will become a punishment of freedom withdrawn.

How bail was from then on to transfer the topology of the law onto money is even more evident in the second case provided by the act of 1679: "security is given by his [the defendant's] own bond to pay the charges of carrying [himself] back."[21] Although the text is somewhat unclear about who is to cover the cost, it precisely calculates most details: the sum to be deposited by the prisoner should not exceed twelve pence per mile for his journey back to the prison. Even deadlines are precisely defined: within a radius of twenty miles a "space" of three days is allowed for his return; from twenty to a hundred miles, the limit is ten days; beyond one hundred miles, he is allowed twenty days. The trade includes the body's transportation, the costs of the journey, or, alternatively, the escape. Whereas the older habeas corpus writ was concerned with topography, the *Habeas Corpus Act* exactly calculates costs in terms of transportation. The local fixation of guilt is translated into a permanent, virtually ubiquitous debt. Indebtedness through surety, tender, or bail is the prescribed bond between body and law; they redefine the law's desire to have the body and to keep it within reach.

The connection between body and law through indebtedness continues the scriptural process; the deposit is "endorsed on the writ." The writing perpetuates and decorporealizes the body at once. The body is dissolved within an economical order, whereas the law's desire to have the body seems suspended by this order. Starting in the seventeenth century, the time gained by the procedure was used for preliminary investigations. The law no longer took an interest in the body as such; it focused on the surrounding network of environment, contact, and movement. Written deposits allowed witnesses to be deposed before the actual trial: those "who have to frame the indictment have the advantage of seeing the whole of the evidence of the depositions [and] if a witness dies, or is too ill to attend, his testimony is perpetuated."[22] Depositions become independent of witnesses' actual performance in court and thus function like bail deposits: they conserve the body wanted by written or pecuniary surrogates. The alternative of "jail or bail" opens up a zone of discretion functionally analogous to the clemency of the king. It is an administrative zone, to be sure, which lends itself to policelike actions without proper legal grounds; like the king's favor, it borders on terror. Social control, it turns out, contains a "zoning" like the king's, a violence that is structural rather than intentional, and the question is how to read its representational ratio.

How was discretion, at first the king's prerogative, discredited in favor of public control? The principal point in this development, the dialectic of punish and pardon, still tends to be overlooked. Foucault, by featuring discipline and control as major forces in shaping the modern subject's "subjectivity," confuses law and sovereignty on the same grounds as the legal positivists against whose conception of progress his work is directed: he leaves untouched or, even gives in to, the fiction of the juridico-discursive formation whose ideology he so effectively criticizes.[23] It may suffice to quote the highly significant account given in J. H. Baker's handbook. For Baker, the "little" irony that the "original purpose [of habeas corpus] was not to release people from prison but to secure their presence in custody," is deepened by another, no lesser irony, namely that of pardon: "Ironically, the existence of this merciful prerogative served to perpetuate a procedure which was far out of line with prevailing notions of criminal responsibility, so that what ought to have been a plain question of law remained for centuries at least nominally a question of favour."[24]

Ironically, "what ought to have been a plain question of law" seems to have escaped and transcended the law's rule, its wish "to have a formal existence."[25] Above all, what it seems to have needed is representation from "above." But to what extent can there reside in this "above" a consideration of representability, which escapes not only the law's representation of itself in its formal existence but transcends its self-understanding with respect to justice? Derrida's "force of law," for example, aims to transcend what is due in the process (and fair in Rawls's sense) in that it always already transcends itself.[26] What could be said about, and in favor of, the mode of self-transcendence that is represented in the presentation of the law as itself?

II

To recapitulate, the *Habeas Corpus Act* is celebrated as a major counter to the king's rule, although the habeas corpus writ had previously been a prerogative of the king. The transition from the king's order to "produce" the body to the liberty of "having the body" is significant, the mistranslation of the original Latin notwithstanding. Shifting from "having" in one sense to "having" in a second one, the Latin idiom of habeas documents a displacement easily overlooked, the literal displacement of the *corpus* in question—its "freedom of movement."[27] Whose is this body? The king's, the law's, the subject's? And whose subject? To whom is this body subject?

Although an important landmark in constitutional history, the act of habeas corpus "in no sense creates any right to personal freedom, but is essentially a procedure act for improving the legal mechanism by means of which that acknowledged right may be enforced." As the *Encyclopedia Britannica* puts it, "It declares no principles and defines no rights, but is for practical purposes worth a hundred articles guaranteeing constitutional liberty."[28] An obvious triumph of legalism, habeas corpus belongs to a set of "legal powers" guarding the application of law.[29] But as Foucault has shown, the consequent turn to control—to "social control over precept," in terms of the particularly British debate on "secondary rules" and "legal powers"—no longer focuses on the body, but on the soul.[30] This turn to the soul, the conversion from body to soul, subjecting the body to the soul, is embarrassed by the violence inflicted and, more precisely, by the traces betraying the violence that remains part of the law's rule, its exercise of power, in spite of the law's explicit disengagement from the body and its pains.

Thus we may have to reconsider a paradoxical side issue of Foucault's story: the discipline imposed in the new era of punishment denies the body under control, in order to control. Against the denial of the body as the object of violence, the story of habeas corpus reads as the reminder of some other, perhaps more fundamental setting, which was superseded by the later function of social control—just as the older, representational function of the law seems to have been superseded by that same controling function. In the case of habeas corpus this perhaps more fundamental setting adds to the picture of the law's bygone representational function to the extent that it contradicts the structure of representation as such, at least in the way we are accustomed to this feature as a primordial mode maintaining and interpreting a world. The understanding of *nomos* as world picture may be merely a belated, metaphorical projection of enlightened times. In other words, the habeas corpus motif may be conclusive for redefining legal progress by an alternative prehistory of what made this progress an ambivalent affair from the beginning.

There is, above all, the scene of the writ as invoked by the writ, the court. This topos, like any, is anything but universal; it is limited (as the writ is limited to the particular grievances at hand, or in view). The defendant must be present for the court or writ to act (as must others, officials). The fact that in Rome exile was equivalent to execution, whereas throughout the Middle Ages the king's body embodied the equivalence of pardon and execution, shows that the court was able to represent itself in giving presence to itself, just as the law was reenacted as "itself." The performance rested entirely in itself without serving any other end—except for the king, who was merely the embodying principle of the body assembled. To a certain extent, the Hegelian monarch resuscitates this principle, and one is tempted to see Hegel as keeping, or rather, reintroducing, the monarch for the very reason discussed here, namely, the "right to pardon [arising] from the sovereignty of the monarch . . . one of the highest recognitions of the majesty of mind."[31] The perlocutionary effect did not simply add to the performative power; rather, when the king's performance weakened and its force vanished, violence had to be brought in to compensate for what had been lost in representational value and therefore had to be re-presented.

In Hegel, the concept of positioning (*Setzung*), presupposed by legal positivists and taken for granted in the pragmatics of the day, is rationally deduced from the *Logic* that is the framework of the *Philosophy of Right*.[32] In this deduction, a logic of representation is revealed and brought into the terms (*auf den Begriff*) of the law itself. According to the nineteenth-century jurist John Austin, such principle was derived from God's positioning power. The representation of this power cannot but present and exhibit the law's own logic as independent of any worldly interest. The emblematic scale of *Iustitia* not only measured the unmeasurable, but decided the undecidable, and the now-forgotten *corda* of *misericordia*, memorable inscription in her name, was meant to remind her of the crucial possibility that justice could be *clementia* (as in the famous mural of *Iustitia* and *Buon Governo* in the Palazzo Publico in Siena).[33]

Quite differently, but still in the same tradition, Chief Justice Coke's "Lady of the Common Law" showed mercy, or the pretense of it, by way of habeas corpus, the writ which ordered a body to court and brought it into place, before justice. This picture has changed: after centuries of shifting meanings, habeas corpus has turned into the awkward name of a petition that in the recent rush to execution in U.S. capital cases has become synonymous with the possibility of successive attempts to delay execution. The function of mere delay is recognizable even in the rough statistics of Shakespeare's England as calculated by Francis Barker, where a rapid rise in the number of executions was still balanced by the fact that between a third and a quarter of those sentenced were pardoned.[34] Where there is no longer any unconditional pardon possible, the conditional delay becomes imperative for those "in waiting" on death row.

The Benjaminian analysis of "overextended transcendence" (*Überspannung der Transzendenz*) had quite naturally taken for granted what Benjamin saw exposed, in the very same century of Justice Coke and the *Habeas Corpus Act*, as the "rotten" original state of "the law itself."[35] "For in the exercise of violence over life and death more than in any other legal act, law reaffirms itself," Benjamin finds, and this reaffirmation of "itself," of its own positional power, makes the law the most effective agent of representation itself and of its power to make present what is not. This, however, may not be, and may not have been, the law's point all along, nor was it the point of the law's acts. In what Foucault describes as the crucial new function of discipline and control from the Age of Reason onward, he offers a significant insight into the law's new need for justification. All of a sudden the legal sphere seems to have lost interest in the body and its pain and transferred legal focus to the soul and its improvement. One is tempted to call this a dangerous supplement indeed, because it takes over what it is meant to support, the law's office of judgment. But while "it," the supplement this time, displaces, even replaces, the functional ratio of representation, it also effaces, disperses, disseminates the topos and the scene of writing the sentence, including the law's own performative force, the force of law, itself.

Against this effacement, the writ and the act of habeas corpus cite and re-cite the law's condition of being effective, its performativity. What else but its desire for the body could make its performance effective? While the law's execution seems to give up the body and ask for the soul instead, the sentence whose execution is thus excused with respect to the soul's improvement and final salvation still needs a referent. As Foucault is able to explain, it both transcendentalizes and literalizes this referent *as* the body; it identifies the body in question, the body "to be had," as the referent needed. The body, whose surface was the target of punishment and served its representational function as a vehicle of symbolism in the manifold modes of torture, evaporates, vanishes into the *Ding an sich* of execution, hit by the guillotine at one decisive point in one decisive moment. After the event, this coming true of the sentence is embalmed in a multitude of interpretive acts of compensation, repairing for the sake of the surviving world what cannot be repaired for the victim, whose being cut off is nothing but the literal consequence of his or her expulsion from this *nomos* and its narrative.[36] What is decisive here is not the factual consequence of death, which comes with the execution, but the exclusion from memory, *damnatio memoriae*, whose very meaning is illustrated by a doubled death. The ideology of interpretive communities finds itself consoled, and is ideological in its false consolation, to the extent that it conceives of law and order as merely or mainly the outcome and merit of interpretive acts.

Calling for the body in order to establish the scene of law's acts, habeas corpus rearranges the procedural connection between judgment and execution (in speech-act terms, between illocution and perlocution as effect). The point of habeas corpus is to take care of the transfers and displacements necessary to guard the topos of the law's own economy, the conditions of judgment in changing social configurations. Without the body there is no act, although the desire for the body is *not* the desire to have the act executed and power exemplified through violence. Rather, the body is to focus the decision, which itself remains undecided between grace and execution, discretion and representation. It is, however, to be taken. The casuistry of substitutions, of cash and delay, rather than the incessant and monotonous shame of executions, keeps the force of law forceful. What if the law had been calling and citing, invoking and delaying, including and excluding, before it came to institutionalized prosecution and enforcement, punishment and execution? An economy of its discourse rather than a sociology of its effects may be needed.

Hegel's insistence on the subject's standing in court on his or her own feet—"im Gerichte leiblich, mit den *Füßen*, zugegen zu sein"—discarded, displaced but also replaced, the old topics of jurisprudence, the "in iudicio stare" quoted by Hegel as an outdated feudal metaphor for the subject's *Leibeigenschaft* (literally, the subject's bodily submission to a feudal lord).[37] Instead, the subject's mental identity (*Geist*), its own knowledge (*Wissen*), has to take the sentence, and put up with it—but cannot take it, and put up with it, except for some utopian moment, or anticipation, of "absolute" knowledge. How can an economy of grace and discretion, of mercy in the face of what we do not know, or avoid knowing, deal with the displaced desire for a truth that is not the law's but rather philosophy's one and only way of coming to terms with what it perceives as the law's "guise" of a philosophical truth and translates into a "discourse of truth"?[38] Would not such discourse deny the law's positional logic and encrypt it as the secret of its own desire to know, or avoidance of knowing what it "cannot but not know"?[39]

On the Politics of Pure Means: Benjamin, Arendt, Foucault

BEATRICE HANSSEN

When Walter Benjamin's "Critique of Violence" first appeared in the journal *Archiv für Sozialwissenschaft*, it looked "quite
out of place," as Gershom Scholem recalls in his *Story of a Friendship*.[1] It had originally been commissioned for the journal *Weiße
Blätter*, whose editor, Emil Lederer, deemed Benjamin's treatise on
violence far too long and difficult. In it, as Benjamin noted in a
letter to Scholem, he aspired to have captured the essence of violence: "There are still questions concerning violence that I do not
touch on in this essay, but I nevertheless hope that it has something
essential to say."[2] Written in 1921, "Critique of Violence" to no
small degree reflects Benjamin's contacts with Hugo Ball and Ernst
Bloch, with whom he repeatedly met in 1919 during his studies at
the University of Bern. Not only did they confront him with the
"question of political activity"[3] in the wake of the Bolshevik Revolution, the collapse of the German empire, and the short-lived 1919
Munich soviet republic, but they also introduced him to the work
of Georges Sorel. Representative spokesperson of French Syndicalism and author of *Réflexions sur la violence*, Sorel was to be foundational for Benjamin's political thought, well beyond the 1921 violence essay.

As the only completed piece in a series of projected texts that
were to become part of Benjamin's broadly conceived *Politik*,[4] "Critique of Violence" survives as an isolated yet seminal fragment of
his politics of violence. But apart from the dubious praise the violence essay would earn him from jurist and later theorist of the
fascist state Carl Schmitt, the text's political effects on the whole
remained rather minimal. Precisely because of its embarrassing
affinities to conservative theorists such as Sorel and Schmitt, it

seemed all too clearly to participate in the tradition of violence that has marked twentieth-century German history. Not until the sixties, at a time when the normative foundations and legitimacy of German liberal democracy were radically shaken by an upsurge of left-wing violence, would "Critique of Violence" become the subject of much debate, notably in the writings of Oskar Negt, Jürgen Habermas, and Herbert Marcuse—with the notable exception of Hannah Arendt, from whose 1969 polemical treatise *On Violence* Benjamin remained conspicuously absent. But even then the fronts were divided. Writing in response to the assassination attempt of Rudi Dutschke, the ensuing *Springer* blockades, and student revolts, the sociologist Oskar Negt interpreted Benjamin's essay as an early reflection on the nature of structural violence. Advocating the legitimate use of counterviolence (*Gegengewalt*), the essay, Negt suggested, could serve to unmask the dissimulation of liberal-democratic systems, which, while holding that violence ought not to be used as a means in politics, in reality sustained structural or institutional violence.[5]

If Negt and Marcuse interpreted Benjamin's revolutionary violence in materialistic-political terms, Habermas, by contrast, cautioned against seeing Benjamin as the theologian of the revolution. In his 1972 essay "Walter Benjamin: Consciousness-Raising or Rescuing Critique," he pointed to the covert connection between Benjamin's theory of violence and the politics of surrealism, placing him squarely in the camp of conservative revolutionaries.[6] More recently, Habermas's 1987 review of Schmitt in translation warned that Benjamin's violence essay was indebted to Schmitt's theory of sovereignty and the aesthetics of violence in that both authors championed "the violent destruction of the normative as such."[7] Thus, if Habermas's analysis from the 1970's maintained that Benjamin's "politics of pure means" put an end to all purposive rationality and therefore was counter to political praxis, the later essay went even further, charging that he in fact had crossed over to the side of Schmitt's conservative antiliberalism. This shift in interpretation should not be surprising. Benjamin's intellectual debts to the contested jurist have been no secret since the 1977 publication of a formerly suppressed letter to Schmitt, in which he avowed his indebtedness to Schmitt's *Political Theology* for his analysis of the German mourning play. And if, furthermore, the language of decisionism (*Entscheidung, Ausnahmezustand*) can be said to traverse Benjamin's writings—from the *Origin of the Ger-*

man Mourning Play to the theses on history—this only seemed to confirm Benjamin's perilous affinities to Schmitt's conservatism.

That a theory of violence could bring him dangerously close to the battlefront of fascism is a threat Benjamin addressed on only a few occasions, one being an encounter with the French fascist Georges Valois. In 1927, his interview with this former student of Sorel appeared in *Die literarische Welt* in the form of a short article on dictatorship, titled "For Dictatorship" ("Für die Diktatur").[8] Here, on the eve of National Socialism's ascendence to power, Benjamin seemed forced to reflect on how precarious, indeed perhaps nonexistent, the difference between left- and right-wing violence really might be. Praising Sorel for being the "greatest and most truthful theoretician of syndicalism," he also scoffed him for providing the "best nursery" for fascist leaders, as was apparent from recent European events—an allusion, no doubt, to Mussolini, who, as a young socialist, had found inspiration in Sorel's school of thought.[9] Valois's appropriation of unbloody, bloodless revolutions, as well as the workers' insurrection, for the fascist cause provided further evidence of how fluid the demarcation line between the two political factions could be. At the same time, Benjamin was quick to dispel the myth of the fraternal feud propagated by the new fascism, which liked "to confront its movement with bolshevism, as whose hostile twin brother it sees itself."[10] How persistent the myth of a fraternal conflict between fascism and Marxism could be is apparent from Schmitt's 1922 *Crisis of Parliamentarism*, which proclaimed that Proudhon's anarcho-syndicalism converged with the Catholic, counterrevolutionary conservatism of Donoso-Cortes in that both ideologies celebrated the "great battle" or "great struggle" that was to set an end to all forms of parliamentarism. Resolutely rejecting the image of two feuding brothers, Benjamin's short essay nonetheless still begged the question of how the violent tactics of the left were to be justified in light of right-wing violence.

Benjamin's silence on the issue is especially noteworthy in view of "Critique of Violence," which clearly announced itself as a philosophico-political attempt to offer a classification or taxonomy of different modes of violence, insofar as it differentiated divine from inauthentic, human manifestations of force. Following the Kantian philosophical tradition, the term "critique" in the essay's title signaled not only the attempt to lay bare the transcendental conditions of possibility of the phenomenon, but also, as Derrida argues in "Force of Law," critical separation and demarcation.[11] The decisive, cutting force of *Kritik* derives etymologically from *krinein* ("to separate") and is echoed in the essay's preoccupation with the language of *Entscheidung*.

Thus, the following analysis takes up the methodological task Benjamin's text assigned itself, namely, that of providing a transcendental critique (*Kritik*) of violence, as well as a *dia-critical* model on the basis of which just manifestations of force were to be distinguished from their inauthentic counterparts.[12] Benjamin's essay emphatically did not celebrate a monolithic, "substantialist" force or violence that could serve as a dynamic, energic *archē* or foundation, but rather proposed an apology for a *pure*, unalloyed form of revolutionary violence, which was to set an end to all mythic force. In so doing, he introduced a critical praxis of violence that would mark his future writings. Against Ernst Jünger's cultist celebration of eternal war as "the highest expression of the German nation" or against fascism's "aestheticization of violence," Benjamin would hold the predatory Angelus Novus, the anarchistic force of the destructive character, the *schlagende Gewalt* of language, the citational violence of Kraus's aphorisms, or, again, the disruptive, revolutionary force of the *Jetztzeit*, which shattered the false continuum of history conceived as mere progress.

To be sure, these figures of thought by now have become part and parcel of Benjamin scholarship. All the more urgent, therefore, is the task of reexamining them in light of the program for a "politics of pure means" and revolutionary force which "Critique of Violence" mobilized—a force that, Benjamin believed, would radically rupture the eternal cycle of violence and counterviolence that has constituted human history. Benjamin hoped once and for all to break the vicious circle of violence by radically rethinking a long-standing philosophico-political tradition according to which violence was to be conceived as *instrumental* in nature, that is, as a means or implement to be put to the service of (political) ends. This tradition runs from Aristotle's syllogistic definition of the means-ends relation to Kant's qualification of *Gewalt* as a disposition over external objects or means, to the theory of war which the German military strategist Carl von Clausewitz laid down in his well-known dictum that "war is the continuation of politics by other means."[13] Furthermore, such a conception of instrumental violence surfaced in Engels's *Anti-Dühring*, which maintained that the "triumph of violence" depended on the implements it uses, or the production of armaments. Finally, it further constituted the target of

Arendt's *On Violence*, to receive perhaps its most radical critique in Foucault's account of "power."

As a political theory, liberalism abjures all forms of violence that surpass the boundaries of individual self-defense or the legitimate monopoly of violence that the liberal-democratic state exercises. Already in her treatise on revolutions, Hannah Arendt suggested that violence constitutes the limit of the political, so that "a theory of war or a theory of revolution . . . can only deal with the justification of violence because this justification constitutes its political limitation."[14] Mindful of this liberal tradition, my essay nonetheless will ask to what degree the phenomenon of violence, for example in the form of violent anticolonial struggle, also shows up the blind spots of liberalism.[15] In many ways, this essay thus elaborates on the theses that Stephen Holmes established in his *Anatomy of Antiliberalism*. That is to say, if the tradition of antiliberalism—whether in its left- or right-wing forms—embraces violence, then to what extent does (political) violence—under certain circumstances—also constitute a limit to liberalism's model of political analysis? In order to pursue this inquiry, my analysis locates Benjamin's essay at three crucial historical junctures: (1) the Weimar Republic and Schmitt's concept of the political; (2) Arendt's response to the counterviolence of the sixties; and, in conclusion, (3) Foucault's variant of poststructuralism, which spells the end, perhaps, of all (transcendental) critiques of violence.

Benjamin's Politics of Noninstrumental Means

Placed within its historical context, Benjamin's "Critique of Violence" appears to be a timely response to the violence of World War I, the ensuing debates about pacifism and militarism, and the peace settlement achieved by the Treaty of Versailles. Furthermore, to no small degree it contributed to discussions about state theory and the malaise of the Weimar Republic, already apparent in 1921, whose crisis of parliamentarism was to find its most notorious detractor in Schmitt. But in its critique of the mythic violence that was said to inhabit the legal order (*Rechtsgewalt*), the essay also reacted to the crisis that afflicted the value-free discipline of positivistic law. No longer able to assure the legitimacy of the legal order, legal positivism instead attested to the discrepancy between legality and legitimacy that was to become typical of modernity.[16]

By underscoring the mythic, fatelike nature of profane law—a thought already developed in his 1919 essay "Fate and Character"— Benjamin opposed his former teacher, the neo-Kantian Hermann Cohen, whose transcendental project to establish an ethics of pure will defined the science of law as a "theoretical factum," that is, as the mathematics of the human sciences, analogous to the role mathematics fulfilled for the natural sciences. Proposing a "historico-philosophical view of law"[17] instead, "Critique of Violence" charted the genealogy of a profane form of violence, which it traced from the earliest primitive, mythic times, through its institutionalization in jusnaturalism and statutory law, to nineteenth- and twentieth-century forms of vitalism apparent in Darwinism and Kurt Hiller's activism. Thus, while the essay argued that the critique of violence should find its starting point in the realm of law or right, Benjamin ultimately formulated a pure, bloodless and—crucially—just violence, which radically escaped all legal norms. To accomplish this, Benjamin—in stark contrast to Arendt, as we shall see—first needed to show the mutual contamination and duplicity (*Zweideutigkeit*) of two political traditions, those of power and of violence, a contamination indicated by his refusal to separate the meaning of *Gewalt*, used to render the Latin *potestas* or power (evident in such expressions as *Rechtsgewalt* or *Staatsgewalt, Macht*)— from *violentia* and *vis*, or "force."[18]

Although Benjamin's ultimate goal was to devise a transcendental critique of violence as a principle (*Prinzip*), it is noteworthy that in an initial, heuristic stage of his analysis he adopted the historical vantage point of positive law. Unlike transcendental philosophy, positive law historicized the phenomenon, insofar as it offered an implicit typology of different forms of violence, based on whether or not they had been historically sanctioned. In this initial moment of differentiation (*Unterscheidung, Entscheidung*), Benjamin took on what he regarded to be the "substantialism" of natural law, for which the use of force signaled the expenditure of natural, vital energy. Yet he relinquished this preliminary point of departure in positive law when he established that in place of the demonic duplicity and indecisiveness that inhabited *Rechtsgewalt* was to come absolute decisiveness (*Entscheidung*) and justice, anchored in the divine and thetic name of God. In a radical repudiation of the executive, legislative, and juridic division of powers that marks the liberal constitution—what in German is called *Gewaltenteilung* as the critic Horst Folkers has noted[19]—Benjamin ultimately established that "Divine violence, which is the sign and seal but never the means of sacred execution, may be called sovereign violence."[20]

The decidedly antimodern gesture with which the essay located sovereignty not in the *demos* but in divine violence—a gesture that one could perhaps call a de-secularization of sorts if modernity is the product of a radical secularization—has played no minor role in discussions about Benjamin's political theology or decisionism. However, less attention has been paid to his attempt radically to rupture the syllogistic bond that since Aristotle has informed the means-end relationship,[21] to posit, on the one hand, what he called pure, unalloyed means, that is, language and the revolutionary, proletarian strike (in the Sorelian sense), and, on the other hand, pure ends: divine justice or divine violence/power.

While Benjamin's critique appeared to be informed by Kant's fundamental distinction between morality and legality in that he too sought to define the morality of an action by disengaging it from the judicial system, he purported to surpass the correlation between justified means and just ends that still upheld Kant's moral philosophy. To be sure, the second formulation of the categorical imperative offered in Kant's *Foundations of the Metaphysics of Morals* was meant to overcome the arbitrariness of the hypothetical imperative, which defined violence (as Horst Folkers has argued persuasively) as the real and potential disposition of means (expressed in German as *in seiner Gewalt sein*, or *etwas in seiner Gewalt haben*). Yet even this formulation of the categorical imperative, Benjamin contended, did not definitively exclude potentially using the other as a means. The injunction formulated in the *Foundations* ("Act in such a way that at all times you use humanity both in your person and in the person of all others as an end, and never merely as a means") still raised the question, Benjamin wrote, "whether this famous demand does not contain too little, that is, whether it is permissible to use, or allow to be used, oneself or another in any respect as a means."[22] Whereas Kant's *Metaphysics of Morals* established the system of ethics as a "system of the ends of pure practical reason," which comprised the doctrines of virtue and of law (*Tugend-* and *Rechtslehre*),[23] Benjamin, by contrast, not only problematized the very notion of just ends, but also announced the deficiency of the legal realm as such. Finally, though Benjamin, following Kant's *Perpetual Peace*, argued that every individual, singular peace treaty, or *pactum pacies*, reiterated the belligerent potential of war, he could hardly have in mind Kant's call for a federation of nation-states when he invoked the Idea of eternal peace. Seemingly afflicted and even corroded by an insidious form of violence (in the sense of *violentia*), *Rechtsgewalt* no longer could set a halt to the belligerence inherent to the state of nature, or *status naturalis*.

By seeking to advocate a radical destruction of the legal order, Benjamin aimed to overcome the fundamental doctrine that upheld natural law no less than positive law, namely that the means justify the end. Both legal traditions remained locked in an antinomic relation in that for the one just ends were to be attained by justified means, whereas for the other justified means were to be used for just ends—a vicious circle Benjamin sought to break by positing his paradoxical notion of noninstrumental pure means, which were neither lawmaking nor law-preserving. "All violence as a means," Benjamin maintained, "is either lawmaking or law-preserving. If it lays claim to neither of these predicates, it forfeits all validity. It follows, however, that all violence as a means, even in the most favorable case, is implicated in the problematic nature of law itself."[24] One could add, moreover, that it also followed from Benjamin's argument that pure, unalloyed means, insofar as they were no longer "contaminated" by the sphere of profane law, were neither lawmaking nor law-preserving.

The consequences of Benjamin's ingenious formulation of what I will call his "politics of noninstrumental means" are far-reaching. Located neither in the party politics of the compromise nor in the Weimar parliament (which, afflicted by a form of amnesia, no longer recalled its roots in the revolutionary violence of 1918), these means were to be found, first, in the realm of private persons, who, following the "culture of the heart," engaged in unalloyed, uncontaminated speech or nonviolent conference (*Unterredung*), and, second—in rare instances—in the public realm, among diplomats, who, through nonviolent agreement, aimed to overcome conflicts peacefully, thus fulfilling "a delicate task that . . . is beyond all legal systems, and therefore beyond violence."[25] Crucially, the same abolition of lawmaking and law-preserving violence distinguished the proletarian revolutionary strike in that its anarchistic force targeted the abolition of law and, in the final analysis, the annihilation of all state power, or *Staatsgewalt*. The logic of pure means was such, furthermore, that "the violence of an action can be assessed no more from its effects than from its ends, but only from the laws of its means,"[26] so that even if it were to produce bloody or catastrophic effects, the proletarian strike remained fundamentally pure. No longer bound to the thetic force of the legal order, revolutionary violence found its very condition of possibility in divine justice, as it gestured toward the coming of a new historic era, on the other side of all mythic violence.

If the first paradox Benjamin's violence essay sought to think was that of noninstrumental means, the essay's second paradox resided in its endeavor to retain an unalloyed form of discussion, while simultaneously advocating revolutionary force. Put differently, Benjamin seemingly retained the legacy of liberalism in *Unterredung* while also opting for the violence of an antiliberal proletarian strike. To do so, he needed to modify Sorel's revolutionary model and reject Schmitt's variant of antiliberalism. Thus, Benjamin did not adopt Bergson's model of *élan vital*, which centrally informed Sorel's revolutionary spontaneism, nor did he take over the latter's concept of myth as the condition of class identity.[27] The critique of Kurt Hiller's activism at the end of the violence essay exemplarily targeted all forms of biologism and vitalism, which were to be dispelled by divine justice—a justice, as Derrida has argued, which took on a decidedly Judaic form. Furthermore, Benjamin needed to divest the proletarian strike of the bellicose roots in war and military strategy that so clearly still underpinned Sorel's *Réflexions sur la violence*, indebted as it was to Proudhon's "radicial anarcho-syndicalism." Just as Proudhon's monumental *La guerre et la paix* conceived the workers' uprising on the model of the "Napoleonic battle," celebrated for its total annihilation of the enemy,[28] so Sorel compared the strike to military warfare, advocating the total elimination of the class adversary.

At the same time that Benjamin implicitly took issue with Sorel, he also diverged from Schmitt's counterrevolutionary political stance, which would be expressed most clearly in his later *The Concept of the Political* (1927). By arguing that the total, sovereign state found its condition of possibility in the antithesis of friend and enemy,[29] Schmitt first of all established as the common enemy liberalism, whose theory of economic competition and of debating adversaries radically de-politicized and dissipated this fundamental, belligerent duality.[30] But he also took on French syndicalism, which after 1906 and 1907—in the figures of Sorel, Berth, Duguit, and others—proclaimed the strike as the economic means par excellence for incurring the *death of the state* and spelling the end of its sovereignty. Thus, if Benjamin, despite his admiration for

Schmitt, managed to keep the jurist's proto-fascist program at bay, it is because he did not share his political anthropology, which remained anchored in a celebration of a primordially belligerent human nature. Warfare for Schmitt was more than just the strategic brandishing of violent implements. It was eminently an existential mode, a mode of being, as well as the "revelation" (*Offenbarung*) of the originary binary opposition between friend and *hostis*, which founded the political.

It is no coincidence that, in defining the political, Schmitt invoked the military theorist von Clausewitz, whose unfinished *On War*, published in 1832, drew on the terminology of means and ends to offer a quasi-Kantian critique of war. Defining war as a "duel [*Zweikampf*] on a larger scale," Clausewitz argued that if the "maximum use of physical force" constituted the means of war, and war in turn aimed at the total destruction of the enemy, then war itself could never amount to "a complete, untrammeled, absolute manifestation of power." Never to be considered in isolation, war instead remained a "political instrument" and thus eminently "a continuation of political activity by other means."[31] Going against the interpretive tradition in Clausewitz scholarship, Schmitt emphasized not the instrumentality of warfare, but its role as the extreme instance of the decision (*Entscheidung*) about who counts as a friend, who as a public enemy. "The military battle itself is not the 'continuation of politics by other means' as the famous term of Clausewitz is generally incorrectly cited. . . . War, for Clausewitz, is not merely one of many instruments, but the *ultima ratio* of the friend-enemy grouping. . . . As the most extreme political *means* it discloses the possibility which underlies every political idea, namely the distinction of friend and enemy."[32]

Clearly, counter to Schmitt's decisionism, Benjamin's "Critique of Violence" opposed founding the political in belligerent violence, for to do so would risk installing violence as an absolute end in itself. All the same, a number of lingering, troubling questions remain. Thus, one must ask what the critical, even *dia-critical*, force of the "pure" violence Benjamin advocated might be. Did it truly succeed in disengaging pure means from (political) ends and thus accomplish his ambitious, indeed utopian, program of rupturing the vicious cycle of violence? Didn't the essay rather reintroduce a theological foundationalism, that is, a decisive, authoritative ground, which was to shore up secular forms of violence?

Benjamin's ill-fated "politics of pure means" remained indebted to the Blochian Judeo-Marxist messianism expressed in his "Theo-logico-Political Fragment," which defined the Kingdom of God not as the goal (*telos*) but the end (*finis*) of history.[33] Seeking to think through the paradoxical politics not of a legal but a *legitimate* form of violence, he speculated that pure violence no longer remained trapped in the circularity of means and ends. Needless to say, in the course of doing so his essay fell short of providing an incisive differentiation between just and unjust uses of violence, and, therefore, of offering a credible critique of violence.[34]

How important this thought pattern was to remain in his later work is evident from the fact that the early politics of pure means re-emerged in the thirties, notably in his celebrated "The Work of Art in an Age of Mechanical Reproduction," a text that, I would suggest, also can be read as an extended reflection on the relations between means, the mediality of the (film) medium, and political ends.[35] In this Marxist attempt to re-appropriate the means of (re)production, Benjamin hoped to separate the pure, unalloyed use of technological means, that is, film as revolutionary medium, from its exploitation in fascist propaganda. War itself, in the final analysis, testified to the abuse of technological means, enacting the slave rebellion of technology. Much as in "Critique of Violence" the essay's afterword again tried to demarcate left- from right-wing politics. The extent to which this project proved fated, even duplicitous, is evident in Benjamin's oft-cited chiastic phrase that in place of the aestheticization of politics is to come the politicization of aesthetics. Read against "Critique of Violence," this statement now can be interpreted not only as a call for the politicization of a *"pure"* film medium, but also as an injunction to revolutionize pure violence.

Arendt's Instrumentalization of Violence

Clausewitz's dictum about means and ends to no small degree also served as a foil against which Hannah Arendt formulated her theory of violence as mere instrumentality and power as an end in itself. Thus, when her polemical pamphlet *On Violence* first appeared in 1969, it sought to characterize a post-Holocaust and post-nuclear world in which all differences between violence and power had been erased. The destructive potential of the century belied the ostensibly marginal position to which the phenomenon of violence had been relegated in nineteenth-century social and political theory. Thus, she argued:

> Whether it is Clausewitz calling war "the continuation of politics by other means," or Engels defining violence as the accelerator of economic development, the emphasis is on political or economic continuity, on the continuity of a process that remains determined by what preceded violent action. . . . Today all these old verities about the relation between war and politics or about violence and power have become inapplicable.[36]

Coming at the height of the cold war, the nuclear arms race, the violence of decolonialization, and the student revolts of the sixties, Arendt's treatise diagnosed what she regarded to be a global, all-pervasive state of violence. Held against these spectacular scenes of violence, it seemed as if Clausewitz's and Engels's "nineteenth-century formulas" or "old verities" had been inverted to the point where peace itself now appeared to be the continuation of war by other means.[37] The nuclear arms race in particular confirmed the arbitrariness and "all-pervading unpredictability" inherent in all violence.[38] As the disturbing sign of an aberrant instrumentality gone awry, it announced the end of *all conventional, strategic* warfare, thus rendering the old dictum of war as the *ultima ratio* obsolete. The relapse into a state of pure, absolute war or nature seemed imminent, for "where violence is no longer backed and restrained by power, the well-known reversal in reckoning with means and ends has taken place. The means, the means of destruction, now determine the end—with the consequence that the end will be the destruction of all power."[39]

Crucially, Arendt's diagnosis did not merely call for the undoing of this reversal. Instead, the postwar malaise provided her an occasion to analyze the liberal-democratic model of power. Contemporary political thought seemed to be marked by a confusion of power with violence, of *potestas* with *violentia*, she argued, because it equated power with coercion, thus implicitly adhering to Clausewitz's definition of war as "an act of violence to compel the opponent to do as we wish."[40] Arendt's argument was, above all, with social scientists, particularly Max Weber, who regarded "the body politic and its laws and institutions" as "merely coercive superstructures, secondary manifestations of some underlying forces." At issue was Weber's influential definition of the state in *Politics as Vocation* as "the rule of men over men based on the means of legitimate, that is allegedly legitimate, violence," which according to Arendt limited the concept of power to "the power of man over man."[41] As such, Weber's theory of power was a relic of the age of absolutism, as it "accompanied the rise of the sovereign European nation-state."[42]

Seeking to overcome these terminological inadequacies, Arendt radically separated power from violence, arguing that they stood to one another in a nondialectical, asymmetrical relationship.[43] Thus she adopted the (Aristotelian/Kantian) means-ends model to define violence, which always needs implements, as instrumental:[44] "Phenomenologically, it is close to strength, since the implements of violence, like all other tools, are designed and used for the purpose of multiplying natural strength until, in the last stage of their development, they can substitute for it."[45] To the extent, further, that violence was "effective in reaching the end that must justify it,"[46] it was fundamentally rational in nature—a statement directed against psychological and anthropological theories of violence, particularly those advanced by Konrad Lorenz—which qualified violence as natural, irrational aggression. By contrast, power was the very condition of possibility of all political action, "the very condition enabling a group of people to think and act in terms of the means-end category."[47] Invoking, in turn, Kant's *Perpetual Peace*,[48] which qualifies eternal peace as an end in itself, Arendt defined power as an absolute or pure *Ziel* (end):[49] "The end of war—end taken in its twofold meaning—is peace or victory; but to the question And what is the end of peace? there is no answer. Peace is an absolute, even though in recorded history periods of warfare have nearly always outlasted periods of peace. Power is in the same category; it is, as they say, 'an end in itself.'"

Arendt's revision of the means-end model is part and parcel of her theory of communicative action. Thus, in her 1963 study *On Revolution* she wrote that "violence itself is incapable of speech," for "where violence rules absolutely, as for instance in the concentration camps of totalitarian regimes, not only the laws . . . but everything and everybody must fall silent."[50] Anchored in Aristotle's double definition of man as a "political animal" and a "being endowed with speech," the statement is indicative of Arendt's conviction that violence was to be located outside the political and political speech. In line with her *Human Condition* (1958), which sought to replace Gehlen's anthropology of purposive action with an anthropology of linguistic action,[51] Arendt—as Habermas put it in his 1976 Arendt essay—dissociated power from the teleological model, to project the "consensus-building force of communication"[52] as a "coercion-free force" or end in itself. Language was to be used in an illocutionary way, "i.e. to establish intersubjective relationships free from violence."[53] At the same time, however, as Habermas emphasized, Arendt narrowed "the political to the practical" on the basis of an outmoded Aristotelian notion of praxis, thus reducing politics to a pristine, violence-free realm. "For this," Habermas continued, "Arendt pays the price of screening all *strategic elements* out of politics as *"violence,"* severing politics from its ties to the economic and social environment in which it is embedded via the administrative system, and being incapable of coming to grips with appearances of *structural violence,"*[54] for "structural violence is not manifest as violence; instead [as ideology] it blocks in an unnoticed fashion those communications in which are shaped and propagated the convictions effective for legitimation." Not only did her political theory not recognize the presence of structural violence in the political arena, but since strategic action, which, like the warfare of the ancient Greeks, was located outside the walls of the *polis*, must appear as a form of violence, I would argue that within Arendt's framework all strategic violence amounted to nothing more than a tautology.[55]

Arendt's blindness to structural violence, of the sort Oskar Negt found thematized in Benjamin's critique of *Rechtsgewalt*, as well as her assertion that violence occured "outside the political realm,"[56] have as their flip side a rejection of all forms of "counter-violence" (*Gegengewalt*), which are seen as the glorification of violence, its anti- or even non-political justification. At stake in Arendt's analysis were not only Sorel's and Pareto's politics of violence, but also, as mentioned earlier, the representatives of the New Left, that is, Sartre, Fanon, and the leaders of the student movement, whose use of force found its philosophical justification in Marcuse's *Critique of Pure Tolerance*.[57] As the heirs to a left-wing revolutionary tradition, these insurrections, Arendt maintained, found their dubious theoretical foundation in a Hegelian and Marxist "trust in the dialectical 'power of negation'"[58] and an accompanying, erroneous concept of history, the offshoot of nineteenth-century conceptions of progress. As she added:

> If we look on history in terms of a continuous chronological process, whose progress, moreover, is inevitable, violence in the shape of war and revolution may appear to constitute the only possible interruption.

> If this were true, if only the practice of violence would make it pos-
> sible to interrupt automatic processes in the realm of human affairs,
> the preachers of violence would have won an important point. . . . It is
> the function, however, of all action, as distinguished from mere behav-
> ior, to interrupt what otherwise would have proceeded automatically
> and therefore predictably.[59]

The student revolts amounted simply to depoliticized "behavior,"
not to be confounded with true political "action," through which
man distinguished himself from animals. At issue in these lines was
nothing less than the politics of mimesis or the return of an aberrant, natural mimicry. Inasmuch as the German student leaders
aimed to unmask the hypocritical practice of state violence, Arendt
found them to be the heirs of Robespierre's despotic "war on hypocrisy," which led to the Reign of Terror as the revolution began
to devour its own children.[60]

In Arendt's reading of Fanon's *Wretched of the Earth*, the limitations of her liberal model of instrumental violence become apparent. Tellingly, in taking position against the antiliberal program
of the New Left and anticolonial violence, her political tract did
not incorporate a moment of reflection of the sort that seemed to
characterize Sartre's contemporaneous reception of Fanon.[61] True,
Sartre's model equally remained caught in a problematic dialectic,
when he maintained that the European (colonial) "masters" were to
learn from the violence thrown back to them by their former slaves.
Nonetheless, Sartre's endorsement of Fanon's liberating "mad fury"
can be read differently, that is, as an awareness that the violence of
decolonialization spelled an end to Western humanism's monopoly
of violence.

Foucault's Radical Destruction
of Instrumentality

In conclusion, let me briefly turn to Foucault, whose historiciz-
ing analysis of force relations not only announces the end of all
critiques of power, but, by implication, also of a (Benjaminian) "critique of violence." His notion of a proliferation of technologies
(*technē*), set forth in *History of Sexuality*, I would argue, especially served to destroy an old, humanist notion of instrumentality,
at the cost, however, of conflating war and politics. Indeed, not
only has Arendt's model of instrumental violence, insofar as it remained anchored in action theory, been taken to task by Habermas,

who queried it from the perspective of systems theory. Foucault's theory of force relations likewise sought to provide a corrective to Arendt's model, already apparent when he addressed epistemic and discursive forms of violence.[62] Whereas Arendt presented legitimacy rather than justification as the diacritical moment in her definition of power, and dissociated communicative power from purposive instrumentality, or means and ends, Foucault aimed to explode the means-end relation altogether. Thus, his anti-humanistic rejection of *power* ended up presenting both war and politics as radicalized forms of instrumentality. In volume one of his *History of Sexuality*, Foucault, like Benjamin, rejected the conventional Western juridico-political model, which located legitimate power in the state apparatus. Unmasking such power as the problematic legacy of monarchical notions of sovereignty, he instead turned to those power mechanisms and operations that surpassed *Staatsgewalt*, thus demonstrating the inability of the judicial mode to codify power absolutely. Discarding all monolithic conceptions of power, whether institutional power, or, in Weber's version, a legalized mode of subjugation and system of domination, Foucault instead thematized what he called a multiplicity of force relations.

Not surprisingly, in the course of his analysis Foucault likewise glossed Clausewitz's famous statement on war, when in the *History of Sexuality* he posed the following question:

> Should we turn the expression around, then, and say that politics is war pursued by other means? If we still wish to maintain a separation between war and politics, perhaps we should postulate rather that this multiplicity of force relations can be coded—in part but never totally—either in the form of "war," or in the form of "politics"; this would imply two different strategies (but the one always liable to switch into the other) for integrating these unbalanced, heterogeneous, unstable, and tense force relations.[63]

That is to say, the relation between war and politics was no longer one of possible reversal or ascendancy, as Arendt still held, but war and politics now appeared as the very encodings of force relations, strategies, or micro powers.

Pace Arendt, Foucault here pushed the political to the point where it became mere strategy or the "strategic codification of these points of resistance."[64] War, violence, and politics were different noninclusive encodings or strategies, ways of coding points of resistance in the strategic field of power relations, which could "circulate without changing their form from one strategy to another, opposing strategy."[65] While these strategies remained rational technologies, they were divorced from a liberal, humanistic subject, which used certain means to achieve certain ends. Discarding the notion of a generative principle, implicit in Clausewitz's emphasis on war as the continuation of politics, Foucault instead assumed a relativistic, nominalistic perspective by reducing power to "the name one attributes to a complex strategical situation in a particular society." Adopting a radically historicist point of view, Foucault refused to take the inherently Kantian step from the analysis of historical force fields of power to a regulatory principle, a "general analytics of every possible power relation." Ultimately, Foucault's *History of Sexuality* thus replaced a *theory* or *critique* of power with a radically *historical* "analytics of power."[66]

Despite the limits that mark the Foucaultian model when it comes to discriminating politics from warfare or strategic violence, it might be valuable to retain his insight that power ought not be seen as a regulatory principle and that violence, too, in its many, even intractable, forms ought to be analyzed locally. Indeed, along the same lines, Clifford Geertz recently has argued against the pervasive use of a globalizing or universalizing notion of nationalistic violence, at the expense of the particularism or specificity of ethnic violence. As a typical occidental concept—indicative of how epistemic violence eliminates ethnic and multicultural differences— the term remains the offshoot of nineteenth-century nationalism, dependent on the liberal nation-state, so that it is worthy of being replaced by more anthropologically refined concepts such as "primordial loyalties." Without wanting to conflate conceptual differences in turn, it seems to me that his position corroborates what I conceive to be a lasting insight that can be gleaned from Benjamin's otherwise flawed "Critique of Violence": that even if the critique of violence must fall short of reaching its goal or end, one would do well to discard all monolithic analyses of violence. It is perhaps this insight, more than anything else, that Benjamin aspired to have communicated when he wrote to Scholem that he hoped to have said the essential about violence.

Marx, Mourning, Messianicity

PETER FENVES

This essay was written in response to Derrida's *Specters of Marx*. That book gives shape to the question I pursue: how the "spirit of Marx" is related to the work of mourning, on the one hand, and something called a "messianic promise," on the other. Like Derrida, I pursue these questions with constant reference to *Hamlet*— not, however, to Shakespeare's *Hamlet* (which haunts *Specters of Marx* from its opening epigraph onward) but rather to Benjamin's, for Benjamin's *Hamlet* has something to say about mourning, messianicity, and perhaps even Marx.

This essay has one further motivation: *Specters of Marx* has little trouble aligning Marx and the legacy of Marxism with the experience of mourning and the return of certain ghosts, but only in his reading of Blanchot's "Marx's Three Voices" does Derrida bring Marx into any relation with what he calls "the messianic." Nowhere does Derrida point toward something in Marx's writing that would correspond to this word. Instead, he speaks of a "spirit of Marxism,"[1] and this spirit, like all spirits, must distinguish itself from the letter—especially when it, this "spirit," is understood as a "messianic eschatology." Derrida presents the latter, in turn, as a promise; more exactly, he presents the messianic in terms of the "formal structure of promising."[2] By contrast, I take my point of departure from the letter of Marx, in particular, a letter he wrote to the German Worker's Party, and in this letter I locate something like a messianic moment in Marx. Since this moment is anything but a promise, I do not so much pursue as pose once again a question concerning the relation—or absolute nonrelation—between mourning and messianicity in the spirit of Marx.

Marx

"This right is thus in its content one of inequality like any other right." Marx underlines these words in the letter in which he launched a critique of the "Gotha Program" and then adds: "A right can by its nature only consist in the application of an equal standard, but unequal individuals (and they would not be different individuals if they were not unequal) can only be measured by the same standard if they are looked at from the same aspect, if they are grasped from one particular side, for example, if in the present case they are regarded only as workers and nothing else is seen in them, everything else is ignored. . . . Right [*Das Recht*] can never rise above the economic structure of a society and its contingent cultural developments."[3] The right of which Marx writes is an "economic" one: it is the right of workers to receive back a share of the total social product equal to their contribution in terms of labor-time to this product. This right cannot be incorporated into the system of juridical rights to which the bourgeois state owes its legitimization. This right, or any "economic" right, can establish itself only at a threshold moment: after the workers have seized the means of production, on the one hand, and before "a more advanced phase of communist society," to use Marx's words, has erased the marks of its laborious and painful birth from the "old womb" of capitalist society, on the other. The right of which Marx writes is therefore untimely. Rights, which belong to the "old womb," outlive themselves, and in the form of this, the last right, they return to their heir. Even if the commodity-fetish has lost its power, something of the fetish, without the commodity, survives: the ability of certain forms, formal structures, and form-giving agencies to equalize (or formalize) unequal individuals, and from the perspective of their time spent in labor, to make them identical. Using labor-time as a measure for all goods does not give rise to a "just distribution," as the drafters of the Gotha Program maintain, but, according to Marx, bespeaks injustice: insofar as labor-time is equalized according to a formal standard for the purposes of distributive justice, the right to an equal share of the total social product is, like all supposedly equal rights, "in its content" unequal. Setting things right, making the postrevolutionary time correspond with itself, making this after-time finally timely—all this means doing away with the "right" to receive back an equal quantity of labor-time. But this, the last right, is in principle no different from any other: each right

is in its own way untimely, for each one applies a standard, indeed the standard of another time, to unequal individuals. Setting things right means not only doing away with rights in general, not only doing away with the legal structure that legitimizes itself through its appeal to the "equal rights of the individual," but, in the end, also doing away with labor-time as a standard, that is, with labor in the service of quantifiable time. Each right is limited to its own time and so is at least potentially untimely. The last right realizes this potential, and for this reason, it demands the most vigilant critique. The "certificates" for labor-time, the *Scheine* that, according to Marx, are supposed to replace money, can at any moment turn into something else: the representative of money, the recurrence of currency, a fiscal return. These *Scheine* can show up (and have in a sense already done so) as ghosts of money and, therefore, as specters of the fetish, reminders and remainders of its conjuring power.

The last right is not only a birthmark; being a mark in which the "old womb" dies, it gives rise to ghosts. These ghosts congregate around places where "unequal individuals" are equalized. Marx does not leave this phrase "unequal individuals" unexplained. On the contrary: in a parenthesis (and many of the later Marx's philosophical theses insert themselves in such parentheses) he explains this phrase. The explanation is radical, for it goes to the root of all explanation, that is, to the principle of reason: "unequal individuals (they would not be different individuals if they were not unequal)." Individuality, in other words, implies nonequality: no two individuals can be exactly alike, differing only numerically. As Marx proceeds to explain, under certain aspects individuals can be treated alike; they can even appear to be alike from certain perspectives, but they cannot be alike under all aspects and from all perspectives, that is, in view of the totality of their characteristics—or, one might add, as monads. The reference to Leibniz is not gratuitous, for Marx's statement "they would not be different individuals if they were not unequal" reinstates the principle by which the monadic character of each monad is deduced and presented: the principle of the identity of indiscernibles. Marx's familiarity with atomism and monadism made him no stranger to this principle: "It is not true," Leibniz writes, "that two substances can be exactly alike and differ only numerically, *solo numero*, and what St. Thomas says on this point regarding angels and intelligences (that among them every individual is a lowest species) is true of all substances."[4] "There is no such thing as two individuals indiscernible from each other."[5]

Individuality therefore consists not in numerical distinction but in qualitative difference, hence in nonequality. How can this principle be justified? Not on the basis of empirical findings, since the principle by which an individual is constituted makes things— individuated things—findable in the first place. But it cannot be justified on the basis of the principle of reason alone, for there is no reason anyone, including God, can give for a decision to create individuals that are not to be distinguished *solo numero*. Justification for the principle of the identity of indiscernibles must then be sought in a certain "taste" in something beyond, or before, or in any case, on the hitherside of mere reason: a taste for difference other than numerical difference; a taste, in short, for incalculable difference to which every differential calculation, every effort to account for differences, however infinitesimal, remains indifferent. Justification on the basis of a taste is, however, no justification at all. Justice nevertheless demands this: individuals must not differ *solo numero*. This unjustifiable taste grounds God's creative calculus and is itself, for this reason, incalculable. Marx may not need a Leibnizian God to justify his parenthetical statement, but he cannot do without a reference to the decision from which the character of this God is deduced: a decision, that is, for difference; a decision in favor of letting each individual be its own species *in the world to come*, in the *to-come*, a decision that in a sense is this to-come, this *à-venir* or *Zu-kunft*. Nothing, not even a taste, grounds this decision, for the word "taste" simply marks the space of a decision for which there is no justifiable standard, no norm, no rule. Thanks to this decision, however, individuals are not only comparable to St. Thomas's angels, each one being an *infima species*, a lowest species; each one is so completely comparable to these angels that they become incomparable to, or "below," everything else, including themselves. For if they are defined, or identified, as one of many, even if they identify themselves as one of many, they are no longer themselves, that is, singular, one of a kind.

Since each one is its own kind—or, to use a perhaps misleading term, its own class—no kind (or class) can subsist on its own. Because no kind can secure itself as itself (under a concept or a rule), because every kind owes its ownness to something for which there is neither kind, class, nor species, every kind—which is to say, every one—is disowned. This "something" to which every one of a kind owes its ownness does not easily lend itself to language, least of all to a philosophical language that has undergone a thoroughgoing critique of religious practices and theological discourse, and for the most part Marx remains silent about it. But when it comes time to critique this critique of theology—and not simply take its results for granted—it is impossible not to speak of this "something" to which every singularity owes its ownness, its property and propriety: the being of a "lowest species" is "species-being" (*Gattungswesen*).[6] Every one of a kind is a "species-being" because its being— its nature, activity, and power—consists in being a species, its own species. But it can be its own species, "itself," only as long as it repudiates being a specimen of a species, and thus "treats" itself (Marx's word) as more than a specimen, as something universal, indeed more universal than any supposed, presupposed, or postulated species. This "more" not only defines the activity of the constitutively incomplete "species" (in quotation marks) of a species-being but indicates the origin of the "more" of value, *Mehrwert*, under whose regime every one of a kind is turned into a specimen of species, a member of a class. The singularity of every one of a kind implies—and implicates every singularity in—a certain universality: a universal inability to make anything once and for all one's own and therefore a universal versatility. Angelic thanks perhaps consists in this: thanks to the other of every kind that makes possible and to this extent virtually inhabits every one of a kind, every versatile "individual," every kind-one. But this thanks cannot be distinguished from a demand to dismantle whatever turns this other of every kind, which has been called, however inadequately, "species-being," into kinds, species, classes. Or as the one whom Marx never ceased to thank—his guardian Engels—writes: "the real content of the proletarian demand for equality is the demand for *the abolition of classes*."[7]

"They would not be different individuals if they were not unequal"—this unpromising remark sets itself off from the rest of Marx's critique, for it—perhaps un-, pre-, or post-critically—exposes in the very form of time, not just in labor-time, a nonequality for which there is no general measure. There is, in other words, no time in general: each individual has its own time, which does not simply mean each one is of a different age or generation. Marx's parenthetical remark is thus absolved of all organicism, including a more inclusive organicism that would allow untimely elements to organize, inhabit, and overdetermine an entity's structure. Instead of supporting a thesis of this kind, the parenthesis gestures toward—better yet, radiates—an altogether untimely and to this extent messianic time in Marx, a *to-come* that is already, virtually, in everyone.

Mourning

Once again, however: the principle of the identity of indiscernibles is valid only as long as there is an unjustifiable decision for a world to come in which each individual is exalted to a lowest species, each an angel. Otherwise, individuals are not only distinguished *solo numero*, each one appears as a specimen of a species, one of its kind, a kind to which it belongs and which subsists independently of its existence. When the principle of the identity of indiscernibles is valid, each individual is like an angel, which is to say, unlike everything else, including itself; each one, as a result, defies the identification by which it is recognized as such. This defiance of identification, including self-identification, is the violence—or force—every one of a kind shares. When, by contrast, the principle of the identity of indiscernibles is no longer valid, there are ghosts, for ghosts are those "things" or "nothings" to which this principle does not apply: they are distinguished, if they can be distinguished at all, *solo numero*. That's why there are so many of them: their being, if they can be said to be at all, lies in being many, returning to one, returning as the same one, again and again. If each night a different ghost haunted a house, that house would not be haunted.

So then: angels or ghosts.

It is no accident that this disjunction corresponds to a certain baroque temperament. Yet the baroque may not simply be a time or a temperament. It may well be the time of this disjunction, which is to say, a time (or a temperament) "out of joint." The architectonic of *Capital* is as baroque as that of the "Monadology," and in at least one respect Leibniz and Marx are in agreement. In our world, or at this time, it is possible, and indeed even necessary, to distinguish things *solo numero*: money, for instance, or commodities of equal value, including labor as a commodity and workers in their capacity as merchants of their own labor power. Things not only can differ in this way, by number alone, they must do so—that's the law, or the apparent law, the law of appearances, a *Scheingesetz* or *das Recht*. In *The Origin of the German Mourning Play*, Benjamin defines this world with great precision: it is "a world in which detail, in any rigorous sense, is of no importance."[8] *The Origin of the German Mourning Play* could be seen as an experiment in, or the

258

experience of, this world. But "baroque" cannot then simply designate a certain time. It is, rather, the time of disjunctions—a disjunction, on the one hand, between an area in which the principle of the identity of indiscernibles holds and a realm in which it does not and, on the other hand, this very disjunction reinscribed into the latter realm, in our time and temperament, in time and temperament itself. The temperament of this time is that of mourning.

"There is no baroque eschatology," Benjamin writes (1: 246), and the consequences of this absence—the absence of an *eschaton* as well as a *logos* of this *eschaton*, a reason or gathering in which "all earthly things are brought together and exalted until they are consigned to their end" (1: 246)—are inestimable. The play of mourning has, as it were, no other subject. If the eschatological or, to use a term Benjamin avoids in *The Origin of the German Mourning Play* but not, of course, elsewhere, the messianic is indissociable from singularity, if it indeed consists in the society of every singularity as such, that is, not according to the rules under which they can be identified and associated but only in their singular relation to each other and in their universal defiance of every form and force of identification, then the phrase "no eschatology" implies more than an inability to secure access to a "saving grace," however this may be construed. It implies the absence of singularity as such, including—but this is not just an inclusion, since the logic of inclusion is a calculus of generalities and particularities—the singularity of time, namely, a date, and in the end the date of death. If death is defined by its uniqueness, each one dying once, then the absence of eschatology is at the same time the absence, or better, the indiscernibility of death. This indiscernibility then takes refuge in the temperament of mourning.

The mourner, from this perspective, mourns less for the dead than for the indiscernibility of death or—but this "or" is more expansive than exclusive—the absence of the messianic, the inaccessibility of justice. And mourners mourn in this way because in mourning the dead are not discernibly dead: they come back again and again, as ghosts, and they come back in this way even before they depart from "this life." Coming back is their life from the start. Benjamin's description of mourning in terms of "revivification" tries to do justice to this phenomenon: "Mourning is the temperament [*Gesinnung*] in which feeling revivifies by means of masks the emptied world in order to have an enigmatic satisfaction in gazing upon it" (1: 318)—upon, that is, a world in which detail is of no great importance, therefore, a world in which work has ceased to be of decisive significance. "Every value was taken from human action," Benjamin writes in conjunction with a doctrine that, like Hamlet, comes from Wittenberg: "Something new emerged: an empty world" (1: 317). The work of mourning consists in filling up this empty world, but since this work is infinite, since there is no end to the depths of this emptiness, since nothing is done by this work but reproduce its original conditions, this work is, for all its gravity, "play."

The play of mourning does not, therefore, take root simply in a doctrine that grants no justification to works; the very nature of mourning denies any relation to justice. This may come as a shock, and it by no means makes mourning any less imperative, but if Benjamin's analysis is to be trusted, there is no equivocation on this point: mourning has no relation to the messianic. Mourning and the messianic are mutually exclusive. What the ghosts who appear before the mourning demand is vengeance, and the spirit of vengeance plays itself out in the act of expiation. Accordingly, the mourning play presents the incessant disasters to which history, represented by the sovereign, falls prey.[9] Instead of justice, there is only endless, "fateful" retribution: an eternal return of the same in which the same returns as inherited "debt," as a *Schuld* everyone must pay in the end. But there is no end: this inherited "guilt" is in advance of the living; it is their provenance, fate, and fortune. The play of mourning—and mourning, again, is never anything but this play—thus consists in an interminable interplay of vengeance and expiation. No play, according to Benjamin, is more adept at presenting this mourning and the melancholia of the prince in which and for whom the spectacle of mourning plays itself out than *Hamlet*.[10]

Benjamin presents *Hamlet* as a "mourning play," or a "play of sorrow," not a tragedy, least of all a representation of "tragic existence" or, to use Nietzsche's words, "Dionysian man." The criterion for the distinction between tragedy and mourning play derives from the more rigorous, more intractable, more irrevocable distinction between mourning and the messianic—and so does the force of Benjamin's treatise, its "critical *Gewalt*" (2: 242). Only with reference to the "real" difference, or mutual repugnance, between mourning and the messianic does the generic distinction between mourning play and tragedy take hold.[11] Distinguishing one dramatic genre from another was not—and is perhaps still not—simply an aesthetic diversion: many of Marx's expositions of revolutionary times and tasks, if not his entire theory of revolution, take their point of departure from dramatic distinctions: the difference between Aeschylean tragedy and Lucian comedy, for example, or, most famously, between the tragedy of the French Revolution and the farce of its repetition.[12] For Benjamin, the force of his analysis of genres is critical from its inception: at a time in which "the return of the tragic" was a dubious political and cultural slogan — dubious at the very least because this slogan sought to solidify a certain Greco-German axis[13] — Benjamin insisted on the uniqueness of Greek tragedy.

Tragedy is a one-time, "epoch-making" Greek affair, never to be repeated, least of all to be reborn out of the spirit of German music. If tragedy does return (to Germany or Germania), it comes back as the mourning play or, to use Marx's term, as farce. This is the law of the mourning play, and of farce as well:[14] everything returns — the dead, the living, the gods — nothing new and nothing decisive take place. But tragedy, for Benjamin, is not simply a genre unique to fifth-century Athens. Within the context of *The Origin of the German Mourning Play*, it assumes the paradoxical function of representing singularity as such. The singular destiny (*Einzelgeschick*) of the tragic hero is to live his death, and from this death — or better, from its singularity — the advent of justice resonates: not in the words of the tragic hero, but in his silence. The silence of the hero makes tragedy into what Benjamin calls (with special reference to Aeschylus and in particular to *Prometheus Bound*) "the preliminary stage of prophecy [*Vorstufe der Prophetie*]" (1: 297) — preliminary, that is, to prophetic speaking, if there is any. Instead of the speech of the prophet, there is the silence of the tragic hero, and this silence makes the hero into a hero, that is, makes him "meta-ethical" in the sense Franz Rosenzweig lends this term: beyond the *ethos* of the *ethnos*, he is one of a kind, no longer of the kind but defiantly opposed to every kind and, because of the violence of this defiance, unable to engage in speech.[15] The inability of the hero to raise his voice and to say, above all, "I am better than the gods," defines tragedy as agonistic infantilism and distinguishes it from all other dramatic forms.

Tragedy stages the singularity of the hero whose silence consolidates the legal regime but at the same time — and this is the time or interruption of tragedy, its caesura — indicates another time altogether, a time to come, the end of mythico-legal ambiguity, the collapse of the Olympian order, and the advent of justice. Greek tragedy is thus defined by its relation to the messianic: if heroes could speak—but they cannot, this is the tragic character of tragedy —they would not speak *of* the coming community but in its language. Indeed, the silence of these "idiots," these metaethical ones, because of its idiomaticity, already speaks in this language: "Out of the distant, new commands of the gods [*Göttergeheiße*], and from this echo coming generations learn their language" (1: 293). Coming generations do not simply learn to speak from the "uncanny emptiness" of this echo; the language they learn, which is not our language and certainly not the language of posttragic society, is likewise empty, uncanny, and, like the gods and their commands, multiple.

Hamlet, according to Benjamin, is not a tragedy, and yet it is not simply a mourning play, either. Something of tragedy comes to *Hamlet*—not his death, which, like all deaths in the play of mourning, is "communal fate," but a certain silence. Benjamin's attention is thus drawn to the end of the play, for it is a striking achievement that *Hamlet*, alone among mourning plays, has an ending at all. This ending stamps *The Origin of the German Mourning Play* down to its final paragraph. Benjamin concludes his analysis of tragedy with a discussion of Hamlet's death; he ends the section "Mourning Play and Tragedy" with an excursus on the play; and, finally, the book closes by recalling this excursus, in which, for the first and last time, mourning turns into blessedness, a conversion (or revolution) that Hamlet alone is able to achieve. In the section entitled "Hamlet," Benjamin sets out the terms for this conversion:

> The secret of his person is enclosed in the playful but, for this reason, measured [or grave: *gemessen*] passage [*Durchgang*] through all the stations of this intentional space [of melancholia], as the secret of his fate is enclosed in an event [*Geschehen*] that is entirely homogeneous to this, his gaze. Hamlet alone is, for the mourning play [*Trauerspiel*], spectator of/by the grace of God [*Zuschauer von Gottes Gnade*]; he cannot, however, find satisfaction in what plays before him but singularly and alone [*einzig und allein*] in his own fate. His life, the model object his mourning lends him, before it expires, points toward Christian providence, in whose womb his mournful images are converted [*verkehren*] into blessed existence. Only in a life of this kind, a princely one, does melancholia redeem itself [*sich erlösen*] by encountering itself. The rest is silence [*Der Rest ist Schweigen*]. (1: 334–35)

Hamlet's mourning lends him a life so that he can play this mourning out to its end. He has no other task than this, to watch the play of mournful images, and by completing this task, by standing opposed not to a "sea of troubles" but to all the images of trouble, each in its turn, he puts an end to mourning—and so to his life. This singles Hamlet out: he alone comes to an end. Once singularity is provided for—or, to use the words to which Benjamin alludes, once "there is a special providence"—the play of mourning likewise comes to an end. "The rest is silence": there is rest— an ending, a remainder—but it cannot be spoken of. Not even the sentence "the rest is silence" speaks of the rest, for it, of course, is not silent: this, the last sentence, does not belong to the "rest" (the silence), and yet saying this—"the last sentence doesn't belong to the rest"—also means: this sentence of Hamlet, his last, is his last; he does not come back; he does not come back as a ghost; the play of mourning is over because at least one sentence, its last, does not belong to the rest. The silence of this rest is so absolute that the rest is released from all predicaments and all promises, from all debt as well as from guilt: no one need be silent so as to let, for example, a "perturbed Spirit," an "Old Mole," or Hamlet's father rest undisturbed.[16] The rest, the silence, cannot for this reason return in the same form, or under any form, and so it cannot be known to come even once. It comes, when it comes, without anticipation and without recognition. The silence of this sentence, which Benjamin cites without quotation marks, as if he wished to note the impossibility of noting it and thereby marking it off, does not signal the return of the tragic, for it is, after all, spoken. Yet it does not signal the start of another mourning play, either. At stake in this silence is the logic, or the sigetics, of "the rest." The "rest" of which Hamlet—or Shakespeare or Benjamin—speaks not only threatens to abandon the play of mourning but also the very language in which this play is enacted. For who can say with any degree of certainty that when Benjamin writes "Der Rest ist Schweigen" the word *Rest* belongs without remainder to German and does not mean beyond "remainder" also "rest," *Ruhe*, the sleep of death? The last sentence does not belong to the rest, and the nonbelonging, the singularity, is so absolute that "the rest" perhaps absolves itself of its language, the language to which it belongs, and the rest is, if not silence, then no longer what has hitherto been known as speech.

In sum: Hamlet's life is singular; his death, "communal fate." The very singularity of his life makes it—which is to say, its end— unrecognizable. If it is recognized, if it is known according to a rule or as a role, if it is recognized as this or that kind of life, it will, Benjamin writes, "flare up again [*aufleben*] undiminished in the world of spirits [*Geisterwelt*]" (1: 315). If there is a rest to mourning, an end, there is no rest, and if there is no rest to mourning, no remainder, there is rest. "The rest" is restless in this way: under no condition can the rest mark itself as "the rest," the silence, because it is the condition for the possibility of marking. "The rest" cannot mark itself, but it can be remarked upon—and this is precisely what Horatio, the scholar and spokesman, is designated to do:

> Good night, sweet prince,
> And flights of angels sing thee to thy rest.

"Rest" is no long restless; it means "sleep," dreamless, unhaunted sleep, the end of mourning. Angelic song puts "the rest" to rest, makes "the rest" into "thy rest," marks the end, and, by so doing, becomes a remainder of another kind: what escapes, or flies away from, the play of mourning; what, in other words, works.

Messianicity

Flights of angels put mourning to rest. Or rather: their song would mark the end, the "rest" of mourning—its end, not its remaining— if the angels hearkened to Horatio. The angels, unlike the ghost, are never heard, much less seen, and Benjamin, who does not always shy away from invoking angels, is silent about the concluding plea of this skeptic and scholar. Benjamin does, however, speak of ghosts or, better, two modes of *Geist*, two ways for "spirits" or "specters" to come and go:

> The rest is silence. For everything unlived falls without possibility of salvation [*unrettbar*] into this space in which the word of wisdom only deceptively wanders [*das Wort der Weisheit nur trügerisch geistert*]. Shakespeare alone was able to stroke Christian sparks from the baroque, un-stoic as well as un-Christian, pseudo-ancient as well as pseudo-pietistic rigidity of the melancholic. If the deep gaze [*Tiefblick*] with which Rochus von Liliencorn reads the ascendancy of Saturn and the marks of acedia in Hamlet's features is not to be defrauded of its best object, then the same gaze will see in this drama the only play of their overcoming in Christian spirit [*das einzigartige Schauspiel ihrer Überwindung im christlichen Geist*]. Only in this prince does melancholic absorption come to Christianness. [*Nur in diesem Prinzen kommt die melancholische Versenkung zur Christlichkeit*]. (1: 335)[17]

Benjamin elucidates the almost tautological sentence "the rest is silence" by speaking of what continues to speak, namely, "everything unlived, everything that has not been lived" (*alles nicht Gelebte*). After Hamlet's end—but, once again, this end remains unrecognizable—every word wanders about in a ghostly manner. Hamlet's "life," by contrast, escapes the intentional space of melancholia. It does not come back, which is to say, his words no longer wander (*geistern*). If his words escape the motility of *Geistern*, if the rest is silent after all, it is because of another mode of *Geist*, a mode in which ghostly wanderings—and thus the eternal return of the same—are overcome. A gaze deep enough to read the melancholic features of Hamlet matches the gaze of the melancholic itself: a reader of this depth is Hamlet and is, for this reason, threatened with the loss of not only this, its "best object," but the object by which this reader is defined and thus of itself. Hamlet will have to be seen otherwise, or his features will have to be read as unreadable—not as features that can be read without remainder as representations of "all the stations of this intentional space" but as the overcoming of these features, these traits, the marks by which Hamlet plays out his role, recognizes and identifies himself in the mirror. This, then, will be seen: a featureless Hamlet, or one who has no marks by which he is known, a Hamlet who, strictly speaking, would no longer recognize himself. The overcoming of these features takes place in *christlichen Geist*. But what is "Christian spirit"? And how does it relate to its counterpart, the wandering "word of wisdom"? When Benjamin, who was not a Christian, although the only "authentic reader" of his treatise—Florens Christian Rang[18]—was very much a Christian, stops reading the features of Hamlet, he may then turn to the name "Hamlet," that is, begin to read Hamlet as "hunchback," perhaps even the hunchback who, according to a story Benjamin tells more than once, wanders about, vanishing only "when the messiah comes" (2: 432). For this Benjamin, at least, *der Geist geistert nicht*—spirit does not go about like a ghost. Spirit does not wander. It comes to a stop, and Hamlet comes to it. Only in this life, which, for all its singularity, is still, Benjamin insists, a life of a kind, a life of its own "princely" kind, a singular life because of its incalculable generality—only in a singularity of this kind does melancholia, as the experience of mourning in the most extreme sense, "come to Christianness [*kommt zur Christlichkeit*]." To Christianness or Christliness, not, as the English translator perfunctorily writes, "to Christianity," and even less to Christendom. In this life, mourning comes to the essence, or being, of the Christly,[19] which is to say, if we are allowed to translate this Greek word into a language Benjamin hardly knew and one that remains almost entirely silent in the *Trauerspiel* book: the messianic. Mourning comes to messianicity. This "coming to" is the "to-come," which no longer need refer to a second coming and cannot therefore refer in any rigorous sense to a first.

The end of Hamlet—of the mourning play and this life in mourning—constitutes something like a model of conversion or perhaps an image of revolution: from endless sorrow to *Christlichkeit*; from mourning to messianicity; from the "from-ness" of everything mournful to the "to-ness" of a "to-come." This end is something like a model of conversion or revolution because the singularity of *Hamlet*, the play or the life, means that it cannot serve as a model. If it does so, the model immediately betrays itself, as indeed it does: the *Verkehrung* of which Benjamin speaks could just as well mean "perversion." And a more perverse, more violent ending is scarcely possible: the ending is brutal, sheer "havoc," as Fortinbras says. No wonder there have been careful readers of Benjamin's treatise who could not accept his exposition of *Hamlet*. On the point of *Hamlet*'s Christianity, Carl Schmitt published a response to Benjamin entitled *Hamlet oder Hekuba*. According to Schmitt, who welcomes Benjamin's treatise, especially its attempt to distinguish tragedy from mourning play, and who even takes time (in 1956) to thank Benjamin for having sent him a copy (in 1930),[20] *Hamlet*, far from being Christian, is "barbaric," and he has no trouble specifying the reason for its barbaric character: the play belongs to the barbarism of its time, a time of potentially violent succession, a time in which the new "law of the earth" (*Nomos der Erde*) had not yet established itself, and thus a time in which certain "taboos" were still actively in force.[21] The "taboos" are, for Schmitt, what makes this play—and among modern dramatic works, this play alone—a tragedy, not a mourning play: history in the form of Mary Stuart "breaks into the play" (this is the subtitle of Schmitt's book), and by breaking into the sphere of play, which is to say, of mere "invention" (*Erfindung*), a violent and scandalous historical moment stamps *Hamlet* with a mythic character, bestowing upon it a value beyond that of mere play, a "surplus value" (*Mehrwert*) by virtue of which it attains the status of a tragedy. For only the gravity of this historical moment—a moment about which everyone in *Hamlet* must remain silent—grants the play its seriousness, lifts it out of the realm of mere play, and brings it into that of tragedy. Benjamin, according to Schmitt, senses the uniqueness of *Hamlet* but does not see how "history breaks into the play." His is therefore guilty of anachronism, and never so much as when he seeks to convert *Hamlet* to the cause of Christianity.[22]

But Benjamin, as we saw, never made Hamlet into a Christian. Schmitt's response to Benjamin deserves more careful treatment, and his deployment of the term "surplus value" in the field of aesthetics is of particular interest from this life-long foe of Marxism. But the conflict between the two comes down to a single point: for Benjamin, the end of *Hamlet*, its "silence," touches upon the eschatological; for Schmitt, the silences or lacunae of the play— its "taboos"—grant it access to the mythic. Since the eschatological is by its very nature "untimely," the accusation of anachronism holds no force; it is an accusation perhaps borne of certain mythico-juridical ambiguities. But these terms hardly do away with the question of anachronism, and Benjamin does indeed assign *Hamlet* to the time of the baroque.[23] To say that this is the time or temporality of disjunction only goes so far. If "there is no baroque eschatology," and if *Hamlet* belongs, however ambiguously, to a baroque time or temporality, then the eschatological, "Christic,"[24] or messianic character of the play can be described in only one way—as an eschatology without eschatology, a messianicity without messiah, *Christlichkeit ohne Christ* (to recall a Kantian formula). But can this eschatology without an "anointed one" distinguish itself from the eschatologies named in honor of certain historically determined manners of applying ointments, that is, of touching and being touched? More generally, can this baroque messianism, this messianicity without messiah, even be thought, which is to say: can it be handled, touched, and acted upon; can it act in its own right? The "without" in the phrase "messianicity without messiah" means at the very least: in the absence of; in the very place of this absence, being-outside-with. But the place of this absence cannot, for Benjamin, be just another stage of mourning; it cannot be experienced as a *loss*. Without mourning, then, and without messiah as well. Does this double "without" only mean good conscience and a "scientific worldview"? Or is it perhaps in this double "without" that, if only for a moment, mourning and messianicity meet?

These questions are all undertaken in response to *Specters of Marx*. The danger to which this work is in large part directed comes from the convergence of good conscience and a certain scientism under the slogan: "Without Marx or Jesus—and without mourning, too!"[25] Derrida emphasizes the work of mourning at the very least because it leaves no room for either good conscience or scientism: the specters of *Marx* cannot be conjured away by appeals to the success of so-called liberal democracy, and the *specters* of Marx, including the phantoms and fetishes he made every effort to track down, expose, and bring to the light of science, cannot be exorcised by appeals to the ontology of the "living present." But if mourning has no work, if mourning cannot work precisely because it is endless, if there is no work of mourning, only ostentatious plays of mourning and plays performed for the sake of the mournful, can this, the work of mourning, work toward these ends? If specters always return to the mournful because mourning never ends, then they are precisely what cannot mark the end of mourning, which is to say, the end *tout court*, the eschatological or messianic. The question to which each of these others then leads comes from the stroke of another slogan: "without messiah and without mourning." Could this constitute a messianicity "for Marx"? In Benjamin's hands, the end of *Hamlet* gestures in this direction: the *Christlichkeit* to which Hamlet comes (it is his to-come) is Christless. The end of the mourning play likewise comes without the ratification of "good conscience" but also without the haunting of "bad conscience," without conscience, which makes "cowards of us all," and yet without heroic self-assertion either. Being without mourning cannot be a matter of conscience or consciousness at all—nor of the unconscious as long as it presents itself as the locus of melancholia's "work of mourning." And being without mourning can just as little present itself as some kind of "ideal" toward which one strives by more and more work or by freer and freer play. As Derrida explains in section 3, paragraph A of *Specters of Marx* (the last of the book's many tables), to be without a determinate messiah may not only be possible, it may be the condition for the possibility of messianic expectation, a dry and deserted condition, the desert itself.[26] But to be without mourning and not to be so in order to make room for a "true 'mourning' "[27] or to make way for a mourning that, overjoyed with a Zarathustrian pathos, only mourns for its lack of anything left to mourn—this seems not only impossible, not only the impossible, but also not necessary, not an imperative, not a condition, not a priority for either action or thought.

If there is no imperative of any sort—hypothetical, categorical, or hyperbolic—to put an end to mourning, then the question returns: How does the play of mourning come to an end? For *Hamlet*, at least one answer is near at hand: it ends in sheer "havoc," in brutal violence, in near-total devastation. From this perspective Carl Schmitt's description of *Hamlet* in terms of an inarticulate, impolite, and therefore unpolitical "barbarism" is surely not in error. Nihilism might be the name of a politics of such barbarism, and nihilism, as everyone who is familiar with the last sentence of Benjamin's "Politico-Theological Fragment" knows, is also the name for a certain nontheocratic and thoroughly messianic politics.[28] But these two nihilisms can be associated only if one decisive point in Benjamin's exposition of *Hamlet* is overlooked: the brutal closing scene does not constitute the end of the mourning play but quite the opposite: it *could* constitute the starting point for a new one, perhaps called *Fortinbras*.[29] The nihilism of which Benjamin speaks at the end of the "Politico-Theological Fragment" has no place for revival, no place for return, and thus no place for scenes of sorrow: "Nature is messianic from its eternal and total transience [*messianisch ist die Natur aus ihrer ewigen und totalen Vergängnis*]" (2: 204). This means at the very least: everything must go, including, as Claudius says—but says only to legitimize his holding onto power—fathers. Everything must go without hope or fear of return—this is a "nihilism" in which there is no room for vengeance or expiation, *Rache* or *Sühne*. But such a nihilism, a nihilism *ex nihilo* that leaves nothing behind, cannot mark itself: it remains silent. On the point of this silence, it corresponds with the end of *Hamlet*, if there is one. Whether *Hamlet* comes to an end is infinitely more undecidable than Hamlet is indecisive. For the end of mourning cannot mark itself, and the mark of this impossibility is, in *Hamlet*, the figure of angels in flight: a collective of singularities, innumerable singularities collectively fleeing. These angels cannot be numbered among the specters, ghosts, or phantoms, particularly if the latter include among their ranks the "Old Mole," Hamlet's father, who, as he confesses, was no angel. Angels are different, and there difference lies, or flies, in this: they mark—without our being able to discern their marks, to hear their "songs"—a rest to the "rotten state" of debt,[30] the end of mourning.

Benjamin presents the structure of the messianic, or messianicity, in Hamlet's last words: "the rest is silence." Marx could be understood to paraphrase this famous phrase when, in the course of distinguishing the tragedy of the French Revolution from its repetition as farce, he remains silent about the dramatic form to which the "social revolution of the nineteenth century" will belong, the dramatic form of the one revolution, in other words, that draws its "poetry" entirely from the future: "There the phrase goes beyond the content, here the content goes beyond the phrase."[31] Here, beyond the phrase—"the rest is silent." This almost tautological sentence is not a command to keep silence, an injunction to say nothing, or a swearing to secrecy, and so this sentence cannot generate a taboo, a secret society, a sect, a crypt—or a play of mourning. These last words do not, in other words, conform to the structure of a promise or its prior, indeed a priori, demand for responsibility, for speaking back, even in the mode of keeping silent. "The rest is silence" incurs no debt; it is merely a statement that, as such— if there could be such a state—does nothing, has neither past nor future, and so refutes itself. It is a statement that, as such, makes no claim to being a name, and Benjamin emphasizes its propositional character by not citing it, by not marking it off as a citation, which is just another name for the name. For a name, even a divinely given one, as Benjamin remarks in a concluding section of *The Origin of the German Mourning Play*, incurs a debt, makes a demand, interpellates the one it names, and is therefore always on this side of mourning.[32] "The rest is silence" exhibits, by contrast, a certain *resting in language* or *arresting language*, not a speech act but a speech idling. So, finally, I ask whether the structure of the messianic should be sought in the "formal structure of promising"[33] or whether, instead, messianicity—or what Benjamin incongruously called *Christlichkeit*—does without debt, without its relation to the other, and does without, or undoes in an arresting language, the linguistic acts to which every debt is finally indebted.

I ask this question knowing, of course, that "the rest is silence" —these remarkable words of wisdom, which, because they remain remarkable, still wander—is also a promise. Not only does the very readability of this statement imply a promise; but, more to the point, my last, it is a promise made by the most loquacious of all Shakespeare's characters finally to shut up.

Violence, Identity, Self-Determination, and the Question of Justice: on *Specters of Marx*

PEGGY KAMUF

Jacques Derrida's *Specters of Marx* bears a three-part subtitle: *The State of the Debt, the Work of Mourning, and the New International.*[1] This subtitle announces three complex sites around which are clustered the text's spectral analyses. In this essay, I propose to consider how the text arranges itself according to other clusterings, as well, which will also be three in number: violence, identity, and self-determination. The trajectory followed here does not attempt to displace the book's own central concerns but rather to link these to the inter-related questions addressed in the present volume. Even so, it will be but a brief prolegomenon, an outline of the possible terrain on which *Specters of Marx* places a discussion of these questions. To call them questions, however, is perhaps already to disregard one of the most insistent appeals made in *Specters of Marx*: an appeal to question questioning itself. How such an appeal can open onto something beyond its performative contradiction or infinite regression will lead us, in conclusion, to consider what kind of gesture the text enacts, a gesture toward justice.

The strongest and most decisive link between *Specters of Marx* and our three themes is with the notion of identity, by which is always presupposed or understood a self-identity or identity with (it)self and without difference. In practically everything Derrida has written over the last thirty years, this figure of circular appropriation of the self to itself without difference is shown to submit to the implacable work of deconstruction, by which is meant a transforming historical inscription that allows us to indicate with the term of identity only a relatively stabil*ized* and never thoroughly stable state of being. Now, any minimal description of *Specters of*

Marx would have to acknowledge that it is initially set in motion by the claims being advanced in so many quarters for the stability, the stable identity, achieved by a new world order in the wake of the demise of the European communist states. According to the ideologues of the new so-called order, Western-style liberal democracy and market economics have achieved the end of history and proved that Hegel, rather than Marx, had gotten things right. But Derrida detects clear symptoms of anxiety disturbing this triumphant rhetoric, leading him to compare it to the initial stage of mourning work that Freud labeled the triumphant phase. *Specters of Marx* is a book of mourning, by which is meant, not a doleful regret over someone's or something's death, but rather and even on the contrary a work that sets itself over against the triumphant declarations of a death—of Marx or Marxism—and assumes the necessity of an interminable mourning, a lifelong mourning, work as always and first of all a work of mourning, and life as always and first of all a living-on of those already dead or not yet born.

It is in these terms of a survival or *survie* of the already-dead and the not-yet-born, but also of simulacra, prostheses, and supplements, that Derrida first introduces his principal theme here, that of specters, ghosts, phantoms, spirits, spooks, revenants, in short, all that lives on in the mode of spectrality. This mode is that of "a *living-on* [sur-vie], namely, a trace of which life and death would themselves be but traces and traces of traces, a survival whose possibility in advance comes to disjoin or dis-adjust the identity to itself of the living present" (xx). Spectrality, then, as the dis-adjustment of identity, the being out-of-joint, as Hamlet says, of time. Identity is always haunted by this disadjustment. The haunting figure of Marx and Marxism, which must be conjured away by the celebrants of the new world order, establishes a first sense of the title *Specters of Marx*.

To this troubled, anxious, and necessarily unsuccessful conjuration, Derrida devotes the first three chapters of the book. The latter two chapters are given over to the other sense of his title, not Marx as specter but the specters that Marx, too, would have sought to conjure away, his own specters and his own hauntings. It is one of the principal arguments of the book that Marx, no less than, for example, his great enemy Max Stirner, and Marxist communism, no less than its great enemies Nazism and fascism, sought to put an end to the specter of the other so as to assure the identity of the living present. This argument is first formulated in these terms:

opened with Marx's signature as a question, but also as a promise or
an appeal, the spectrality whose "logic" we are going to analyze will
have been covered over . . . by Marx's *ontological* response. The response of Marx himself for whom the ghost must be nothing, nothing
period (non-being, non-effectivity, non-life) or nothing imaginary. . . .
But also the response of his "Marxist" successors wherever they have
drawn, practically, concretely, in a terribly effective, massive, and immediate fashion, its political consequences. (30)

The link to the notion of self-determination appears less evident. Yet the exacerbating relation between an irreducible spectrality and struggles for territory in the name of ethnic (or religious
or other) self-determination is implied throughout *Specters of Marx*
and explicitly named in its third chapter. There Derrida draws up
a list, a black list on a blackboard, of what he calls the ten current plagues of humanity. The point of this exercise is to blacken
the rosy picture painted by certain avatars of Kojève who celebrate,
in the words of one of them, the "universalization of Western liberal democracy as the final point of human government."[2] This
universalization, which Derrida prefers to call "mondialisation,"
the becoming-worldwide, of market liberalism and liberal "democracy," necessarily marks the limits of self-determination when it
is understood as synonymous with national sovereignty. The ten
plagues Derrida goes on to list are an ironic reversal of the ten
plagues called down on Egypt before it granted self-determination
to the enslaved people of Israel. Here, on the contrary, the plagues
plague precisely the determination to enforce any national, ethnic,
or territorial frontiers against the incursion of forces from without, indeed, against all the new forms of enslavement invented by
economic liberalism and its offshoots or parasites. The ten plagues
are briefly indicated: unemployment, homelessness and forced immigration, economic warfare, the uncontrollable contradictions of
free-market protectionism, the spiral of third-world indebtedness,
economic reliance on an expanding and increasingly sophisticated
arms industry, the uncontrollable spread of nuclear armaments,
inter-ethnic wars, the growing power of the Mafia and drug cartels,
and, finally, the dominance of certain states over international law
and international institutions.

In his sketch of the eighth plague on this list, inter-ethnic wars,
Derrida brings out specifically the link to the spectrality that is his
concern throughout. The primitive conceptual phantasm of community or nation-state that guides such conflicts supposes what

273

Derrida calls an "ontopology," by which is meant "an axiomatics linking indissociably the ontological value of being-present [*on*] to its *situation*, to the stable and presentable determination of a locality, the *topos* of territory, native soil, city, body in general" (82). Now the archaism of this ontopological phantasm is rendered more archaic than ever by the accelerated dislocation of tele-technology. The tie to soil, territory, national frontiers—all that may delimit a self for self-determination—is increasingly and ever more spectacularly spectralized, displaced by a spectral image. Given that this spectralization is itself archaic, or arch-originary, what is at stake is not an ontopological rootedness versus a spectrological dislocation but rather the conditions under which, once again, stabilizations are possible. Arch-originary spectrality is also, writes Derrida, "the positive condition of the stabilization that it constantly relaunches" (ibid.). Here one may recall that, elsewhere in the same book and in other recent texts, Derrida underscores this positive condition of the tele-technological force of displacement—for example, the penetration of Western media transmissions within the former Soviet bloc. Likewise, in an essay published after *Specters of Marx* which pursues many of the same concerns with spectrality and geopolitics, Derrida has insisted on the basic alliance between the phenomenon of fundamentalist revival in religion and tele-technological advances.[3] With the accelerated dislocation or spectralization of place through tele-technology, that which makes this technology increasingly less subject to the control of any centralized, which is to say localized, apparatus, what has been called self-determination, though no doubt always with nostalgia, will doubtless have to give up the ghost, in other words, invent a living-on in its new, ghostly simulacra.

To connect with violence, I will cite a page of *Specters of Marx* where Derrida risks a spectral interpretation of the totalitarian violence that has characterized our century. That violence would be driven by a specific fear, the fear of the specter, but this specter appears in the other's camp no less than in one's own:

> one could be tempted to explain the whole totalitarian inheritance of Marx's thought, but also the other totalitarianisms that were not just by chance or mechanical juxtaposition its contemporaries, as a reaction of panic-ridden fear before the ghost in general. To the ghost that communism represented for the capitalist (monarchist, imperial, or republican) States of old Europe in general, came the response of a frightened and ruthless war and it was only in the course of this war

that Leninism and then Stalinist totalitarianism could have constituted themselves, hardened themselves monstrously into their cadaverous rigor. But since Marxist ontology was *also* struggling against the ghost in general, in the name of living presence as material actuality, the whole "Marxist" process of the totalitarian society also responded to the same panic. We must, it seems to me, take such an hypothesis seriously. . . . It is as if Marx and Marxism had run away, fled from themselves, and had scared themselves. . . . More precisely, given the number and the *frequency*, it is as if they had been frightened by *someone* in them. They should not have done so, we might think a little hastily. Nazi and fascist totalitarianisms found themselves now on one side, now on the other in this war of ghosts, but in the course of a sole and same history. And there are so many ghosts in this tragedy, in the charnelhouses of all the camps, that no one will ever be sure of being on a single and same side. It is better to know that. In a word, the whole history of European politics at least, and at least since Marx, would be that of a ruthless war between solidary camps that are equally terrorized by the ghost, the ghost of the other, and its own ghost as the ghost of the other. The Holy Alliance is terrorized by the ghost of communism and undertakes a war against it that is still going on, but it is a war against a camp that is itself organized by the terror of the ghost, the one in front of it and the one it carries within itself. (104–5)

What seems most important here for any critique of violence is the apositionality or indetermination of the ghost or specter whose apparition could have the power to set off such destructive exorcisms. Derrida insists that the panic-ridden fear is a reaction before "the ghost in general." But the ghost in general is not, if indeed it is a ghost, a conceptual generality; it is not, for example, the *idea* of ghost or ghostliness. The ghost is not the same thing as the spirit, or at least it is not *supposed* to be. In his reading of the critique of Stirner in *The German Ideology*, Derrida isolates the nerve or axis of that critique in such a differentiation of *Geist* and *Gespenst*, but this difference keeps slipping away in Marx's relentless indictment of Stirner. The specter would be a certain incarnation of spirit or idea or thought, according to Marx; its specificity is "as incorporation of autonomized spirit, as objectivizing expulsion of interior idea or thought" (203). For Derrida what unites Stirner and Marx despite the battle lines drawn by the latter is the effort to reduce this spectral incarnation, to reappropriate life in a proper, rather than a ghostly, prosthetic, or simulated body. To reduce, therefore, the ghost in general. This reappropriating movement, in both cases, would seek to kill the ghost by giving it life: for Stirner the subjective life of the ego, for Marx the real life of effective reality and work. What remains indistinguishable, however, between these two reappropriations is the drive to rid the living life of a nonliving other, or specter. And in that, they both undertake a work of mourning which is never one kind of work among others.

If we look now again at the passage we read a moment ago, we can see how the panic before the ghost in general is inflected by the work of mourning just isolated and thereby how this general spectrality is specified even as it remains unlocalizable or indeterminate. It is "as if [Marx and Marxism]," writes Derrida, "had been frightened by *someone* in them." This hypothesis, which succeeds the hypothesis of the fear of the ghost in general, follows the spectrogenic process of a certain kind of incarnation: the ghost in general, as ghost and not pure idea, has a kind of body, it is a *someone*. And this incorporation is also an interiorization, it is a "someone *in* them." This positioning of the ghost, however, is also an equivocation on the identification of that position, since the ghost is an outside inside, an exteriority within. Whose ghost is whose is now a question, since no certain line can be drawn between, as Derrida writes, "the ghost of the other, and its own ghost as the ghost of the other," or again in the final line quoted, "the ghost, the one in front of it and the one it carries within itself." The ghost is both specified, it is a some*one*, and at the same time of uncertain location or provenance. The violence this provokes would, so to speak, put the ghost in its place. "Let the dead bury their dead," wrote Marx.

The worst violence is that which would put the dead in their place outside of life, which would determine, therefore, the limits of life: "Step over the line and you're dead." It is the violence of the law as much as of the unlawful or the outlaw. If, however, we would continue to distinguish between law and justice, as Derrida insists we must, then it is because by justice we mean justice for more than the living, the presently living. This affirmation is put in place in the exordium that opens *Specters of Marx*, and it orients everything that follows. "No justice . . . seems possible or thinkable without the principle of some *responsibility*, beyond all living present, within that which disjoins the living present, before the ghosts of those who are not yet born or who are already dead, be they victims of wars, political or other kinds of violence, nationalist, racist, colonialist, sexist, or other kinds of exterminations, of the oppressions of capitalist imperialism or any of the forms of totalitarianism" (xix). This radical definition or, more precisely, injunction of justice immediately raises questions, and not only the question of how there can be responsibility for justice answerable to anything other than the life of a living being.

That question, which is anticipated by Derrida, is answered by the very irrefutability of the value of life, which it assumes and which carries life beyond its empirical or ontological definition toward the living-on or *sur-vie* we spoke of at the outset. But there remains the question of justice as responsibility and therefore as decision that must be taken, as act that, in effect and perhaps like the very worst violence, separates the living from the dead. Here one may think in particular of Derrida's constant reminders in *Specters of Marx* that inheritance of the past and thus from the no-longer-living (for example, Marx) is always an act of deciding and sifting among heterogeneous and conflicting legacies. Likewise, responsibility before the not-yet-born and before the future demands a decision without certain rule. Numerous examples, several of which Derrida does indeed cite, could be found within the domains of medical practice and technology (euthanasia, therapeutic abortion or abortion in general), genetic engineering, reproductive technology, animal experimentation, and so forth—in other words, those domains where the so-called life sciences operate on the edge of any definition of life or the human.

Such a summary review of these three possible intersections with *Specters of Marx* perhaps raises more questions than it answers. Most evidently it elides the question of justice, which is at the center of this book, that is, at the place Derrida has identified as the undeconstructible ground of possibility of deconstruction.[4] *Specters of Marx* approaches this question in a number of ways, which are specifically inflected here by the condition of irreducible spectrality analyzed through Marx's texts and the legacies of Marxism. Or rather, Derrida takes up the question of justice here in its form *as* question, a question that is posed to a ghost. What is one doing when one questions a specter? Is such a question at the same time a suspension of the very mode of the question?

These questions about the question (of justice) can be traced throughout *Specters of Marx*. Indeed, the book might be described as itself suspended or supported between two interrogative moments, which thus form the most immediate frame of Derrida's text. Not only, then, does the word or the subject of the question return with insistence and get remarked at several of the most stressed points of this text, but the question of the question inaugurates the trajectory of the text and gives impetus to its final gestures. There is first an exordium in which the question of the future, that is, both about the future and coming to us from the future—"Whither Marxism?" the title of the colloquium for which Derrida originally wrote *Specters of Marx*—is translated into what "is perhaps no longer a question":

> This question *arrives*, if it arrives, it questions with regard to what will come in the future-to-come. . . . If it is possible and if one must take it seriously, the possibility of the question, which is perhaps no longer a question and which we are calling here *justice*, must carry beyond *present* life, life as *my* life or *our* life. (xx)

Likewise, at the other end of the book, in the penultimate paragraph, a question is asked about the very act of questioning: "Can one, in order to question it, address oneself to a ghost? To whom? To him? To *it*, as Marcellus says once again and so prudently? 'Thou art a Scholler, speake to *it* Horatio. . . . Question *it*'" (175). This quotation from *Hamlet* will be repeated one more time in the italicized last words of the book, but without the final injunction to "question it." "*Thou art a scholar; speak to it, Horatio*" (176). Between these two citations, in the space where the demand or the injunction to question the ghost has been effaced, the first question ("Can one, in order to question it, address oneself to a ghost?") gets reformulated as follows: "The question deserves perhaps to be put the other way: could one *address oneself in general* if already some ghost did not come back?" (176).

With these minimal indications, which are privileged by their framing position in the book, one sees the suspension of the question being put in place. One could say that there is nothing surprising about this in a book that, in more than one way and first of all in its title, is closely related to Derrida's earlier essay *Of Spirit*, which bears the subtitle *Heidegger and the Question* and which questions the privilege Heidegger seems to grant to questioning as a mode of thought. Moreover, well before this latter text, Derrida had proliferated questions about the question, especially in its ontological form, "What is . . . ?" It is precisely the ontological response to a certain spectrality that is being tracked throughout *Specters of Marx* ("the hypothesis that we are venturing to put forward here: opened with Marx's signature as a question, but also as a promise or an appeal, the spectrality whose 'logic' we are going to analyze will have been covered over . . . by Marx's *ontological* response" [30]). But it seems that *Specters of Marx* also advances, so to speak, the suspense of the question in another manner. Or rather, the suspense is otherwise suspended and with different effects. To attempt to narrow down or specify this "otherwise," we can look more closely at two other passages in the book.

They are both found toward the end of the text and echo each other in a somewhat muffled way. The first passage follows on Derrida's reading of the opening of *Capital*. He wonders whether these pages stage a "great scene of exorcism" without ever answering definitively or simply "yes" to this question. Dictating this suspension of the answer is an unwillingness to consign Marx's thought to the enclosure of the frightened reflex that is called here *se-faire-peur*, "make-oneself-fear." But beyond this generosity toward the spirit or specter of Marx, Derrida speaks also of thought or thinking itself as *necessarily* a form of conjuration.

> For we are wagering here that thinking never has done with the conjuring impulse. It would instead be born of that impulse. To swear or to conjure, is that not the chance of thinking and its destiny, no less than its limit? The gift of its finitude? Does it ever have any other choice except among several conjurations? We know that questioning itself—and the most ontological, the most critical, and the most risky of all questions—still protects itself. Its very *formulation* throws up barricades or digs trenches, surrounds itself with barriers, increases the fortifications. It rarely advances headlong, at total risk to life and limb [*à corps perdu*]. In a magical, ritual, obsessional fashion, its *formalization* uses *formulas* which are sometimes incantatory procedures. It marks off its territory by setting out there strategies and sentinels under the protection of apotropaic shields. Problematization itself is careful to disavow and thus to conjure away (we repeat, *problema* is a shield, an armor, a rampart as much as it is a task for the inquiry to come). Critical problematization continues to do battle against ghosts. It fears them as it does itself. (165)[5]

By proliferating with so much energy the traits of the analogy, this characterization of questioning or problematization as a warlike defense against ghosts seems itself to be mounting a defense against a threatening figure, armed *cap à pied*, which advances behind a shield. It is as if they wanted to conjure this conjuring question and, by denouncing its weapons, force it to lay them down. There would thus be a battle played out *en abyme*, without any possible victory that does not have to appeal to some conjuring mechanism, in other words, to that against which one is defending oneself. To question the question would therefore come down to repeating its conjuring stratagems. That much is clear. But the passage we are examining does more than illustrate this auto-defensive structure of critique, by letting itself or pretending to let itself get taken in by it. It is also a matter here of a certain *wager*: "we are wagering here that thinking never has done with the conjuring impulse."

Why this wager? Why the verb "wagering"? The answer may be quite simple: it is used as a synonym of "think," a substitution made necessary (or at least desirable) because the subject of the next clause is "thinking." But the explanation of "style" is hardly satisfying. Wagering puts something at stake in a different way than thinking. If the sentence in question affirms that thinking can never "have done with the conjuring impulse," then it does so in what is not simply a theoretical or falsifiable proposition. To have done with conjuration would be, if it were possible, a future state. But to have done with conjuration, to put an end once and for all to ghosts—all ghosts—is to put an end to the future, to bar it by and in a present entirely present to itself, without difference. And it is against this present without future (what the last pages of the text call this impossible that "can nevertheless *take place*" as "the ruin or the absolute ashes" [175]) that this wager is wagering, which is to say, taking sides. This wager, therefore, sums up the principal gesture or act of the book, the taking of sides that Derrida constantly assumes and affirms throughout. But the gesture is anything but a simple one, for it is a wager that one will not have done with the conjuring effects of the question even as one continues to question that question and those effects.

Skipping over several pages, we come to the second passage questioning the question. Marx's "critical but pre-deconstructive ontology" has just been named as that upon which he sought to ground his exorcism of the spectral. Derrida then comments:

> Pre-deconstructive here does not mean false, unnecessary, or illusory. Rather it characterizes a relatively stabilized knowledge that calls for questions more radical than the critique itself and than the ontology that grounds the critique. These questions are not destabilizing as the effect of some theoretico-speculative subversion. They are not even, in the final analysis, questions but seismic events. *Practical* events, where thought *becomes act* [se fait agir], and body and manual experience . . . labor but always divisible labor—shareable. . . . These seismic events come from the future, they are given from out of the unstable, chaotic, and dis-located ground of the times. A disjointed or dis-adjusted time without which there would be neither history, nor event, nor promise of justice. (170)

The passage contains one of the numerous difficulties encountered in translating this text: the expression *se fait agir*. That expression echoes another locution in the lexicon of *Specters of Marx*, *se faire peur* (translated as "make oneself fear"), in which is concentrated the action of ontologizing exorcism. Between the two, between the *se-faire-peur* and the *se-faire-agir*, there is the difference between what constitutes a present for itself by fixing or freezing itself in fear of the specter and what lets itself be approached and even exceeded by what is not the same: an event. It is a matter therefore in this *se-faire-agir* of a mutation or transformation rather than a self-constitution. It is thinking that becomes act by making itself into act. Thinking becomes act or rather *agir*, acting, but also "body and manual experience . . . labor." Note as well that this *se-faire-agir* of thinking takes place in the suspension of the question, there where, "in the final analysis," questioning gives way to the seism of the event. As we read in the previous passage, questioning or problematization would be on the order of the "make-onself-fear" that protects itself from everything that is coming with the event.

But if thinking becomes act and body and labor where questioning gives way to the event, is it not still a kind of conjuration, this time a conjuration of questioning? Can one, in other words, recognize in this *call* for a thinking that becomes act and body (for it is indeed a call, or a wager) a movement of the conjuring impulse that, as we just read, thinking can never have done with? And if so, if in fact thinking has no "choice except among several conjurations," how can this call call for something other than the coming of the future as the future of a conjuration? To put it in other terms: can one finally distinguish, "in the final analysis," between the "make-oneself-fear" of the conjuration and the "make-oneself-act" of the transformation or the deconstruction?

It is possible that this question makes little sense, for the essential reasons that we have tried to explicate by going back over some of those places in *Specters of Marx* where the abyss of questioning the question opens up so clearly. It would make little sense because it persists in questioning a future, a future-to-come, and thus a past, which will never answer "present" in the present. For that reason, the text seeks what it calls "another structure of 'presentation,'" other, that is, than the question ("perhaps it is no longer at all a matter of a question and we are aiming instead at another structure of 'presentation,' in a gesture of thinking or writing" [29]; this sentence is followed by a passage from Blanchot's essay "The Three Voices of Marx," which also speaks of a certain "absence of the question"). What has to be "presented" otherwise, according to "another structure," is, of course, the spirit or the specter, that which does not present itself but divides the presence of every present. Would the spectral, therefore, be that which one cannot question or interrogate without dissipating or conjuring it by demanding that it answer? The question would be something like a mirror held up before the ghost—which can be recognized by the absence of its reflection there. It would be a mirror-question, therefore, which can only reflect back to the questioner his or her own image. This is indeed what Hamlet will discover when he is reduced to *asking himself* if the ghost speaks truly and if he, the heir of a dead father, is indeed obliged by its words "to set it right." The question Hamlet asks himself is the question of justice, or rather, that which "is perhaps no longer a question and which we are calling *justice*." If justice is not a question, if it is out of the question or unquestionable, it nevertheless situates us in the space opened by a question that has been posed and that *Specters of Marx* formulates in Hamlet's terms. This is a moment in which one may read the highest stakes of the text, of its wager.

> How to distinguish between two disadjustments, between the disjuncture of the unjust and the one that opens up the infinite asymmetry of the relation to the other, that is to say, the place for justice? . . . Whether he knows it or not, Hamlet is speaking in the space opened up by this question—the appeal of the gift, singularity, the coming of the event, the excessive or exceeded relation to the other—when he declares "The time is out of joint." And this question is no longer dissociated from all those that Hamlet apprehends as such, that of the specter-Thing and of the King, that of the event, of present-being, and of what *there is to be, or not,* what there is *to do,* which means *to think,* to make do or to let do, to make or to let come, or to give, even if it be death. How does the concern with what *there is to be* intersect, in order perhaps to exceed it, with the logic of vengeance or right?
>
> A trajectory that is necessarily without heading and without assurance. The trajectory of a *precipitation* toward which it trembles, vibrates, at once orients and disorients itself the question that is here addressed to us under the name or in the name of *justice.* (22–23)

We must conclude, although we have done nothing more than re-pose the questions that *Specters of Marx* scatters in the path of our reading. Above all, the question of justice, which is not a question. We spoke of a suspension of the question, but this is perhaps incorrect. This question that is not one constantly interrogates us urgently and without possible delay. As everyone knows, not to hear it or answer it is already an answer. But does not what is called here "precipitation" call for a question, at least in order to gain some time? Absolute precipitation, without suspension, the instant without interval, "real time," which means time that would not know the difference made by another time and the time of the other—this would be the most total injustice. We say "would be" in order to place this catastrophic precipitation under the sign of a hypothesis, the very hypothesis that must be rejected as impossible. But in order to do that, can one suspend the most dangerous question, the one we have just cited and that asks "How to distinguish between two disadjustments"? Is that not a just question? Which also means a true question, one that must not be suspended even if one is absolutely unsure of being able to answer it without undue precipitation?

One 2 Many Multiculturalisms

WERNER HAMACHER

Culture—. And many—.

It is always the other who has culture—if indeed culture can be had. Culture is the art of nonnaïveté, the shame one experiences before what is one's own, a turn away from oneself; it is the dignity of nonegotism—and it would indeed be uncultured to rule out the possibility that culture, defined thus, could be a ruse of egotism, a barbarous technique of domination.

Culture, then, is always also culture's shame for perhaps not being sufficiently culture, for being perhaps still naive, nativist, natural, nationalist, egocentric, and for not corresponding to its own concept. The very concept of culture prohibits simple iden-tification with it or with any of its forms. No culture is Culture, culture itself, no culture can measure up to its claim to be culture. It is in this failure, in its insufficiency and discontent with respect to culture, that the pathos of culture resides—a pathos of distance, but nevertheless a pathos. It is, therefore, not a possession, this cul-ture, but a projection and a reproach, an attempt to reach a goal—itself, that other—that is by definition unattainable: ever another culture, and each time guilty of not being the other culture and of not being whole. It thus *is* not, but becomes. Nor does it *become*, but will always *have been* something other than what its own be-coming is capable of attaining: the social form of a dysfunctional *futurum exactum*, a priori outlived, a defunct body which it has already again surpassed. Culture, in short, is not *a* culture and not *one* culture, unless its unity consists in its not having arrived. Cul-ture—this could be its minimal definition—is its ex-position: its

Translated by Dana Hollander

interruption (the interruption of its labor, its strike), its imminence, its refusal or incapacity to be what it only promises to become.

It is in this sense—in this double sense and thus as an indication of the unavoidable fracture of sense—that we may understand an aphorism from Nietzsche's *Human, All Too Human* that speaks of the dichotomy between seeking and having, between research and teaching, between pleasure and pain, giving and taking, production and reception. It reads: "To the man who works and searches in it, science [*Wissenschaft*] gives much pleasure; to the man who *learns* its results, very little. . . . Now, if science produces ever less joy in itself and takes ever greater joy in casting suspicion on the comforts of metaphysics, religion, and art, then the greatest source of pleasure, to which humankind owes almost its whole humanity, is impoverished. Therefore a higher culture must give man a double brain, two brain chambers, as it were, one to experience science, and one to experience nonscience. Lying next to one another, without confusion, separable, self-contained: our health demands this."[1] Rescuing culture—this is the task that Nietzsche assigns to what he calls "higher culture." But what must be rescued is the particular culture that is declared to be coextensive with science [*Wissenschaft*] in the broadest sense, with *tekhnē*; what must be saved is science—from itself: for it consists not only in the "comforting" practices of metaphysics, religion, and art, but also in the unpleasant practices of suspecting and destroying these practices. What it has given with one hand, it takes with the other; it is its own sickness. "Higher culture," the rescue of culture from itself and from its ruinous duplicity, would not consist, for Nietzsche, in turning away from culture—this would only bring about the barbarism diagnosed by him under the names *Bildungs-Philistertum* [the philistinism of the educated], positivism, and nihilism as suicidal cultural phenomena. The rescue of culture lies in the affirmation of cultural self-suspicion, in the explicit split of culture into itself and its suspicion of itself, that is, in the regulated distribution of its forces into a dyad of science and nonscience, culture and nonculture. The schizophrenia of "higher" culture, its "double brain," as Nietzsche calls it, is its sickness as well as its convalescence, it is its sickness unto convalescence. Only as a double culture is culture rescued; with its "double brain," culture reaches beyond itself as its own destruction. Therefore, culture is always in crisis, because it is itself this crisis, because it is crisis itself. But it is precisely because it only lives as this crisis, as a splitting-off, a separation, a division from itself, that it lives as its own survivor: as that culture which, being a head and ahead of itself, comes back to itself as a revenant, spirit, and ghost of culture. Scientists, the producers of culture, writes Nietzsche, "are haunted by ghosts of the past, as well as ghosts of the future."[2] Culture is always a matter of the survival, of the more than merely living, of the living otherwise and the living elsewhere of culture. It is organized aporia and the aporia even of organization and disorganization; since it does not stand still in this aporia—paralyzed like Hercules, the cultural hero of Greek mythology, before the trivium in Renaissance paintings— since aporia is rather the form of its very movement, it is diaporia, the movement of pathlessness, the pathlessness of movement.[3]

What is called culture is never the one without being also an other, and it is never something other than culture without at the same time being its impossibility. This is why it cannot be localized or appropriated, cannot be reserved for anyone—neither sociologically for a given stratum or class, nor in the realm of national politics for a given terrain or a given language, nor historically for a given epoch. But just as the concept of culture is a concept of distinction, of differentiation from itself and of the crisis constitutive of its structure, so too it has always been used at the same time as a polemical term for the distinction between culture and nonculture, culture and nature, culture and barbarism or uncultivatedness, and thus as a weapon in the struggle against other cultures, as an instrument of the denunciation and barbarization of cultures. Just as no one can say of himself that he is cultivated without having thereby already denied himself culture, so too it cannot be said of others— least of all in their presence—that they have culture, without this compliment being necessarily taken as dupery and denunciation. Culture is always also a declaration of war.

The reason why any judgment as to whether someone is cultured or not must, strictly speaking, be taken as impertinent is evident: whoever judges in this way himself presumes to control the standard for what is culture and the right to accord to the judged party the role of object, or even victim, of this judgment. But culture knows neither an objective standard nor anyone who could presume to represent one. Culture is the taboo against speaking of it in assertions. One does not speak of culture—this is its definition and its self-definition. But one does not speak of it, not because one has it (as this saying has gone at one time or another), but because it is culture itself that speaks and because it is not possible—

286

yet certainly also unavoidable—to speak about speaking without thus already speaking of something *else*. This is the dilemma, the "double brain" of culture: it permits and demands that one speak, name, say the truth about it and about everything, but only under the condition that one not speak about culture itself "as such." If it can be characterized as the art of nonegotism, then it must also be determined as the art of nonobjectivity and nonobjectification: culture is not an object. It is our way of being there with ourselves and others in language and languages, and it is our way, before any subject or object, of going beyond all conceivable subject- and object-fixations.

This is not to say that culture has not been spoken of and that one mustn't indeed speak of it. In fact, everyone who speaks, under whatever conditions he or she or it speaks, speaks already, inevitably, also of culture: not only in the institutions designated for this purpose, the institutions for the archiving, production, and distribution of culture; not only in scientific and, as they're called, literary writings; not only in words, gestures, actions, and movements; and not even only explicitly and thematically; but first of all, and most of the time, implicitly, tacitly, and circuitously. One speaks of culture—speaks, writes, articulates culture—always in its double and contradictory movement as affirmation and as transformation: that is, always also in a way that is distancing, neutralizing, inventive, in a way that makes out its deficits and works toward its perfection, toward what one might call (I shall return to this word) its acculturation.

Freud, who devoted a large part of his work to just this acculturation, writes in *The Future of an Illusion* in 1927: "Human civilization [*Kultur*], by which I mean all those respects in which human life has raised itself above its animal conditions and differs from the life of beasts—and I scorn to distinguish between culture [*Kultur*] and civilization [*Zivilisation*]—presents, as we know, two aspects to the observer. It includes, on the one hand, all the knowledge and capacity that men have acquired in order to control the forces of nature and extract its wealth for the satisfaction of human needs, and, on the other hand, all the institutions necessary in order to adjust the relations of men to one another and especially the distribution of the available goods. The two trends of civilization are not independent of each other: firstly, because the mutual relations of men are profoundly influenced by the amount of instinctual satisfaction which the available goods make possible;

287

secondly, because an individual man can himself come to function as wealth in relation to another one, in so far as the other person makes use of his capacity for work, or chooses him as a sexual object; and thirdly, moreover, because every individual is virtually an enemy of civilization, though civilization is supposed to be an object of universal human interest."[4] This is not the place to examine in detail the difficulties of this definition of culture: the differentiation between human and animal; the distinction, rejected by Freud, between civilization and culture, which was propagated in the 1910's, especially by Spengler, with disastrous consequences; the distinction between needs and drives; the at once economico-technical and ethical concept of the good and of goods; the concept of the domination of nature, etc. What is important for the time being is the notion of hostility toward culture, which establishes between the two "aspects" or "trends" of human civilization—the domination of nature and the regulation of social relations—a connection: that "every individual is virtually an enemy of civilization" takes that individual out of the human community, makes him into a part of nature and thus into an object—Freud also says "victim"—of the labor of cultivation which he rejects. Freud regards this virtual enmity toward culture on the part of every individual, the individual's "destructive, and therefore anti-social and anti-cultural, tendencies,"[5] not only as impossible to pacify, but also as a particularly powerful cultivating factor. He ascribes to these "anti-cultural tendencies" the emergence of conscience and thus of the consciousness of justice and of morality in general; he attributes to the pressure they exert the "great experiment in civilization"[6] of the Bolshevist revolution, about whose prospects he is careful and liberal enough to suspend judgment. To these tendencies, and thus to "brute violence," he finally traces all the great cultural creations of humanity and thus the very humanity of man.[7] Anticultural violence, since it is essentially unstable, multiple, unhomogeneous, and capable of turning against itself, since it is vertible and invertible, founds culture by turning against itself. Culture is not a pole that turns against another pole that is opposed to it; rather it is the pole that, by its very turn against itself—that is, by its splitting and turning—first erects the other pole. The pole of the violence of all against all erects another pole through which a community, the unity of a community, is supposed to be established: the pole erects its counter-pole, erects itself as its opposite and thus first establishes the political, communal life in which its movement is supposed to be brought to a standstill and in which all destructive, antisocial, and anticultural tendencies are supposed to be pacified. The work of cultivation, acculturation, as real and efficient as it may be, remains—in Freud's word—an "illusion," because it must be driven by the forces that work toward the destruction of all culture, the destruction of politics and of moral ideals, and that allow themselves to be bound together only in a partial and problematic pact. If the war of all against all—and this Hobbesian notion of the state of nature serves as the model for Freud's genealogical mythology of acculturation—secures peace, then war will soon dissolve again the ties that it has bound.

Culture, as real and efficient as it may at times appear, is for Freud a delusion because it always consists of a linkage of mutually hostile elements. Freud therefore conjures up *two* apocalyptic fantasies, also polar opposites of each other. The first is the destruction of human cultures by uncultivated destructive drives in devastating wars; the other is the "extinction of the human race" by the very process of cultural development. The process of civilization, Freud writes, "may perhaps be leading to the extinction of the human race, for in more than one way it impairs the sexual function; uncultivated races and backward strata of the population are already multiplying more rapidly than highly cultivated ones."[8] Culture, having originated out of the mythical antisocial state of nature, can have only a precarious existence under the pressure of the forces it seeks to control. But even if it should be possible to attain the "ideal condition" of culture in the form of a "community of men who had subordinated their drives [*Triebleben*] to the dictatorship of reason,"[9] we cannot, according to Freud, expect anything other than the extinction of humanity and of its culture. Its survival would depend on those whom Freud calls, with an astounding gesture of jealous contempt, "uncultivated races" and "backward strata."

Culture, in short, leads to death and to the death of culture: first, because it is never sufficiently culture; second, because it is too much culture; and in any case, because it is not itself, but a disguised, transformed, complicated nature, because it is a culture of death, a detour of death and the detour toward death. The same is true—the formula is familiar from "Beyond the Pleasure Principle"—of life: a detour toward death, it is always the life of death. Likewise for politics: it is a politics of death, a necrocultural politics, a linking of that which in principle resists any linking—an aporia, an apolitia, an aporopolitics.

Freud suggests that culture is a marginal phenomenon of natural as well as civilizational processes. It exists only on its own margins, on the limit between its ideal and its disappearance. And on the limit between the ideal and that which it is not, thus on the limit of the ideal—but since this ideal is itself nothing but its limit, culture exists only as the transgression of this limit in itself, as auto-affection and as auto-destruction. The ideals of a culture, Freud argues, are formed according to "the first achievements which have been made possible by a combination of internal gifts and a culture's external circumstances"; the satisfaction "which the ideal offers to the participants in the culture is thus of a narcissistic nature; it rests on their pride in what has already been fortuitously achieved [geglückte Leistung]." Freud continues: "To make this satisfaction complete calls for a comparison with other cultures which have aimed at different achievements and have developed different ideals. On the strength of these differences every culture claims the right to look down on the rest. In this way cultural ideals become a source of discord and enmity between different cultural units, as can be seen most clearly in the case of nations."[10] Culture originates in the "fortuitously successful" (geglückt)—and thus contingent—identification with an object, an object which is thus adopted as an ideal. Initially, it is less a process than it is the instantaneous, punctual event of an appropriation, in which idealization and identification, self-identification and self-idealization, coincide. The ideal, the identical, is the center of culture, its origin, its figure, its contour or limit—and thus also already its end. It is the momentary appearance of Narcissus in a deadly mirror. The ideal is the source of appreciation only because it is the source of self-appreciation. What does not belong to the ideal, what one cannot identify with, can, according to Freud's portrayal, only be looked down upon or regarded with contempt. The culture of recognition is thus a culture of self-recognition and self-idealization, of self-affection—and of the mere affectation of a self—with respect to another who is regarded as pertaining to one's own self, as belonging to oneself alone, as reducible to oneself. As a system of narcissism, of ego-constitution and ego-stabilization, culture is nothing but the idealization of the ego in the other. Thus, for Freud, culture is always defined as the ideo-egological constitution of a community. It obeys one sole principle, that of identity, and is, to use a somewhat more recent term, identity politics.

It follows from this, however—and here Freud comes to the

second constitutive feature of self-idealization and thus of culturization—that every culture must also be a culture of contempt; of contempt for the other as well as contempt for the self, insofar as it does not live up to its own ideal. "To make this satisfaction complete," Freud goes on to explain, "calls for a comparison with other cultures which have aimed at different achievements and have developed different ideals. On the strength of these differences every culture claims the right to look down on the rest."[11] To make its satisfaction "complete": no culture, no narcissism, no satisfaction, no identity, no ideal is complete, fulfilled, or consistent if it does not compare itself with *other* cultures, identities, and ideals, if it does not set itself off from them, set itself above them, or exclude them from itself. For the sake of its own identity and ideality, every culture thus becomes, in a manner of speaking, a comparative science of culture and pursues a politics of segregation, of deprecation, contempt, and defamation. Culture is, again, anticultural. Hostility to culture becomes a factor in cultivation, Freud explains, wherever it is directed at foreign cultures rather than at its own. In this, it does not cease to be antisocial, anticultural, and destructive, but its destructiveness is in the service of the ideal, which, itself destructive, brings into view an end to destruction. The ideal itself, as cultural as it might be, acts as anti-idealization. For the sake of narcissistic satisfaction with their own ideal, the aggressive, vengeful tendencies that resist idealization must attack all that lies at the limit of the ideal: they must therefore attack the limit itself and, along with it, the ideal. What is called a cultural ideal is not a peaceable, unified entity but a battleground.

The hatred of the foreign is a part of self-hatred, a part of the hatred triggered by the compulsion to be oneself. Xenophobia derives from the fear of oneself, the fear of the violence required for becoming and remaining oneself, for becoming familiar with oneself—an other, something inassimilable and foreign to the point of invisibility and impalpability. Thus, the ideal, and consequently culture as well, has two aspects according to Freud—or rather one aspect and one nonaspect, a face and a nonface. On the one hand, it represents its identity with itself, presents it, exhibits it, and makes it available to others as an object of speculation. On the other hand, it excludes the other, which it experiences as threatening and lethal, and thus directs itself against precisely the ideality that is constitutive of the concept of culture itself. The definition of the ideal is, like all definitions, a separation. It separates the one ideal not only from another ideal of culture, but at the same time also from itself. It erects a limit at which it departs from itself and declares itself to be contemptible, defunct, and dead. An ideo-egological community always forms itself as a necrological one. Its formula is: "other than itself."

With this very incomplete and formal sketch of what culture is for Freud—and not only for Freud, but for a long line of theoreticians, philosophers, anthropologists, psychologists, and sociologists before and after him—with this sketch, at least the following four points should become somewhat clarified:

1. Even the tradition of Enlightenment, of which Freud in this century was and remains (all death sentences to the contrary) the avant-garde, even this tradition, which, more than any other, eased the opening toward non–Central European cultures, falls short, in its definition of the cultural as an ideal, of its own claims and insights. It does so most blatantly where it speaks, as Freud does in the quoted passage, of "uncultivated races" and "backward strata." These denunciations are no momentary slips but are programmed into the very concept of an ideal that determines itself as an ideal of the self and of an egologically constituted community. The seemingly unprejudiced description of sociological or ethnographical states of affairs in fact follows the prescription given by the structure of the narcissistic ideal and thus follows a logic of definition, of demarcation and segregation, that is itself insufficiently articulated and thought through.

2. Enlightenment about the Enlightenment cannot content itself with turning the ideals of anthropology and of its subdisciplines —of historiography, psychology, sociology, ethnography—against themselves. Proceeding thus would only repeat the founding gesture from which these ideals themselves emerged. On the other hand, the critical radicalization of the Enlightenment cannot simply renounce these ideals, for it cannot simply leap out of its own history. It can, however, and must contribute to the further transformation of these ideals, to their mobility and their redefinition in an open field of possibilities. As long as the anthropological disciplines proceed from a determinate *ideal* that is immune from redefinition, they will also proceed from a "human being" that produces itself according to its own image, subjectivizes itself, and, at the same time, manipulates itself as an object or a victim. Their history of man and of culture, politics, and economics is in essence

a history of self-production and self-idealization. But insofar as it is a history of self-domestication, it must be a history not only of subjectification, but also of the subjugation, colonization, and enslavement of the other. As a history of the domination of the self, it must also be that of the sacrifice of the other, and even of the other in the self. The *prescription* of its ideal operates, implicitly or explicitly, by delicate or brutal means, the *proscription* of whatever does not conform to it. The law of proscription, which governs the logic of identification, idealization, and cultivation, cannot be turned against itself without disastrous effects. What is needed is another, transformative form of analysis.

3. The empiricism on which this style of Enlightenment (Freud's, for example) about culture, and thus this style of cultivating culture, is based can no longer be a positivism; there are no statistical data, no quantitative studies, no *polls* from which one might glean the truth about culture. In order to account for the formative structures of the cultural ideal, Enlightenment must rather—and Freud emphasizes this repeatedly and explicitly[12]—have recourse to speculation and to myth. The structure of speculation and myth, however, is none other than that of specular self-constitution in narcissism, of the myth that repeats what has already been said, of the recognition of what has supposedly already been cognized. Speculation and myth thus depend on a stipulation which they can never control. Freud called it "fortuitous achievement" [*geglückte Leistung*], and by this strange combination of chance success [*Glücken*] and achievement [*Leistung*] he concedes that this achievement cannot be regulated but is essentially contingent: it is prior to the formation of the I and of its ideal. It is not that the I experiences good fortune or happiness [*Glück*]; rather, it is through happiness that an I first begins to experience "itself." Happiness is constitutive of the I, but no happiness could be "constituted" by the I. Ideals serve to preserve happiness, to stabilize, to rationalize and ration it—this is why they are just as much *promesses de bonheur* as they are regulators of unhappiness. Happiness cannot be rationed, recognized, or retold. It may be the object of myth and speculation and the center of culture; but if it remains, it does so as something that comes along by chance, as something that has been found or received, as a felicitous or "fortuitous achievement," not as the result of deliberate efforts. Nothing can be known of happiness before it has been found. It is an unconscious of speculation and its culture, an unconscious of any ideal that allows itself to be erected

by it, of any I that owes its existence to it. This unconscious—
which is perhaps another than the one mapped out by Freud—must
lie in the setting apart of the ideal from the ideal, in the ex-position
of identification in the very moment of identification, and thus in
that which allows neither for complete idealization nor for identification, which can be accessed neither by speculative methods
nor by those of a myth-generating empiricism. This unconscious
must be each time singular and can be encountered only in a manifold of incommensurables—only in cultures, in many, never in one
"Culture." Luck is the other of culture—hence the myths of "noble
savages," hence the xenophobia directed against them, denouncing
them as barbaric and nonhuman as soon as they, or their happiness,
appear threatening.

4. The theoretical and practical transformation which tries to
uncover this other of culture within culture cannot simply be a
metamorphosis into another form of culture, nor can it be the formation of the trans- of culture and thus the perpetuation of idealiza-
tions and identifications. It must also be a movement that *breaks
off* any formation and *opens* something other than itself: it cannot
be only formation, nor only aformation, but must be *afformation*.
Afformation, however, cannot do otherwise than call into question
the ideal forms even of the multitudes, of the pluralities and multi-
plicities and thus also even of a countable and calculable multiculturalism: not in order to negate it and thus the idea of pluralism—
nothing could be more pernicious—but in order to speak about that
which is still denied and suppressed in these ideal forms, and in a
language that is not only cultural and not only politico-economical.
But if this happens—and it will be shown that it can happen only in
an antinomic, inconsistent, or aporetic form—then the culturalism
of multiculturalism will also have to expose itself to an experience
that all cultures live on and that each culture seeks to temper, to disavow or discard: the pain, that is, of being unable to be what it promises, of not being able to anticipate or plan what it is to become; the
pain of not being the happiness which its ideals seek to preserve.

In order to recall this pain of culture and in relation to culture,
this culture and any culture, and in order to recall again the rupture
of aporia, here, without further commentary, a passage from the
"Meditations on Metaphysics" in *Negative Dialectics*.[13] Adorno, in
every respect one of the most cultivated philosophers of modernity
and of the failure of its cultures and cultural critiques, writes:

An innkeeper named Adam clubbed the rats pouring out of holes in the courtyard before the eyes of the child who loved him; it was in his image that the child made its own image of the first man. That this has been forgotten, that we no longer know what we used to feel before the dogcatcher's van, is both the triumph of culture and its failure. Culture cannot bear to be reminded of that zone, because it keeps emulating the old Adam, and precisely this is irreconcilable with culture's conception of itself. It abhors stench because it stinks—because, as Brecht put it in a magnificent line, its mansion is built of dogshit. Years after that line was written, Auschwitz demonstrated irrefutably the failure of culture. That this could happen in the midst of the traditions of philosophy, of art, and of the enlightening sciences says more than that these traditions and their spirit lacked the power to take hold of men and work a change in them. . . . All post-Auschwitz culture, including its urgent critique, is garbage. In restoring itself after what happened without resistance on its own premises, culture has turned entirely into the ideology it had potentially been—had been ever since it presumed, in opposition to material existence, to inspire that existence with the light denied it by the separation of the mind from manual labor. Whoever pleads for the maintenance of this radically culpable and shabby culture becomes its accomplice, while the man who says no to culture is directly furthering the barbarism which our culture showed itself to be. Not even silence gets us out of the circle.

ɣ   ɣ   ɣ

Many cultures—. Others—.

Multiculturalism is a term of struggle. It does not mean to describe a given relation between cultures, but to call for one that is not yet given. What this term calls for—if only by implication—is not already true, but is supposed to yet become true. Therefore one cannot reproach it for not telling the truth.

But it fails to be precise in at least two ways. First, it suggests that the culture in which we work, make connections, establish, follow, alter, and break rules, and in which we perhaps even live, is a monoculture, a monolithic totality that is neither genetically nor structurally co-determined by other cultures, structured by them, nor even "cultivated" by them. The opposite is true. There is no single culture that constitutes an autarchic, self-established, and self-sufficient unity. Every culture cultivates itself with regard to other cultures and is cultivated by other cultures. There is no culture that has not emerged from the configuration of others—and thus *a limine* from the configuration of all others—and has not been co-determined and transformed by these others at every moment of its history. This means: there is no one culture. Culture is a *plurale tantum*: it exists only in the plural, and it exists only as given also by other cultures—and thus as withheld, impaired, diminished, or threatened by other cultures. Culture already means multiculture, and it means the culture of the multiplicity of cultures.

That culture is historically and structurally possible only in the plural means further that no culture is purely and simply, completely and essentially Culture. Whatever is Culture in any given individual culture is constitutively lacking in what separates it from other cultures. Because every one is dependent on others, no single one is determined—by either its substance or the totality of cultures. The one substance of a culture—its particular ideal—and the one totality of all cultures are ahistorical chimeras. If there were one substance, an immovable essence immune to transformation, for every single culture, not one of them would be capable of historical change, none could refer to another, and each would be its own grave, a necroculture, a culture of the disappearance of culture in its pure ideal, and thus a culture of nihilism. However strong the tendencies of decontextualization, idealization, and fetishization in every culture, pure monoculturalism is an ideological phantom, regardless of who invokes it, or to what ends.

Just as there is no essence of culture, there is no integral totality of all cultures in which they could coexist peacefully or in which they could blend into one another. If there were such an integral totality, we would have to be able to give the noncontroversial rules according to which it is organized, any historical transformation of its ideal would be impossible, and this totality would, here and now, be at its end.

Like culture—which is itself already not one—the multiplicity of cultures is not a function of those who are engaged in its project and who generate it, always anew and differently, by the transformation of their traditions. Cultures, in the plural, were not and are not, as their name would have it, "cultures," but rather cultivations; they are multiplications, *multicultivations*. To characterize this process, the term "acculturation," employed by sociologists and ethnologists since the end of the nineteenth century to mean the incorporation of elements from one culture into another, must be pluralized and made more dynamic. No culture reacts to another merely passively through assimilation, but rather transforms the other culture along with itself, splits and diversifies, multiplies it and itself and thus contributes to the emergence of not only one, but a multiplicity of new cultures. *Acculturations* and *multicultivations* are movements of opening, movements in which what appeared only retrospectively as a secure possession gives itself over to what is not yet "there," to what has not yet been appropriated, what is not even known "as such" but nonetheless announces itself. They refer to a multiplicity—thereby multiplying themselves—that is not yet *given* [*gegeben*], but is first given and remains given as a *task* [*aufgegeben*]. But in order for it to multiply in this way, every cultivation must, whatever the traditional context in which it takes place, abandon its restrictive prescriptions—and thus its origins and the futures they prescribe: it must, in principle, break with what has hitherto been known as culture in favor of its multiplication, and thus in favor of its acculturations. It can never be *acculturation* without at the same time being, under the guise of culturelessness or of the utter loss of culture, *a-culturation* and decultivation.

This moment of the interruption of cultivation in the opening up toward another, yet unknown and unacknowledged culture, this interruption of the process of civilization, an interruption without which this process would be nothing but a smooth passage through an essentially homogeneous continuum of given cultures, marks the point of the de-idealization of both one's "own" and of the "foreign" culture; it marks, therefore, the moment of *anxiety* that provokes the notorious symptoms of self-defense and stabilization—demonizations, defamations, segregations, and worse. But it also marks a *chance*: of seeing the other not as an already familiar and thus cognitively and practically dominated other, not as an already homogenized other, but as the other in its singularity, its incommensurability and therefore (I shall return to this) in its dignity—to see other cultures not as subject to their repressive ideals, but as subjects of their emancipation from it. *Acculturations* are thus processes, and, more precisely, events of alteration, singularization, and pluralization, in which cultures not only open up to each other, but in doing so also open up to what none of their ideals yet conforms to and what, *a limine*, no ideal could ever conform to. Acculturations open, within cultural systems and within culture as a system, gaps which no amount of cultural activity can fill. The more expansive and accelerated these processes, the more such gaps open up, the more intense are the defensive reactions—anxiety, hate, and above all indifference—and, perhaps too, the greater the chances of finding a new relationship between cultures, a new relationship to the between of cultures and to these gaps of sheer existence. These are the chances which it is incumbent upon the multiculturalisms to realize.

Multiculturalisms: if the historical and structural *a priori* of every culture is its multiplication, then *one* multiculturalism cannot be enough, and there need to be *many* multiculturalisms. There *must* be more than one, there *must* be more than *many*, and thus, across cultures, there must be the possibility of more than that which today we still call cultures: this is the imperative of the *ac*culturations, alterculturations. There must be something *other* than culture and its mere multiplicity. It is the imperative of autonomization. This imperative must count, and must count many, but it cannot do so unless it exposes the countable cultures, in and beyond counting, to what cannot be counted.

The concept "multiculturalism" is imprecise and insufficient in a *second* respect. It suggests that it is itself already a multicultural concept, that it already lies beyond the confines of a particular tradition of historical cultures, and that it is untainted by the principles and interests by which this culture has, at least until now, operated. But the concept of cultural diversity, and especially the concept of its desirability, itself has a relatively precise historical context: it belongs, like the concept of democracy, to the European-American cultures and has, to my knowledge, never appeared as a descriptive category nor, even less, as an imperative, in any other culture. The word "multiculturalism" speaks a European language—a dead language, in fact, one which, precisely because it is dead, claims to provide services that are just as useful (that is to say, apparently neutral) for international and intercultural communication as do comparable concepts in the technologies of clone biology, for example, or microphysics. But this concept not only speaks a particular national language, thereby already monopolizing and prejudicing, however implicitly and in however restrained a fashion, the decisions as to *whose* "multiculturalism" is, and should be, at issue; it speaks, furthermore, the language of the concept. But it is anything but self-evident that the effective praxis of multiculturalisms—their social as well as political, their everyday as well as their theoretical praxis —would mainly rely on an abstract, technological, neutralizing, conceptual language. Rather, it is more likely that this concept, and conceptual language in general, will do its share to expand to all cultures the privileges of conceptual abstraction and of the logic of subsumption characteristic of North American and European cultures.

However anticolonialist its intention, the concept of "multiculturalism" might well still be a concept with colonializing effects.

The perpetuation of colonialization under the guise of anticolonialist slogans may certainly take other forms than those suggested by Herman Melville in *Redburn*, a hymn to the only nominally international federation of America, but these forms will never be far removed from the ideology praised in *Redburn* and from that ideology's economical background. Melville, convinced that the American constitution "should forever extinguish the prejudices of national dislikes," sees "on this Western Hemisphere all tribes and people . . . forming into one federated whole; and there is a future which shall see the estranged children of Adam restored as to the old hearth-stone in Eden." This multinational America is, for Melville, a pre-Babelian Eden; its unity, however, is very precisely determined: it is the unity, not of languages in their process—in the process of their *translation*, for example—but of a particular national idiom, the British, and of a particular mythology, the Christian. Melville writes: "Then shall the curse of Babel be revoked, a new Pentecost come, and the language they shall speak shall be the language of Britain. Frenchmen, and Danes, and Scots; . . . Italians, and Indians, and Moores; there shall appear unto them cloven tongues as of fire."[14] The millenarian unity of nations that is here inspired by a single national language has, at the beginning of this chapter, a different genius: not Anglo-Christian, but Greco-Roman, and this too is a genius of colonialist internationalism and multiculturalism. In the docks of Liverpool, Melville writes, "all the forests of the globe are represented, as in a grand parliament of masts. . . . All climes and countries embrace; and yard-arm touches yard-arm in brotherly love"—but they do so "under the beneficent sway of the Genius of Commerce."[15] The Holy Ghost of multicultural unity thus has a prosaic name: it is called Mercury, its profession—Merchant.

The question, therefore, is: Who counts, who pays? And further: Is it still possible, here and now, simply to count?

Over a century ago, Melville was singing the praises of what is sharply, and cynically, recalled by David Rieff in a 1993 article in *Harper's*. He asks: "Are the multiculturalists truly unaware of how closely their treasured catchphrases—'cultural diversity,' 'difference,' the need 'to do away with boundaries'—resemble the stock phrases of the modern corporation: 'product diversification,' 'the global marketplace,' and 'the boundary-less company'?"[16] They are indeed aware of these compromising alliances, "the" multiculturalists. But it is nevertheless important to keep calling attention to the commerce between commerce and multiculturalization, to the objective pact between culture and "corporate culture," and to the fact that the emancipation of cultures has thus far always *also* been an emancipation *toward* the culture of capital. This must be pointed out, whether cynically or not, so that this emancipation may become more than the mere veil or train of an economic rationality whose effects will likely be no less devastating in the future than they have been in the past. But just as the rationality of capital has in the best of cases also unleashed resistance against it—by dissolving repressive traditional alliances, by establishing democratic and judicial processes, by creating unions, etc.—so, conversely, one cannot attack the rationale of capital without also reckoning with it: this is the aporia both of capital and of the cultures that transform themselves under its aegis and against it.

This aporia can be *interpreted* in various ways; the point, however, is also to *mobilize* it.

Without a clear awareness of the borders it sets and the chances it offers, and without the determination to make use of these chances, the politics of multiculturalism will be cultural politics, managerial politics, puppet politics.

What counts? And what does it mean to count?

In the debates on multiculturalism, on the principles of liberalism and of democratization, on the politics of identity and of difference, there are essentially two positions: on the one hand, an abstract universalism of rights that takes the principles of autonomy and equality as the basis for its arguments; on the other hand, the position of historical particularism, which calls for the restoration of the violated principles of autonomy and equality. What is the status of the principles of equality and autonomy espoused by both positions? Despite the universalism of these principles, they always began as principles of the struggle of particular groups against their particularism and against the segregationist and exploitative politics of other groups. They were the principles of social production and self-production activated against the confinement to repressive and paralyzing forms of life. But not only the principles of newly emerging private property and of the individualized forces of production, not only the historical principles of labor were mobilized against feudal economics based on inherited property. Principles of capitalization and self-capitalization that were at first regionally limited, *European* principles of the autonomy of labor—of labor becoming autonomous and of labor as a platform for citizens' claims to autonomy—were also mobilized. That they have not remained so, that the politically and juridically asserted democratic rights to self-determination first proclaimed in England, France, and the United States did not remain limited to Europe and the United States is, *among other things*, the paradoxical success of a murderous politics of colonialization, of oppression, and of economical and ideological enslavement—and thus of the destruction of autonomy. The process of the practical universalization of individual and social liberties has, in the last centuries, gone hand in hand with a process of oppression, disenfranchisement, and the massacre of countless persons and peoples. And this process—one hesitates to call it a process of civilization—has to this day not ceased to feed on the massive exploitation of individuals and peoples. The universalization of the principles of autonomy, self-determination, and self-production, the universalization of the principle of individual and social *labor*, was, in its political and socioeconomic practice, *at the same time* the universalization of particular interests—of interests, that is, that had increasingly become detached from human agents: the interests of capital. The process of "cultivation" was, and still is, *also* a process of capitalization. The formation of cultural ideals, which is supposed to culminate in the *autonomy* of the self, is at the same time a process of the *automation* of the mechanism of capital—of paying and counting. It is a process of the obliteration of labor, the obliteration of history and of the heteronomous particularity of the socio-economic and politico-cultural forces that sustain this autonomy and automation, a process of the erasure of those who are always insufficiently paid and of that which cannot be counted. Whoever invokes the universalism of *this* freedom and *this* equality—both as yet unattained—invokes, whether or not he acknowledges it, always *this* history of automatization, colonialization, and exploitation. Whoever appeals to equality does so within a history of inequality. Whoever appeals to his autonomy appeals to it as something that is itself not autonomous. He appeals to an aporetic self, to an aporetic equality, and to an aporetic principle of universality—and even the form of his appeal is aporetic.

Marx, who wrote the history of this contradictory movement—the movement of capitalization and autonomization, of automatization and the struggle against it—probably had fewer illusions about the form of the demand for autonomy than did most of the social and historical theorists who succeeded him. His observations, it seems to me, are still operative today in the politics of multiculturalisms. In the *German Ideology* he writes: "Each new class which puts itself in the place of one ruling before it is compelled, merely in order to carry through its aim, to present its interest as the common interest of all the members of society, that is, expressed in ideal form: it has to give its ideas the form of universality, and present them as the only rational, universally valid ones. The class making a revolution comes forward from the very start, if only because it is opposed to a *class*, not as a class but as the representative of the whole of society, as the whole mass of society confronting the one ruling class."[17] The claim to universality is thus "illusory" or "ideological" in that it exceeds the interests of the revolutionary masses; it can "become true" only to the extent that these masses universalize themselves under the pressure of the capitalist means of production, that they detach themselves from "separate national interests," religions, moralities, and cultures, thereby making "not only their relationship to the capitalist, but labor itself, unbearable" for them.[18] Marx leaves no doubt that he believes in this becoming-true, that he wants to make others believe in it, and, at the same time, that he can make others believe in this becoming-true of internationalization and universalization only because he also believes that already its idea—a surplus that exceeds the interests of capital and labor—along with the unbearableness of labor and of capitalist formal universalism, are an "ideal" reality. This is more pronounced in the "Holy Family," where he writes: "The 'idea' was always an embarrassment insofar as it differed from the 'interest.' Yet it is easy to understand that every massive, historically effective 'interest,' when it first comes on the scene, goes far beyond its real limits in the 'idea' or 'imagination' and mistakes itself for human interest in general. . . . Thus if the revolution, which can represent all great historical 'actions,' is a failure, it is so because the mass within whose living conditions it essentially came to a stop was an exclusive, limited mass, not an all-embracing one. . . . because the most numerous part of the mass, the part distinct from the bourgeoisie, did not have its real interest in the principle of the [1789] revolution, did not have a revolutionary principle of its own, but only an 'idea,' and hence only an object of momentary enthusiasm and only seeming uplift."[19] The advantage [*Vorsprung*] that the idea of the whole has over the interest of the whole, the advance, the credit, one might say, that capital gives itself,[20] the idea's bad check "bounces" in the face of interests—but it also brings about

302

the collapse of interests. The transgression of the "real limits," the violation of the exclusivity of bourgeois interests by the idea of a "human interest in general," this advantage, this excess, this hyperbole of the idea is for Marx not only a source of embarrassment but one of the driving forces of social and economic emancipation. The idea *is* nothing but the interest's advantage over itself; it is the opening of special interests toward other, nonexclusive, universal interests. It is interest's interest in going beyond itself.

Universalization thus inevitably has two faces: on the one hand, it is a potential embarrassment, contained within the limits of particular interests, and itself a particular universalization. At the same time it is a socially, politically, and theoretically productive force for the attainment of rights and for the realization of the claim to a no longer merely particular freedom. What universalization ("human interest in general") thus initially means, what it means for Marx in 1844–45, is that *this* universalization, *this* emancipation, being not yet enough, promises a *further* one. Marx participated in this movement of the historical "bad credit" of the idea, this movement of historicization, socialization, and universalization, with his announcement of a "reign of freedom." This idea (which was not only his) has until now been an embarrassment (one for which he is not entirely without fault), but, conversely, its incalculable, "enthusiastic," advantage has not ceased to embarrass "the interests." Which *also* means that capital credit does not stop discrediting itself, miscounting and counting itself out. Its *ratio*, above all, is a *ratio* of excess, of asynchrony, of its "own" anachronization, and thus of both its projection and rejection.

Automatization *and* autonomization are open processes of transformation. There is neither pure historical automatism nor pure transhistorical autonomy. The process of appropriating what is one's own, the *autos*, is a discontinuum of unreached advances. Self-advance, self-crediting, and anachronism are not simply historical phenomena, but define the structure—or distructure—of becoming-historical and phenomenalization. Without the aporia, without the tear that runs through interest as well as through the idea, there would be no history and no culture. Both history and culture, and thus the movement of autonomization in both, are aporetic.

One must call to mind the history of the universalization of the principle of autonomy, this colonial history of the concrete universal of capital culture, not in order to discredit the universalist ethics of the claim to freedom—this claim can be imperative only because it can never be simply fulfilled and never completely discredited—but rather in order to see the paradoxes of its principle clearly wherever they become political realities in history, that is, where they make history. But one must also call this history to mind in order to understand the motives and risks of the politics of difference or of identity. The politics of difference, as it is characterized by some of its theorists—I shall limit myself here to its dominant features—is a politics of resistance to the assimilation to a *formal* principle of equality and at the same time a politics of the reparation of *historical* injustice. These "politics of the particular," or at least most of them, are, as they appear today, essentially reactive: they are responses to the injustice perpetrated against persons, groups, and cultural ideals. "Measures of reverse discrimination" are supposed to contribute to a historical evening of the score, and thus to the realization of formal law in a situation of historical injustice. Such measures are part of a politics directed against the preservation of legal and structural inequalities which existed in the past and which continue into the present; they are thus part of a politics that is perhaps the first in history to regard itself as a genuinely *historical* politics and as a politics of a *historical* consciousness of justice.

The "risks" of this politics, which do not call into question its urgency, have been identified, more or less clearly, and more or less tendentiously. First, such a politics condenses the history of injustice into a space of simultaneity and makes it into an object of "social engineering" or technology, of assimilation to a common legal space of supposedly symmetrical relations. Second, this politics could continue, in reverse, the discrimination it struggles against (the idea expressed by the term "reverse discrimination"), and the hitherto "underprivileged" could be reduced to showpieces of a ghetto, or mausoleum, culture.[21] Finally, such a politics could channel the rage, the raw material of revolt, onto the treadmills of the existing system.[22] The real problem, however, which these risks exhibit only in a confused fashion, lies in that autonomy cannot be a merely formal legal equality or formally equalized history. One can speak of autonomy only where each individual and each individual society gives *itself* as an individual or as a society, establishes itself (as) its law, a law decreed by no one but itself. The search for what gives, erects, or decrees can quickly lead to a retreat into what is supposedly already given: this is the reason for the cultic restorations of past ideals, the regressions into nostalgia, the retreats to "one's own" land—land which in fact was never one's own—the phantasmatic revival of pasts that were never present, the appeal to roots and other fetishes. But it is also the reason for the recourse to what is already given, to posited law, which, in the debates on cultural politics—especially in the United States—functions precisely as a cultural ideal, with all the narcissistic and destructive trimmings that Freud attributed to such ideals. But the given, the posited law must, in order to be given, always be given anew. It must not only be interpreted anew with a view to the future, and thus be interpreted otherwise than by those who decreed it, but must, if it is to measure up to the claim for autonomy, above all be given and re-given by those to whom it is supposed to apply. The task of multicultural—that is, of any emancipatory—politics can thus lie in nothing less than the transformative renewal and expansion of the same autonomy that serves as the idea of democratic constitutions. Its task must be a renewed invention of this idea—that is, its renewed, first, self-invention.[23]

According to the claim of autonomy, the giver must give himself. Who else could give him, the one who is not given, in the absence of the giver? Who or what could give him- or itself without already having, or having received, itself? Is there an interest in freedom without an idea that exceeds particular liberties? Is there an idea of freedom that is not an interest? And must there not be a freedom that exceeds even its idea? Any politics of autonomy, of democratization and multiculturalization will have to ask itself these questions. They are questions that present themselves for the theory of legal autonomy as well as for the vindication of the right to historical equalization and reparation. And these questions, once again, lead to an aporia: the aporia not only of the cultural idiom and its intercultural genesis and transformation, the aporia not only of special interests and their universalization in the idea, but the aporia also of autonomy and thus of every possible politics of change that is founded on it. The aporia in self-determination stands for the *other* self and the *other* of every possible self.

Y   Y   Y

Others—. Otherwise than many—.

The two radical positions among theories of multicultural politics—abstract universalism and revertive particularism—are in an aporetic relation, not because they contradict each other, but because both of them must finally appeal to a claim to autonomy that precedes any positive law and any given authority, any self that is already given. This aporia not only springs from the historicity of the idea of autonomy; it is not only an aporia of the historicity of cultures, but it is also an aporia of their historicization. Because the fundamental ethical and political claim to autonomy—fundamental in that it first *gives* a ground—is essentially a claim for its realizability in history and society, because, therefore, the decision concerning what qualifies as historical and social change, and as history and society in general, depends on this claim, everything in the theory and politics of multiculturalism depends on determining as precisely as possible what is to be understood by autonomy in the first place.

One of its gravest misunderstandings may be clarified with relative economy by examining Charles Taylor's discussion of some of the problems outlined here in his *Multiculturalism and "The Politics of Recognition."*[24] Taylor subsumes all of these problems within the schema of recognition, particularly recognition by way of images. From the very first sentence of his essay, Taylor speaks of "the need, sometimes the demand, for recognition," noting a link between "recognition" and "identity," and linking both these notions in turn to the image that dominates his entire text: oppressed, marginalized groups, peoples, or genders have, he explains, "internalized a picture of their own inferiority" and thus an "imposed and destructive identity."[25] The distortion of the picture one has of oneself is for Taylor an effect of the "close connection between identity and recognition," and this connection is itself not merely unavoidable, but constitutive, or, as he puts it, "the crucial feature of human life." He speaks of the "fundamentally dialogical character" of human behavior, which he describes as a "balanced reciprocity that underpins equality."[26] "Reciprocal recognition among equals" is, according to Taylor, the aim of a politics of undistorted social identity formation, such as he claims can be found in Hegel.[27] He equates this reciprocal recognition, without further explanation or differentiation, with a program of a "politics of equal dignity."

Taylor finds in Rousseau, whom he cites as an existential theorist of authenticity as well as a political theorist of social relations of symmetry, and whom he considers one of the first and decisive figures of the politics of "reciprocal recognition" and "equal dignity," an early form of the schema that he himself follows in a modified form. Taylor again insists upon the motif of an image when

he emphasizes, in the "Letter to d'Alembert," the example of public, political *spectacles* by which Rousseau defines the structure of
a free society of equals: "Let the spectators become a spectacle for
themselves; make them actors themselves; do it so that each sees
and loves himself in the others so that all will be better united."[28]
Taylor does not engage in a detailed reading of this text and therefore sees in it, as do most commentators, nothing but an image of
pure self-transparency. (But nothing can be seen in a transparent
medium. As Rousseau says, "What will be shown in them? Nothing, if you will.")[29] Taylor regards Rousseau's solution to the problems of a "new politics of equal dignity" as "crucially flawed," first,
because he claims it is incompatible with personal and social role
differentiation and, second, because it subjects particular tendencies within a society to a universal purpose, to the detriment of
the interests of its individual members.[30] (Taylor thus has in mind
a society oriented essentially to competition.)[31] Taylor's critique of
the image he has constructed of Rousseau's society is a critique
of its asymmetry: what dominates in this society is the universal,
to which individuals merely contribute their services. But in Taylor's view, individuals are *social* individuals only as agents in the
give and take of private interests; their individual interests, what
sets them off from society, are at the same time the principle of the
social contract to which they are a party. As a result, the asymmetry and nonreciprocity which Taylor regards as a "flaw" in Rousseau's construction of society also dominate his own construction
of reciprocal recognition. It doesn't occur to Taylor that this interest might be yet another form of domination: of a domination—and
thus of an asymmetry—that is all the more tyrannical for its claim
that it be immediately universal. It is private interest that dominates in public recognition. The politics of recognition is thus, more
or less unwittingly, in conflict with itself. It pleads for differentiation, but the terrain of this differentiation is a recognition to which
even the smallest of movements must conform lest it fall, uncog-
nized and unrecognized, away from the social nexus. Taylor retains
this construction because it represents, in his view, the historical
paradigm of a society of freedom, which for him means, without
further differentiation, not only a society of "recognition," but also
one of "respect."

From Taylor's fundamental assumptions about the recognition
structure of freedom emerges a series of problems, which he solves
with the Romanticist hypothesis of an infinite approximation to-

ward a horizon of intra- and inter-social communality. Taylor fails to see that the very structure of this solution repeats the same "pragmatic contradiction" between intelligible freedom and empirical interest of which he accuses his adversaries: a "particularism masquerading as the universal."[32] The question this raises is, first, whether a society of freedom can be thought as a society of the interest in recognition, including whether it can continue to be thought as a *société du spectacle*—be it in Rousseau's or in Debord's sense—differentiated according to social "roles." Taylor does not pose this question, just as he does not pose a second one: whether a society of respect [*Achtung*] for others—which is for Kant the only society in which the fact of reason, freedom, is realized—can be essentially organized according to the model of recognition [*Anerkennung*]—of *self-cognition through* others and the *knowledge of others*. Furthermore, if a society of freedom—that is, a society founded on autonomy as its only principle—is also the only society capable of doing justice to the individual in his sociality, can this society then still be represented by given (i.e., unfree) "interests" and "intentions," in fixed or fixable (i.e., also unfree) "roles," in figures of positive law or of consciousness? Conversely, what would a free singularity that does not represent itself be? If it must represent itself, can it still do so *as* singularity?

None of these questions is posed by Taylor. Indeed, they are questions which he cannot pose, for he fails to lay out the concepts he regards as fundamental—autonomy and respect—with the necessary precision. For him, these concepts are not only compatible with those of recognition, of intention, of pragmatic interest and social role, but may, as his text demonstrates, even be fused with them. But there are further questions not posed by Taylor, questions that ought to be posed in order to further clarify the structure of interest and of freedom. Can we ever speak of particular interests, even of the interest in recognition, when these interests are not formulated with a view toward their autonomous determination and thus with a view toward freedom and singularity? Must not any interest, in order to define itself as such, clash with and change its own concept? Is not every interest, as an empirical interest, then at odds with itself as conceptually determined? Is not every interest and every experience structurally an interest produced by a contradiction, an experience originating in a tension that threatens it? Do we not continually experience tensions only as irresolvable—and is *experience* in general not possible only as the experience of an aporia—and thus as the experience of an inhibited or, *a limine*, of an impossible experience? Is aporia not always the aporia that shows itself in its empiricism, in its aporetic empiricism, its apo-empiricism? And is the division between the intelligible and the empirical, since it does not neatly separate the two realms of nature and freedom, but rather cuts across both of them, not in need of re-vision? Must not all "solutions," whether analytical or pragmatico-political, lie precisely in this field of apo-empiricism, rather than beyond it in the "idea" of a unity without tension? Is not this unity itself merely an anticipated and thus revisable and transformable entity, or at least something still to come? And would it be ana-lytically and politically justifiable, would it even be possible, to articulate this unity otherwise than as an other and changeable unity, and thus not only as a unity yet to come, but one by which every "interest," every "experience" in every Here and Now, itself becomes something ex-posed?

Taylor, like other authors in the debates on multiculturalism, appeals to Kant numerous times in order to situate the terms "dig-nity" and "respect" in the history of philosophy. He refers par-ticularly, if only in a cursory fashion, to the *Groundwork of the Metaphysic of Morals* and its determination of reason as a "uni-versal human potential."[33] But how does Kant present the relation-ship between respect and cognition and the recognition of another? What is the relation between the law of reason, on the one hand, and empirical data and interests, on the other? And what is the internal structure of this law? Taylor and other proponents of a liberalism hospitable to particularities often speak of equality in the sense of legal egalitarianism. Such equality immediately brings with it, within a system of quantitative-representative democracy, the question of the quanta and amounts to be represented, and of how they will be represented. To take the question further: can minorities and majorities be adequately represented? How is "rep-resentation" possible in general? What, once again, counts, what is counted—and what is counting?

In the passage of the *Groundwork* to which Taylor explicitly refers, one of its canonical passages, Kant differentiates between value [*Wert*] or price [*Preis*] and dignity [*Würde*].[34] A price applies to that for which "something else can be put in its place as an *equiva-lent*; if it is exalted above all price and so admits of no equivalent, then it has a dignity."[35] But only what itself determines its value is exalted above all value, and since this giving [*Gebung*] of value

309

(its "law-giving" [*Gesetzgebung*], as Kant writes) must not depend on any pre-existing or pre-given value, since it must be an unconditional and incommensurable giving, it is entitled to an "esteem" [*Schätzung*] which must, in its turn, be not relative or comparative but unconditional and incommensurable. Kant calls this esteem "reverence" or "respect" [*Achtung*].[36] Dignity and reverence—or respect—are thus not concepts of a comparative quantitative estimate, but concepts constitutive of quantity. They do not count something other, but only, purely, themselves. To be precise, they do not count, but rather *give* number and are, in thus giving and *attributing*, themselves exempt from any number, uncountable, transnumeral. The dignity before which all valuations and measurements fail—because it is in dignity that they first emerge—along with the respect that corresponds to dignity, can only be attributed to what is under the purview of no law but the one it gives itself, to a being that for this reason alone can be called autonomous. Autonomy and, with it, dignity are for Kant the irreducible minimal determination of man as a social being universal in his respective singularity. To speak, as Taylor does, of the "equal dignity" of each reasonable being[37]—and of each being capable of becoming one—makes sense, according to Kant's determination of dignity, only if this equality denotes, not the equality of quantities according to a measure that is heterogeneous to them, but a singular equality given each time anew. Equality according to the moral law means the incommensurable uniqueness of each positing [*Setzung*]. It means marking a number that is each time unique, and thus the numberlessness and uncountability of every number. This is why whatever is counted by another can already no longer count as autonomous.

Kant leaves no doubt that the will gives itself its law only as to another, to a finite will, and that it refers to the self only as to another self. The imperative of autonomy is thus by no means the fact that a self *has* its own law, but the stipulation that, in order to be a self, it must first *give itself* as something not yet given: that it must give itself as another and give the other along with itself. The imperative is not an imperative of an already pre-existing autonomy, but only the imperative of *autonomization*; it is not an imperative of the singular, but of its *singularization*, not an already-universal imperative, but an imperative of *universalization*. The achievement of complete singularity (*omnemodo determinato*, as Kant defines it in late Scholastic terms) would be complete universality.

This singularity and this universality are not given but can, under conditions of finitude, only be commanded. The claim to a never yet achieved universalization of a still incomplete singularization, however, while it may not state the *comparability* of singularities, does *command* it—and thus commands the very *equivalence* that Kant wanted to keep rigorously apart from the incommensurable dignity of autonomy. The incommensurability requirement is at the same time that of absolute commensurability. Unconditional, realized value would be the price set by a market that is itself unconditional; it would be—in Marx's terms—a universal equivalent. The uncountable would be the pure ideality of counting itself.

The aporia of the incomparable, that it must itself still be a category of comparison, colors all of Kant's formulations in the *Groundwork*. But it does not devalue them, for it is the aporia of valuation itself, of self-valuation, the aporia of absolutization. For Kant, autonomy is not given but required or claimed; and it is in this very claim that autonomy gives itself. "But the law-*giving* [*Ge-setz*gebung] which determines all value must for this reason have a dignity—that is, an unconditioned and incomparable worth—for the esteem [*Schätzung*] of which . . . the word 'reverence' is the only becoming expression."[38] This "giving" [*Gebung*] is "a dignity"—and thus a giving of singularity and of universality, not singularity and universality themselves as given. As the giving of the universal it is never itself universal; as the giving of the singular it is never itself singular; it is *pre*singular and *pre*universal. Its autonomy defines itself and defines every self as *heterautonomous*. It commands singularity and universality and thus erects a double command that is doubly contradictory: that it is necessary to count, compare, and represent in terms of equivalents; and, at the same time, that it is impermissible to count, or to measure by equivalents, or to compare. That the uncountable be counted, and that the countable be uncountable, countless, dis-counted.

These relatively abstract considerations—and they are also considerations regarding the structure of abstraction and idealization, as well as the structure of empiricization and socialization—have no *immediate* political consequences, but delimit the space in which political questions both theoretical and practical may be posed regarding the form of democracy, the parameters of a complex and even aporetic mediacy: the field, on the one hand, of counting in political space and, on the other, this political space as one of the uncertainty of counting.

What is counted are *votes* or *voices* [*Stimmen*]. And not each one for itself, but each only in respect to its belonging to a majority or a minority of other votes. Majorities and minorities, the constituents of quantitative representational procedures, are quantities that can be considered only in relation to each other and thus not, at least not at first, as incommensurable and immeasurable. The vote is raised only to fade immediately away, and it becomes a voting voice, a vote that counts, only by losing its singularity. At best, it fulfills its incommensurability by making itself commensurable. But the dialectics of the singular vote—which Hegel describes in his Jena *Realphilosophie*—is a model only for a democracy of sacrifice, not of the liberation of the individual. As long as voting [*Abstimmungen*] and consensus [*Übereinstimmungen*] decide what is and what is not a vote, who has and who is denied the right to vote, there will be no political vote in the sense of a voice which sounds only itself, which is autonomous and counts in the Kantian sense. And as long as votes don't also count when they are not *counted*, democracy will not have been realized. This nondialectizable remainder on the political path from the vote [*Stimme*] to self-determination [*Selbstbestimmung*] has, in the history of democracies, occasioned the most bitter conflicts and the most urgent reforms. The struggles over class- or estate-based electoral systems, over the suffrage of the unlanded and the unemployed, over women's suffrage and voting age were always struggles about the limits of representation, about the concept and the practice of democracy and democratization. The politics of multiculturalization entails the continuation of these struggles. It involves the suffrage, for example, of immigrants, their "naturalization," their citizenship, the representation of their interests; it also involves the proportionality of their representation, the voting districts they belong to, and thus the valuation or devaluation of their voices. It is a matter of who votes and how they count, of which voices and how they are heard and thus how they first become voices and votes, decisive and deciding ones. It is a matter of counting the uncounted, and, in a very prosaic sense, of the commensurabilization of the incommensurable.

But how is one to give oneself a voice if one as yet has none? How can those who do not yet count or who no longer count be counted? These questions mark a systematic limit of the quantitative rationale which grounds representational procedures and thus a limit of the current ideology of democratic nation-states. The question of who represents those who don't or don't yet belong to a democracy—such as immigrants, for example, or children—the question of membership in a democracy, cannot be answered by reference to the quantitative representation of a given number of citizens. Immigrants (even if only virtual immigrants) and children (even possible children) do not belong to this number and can nevertheless justifiably lay claim to representation in democratic institutions. It is the same with the mentally ill, the dead, the imprisoned, the illiterate, those who refuse to "cast" their vote, and those who do not "have" a vote—there are always countless more of them than any given number of citizens "belonging" to a democracy. The claim to autonomy that underlies all democracies regards all of them—all and more—as having a voice; in this claim they have, in a sense, a voice for a voice, a voice even before or after they have one. The claim that is theirs even before—or after—they can speak as civil or legal subjects requires, in a democracy worthy of that name, everyone to be its spokespersons. This means that, within the system of merely quantitative representation by way of equivalence, a voice must announce itself on behalf of those claims that are incommensurable with such representation—another voice and perhaps something other than a voice.[39] The commensurable must incommensurabilize itself, must dis-count and outcount the countable.

In keeping with the claim of the unrepresented or unrepresentable to democratic representation, the borders of democratic states must open again and again, and ever wider: to refugees, asylum seekers, immigrants regardless of origin—what counts is only their future and the future of democratization. But the borders of these states must also open inward: to the suffrage of those who do not yet have it but to whom it must not be denied according to the principle of allowing for self-determination. The juridical reforms required for this—there have been such reforms in the past and there need to be more in the future—were and are, however, only possible based on a representation that regards itself not only as substitution or equivalence, but as responsibility and respect for the autonomization of others. Only such representation is capable—has always and continually been capable, albeit imperfectly, and will be capable in the future—of standing up not only for those who don't *yet* have a political voice but also for those who can *never* have one and who nevertheless lay claim to one. Democratic self-determination thus means: voting for the possibility of another self and of another that would not be the other *of* the self; it means voting, voicing one's claim to *heterautonomy*. And multicultural democracy thus means: a democracy open not only to many cultures but also to that which cannot be assimilated to any familiar concept of culture, to another culture and to something other than culture.

Such a democracy—and Charles Taylor is undoubtedly right about this important point—can only be a democracy of respect. Of course, not simply of *"equal* dignity," as he puts it, but of a dignity that is in each individual case singular and thus incomparable. And not of a respect that restricts itself to the already-recognized legal subjects of a given state, not even a respect that restricts itself to already identifiable entities—individuals, groups, or states—but a respect *before* individuals, one that *precedes* even moral and political personhood and, in doing so, first *makes possible* (in a noncoercive fashion) the contouring and identification of persons. *Before* the individual and *before* the universal there must be the imperative of respect: that the one and the other, the one not *as*, but *with* the other and *for* the other, the incommensurable *and* the commensurable, be possible. The subject of autonomy—if it can still be called that—can, on Kant's account, only be the subject of *autonomization*: a subject *before* its autonomy, one that has not already given itself its law but that is still giving it to itself, a subject *before* the subject: not subject, but project and, since it lacks a project's constituted "pro," not a project, but a "ject," a throw. Every democracy that is not in this sense also a demo*baly* amounts, no matter how well meaning its decisions, to an apology for currently dominant market and majority relations, to the cratodicy of the status quo.

A democracy of autonomy can only be one *before* democracy and *for* democratization. And its responsibility can only be one *before* responsibility, a *pre*sponsibility. The idea of moral—and thus political—personhood, the idea of dignity and the respect it calls for, is therefore paradoxical. It is more paradoxical than the "pragmatic contradiction" feared by Charles Taylor, in the form of "a particularism masquerading as the universal,"[40] because what is involved in the idea of the moral person is the constitution of the individual in his singularity, what is involved is a "particularism" which is not yet particularism and not yet capable of masquerading as something else, what is involved is a "universal" not yet capable of being universal and not yet capable of *being*. This idea involves a contradiction that is not yet contra*diction*, not yet linguistic. What is paradoxical is autonomy *itself*. In it something, any entity, is supposed to prove itself to be reasonable by prescribing for itself the law of its action—but it can prescribe this law as a reasonable one only if it is already capable of this law, of its formulation, and thus of its, if only preemptive, fulfillment. A being, however, that thus fulfills its law has no need for such a law. And if autonomy is aporetic, then identity, singularity, universal applicability, and universality are aporetic along with it. If the lawgiving subject, the subject constituted by the very law that it gives, is aporetic, then so is the object on which this law is imposed, and so is the giving, the good will, and finally the good and the law itself.

Kant did not hesitate to acknowledge this aporia. He spoke of it as a "paradox" and a "circle."[41] He tried to resolve this "paradox" with the hypothesis of the "idea of reason" and the construction of an "empirical character." Yet the aporia of autonomy is not solved but only laid out, ex-posed, and transposed from the pure intelligible character to the outside of language, in the *apodictic* character of the categorical imperative,[42] that is, in the fact that it essentially is spoken (spoken into being: *her-vor-sprechen: apodeiknumi*, to bring to the fore, announce, bring to light in a sign). The aporia of the categorical imperative is the aporia of the apo-dicticity of language: the fact that it already speaks, already pronounces and addresses, without thereby saying something determinate to someone determinate, without already being able to correspond to the categories of the singular or of the universal. The claim of language is formalized in the categorical imperative: to speak in such a way that speech is effectively, permanently, and universally comprehensible. But this claim, this imperative, is still paradoxical, since even its language—otherwise it would not have to be only a *claim* to language—is not yet language, not yet singular and not yet universal. Even the imperative is only the imperative of an imperative. Kant expressly says of the maxim as the subjective principle of action that it itself contains a maxim, that it is thus always the maxim of a maxim.[43] Language is our only autonomy—and this autonomy is not only aporetic, it is aporia "itself." The "paradox" of which Kant speaks is not one among the possible predicates of autonomy, nor is it a predicate that can be denied to autonomy; it indicates autonomy's own pre-dication, its apo-diction, its heterautonomy.

Aporia is autonomy—it *opens up* the determination of the self as self and through the self, without a self already having been given; it *gives* itself to the self and gives itself to it, paradoxically, only in retreat; it *exposes* the self to itself and *lets* it *be* exposed to itself as always another. The experience of aporia is the only possible experience of self-determination that does not deceive itself about the fact that a self, in order to be capable of determining itself, must already be given, and that, in order to be given, it must have been given by itself, but can never be a *given*. It is the only experience that does not deceive itself about the fact that self-legislation (*Selbstgesetz*gebung: the *giving* of law to oneself) must correspond to a self-apprehension, but that only one who is already a self can apprehend himself, and no one can *be* himself without already having apprehended himself. If Kant calls pure spontaneity "reason" and by way of this "reason" solves the "paradox" of autonomy, then this may be understood first in such a way that "reason" [*Vernunft*], the capacity for "apprehension" [*Vernehmen*], is nothing but the experience of the paradox of self-apprehension. Reason is the experience of aporia and thus of "spontaneity" as "self-respondence," as responsibility before oneself not as a given, but as something *to be* given, not as something already perceived, but as an other that is yet *to be* perceived. Reason: this is not what we are ourselves; it is rather the name of the aporia of "our" self-apprehension, the name of the aporia of "our" hearing, of "our" belonging and nonbelonging to "ourselves," even the name of the aporia of every name.

One needs to recall this paradoxical structure of reason if one advocates a politics in the name of reason, or even just a reasonable politics. For reason does not mean this or that partial reason, it does not refer to a sociologically fixable *ratio* of groups or classes, and least of all to the *ratio* of a specific political economy, the capitalist one in particular. Rather, it refers to the claim directed toward the utmost possible universality and thus to the minimal universality of autonomy: but it is a *claim* addressed to itself and as such never a stable, fixed, and finished thing, but always only on the way to itself, a thing of distance.[44]

Autonomy is the autonomy of aporia, it is the autonomy only of a law *giving* which gives the self without having it, and which therefore always only *claims* to give it as an other. This is why autonomy has the dignity and the respect that Kant ascribes to good will, for it is only as an aporia that it is incommensurable, even with its "self," its *autos*. The incommensurable is the only measure that is not given but that gives "itself" and thus does not cease to give and to withhold itself. Only in this way does it bear witness to, and demand respect for, the other person, and for the other, for autonomy itself. It does not count, does not allow itself to be counted—least of all by "itself"—but for this very reason always allows an opening both for numbers or quantifications and for the supernumerary or the innumerable, for the multitudes of politics, economies, and cultures and for their capacity to retreat, again and again, from the system of numbers and valuations, of numberings and namings, of identifications and definitions.

This interpretation of the Kantian minimal law of an ethics of autonomy is not, at least not in all respects, the one that Kant himself gave of it. It is an active interpretation of the "paradox" emphasized by Kant himself, and it is an interpretation that links this paradox to the notions of reason and autonomy without having recourse to the untenable split between the empirical and the intelligible character. It insists on autonomy's being an apo-empirical movement. It is thus an interpretation that gives up neither the aporia nor the autonomy of reason, but which views one in the light of the other and thereby opens the self to the other—to another not reducible to any self. This interpretation thus relates to the philosophical tradition of the politics of autonomy, to this tradition of a *culture* of the *claim* to autonomy, not as to a self-contained canon, not as to *one* tradition and not as to *one* culture. Still less does it relate to this culture as to a *given* and henceforth established one but as to one that itself opens up and demands its transformation. It detaches itself from this culture and tries to continue it. Continue it, that is, with a view toward the theoretical and practical demands, including the political ones, that arise, not only today and not today for the last time, from the idea of autonomy.

But what are the consequences of these very abstract and still too provisional reflections on the logic of autonomy for a politics of democratization? To begin with, there are consequences that are themselves very abstract, but that concern precisely the abstractness and the ideality of Kantian and Kantianizing social and political theories. They concern, among other things, the counterfactual *ideal* of an unlimited communicative community, such as the one envisioned by Jürgen Habermas. This ideal is inevitable since it is a structural feature of finite languages to project their comprehensibility, and even their validity, beyond situational barriers, but it is problematic and even dangerous as soon as it is posited as the ideal of a communication that remains essentially limited to "arguments." Such a limitation amounts to an axiomatic determination that all socially and politically relevant language is and must remain an already-constituted language—meaning a language essentially constituted as argumentation.[45] The ideal of this communicative community is for Habermas dictated by the logic of the argument—but with this reason's claim to unlimited and unconditional autonomy, and thus the very claim that is supposed to found this ideal, has already been given up. Likewise, in the debate on multiculturalism, in which Habermas has participated with a response to Charles Taylor's "politics of recognition," he affirms the claim to autonomy in the abstract, only to negate it *in concreto*. Thus, he insists, along with John Rawls and Ronald Dworkin, on the "neutrality of law" with respect to what he calls, surprisingly, "ethical differentiations within a given society" and declares that "in complex societies"—but why only in these?—"the totality of citizens can no longer be bound together by a substantive value consensus, but only by a consensus about the procedure for legitimate legislation and the exercise of power."[46] Just as socially relevant communication is reduced by Habermas to argumentation, so the presumed neutrality of the law and the formalism of legislative procedures is reduced to a historically, regionally, and culturally limited consensus about the conservation of existing lifeforms. The "procedural consensus" must, Habermas claims, "be embedded, by means of what might be termed constitutional patriotism, in the context of a particular, historically determined, political culture,"[47] and this consensus finds its expression in the "right of a political community to keep its politico-cultural lifeform intact," in "a nation's right to assert its identity."[48] This consensus, the "procedural" one that is "embedded" in "constitutional patriotism," finds its expression, according to Habermas, in the "identity of the community, which must not be affected even by immigration," in the "legitimately asserted identity of the community,"[49] which must protect itself against the influx of immigrants from other cultures. Finally, this consensus finds its expression in the formula of the "limits of capacity" for immigration.[50]

But can the "identity of a community" be de facto left untouched by immigration? Habermas the sociologist ought to know that there is no single argument in favor of this possibility. And can a particular "politico-cultural lifeform," as Habermas asserts, de jure claim the right to remain "intact"? Habermas the moral philosopher ought to know that there is no single tenable philosophical argument for such a right to intactness. Finally, can one appeal, by the principle of democratic autonomy, to "limits of capacity" for absorbing immigrants when what is at issue is the admittance of refugees and asylum seekers who are fleeing either terrorist regimes or countries with a disregard for their democratic claim to self-determination and thus also for the preservation of their lives? Whoever counters the claim to self-determination on the part of refugees and asylum seekers—and every emigrant is a virtual refugee—with the argument of the "limits of capacity" or with the equivalent argument about the positive legal determinations of a consolidated nation-state thereby gives up the claim that is the sole principle of the democracy for whose intact preservation he purports to plead: he gives up the claim to autonomy. Every democracy and every theorist who claims to speak in its name becomes corrupted by resorting to the argument of the "limits of capacity" and for "constitutional-patriotic integrity," for it or he thereby betrays the claim to autonomy, which is always also the claim of an other for autonomy, and the claim for respect, which is always a claim for the unconditional respect for the other. By the "capacity" argument, the sole principle of democracy—active respect for the autonomization of all others—is perverted into the claim for the interests, both the profit interests and the interest in identity, of its "legal community."[51] The transcendental pragmatics of the community of argumentation turns out, at its limits— where it defines itself and differentiates itself from others, where it must show its true colors—to be a transcendental-utilitarianist, profit-motivated egotism and not a new, reasonable foundation of the principle of democratic autonomy. At this limit it also becomes evident that the ideal of argumentation is an ideal of the symmetrical weighing of interests and of an economy of *do ut des*: precisely the economy of the trading of equivalents which Kant had rejected on ethical grounds. This ideal must fail those who can offer no argument other than the threat to their own lives.

Linked to the ideal of argumentation is another, no less questionable ideal, which is held high by theorists of liberalism and which is, it seems to me, not radical enough to be consistent with the principle of a democracy of respect. It is, and here we return to Taylor's reflections, the ideal of recognition. Recognition, a concept which Taylor invokes more than he explains, is taken by him to be the knowledge or cognition of the other, particularly of the other in his value, and, in the case under discussion, of other cultures in their value. Although Taylor explicitly, and with a footnote reference to Kant's *Groundwork of the Metaphysic of Morals*, refers to the above-mentioned definition of dignity and thus to dignity in its difference from value, and although he speaks repeatedly and emphatically of the demand for respect, he assimilates respect to cognition just as he takes dignity and value to be essentially equivalent. Which means nothing less than that Taylor not only flattens the conceptual differentiations in his own text, but also that he obliterates the differences within the philosophical and political culture to which he refers and which he regards as his own—the "North Atlantic civilization."[52] Obliterates them, that is, to his double and triple advantage. First, he can dispense with claims for the differentiation of his "own" philosophical tradition; second, he can write off as contradictory the demands of those he calls multiculturalists; and, third, he can phantasmatically assimilate the two demands to each other: the hollowed-out demand of his "own" culture and the stylized demand of "foreign" cultures.

How, then, does Taylor's liberalism relate to the philosophical tradition he regards as his own, and how does it relate to this tradition such that he need conceive of neither this nor any other tradition as a culture of dissent? For Kant, respect is a "self-produced feeling" that "demolishes my self-love";[53] it is therefore immediate auto- and hetero-affection, auto-as-hetero-affection, and therefore always respect for an other irreducible to any self. This respect for the other always precedes the cognition of the other—as well as its recognition—because the other only ever appears in the perspective of respect, his arrival only occurs in respect, he cannot exist as the object of comparative theoretical cognition and can never exist merely as an object, but only in his pre-objective and pre-subjective arrival. The other is incommensurable only for respect; for cognition it is one among other comparable objects which can be assigned a determinate exchange value. Taylor erases this fundamental difference between respect and cognition, or recognition, when he says, on the one hand, of the spokespersons of other cultures that "they want respect" and, on the other hand, paraphrases their demand as urging "that we all *recognize* the equal value of different cultures; that we not only let them survive, but acknowledge their *worth*."[54] From this difference, which he himself fails to respect, between respect and the attribution of value, between the alterity of the other and his equality, Taylor can then construct, among the claims of other cultures, a contradiction that allows him to dismiss these claims as unacceptable. Taylor writes (thereby pointing out the paradoxical structure of every relationship between supposedly already-constituted identities, values, and standards of value): "The peremptory demand for favorable judgments of worth is paradoxically—perhaps one should say tragically—homogenizing. For it implies that we already have the standards to make such judgments. The standards we have, however, are those of North Atlantic civilization. . . . By implicitly invoking our standards to judge all civilizations and cultures, the politics of difference can end up making everyone the same."[55]

But is it really value judgments that are advanced here, as Taylor claims? Based on his own reference to the demand for "respect," apparently not. And do "we" "have" simple and straightforward measures of value for these supposedly required value judgments? "Have" "we" the "standards" for what Taylor calls "North Atlantic civilization," to which Kant and the declarations of the French Revolution and subsequent emancipation movements also purportedly belong? Again, apparently not, for Taylor himself no longer "has" them—no longer remembers them, no longer has them in mind—when he forgets the Kantian "standard" for the other's dignity, which is a measure no longer of value, but of a value beyond all values, and a measure beyond all measures, the incommensurable, absolute, and absolutely other measure of the other, assimilating it to the "standard" of the exchange of equivalents. Taylor's evocation of "paradoxical"—"and perhaps tragic"—homogenization is therefore possible only because he homogenizes first his "own" philosophical culture and then goes on to homogenize other cultures, assimilating them to his own by redefining the claim to respect as a demand for equal value attribution. On both counts, the claim to respect—indeed, the very concept of respect—falls prey to this homogenization. The only trace left of it in Taylor's argument is his perception of a paradox: the other's demand for equality is paradoxical—or tragic—if at the same time it insists on its alterity.

This is at once true and false. It is true that there is a paradox of recognition and an even graver one of respect for the other. What is false is Taylor's conclusion concerning homogenization. A paradoxical homogenization is simply no longer a homogenization, it is a heterogenization, and this is why it is rejected by Taylor in its logical form, in the form of paradox. "In this form," he reasons on the basis of the law of the excluded middle (*tertium non datur*), "the demand for equal recognition is unacceptable."[56] With this it is clear that Taylor does not accept heterogenization in the form of paradox, does not admit it despite his liberalism of hospitality,[57] because according to the principles of the classical logic "of North Atlantic civilization" he cannot allow a logical inconsistency to stand. Taylor thus argues, according to the primacy of cognition and recognition, as a logician, not as an ethicist of political and cultural claims. His rejection of logical paradox, however, is only possible against the background of the homogenization of logic and ethics and, in addition, the homogenization of logic itself: Taylor "forgets" that at the latest since Cantor's discovery of inconsistent sets, since the formulation of an unsolvable aporia by the logician (and radical liberal) Bertrand Russell, and since Gödel's theorem of undecidability, there is also a logic of aporia in "North Atlantic civilization" and that, since then at the latest, it is not simply possible to reject paradoxical demands on the basis of the "logical" law of contradiction.[58]

Taylor doesn't reject it completely. He rejects it in the logical form of paradox and in the multicultural form of heterogenization, "but," he writes, "the story doesn't simply end there."[59] The story doesn't end in an aporia; it proceeds, according to Taylor, toward an infinite horizon of fusions of value. Having previously cited Gadamer's hermeneutics of the "fusion of horizons," he concludes from the paradoxes of multiculturalism that what is needed is "a willingness to be open to comparative cultural study of the kind that must displace our horizons in the resulting fusions. What it requires above all is an admission that we are very far away from that ultimate horizon from which the relative worth of different cultures might be evident."[60] Taylor thus "solves" the paradoxes, the logical ones as well as the political and ethical ones, by the ideal of fusion. Just as he earlier fused together respect and cognition, dignity and value, the claim to autonomy and the claim to equivalence, just as he quietly fused a strand of a tradition in his "own" culture with another one diametrically opposed to it, the final and only possible solution he counterposes to multiculturalism is a cultural fusionism—and even in it he discerns nothing other than the possibility of assessing "the relative worth of different cultures." He solves the paradox of the relation to the other by a fusion in which the other is forced to give up its alterity and the dignity of its singularity to relative value, the value of equivalence. Taylor counts cultures, and at their horizon, at the limit where they melt, he counts only one, the culture of counted, relative value, the culture of counting.

Each of the "fusions" practiced by Taylor—and this is why he succeeds in them—is in truth an oppression, a marginalization, a disregard precisely for what resists any fusion: a disregard for respect and for dignity, for the claim to singularity and autonomy, and for the excluded middle that can be neither equal nor unequal, and that thus shatters the logical and political economy of the Either/Or. But what is first of all disregarded, marginalized, and domesticated in Taylor's presentation and solution of the paradoxes of multiculturalization are the paradoxes and the tensions in his "own" culture, in the tradition of "his" philosophy and thus precisely that within this tradition which has already taken sides with the other, with other cultures and other possibilities of these other cultures. As always, domestication begins at home. And it is continued "outward" vis-à-vis other cultures by essentially the same means by which dignity is devalued into relative worth, by which autonomy is perverted into quantitative equality, and by which alterity is erased by its fusion: a "politics of fusion" as a continuation of endogenous colonialism, and by the same means.

The principles of radical democracy formulated by Habermas are not democratic enough; the liberalism of hospitality recommended by Taylor is not hospitable and not liberal enough. Both seek a place for the other that will make this other into a partner in dialogue, that will lead to his legal equality, that will secure for him the recognition of his singularity. This is indispensable and urgently necessary. But it presupposes that today's democracies, especially the American and European ones, *begin* by respecting the other as one who is not yet a partner in a dialogue, not yet a partner in trade or in the exchange of commensurable arguments, and who does not yet enjoy the legal equality which a symmetrical relation to those who are still privileged could grant him—who therefore, in brief, is not yet recognized. In order for the recognition of the other to be possible, there must first be respect for the other. For the other to be recognized as having a position of equality, he must first be esteemed, protected, supported, and in some cases protected from himself as an other with no determinate position and outside all forms of symmetry and reciprocity. There can be no recognition without respect: without asymmetry, without nonreciprocity, without a gift that precedes exchange, that opens dialogue, that gives arguments a chance.[61] This respect cannot already be teleologically directed toward reciprocal recognition and dialogical argumentative exchange. It must open up the possibility of recognition under "current" legal conditions, but it must also keep open the possibility of a recognition not limited by such conditions, and thus of a transformation of recognition, a transformation of the paradigm of specular identification, of constitutional narcissism, of the idealization of the given. It must open up the possibility of a dialogue, but must in doing so keep open the possibility that the dialogical form might transform itself. It must make room for arguments, but must concede the possibility that the restrictive form of argumentation might give way to another, more generous, one. Democracy must be democracy for *another*, more just, democracy; and multiculturalism has a real political chance only if it acts as the representative of this other democracy—that is, if it acts not only (but only *also*) as the slow revolution of the third worlds within the first.

Multiculturalism *cannot* be a cultural fusionism. The latter not only allows the culture of others to be pushed aside to the unattainable "horizon" of an "authentic" encounter, it also permits every other culture, the other of the "own" culture or the other of "culture" *tout court*, to be perceived no longer in its alterity but only as a variant of one's own culture. Cultural fusionism permits treating one's own culture as a homogeneous, given fact, ignoring its internal tensions, contradictions, and struggles, and giving oneself over to the fantasy that it is a logical continuum without history and does not always *also* contain the demand to transform that history. But every culture is culture only because it is history: the history of dissent and of separations from previously attained stages of culturization. Each is transculturation, is thus *ac*culturation and *a*culturation, the *interruption* of a culture in its *opening* to another and something other than merely culture. The dissent from every previous, every "given" culture belongs to the project of culture itself: it is not itself if it makes itself conform to the culture already established, it is itself only where it *afforms* itself, where it allows its forms and the form of form itself to be interrupted and to take on other forms, other than the familiar and recognized forms and perhaps something other than a form. Culture is autonomous only in autonomizing itself: in referring first and foremost to that which it is never already itself. But the demand to respect the other in its singularity means respecting this other ever otherwise and thus not in the chimeric unity of its ideal but in its possibilities, in its multiplicity, not by a rule, but in its unregulatability. Always as that which may be still otherwise than other and still more than more.

A multiculturalism for which the unity of a given culture counts as an established fact is still a disguised monoculturalism. A democracy which conceives its unity as a nationally based legal union closed both inwardly and outwardly, and which therefore rejects further demands from inside and from outside is still a mono-democracy; it is not yet a democracy for other—possible—democracies, not yet polydemocracy. As long as this is so—that is, as long as it does not stand up also for the rights and protection of those who "don't belong to it," as long as it is not a dynamic democracy fighting for democratization—its autonomy remains autism, and the forms of antidemocratism that are, if not promoted, then at least tolerated by it (racism, sexism, classism, nationalism, and fundamentalisms of every provenance) must remain virulent within it and outside it. Democratization must reckon with these threats in order not to be discounted.

Multiculturalism must not be a culturalism. It must be concerned neither with the mere conservation of the purported integrity of cultures, nor with their mere perpetuation. A culture that does only this, that is not active—even if inexplicitly and in a mediated fashion—as a protest against social and political injustice and which does not stand for a social and political praxis of justice is nothing but an amusement park, a technique of entertainment, "garbage," as Adorno writes. Culture has already betrayed what is called culture if it does not consistently work against its own corruption, against itself. Walter Benjamin writes of the historical materialist: "For without exception the cultural treasures he surveys have an origin which he cannot contemplate without horror. . . . There is no document of civilization which is not at the same time a document of barbarism. . . . The historical materialist therefore disassociates himself from it as far as possible."[62] If multiculturalism does not want to throw this counsel to the wind, it will have to define itself continuously against the barbarism which threatens it from within and from without, it will have to define itself always and at once as *acculturation and* democratization. Otherwise it remains a mere piece of the domination machine that has not ceased to place "culture" at its service, cunningly or brutally, on all conceivable fronts.

Multiculturalization and democratization can only be an aporetic praxis and a praxis of aporia. They must be the fight for an autonomy of the more than many, of the singular, but this fight can take place only under conditions unfavorable to such autonomy. Autonomy doesn't exist; it must be brought into existence and must not cease to be brought into existence. There cannot be only one autonomy, there would have to be many, innumerably many, and there is only one that would be one too many, which would be one and one only.

... and pomegranates

JACQUES DERRIDA

. . .

Of a discourse to come—on the to-come and repetition. Axiom: no to-come without heritage and the possibility of *repeating*. No to-come without some sort of *iterability*, at least in the form of a covenant with oneself and of a *confirmation* of the originary *yes*. No to-come without some sort of messianic memory and promise, of a messianicity older than all religion, more originary than all messianism. No discourse or address of the other without the possibility of an elementary promise. Perjury and broken promises require the *same* possibility. No promise, therefore, without the promise of a confirmation of the *yes*. This *yes* will have implied and will always imply the trustworthiness and fidelity of a faith. No faith, therefore, nor future without everything technical, automatic, machinal supposed by iterability. In this sense, the technical is the possibility of faith, indeed, its very chance. A chance that entails the greatest risk, even the menace of **radical evil**. Otherwise, that of which it is the chance would not be faith but rather program or proof, predictability or providence, pure knowledge and pure know-how, which is to say: annulment of the future. Instead of being opposed, as is almost always done, the machinal and faith ought to be thought *together*, as *one and the same possibility*. The same holds for the machinal and all the values entailed in the sacrosanct (*heilig*, holy, safe and sound, unscathed, intact, immune, free, vital, fecund, fertile, strong, and, above all, as we will soon see, "swollen")—more precisely in the sacrosanctity of the **phallic** effect.

Translated by Samuel Weber

➤ This double value—is it not, for example, that signified by a phallus in its differentiality, or rather by the **phallic**, *the effect of the phallus*, which is not necessarily the property of man? Is it not the phenomenon, the *phainesthai*, the day of the *phallus*?—but also, by virtue of the law of iterability or of duplication that can *detach* it from its pure and proper presence, is it not also its *phantasma*, in Greek, its ghost, its specter, its double or its fetish? Is it not the *colossal automaticity* of the erection (the maximum of life to be kept unscathed, indemnified, immune and safe, sacro-sanct)— but also and precisely by virtue of its reflex character, that which is most mechanical, most separable from the life it represents? The phallic—is it not also, as distinct from the penis and once detached from the body, the marionette that is erected, exhibited, fetishized, and paraded in processions? Is this not where one grasps, virtuality of virtuality, the power or potency of a logic powerful enough to account for (*logon didonai*)—counting on and calculating the incalculable—everything that binds the tele-technoscientific machine, this enemy of life in the service of life, to the very source and resource of the religious: to faith in the most living as dead and automatically *sur-viving*, resuscitated in its spectral *phantasma*, the holy, safe and sound, unscathed, immune, sacred, in a word, everything that translates *heilig*? Matrix, once again, of a cult or of a culture of the generalized fetish, of an unlimited fetishism, of a fetishizing adoration of the Thing itself. One could, without being arbitrary, read, select, connect everything in the semantic genealogy of the unscathed—"saintly, sacred, safe and sound, *heilig, holy*" —that speaks of force, **life**-force, fertility, growth, augmentation, and above all *swelling*, in the spontaneity of erection or of pregnancy.[1] In brief, it does not suffice to recall here all the phallic cults and their well-known phenomena at the core of so many religions. The three "great monotheisms" have inscribed covenants or founding promises in an *ordeal of the unscathed* that is always a circumcision, be it "exterior or interior," literal or, as was said before Saint Paul, in Judaism itself, "circumcision of the heart." And this would perhaps be the place to inquire why, in the most lethal explosions of a violence that is inevitably ethnico-religious, why on all sides women are privileged victims (not "only" of murders, but also of the rapes and mutilations that precede and accompany them).

➤ The religion of the living—is this not a tautology? Absolute imperative, holy law, law of salvation: saving the living intact, the unscathed, the safe and sound (*heilig*), which has the right to absolute respect, restraint, modesty. Whence the necessity of an enormous task: reconstituting the chain of analogous motifs in the sacro-sanctifying attitude or intentionality, in relation to that which is, should remain, or should be allowed to be what it is (*heilig*, living, strong and fertile, erect and fecund: safe, whole, unscathed, immune, sacred, holy, etc.). Salvation and health. Such an intentional attitude bears several names of the same family: respect, modesty, restraint, inhibition, *Achtung* (Kant), *Scheu, Verhaltenheit, Gelassenheit* (Heidegger), restraint or *holding-back* [*halte*] in general.[2] The poles, themes, causes are not the same (the law, sacredness, holiness, the god to come, etc.), but the movements appear quite analogous in the way they relate to them, *suspending* themselves, and *in truth interrupting themselves*. All of them involve or mark a halt. Perhaps they constitute a sort of universal: not "religion" as such, but a universal structure of religiosity. For if they are not in themselves properly religious, they always open the possibility of the religious without ever being able to limit or restrain it. This possibility remains divided. To be sure, it is respectful or inhibited abstention before what remains sacred mystery, and what ought to remain intact or inaccessible, like the mystical immunity of a secret. But in thus holding back, the same halting also opens an access without mediation or representation, hence not without an intuitive violence, to that which remains unscathed. That is another dimension of the mystical. Such a universal allows or promises perhaps the global translation of *religio*, that is: scruple, respect, restraint, *Verhaltenheit*, reserve, *Scheu*, shame, discretion, *Gelassenheit*, etc. All halt before that which must or should remain safe and sound, intact, unscathed, before what must be allowed to be what it ought to be, sometimes even at the cost of sacrificing itself and in prayer: the other. Such a universal, such an "existential" universality, could have provided at least the mediation of a *scheme* to the globalatinization of *religio*. Or in any case, to its possibility.

What would then be required is, in the same movement, to account for a double postulation: *on the one hand*, the absolute respect of **life**, the "Thou shalt not kill" (at least thy neighbor, if not the living in general), the "fundamentalist" prohibition of abortion, of artificial insemination, of performative intervention in the genetic potential, even if to ends of gene therapy, etc.; *and on the other* (without even speaking of wars of religion, of their terrorism and their killings), the no less universal sacrificial vocation. It was not so long ago that this still involved, here and there, human **sacrifice**, even in the "great monotheisms." It always involves sacrifice of the living, more than ever in large-scale breeding and slaughtering, in the fishing or hunting industries, in animal experimentation. Be it said in passing that certain ecologists and certain vegetarians—at least to the extent that they believe themselves to have remained pure of (unscathed by) all carnivorousness, even symbolic[3]—would be the only "religious" persons of the time to respect one of these two pure sources of religion and indeed to bear responsibility for what could well be the future of a religion. What are the *mechanics* of this double postulation (respect of life and sacrificiality)? I refer to it as *mechanics* because it reproduces, with the regularity of a technique, the instance of the nonliving or, if you prefer, of the dead in the living. It was also the automaton according to the phallic effect of which we spoke above. It was the marionette, the machine dead yet more than living, the spectral fantasy of the dead as the principle of life and of sur-vival (*sur-vie*). This mechanical principle is apparently very simple: life has absolute value only if it is worth *more than* life. And hence only insofar as it mourns, becoming itself in the labor of infinite mourning, in the indemnification of a spectrality without limit. It is sacred, holy, infinitely respectable only in the name of what is worth more than it and what is not restricted to the naturalness of the bio-zoological (sacrificeable)—although true sacrifice ought to sacrifice not only "natural" life, called "animal" or "biological," but also that which is worth more than so-called natural life. Thus, respect for life in the discourses of religion as such concerns "human life" only insofar as it bears witness, in some manner, to the infinite transcendence of that which is worth more than it (divinity, the sacro-sanctness of the law).[4] The price of human life, which is to say, of anthropo-theological life, the price of what ought to remain safe (*heilig*, sacred, safe and sound, unscathed, immune), as the absolute price, the price of what ought to inspire respect, modesty, reticence, this price is priceless. It corresponds to what Kant calls the dignity (*Würdigkeit*) of the end in itself, of the rational finite being, of absolute value beyond all comparative market price (*Marktpreis*). This dignity of life can only subsist beyond the present living being. Whence, transcendence, fetishism, and spectrality; whence, the religiosity of religion. This excess above and beyond the living, whose life has absolute value only by being worth more than life, more than itself—this, in short, is what opens the space of death that is linked to the automaton (exemplarily "phallic"), to technics, the machine, the prosthesis: in a word, to the dimensions of auto-immune and self-sacrificial supplementarity, to this death-drive that is silently at work in every community, every *auto-co-immunity*, constituting it as such in its iterability, its heritage, its spectral tradition. Community as *common auto-immunity*: no community [is possible] that would not cultivate its own auto-immunity, a principle of sacrificial self-destruction ruining the principle of self-protection (that of maintaining its self-integrity intact), and this in view of some sort of invisible and spectral survival. This self-contesting attestation keeps the auto-immune community alive, which is to say, open to something other and more than itself: the other, the future, death, freedom, the coming or the love of the other, the space and time of a spectralizing messianicity beyond all messianism. It is there that the possibility of religion persists: the *religious* bond (scrupulous, respectful, modest, reticent, inhibited) between the value of life, its absolute "dignity," and the theological machine, the "machine for making gods."[5]

➤ Religion, as a response that is both ambiguous and ambivalent {*à double détente et à double entente*}, is thus an ellipse: the ellipsis of **sacrifice**. Is a religion imaginable without sacrifice and without prayer? The sign by which Heidegger believes onto-theology can be recognized is that the relation to the absolute Being or to the supreme Cause has freed itself of both, thereby losing access to sacrificial offering no less than to prayer. But there as well, two sources: the divided law, the double bind, the dual foci, the ellipsis or originary duplicity of religion, consists in that the law of the unscathed, the salvation of the safe, the humble respect of that which is sacro-sanct (*heilig*, holy) *both requires and excludes* sacrifice, which is to say, the indemnification of the unscathed, the price of immunity. Hence: auto-immunization and the sacrifice of sacrifice. The latter always represents the same movement, the price to pay for not injuring or wronging the absolute other. **Violence** of sacrifice in the name of nonviolence. Absolute respect enjoins first and foremost sacrifice of self, of one's most precious interest. If Kant speaks of the "holiness" of the moral law, it is while explicitly holding a discourse on "sacrifice," which is to say, on another instantiation of religion "within the limits of simple reason": the Christian religion as the only "moral" religion. Self-sacrifice thus sacrifices the most proper in the service of the most proper. As though *pure* reason, in a process of auto-immune indemnification, could only oppose religion as such to *a* religion or *pure* faith to this or that belief.

> ➤ In our "wars of religion," **violence** has two ages. The one, already discussed above, appears "contemporary," in synch or in step with the hypersophistication of military tele-technology—of "digital" and cyberspaced culture. The other is a "new archaic violence," if one can put it that way. It counters the first and everything it represents. Revenge. Resorting in fact to the same resources of mediatic power, it *reverts* (according to the return, the resource, the repristination, and the law of internal and auto-immune reactivity we are trying to formalize here) as closely as possible to the body proper and to the premachinal living being. In any case, to its desire and to its phantasm. Revenge is taken against the decorporealizing and expropriating machine by resorting—reverting— to bare hands, to the sexual organs or to primitive tools, often to weapons other than firearms {*l' "arme blanche"*}. What is referred to as "killings" and "atrocities"—words never used in "clean" or "proper" wars, where the dead are no longer counted (guided or "intelligent" missiles are directed at entire cities, for instance)—is here supplanted by tortures, beheadings, and mutilations of all sorts. What is involved is always avowed vengeance, often declared as **sexual** revenge: rapes, mutilated genitals or severed hands, corpses exhibited, heads paraded, as not so long ago in France, impaled on the end of stakes (phallic processions of "natural religions"). This is the case, for example, but it is only an example, in Algeria today, in the name of Islam, invoked by both belligerent parties, each in its own way. These are also symptoms of a reactive and negative recourse, the vengeance of the body proper against an expropriatory and delocalizing tele-technoscience, identified with the globality of the market, with military-capitalistic hegemony, with the globalatinization of the European democratic model, in its double form: secular and religious. Whence—another figure of double origin—the foreseeable alliance of the worst effects of fanaticism, dogmatism, or irrationalist obscurantism with hypercritical acumen and incisive analysis of the hegemonies and the models of the adversary (globalatinization, religion that does not speak its name, ethnocentrism putting on, as always, a show of "universalism," market-driven science and technology, democratic rhetoric,

"humanitarian" strategy, or "keeping the peace" by means of peace-keeping forces, while never counting the dead of Rwanda, for instance, in the same manner as those of the United States of America or of Europe). This archaic and ostensibly more savage radicalization of "religious" violence claims, in the name of "religion," to allow the living community to rediscover its roots, its place, its body and its idiom intact (unscathed, safe, pure, proper). It spreads death and unleashes self-destruction in a desperate (auto-immune) gesture that attacks the blood of its own body: as though thereby to eradicate uprootedness and reappropriate the sacredness of life safe and sound. Double root, double uprootedness, double eradication.

➤ Double rape. A *new cruelty* would thus ally, in wars that are also wars of religion, the most advanced technoscientific calculability with a reactive savagery that would like to attack the body proper directly, the **sexual** thing, which can be raped, mutilated, or simply denied, desexualized—yet another form of the same violence. Is it possible to speak today of this double rape, to speak of it in a way that wouldn't be too foolish, uninformed, or inane, while "ignoring" "psychoanalysis"? Psychoanalysis can be ignored in a thousand ways, sometimes through extensive psychoanalytic knowledge that remains culturally disassociated. Psychoanalysis is ignored when it is not integrated into the most powerful discourses today on right, morality, politics, but also science, philosophy, theology, etc. There are a thousand ways of avoiding such consistent integration, even in the institutional milieu of psychoanalysis. No doubt "psychoanalysis" (we must proceed more and more quickly) is receding in the West; it never broke out, never really broke out of the borders of a part of "old Europe." This "fact" is a legitimate part of the configuration of phenomena, signs, symptoms that we are questioning here under the title of "religion." How can one invoke a new Enlightenment in order to account for this "return of the religious" without bringing into play at least some sort of logic of the unconscious? Without bringing it to bear on the question of radical evil and working out the reaction to radical evil that is at the center of Freudian thought? This question can no longer be separated from many others: the repetition compulsion, the "death drive," the difference between "material truth" and "historical truth" that imposes itself upon Freud with respect to "religion," precisely, and that works itself out above all in closest proximity to an interminable **Jewish Question**. It is true that psychoanalytic knowledge can in turn uproot *and* reawaken faith by opening itself to a new space of testimoniality, to a new instance of attestation, to a new experience of the symptom and of truth. This new space would have to be also, although not exclusively, legal and political. We shall have to return to this.

➤ We are constantly trying to think, albeit otherwise, the interconnectedness of knowledge *and* faith, technoscience *and* religious belief, calculation *and* the sacrosanct. In the process we have not ceased to encounter the alliance, holy or not, of the calculable and the incalculable. As well as that of the innumerable and of number, of the binary and of the digital. Demographic calculation, for instance, today concerns *one* of the aspects, at least, of the "religious question" in its geopolitical dimension. As for the future of a religion, the question of number concerns as much the quantity of "populations" as the living indemnity of "peoples." This does not merely signify that the religious factor has to be taken into account, but that the manner in which the faithful are counted must be changed in an age of globalization. Whether it is "exemplary" or not, the **Jewish question** continues to be a rather good example (sample, particular case) for future elaboration of this demographic-religious problematic. In truth this question of *numbers* obsesses, as is well known, the Holy Scriptures and the monotheisms. When they feel themselves threatened by an **expropriative and delocalizing** tele-technoscience, "peoples" also fear new forms of invasion. They are terrified by alien "populations," whose growth as well as presence, indirect or virtual—but as such, all the more oppressive—becomes incalculable. New ways of counting, therefore. There is more than one way of interpreting the unheard-of survival of the small "Jewish people" and the global extension of its religion, single source of the two monotheisms which share in a certain domination of the world and of which, in dignity at least, it is the equal. There are a thousand ways of interpreting its resistance to attempts at extermination as well as to a demographic disproportion, the likes of which is not known. But what will come of this survival the day (already arrived, perhaps) when globalization will be saturated? Then "globalization," a term so frequently encountered in American discourse,[6] will perhaps no longer allow the surface of the human earth to be segmented into micro-climates, those historical, cultural, political micro-zones, little Europe and the Middle East, in which the Jewish people has had such great difficulty surviving and bearing witness to its faith. "I understand Judaism as the possibility of giving the Bible a context, of keeping this book readable," says Levinas. Does not the globalization of demographic reality and calculation render the probability of such a "context" weaker than ever and as threatening for survival as the worst, the radical evil of the "final solution"? "God is the future" says Levinas—while Heidegger sees the "last god" announcing himself in the very absence of a future: "The last god: his occurring [Wesung] is found in the hint [im Wink], in the onset of an arrival still outstanding [dem Anfall und Ausbleib der Ankunft], as well as in the flight of gods that are past and of their hidden metamorphosis."[7]

This question is perhaps the most grave and most urgent for the state and the nations of Israel, but it also concerns all the Jews, and doubtless also, if less obviously, all the Christians in the world. Not at all Moslems today. And to this day, this is a fundamental difference between the three original "great monotheisms."

➤ Is there not always another *place* of dispersion? Where the source today divides itself again, like *the same* dissociating itself between faith and knowledge? The original reactivity to an **expropriative and delocalizing** tele-technoscience must respond to at least two figures. These are superimposed upon one another; they relay or replace each other, producing in truth at the very place of the emplacement only indemnifying and auto-immune supplementarity:

(1) violent sundering {arrachement}, to be sure, from the radicality of roots (Ent-würzelung, Heidegger would say . . .) and from all forms of originary *phūsis*, from all the supposed resources of a force held to be authentically generative, sacred, unscathed, "safe and sound" (heilig): ethnic identity, descent, family, nation, blood and soil, proper name, proper idiom, proper culture and memory;

(2) but also, more than ever, the counter-fetishism of the same desire inverted, the animist relation to the tele-technoscientific machine, which then becomes a machine of evil, and of radical evil, but a machine to be manipulated as much as to be exorcised. Because this evil is to be domesticated and because one increasingly *uses* artifacts and prostheses of which one is totally ignorant, in a growing disproportion between knowledge and know-how, the space of such technical experience tends to become more animistic, magical, mystical. The spectral aspect of this experience persists and then tends to become—in proportion to this disproportion, one might say—increasingly **primitive and archaic**. So much so that its

rejection, no less than its apparent appropriation, can assume the form of a religiosity that is both structural and invasive. A certain ecologist spirit can participate in this. (But a distinction must be drawn here between a vague ecologist ideology and ecological discourses and politics, which are often both competent and rigorous.) Never in the history of humanity, it would seem, has the disproportion between scientific incompetence and manipulatory competence been as serious. It can no longer even be measured with respect to machines that are used every day, with a mastery that is taken for granted and whose proximity is ever closer, more interior, more domestic. To be sure, in the recent past every soldier did not *know* how his firearm functioned although he *knew* very well how to use it. Yesterday, all the drivers of automobiles or travelers in trains did not always know very well "how it works." But their relative incompetence stands in no common (quantitative) measure nor in any (qualitative) analogy with that which today characterizes the relationship of the major part of humanity to the machines from which they live or with which they strive to live in daily familiarity. Who is capable of explaining scientifically to children how telephones function today (by undersea cables or by satellite)? The same is true for television, fax, computer, electronic mail, cd-roms, magnetic cards, jet planes, the distribution of nuclear energy, scanners, echography, etc.

➢ The same religiosity is obliged to ally the reactivity of the **primitive and archaic** return, as we have already said, *both* to obscurantist dogmatism *and* to hypercritical vigilance. The machines it combats by striving to appropriate them are also machines for destroying historical tradition. They can displace the traditional structures of national citizenship; they tend to efface both the borders of the state and the distinctive properties of languages. As a result, the religious reaction (rejection and assimilation, introjection and incorporation, impossible indemnification and mourning) normally follows two avenues that compete with each other and are apparently antithetical. Both of them, however, can as easily oppose or support a "democratic" tradition: *either* the fervent return to national citizenship (patriotism of the *home* in all its forms, affection for the nation-state, awakening of nationalism or of ethnocentrism, most often allied with churches or religious authorities) *or*, on the contrary, a protest that is universal, cosmopolitan, or ecumenical: "Ecologists, humanists, believers of all countries, unite in an International of anti-teletechnologism!" What is involved here, moreover, is an International that—and it is the singularity of our time—can only develop through the networks it combats, using the means of the adversary. At the same speed against an adversary that in truth is the same. The same (but) double, which is to say, what is called the contemporary in the blatant anachrony of its dislocation. Auto-immune indemnification. This is why these "contemporary" movements are obliged to seek their salvation (the safe and sound as the sacrosanct), as well as their health, in the paradox of a new alliance between the tele-technoscientific and the *two* sources of religion (the unscathed, *heilig*, *holy*, on the one hand, and faith or belief, the fiduciary on the other). The "humanitarian" would provide a good example of this. "Peacekeeping forces" as well.

➤ Of what should one take particular note in trying to formalize, in a concise manner, the axiom of the **two** sources around each of the two "logics" if you like, or each of the two distinct "resources" of what in the West goes by the Latinate name "religion"? Let us remember the hypothesis of these two sources: on the one hand, the fiduciar*ity* of confidence, trustworthiness {*fiabilité*} or of trust {*fiance*} (belief, faith, credit, etc.), and on the other, the unscathed*ness* of the unscathed (the safe and sound, the immune, the holy, the sacred, *heilig*). Perhaps what ought first to be stressed is this: each of these axioms, as such, already reflects and presupposes the other. An *axiom* always affirms, as its name indicates, a value, a price; it confirms or promises an evaluation that should remain intact and entail, like every value, an act of faith. Second, each of these two axioms renders possible, but not necessary, something like a religion, which is to say, an instituted apparatus consisting of dogmas or of articles of faith that are both determinate and inseparable from a given historical *socius* (Church, clergy, socially legitimated authority, people, shared idiom, community of the faithful committed to the same faith and sanctioning the same history). But the gap between the opening of this *possibility (as a universal structure)* and the *determinate necessity* of this or that religion will always remain irreducible; and sometimes (it operates) within each religion, between, on the one hand, that which keeps it closest to its "pure" and proper possibility, and, on the other, its own historically determined necessities or authorities. Thus, one can always criticize, reject, or combat this or that form of sacredness or of belief, even of religious authority, in the name of the most originary possibility. Such possibility can be *universal* (faith or trustworthiness, "good faith" as the condition of testimony, of the social bond and even of the most radical questioning) or already *particular*, for example, belief in a specific originary event of revelation, of promise or of injunction, as in the reference to the Tables of the Law, to early Christianity, to some fundamental word or scripture, more archaic and more pure than all clerical or theological discourse. But it seems impossible to deny the *possibility* in whose name—thanks to which—the derived *necessity* (the authority or determinate belief) would be put into question, suspended, rejected, or criticized, even deconstructed. One can *not* deny it, which means that the most one can do is to deny it. Any discourse that would be opposed to it would, in effect, always succumb to the figure or the logic of denial {*dénégation*}. Such would be the place where, before and after all the Enlightenments in the world, reason, critique, science, tele-technoscience, philosophy, **thought** in general, retain the *same* resource as religion in general.

➤ This last proposition, in particular insofar as it concerns **thought**, calls for several essential qualifications. It is impossible here to devote to it the necessary elaborations or to multiply, which would be easy, references to all those who, before and after all the Enlightenments in the world, believed in the independence of critical reason, of knowledge, technics, philosophy, and thought with respect to religion and even to all faith. Why then privilege the example of Heidegger? Because of its extreme character and of what it tells us, in these times, about a certain "extremity." . . . Heidegger wrote in a letter to Löwith, in 1921: "I am a 'Christian theologian.'"[8] This declaration would merit extended interpretation and certainly does not amount to a simple declaration of faith. But it neither contradicts, annuls, nor excludes this other certainty. Heidegger not only declared, very early and on several occasions, that philosophy was in its very principle "atheistic," that the idea of philosophy is "madness" for faith (which at the least supposes the converse), and the idea of a Christian philosophy as absurd as a "squared circle." He not only excluded the very possibility of a philosophy of religion. He not only proposed a radical separation between philosophy and theology, the positive study of faith, if not between thought and theology,[9] the discourse on the divinity of the divine. He not only attempted a "destruction" of all forms of the onto-theological, etc. He also wrote, in 1953: "Belief [or faith] has no

337

place in thought [*Der Glaube hat im Denken keinen Platz*]."[10] The context of this firm declaration is, to be sure, rather particular. The word *Glaube* seems to concern *first of all* a form of belief: credulity or the blind acceptance of authority. Heidegger was concerned with translating a *Spruch* (a saying, a sentence, decree, decision, poem, in any case a saying that cannot be reduced to its statement, whether theoretical, scientific, or even philosophical, and that is tied in a singular and performative way to language). In a passage that concerns presence (*Anwesen, Präsenz*) and presence in the representation of representing (*in der Repräsentation des Vorstellens*), Heidegger writes: "We can not scientifically prove [*beweisen*] the translation nor ought we simply by virtue of any authority put our trust in it [accredit it, believe it; *glauben*]. The reach of proof ['scientific' is to be inferred] is too short. Belief has no place in thinking [*Der Glaube hat im Denken keinen Platz*]." Heidegger thus dismisses, back to back, scientific proof (which might suggest that to the same extent he accredits nonscientific testimony) and belief, here credulous and orthodox confidence that, closing its eyes, acquiesces and dogmatically sanctions authority (*Autorität*). Certainly, and who would contradict this? But Heidegger still extends with force and radicality the assertion that belief *in general* has no place in the experience or the act of thinking *in general*. And there we have difficulty following him. First, along his own path. Even if one succeeds in averting, in as rigorous a manner as possible, the risk of confusing modalities, levels, contexts, it still seems difficult to dissociate faith in general (*Glaube*) from what Heidegger himself, under the name of *Zusage* ("accord, acquiescing, trust or confidence"), designates as that which is most irreducible, indeed most originary in thought, prior even to the questioning said by him to constitute the piety (*Frömmigkeit*) of thinking. It is well known that without calling this last affirmation into question, he subsequently explained that it is the *Zusage* that constitutes the most proper movement of thinking, and that without it (although Heidegger does not state it in this form) the question itself would not emerge.[11] This recall to a sort of faith, this recall to the trust of the *Zusage*, "before" all questioning, thus "before" all knowledge, all philosophy, etc., finds a particularly striking formulation relatively late (1957). It is formulated in the form—rare for Heidegger, whence the interest often attached to it—not of self-criticism or remorse, but of a return to a formulation that demands to be nuanced, refined, let us say, to be reengaged differently. But this gesture is less novel and singular than it might seem. Perhaps we will try to show elsewhere (it would require more time and space) that it accords with everything which, from the existential analytics of the thought of being and of the truth of being on, reaffirms continuously what we will call (in Latin, alas, and in a manner too Roman for Heidegger) a certain *testimonial sacredness*, or, we would even go so far as to say, a sworn word {*foi jurée*}.

This reaffirmation continues throughout Heidegger's entire work. It resides in the decisive and largely underestimated motif of attestation (*Bezeugung*) in *Being and Time*, as well as in all the other motifs that are inseparable from and dependent upon it, which is to say, *all* the existentials and, specifically, that of conscience (*Gewissen*), originary responsibility or guilt (*Schuldigsein*), and *Entschlossenheit* (resolute determination). We can not address here the immense question of the ontological repetition, in all these concepts, of a so markedly Christian tradition. Let us therefore limit ourselves to situating a principle of reading. Like the experience of authentic attestation (*Bezeugung*) and like everything that depends upon it, the point of departure in *Being and Time* resides in a situation that cannot be radically alien to what is called *faith*. Not religion, to be sure, nor theology, but that which in faith acquiesces before or beyond all questioning, in the already common experience of a language and of a "we." The reader of *Being and Time* and the signatory who takes him as witness are already situated in this element of this faith from the moment when Heidegger says "we" to justify the choice of the "exemplary" being that is *Dasein*, the questioning being that must be interrogated as an exemplary witness. And what renders possible, for this "we," the positing and elaboration of the question of being, the unfolding and determining of its "formal structure" (*das Gefragte, das Erfragte, das Befragte*), *prior to all questioning*—is it not what Heidegger then calls a *Faktum*, that is, the vague and ordinary pre-comprehension of the meaning of being, and first of all of the words "is" or "be" in language or in a language (§ 2)? This *Faktum* is not an empirical fact. Each time Heidegger employs this word, we are necessarily led back to a zone where acquiescence is *de rigueur*. Whether this is formulated or not, it remains a requirement prior to and in view of every possible question, and hence prior to all philosophy, all theology, all science, all critique, all reason, etc. This zone is that of a faith incessantly reaffirmed throughout an open chain of concepts, beginning with those that we have already cited (*Bezeugung, Zusage*, etc.), but it also communicates with everything in Heidegger's way of thinking that marks the reserved holding back of restraint (*Verhaltenheit*) or the sojourn (*Aufenthalt*) in modesty (*Scheu*) in the vicinity of the unscathed, the sacred, the safe and sound (*das Heilige*), the passage or the coming of the last god that man is doubtless not yet ready to receive.[12] That the movement proper to this faith does not constitute a religion is all too evident. Is it, however, untouched (*indemne*) by all religiosity? Perhaps. But by all "belief," by the "belief" that would have "no place in thinking"? This seems less certain. Since the major question remains, in our eyes, albeit in a form that is still quite new, "What does it mean to believe?," we will ask (elsewhere) how and why Heidegger can at the same time affirm one of the possibilities of the "religious," of which we have just schematically recalled the signs (*Faktum, Bezeugung, Zusage, Verhaltenheit, Heilige*, etc.), and reject so energetically "belief" or "faith" (*Glaube*).[13] Our hypothesis again refers back to the two sources or two strata of religion which we distinguished above: the experience of sacredness and the experience of belief. More receptive to the first (in its Greco-Hölderlinian or even archeo-Christian tradition), Heidegger was probably more resistant to the second, which he constantly reduced to figures he never ceased to put into question, not to say "destroy" or denounce: dogmatic or credulous belief in authority, to be sure, but also belief according to the religions of the Book and onto-theology, and above all, that which in the belief in the other could appear to him (wrongly, we would say) to appeal necessarily to the egological subjectivity of an alter ego. We are speaking here of the belief that is demanded, required, of the faithful belief in what, having come from the utterly other (*de l'autre tout autre*), there where its originary presentation in person would forever be impossible (**witnessing** or given word in the most elementary and irreducible sense, promise of truth up to and including perjury), would constitute the condition of *Mitsein*, of the relation to or address to the other in general.

➤ Beyond the culture, semantics, or history of law—all, moreover, intertwined—which determine this word or this concept, the experience of **witnessing** situates a convergence of *these* two sources: the *unscathed* (the safe, the sacred, or the saintly) and the *fiduciary* (trustworthiness, fidelity, credit, belief, or faith, "good faith" implied in the worst "bad faith"). We speak of these two sources *there*, in one place of their convergence, for the figure of the two sources, as we have verified, proliferates, can no longer be counted, and therein lies perhaps another necessity of our interrogation. In testimony, truth is promised beyond all proof, all perception, all intuitive demonstration. Even if I lie or perjure myself (and always and especially when I do), I promise truth and ask the other to believe the other that I am, there where I am the only one able to bear witness and where the order of proof or of intuition will never be reducible to or homogeneous with the elementary trust {*fiduciarité*}, the "good faith" that is promised or demanded. The latter, to be sure, is never pure of all iterability or of all technics, and hence of all **calculability**. It also promises its repetition from the very first instant. It is involved {*engagé*} in every address to the other. From the first instant it is coextensive with this other and thus conditions every "social bond," every questioning, all knowledge, performativity and every tele-technoscientific performance, including those of its forms that are the most synthetic, artificial, prosthetic, calculable. The act of faith demanded in bearing witness exceeds, through its structure, all intuition and all proof, all knowledge. ("I swear that I am telling the truth, not necessarily the 'objective truth,' but the truth of what I believe to be the truth, I am telling you this truth, believe me, believe what I believe, there, where you will never be able to see nor know the irreplaceable yet universalizable, exemplary place from which I speak to you; perhaps my testimony is false, but I am sincere and in good faith, it is not false {as} testimony.") What, therefore, does the promise of this axiomatic (quasi-transcendental) performative do that conditions and foreshadows "sincere" declarations no less than lies and perjuries, and thus all address to the other? It amounts to saying: "Believe what I say as one believes in a miracle." Even the slightest testimony concerning the most plausible, ordinary, or everyday thing cannot do otherwise: it must still appeal to faith as would a miracle. It offers itself like the miracle in a space that leaves no room for disenchantment. The experience of disenchantment, however indubitable it is, is only one modality of this "miraculous" experience, the reactive and passing effect, in each of its historical determinations, of the testimonially miraculous. That one should be called upon to believe in testimony as in a miracle or an "extraordinary story"—this is what inscribes itself without hesitation in the very concept of bearing witness. And one should not be amazed to see examples of "miracles" invading all the problematics of testimony, whether they are classical or not, critical or not. *Pure* attestation, if

341

there is such a thing, pertains to the experience of faith and of the miracle. Implied in every "social bond," however ordinary, it also renders itself indispensable to Science no less than to Philosophy and to Religion. This source can collect or scatter itself, re-join or dis-join itself. Either at the same time or successively. It can appear contemporaneous with itself where testimonial trust in the pledge {gage} of the other unites belief in the other with the sacralization of a presence-absence or with a sanctification of the law, as law of the other. It can divide itself in various ways. First of all, in the alternative between sacredness without belief (index of this algebra: "Heidegger") and faith in a holiness without sacredness, in a desacralizing truth, even making of a certain disenchantment the condition of authentic holiness (index: "Levinas"—notably the author of *From the Sacred to the Holy*). As a follow-up, it can dissociate itself when what constitutes the "social bond" in belief is also an interruption. There is no opposition, fundamentally, between "social bond" and "social unraveling." A certain interruptive unraveling is the condition of the "social bond," the very respiration of all "community." This is not even the knot of a reciprocal condition, but rather the possibility that every knot can come undone, be cut or interrupted. This is where the *socius* or the relation to the other would disclose itself as the secret of testimonial experience—and hence, of a certain faith. If belief is the ether of the address and relation to the utterly other, it is {to be found} in the experience of non-relationship or of absolute *interruption* (indices: "Blanchot," "Levinas". . .). Here as well, the hypersanctification of this non-relation or of this transcendence would come about by way of desacralization rather than through secularization or laicization, concepts that are too Christian; perhaps even by way of a certain "atheism," in any case by way of a radical experience of the resources of "negative theology"—and going beyond even this tradition. Here we would have to separate—thanks to another vocabulary, for example, Hebraic (the holiness of *kidouch*)—the sacred and the holy, and no longer settle for the Latinate distinction, recalled by Benveniste, between the natural sacredness in things and the holiness of institutions or of the law.[14] This interruptive disjunction enjoins a sort of incommensurable equality within absolute dissymmetry. The law of this untimeliness interrupts and makes history, it undoes all contemporaneity and opens the very space of faith. It designates disenchantment as the *very resource of the religious*. The first and the last. Nothing seems therefore more uncertain, more difficult to sustain, nothing seems here or there more imprudent than a self-assured discourse on the age of disenchantment, the era of secularization, the time of laicization, etc.

➤ **Calculability:** question, apparently arithmetic, of two, or rather of n + One, through and beyond the demography of which we spoke above. Why should there always have to be *more than one* source? There would not have to be two sources of religion. There would be faith and religion, faith or religion, because *there are at least two.* Because there are, for the best and for the worst, division and iterability of the source. This supplement introduces the incalculable at the heart of the calculable. (Levinas: "It is this being-two {*être à deux*} that is human, that is spiritual.") But the One {no} more {*plus d'Un*}[15] is at once more than two. There is no alliance of two, unless it is to signify, in effect, the pure madness of pure faith. The worst violence. The One {no} more is this n + One, which introduces the order of faith or of trust in the address of the other, but also the mechanical, machinelike division (testimonial affirmation and reactivity, "yes, yes," etc., answering machine and the possibility of **radical evil**: perjury, lies, remote-control murder, ordered at a distance even when it rapes and kills with bare hands).

➤ The possibility of **radical evil** both destroys and institutes the religious. Onto-theology does the same when it suspends sacrifice and prayer, the truth of this prayer that maintains itself, recalling Aristotle one more time, beyond the true and the false, beyond their opposition, in any case, according to a certain concept of truth or of judgment. Like benediction, prayer pertains to the originary regime of testimonial faith or of martyrdom that we are trying to think here in its most "critical" force. Onto-theology en**crypts** faith and destines it to the condition of a sort of Spanish Marrano who would have lost—in truth: dispersed, multiplied—everything up to and including the memory of his unique secret. Emblem of a still life, of a *nature morte*: a pomegranate, one Passover evening, cut open on a tray.

➤ At the bottom without bottom of this **crypt**, the One + n incalculably engenders all these supplements. *It makes violence of itself, does violence to itself and keeps itself from the other.* The auto-immunity of religion can only indemnify itself without assignable end. On the bottom without bottom of an always virgin impas-

343

sibility, *khōra* of tomorrow in languages we no longer know or do not yet speak. This place is unique, it is the One without name. It *makes way, perhaps*, but without the slightest generosity, either divine or human. The scattering of ashes is not even promised there, nor death given.

.   .   .

Notes

Notes

de Vries and Weber, "Introduction"

1. The paper that Derrida contributed to the Amsterdam colloquium, "Archive Fever: A Freudian Impression," has been published in *diacritics* 25, no. 2 (Summer 1995): 9–64.

2. The French text of this essay is available in Jacques Derrida and Gianni Vattimo, eds., *La religion* (Paris: Editions du Seuil, 1996), 9–86. (English publication forthcoming from Stanford University Press.)

de Vries, "Violence and Testimony"

1. Emmanuel Levinas, *Difficult Freedom: Essays on Judaism*, trans. Seán Hand (Baltimore: The Johns Hopkins University Press, 1990), 296 n. 4, translation modified. On Weil, see also E. Levinas, *En découvrant l'existence avec Husserl et Heidegger* (Paris: Vrin, 1972) 189.

2. Emmanuel Levinas, *Entre nous: Essais sur le penser-à-l'autre* (Paris: Grasset, 1991), 34.

3. See Emmanuel Levinas, *Totalité et infini: Essai sur l'extériorité* (The Hague: Martinus Nijhoff, 1961), 259.

4. Levinas, *Difficult Freedom*, 6.

5. Ibid., 6–7; my italics.

6. For this terminology, see Eric Weil, *Logique de la philosophie*, 2d ed. (Paris: Vrin, 1967), 59. The important third part of the introduction to this work is entitled "Philosophie et violence," and its first section carries the title "La violence et le discours" (54–86).

7. Jacques Derrida, *Writing and Difference*, trans. Alan Bass (Chicago: University of Chicago Press, 1978), 315 n. 42.

8. Ibid., 95.

9. Emmanuel Levinas, "Transcendence et hauteur," *Cahier de l'Herne*, ed. Catherine Chalier and Miguel Abensour (Paris: l'Herne, 1991) 64; see also 72. See *Totalité et infini*, xii, and Derrida, *Writing and Difference*, 153.

10. See Eric Weil, *Philosophie et réalité: Derniers essays et conférences* (Paris: Beauchesne, 1982), 23 ff., notably pp. 50 and 95 ff.

11. Ibid., 24.

12. Ibid., 49–50.

13. See Weil, *Logique de la philosophie*, 57.

14. Ibid., 56. 15. Ibid., 10.

16. Ibid., 11. 17. Ibid.

18. Ibid., 188. 19. Ibid., 179.

20. Ibid., 65. 21. Ibid., 59.

22. Cf. ibid., 68.

23. Weil, *Philosophie et Réalité*, 56.

24. Derrida, *Writing and Difference*, 315 n. 42.

25. Levinas, *Difficult Freedom*, 7.

26. Emmanuel Levinas, *Collected Philosophical Papers*, trans. Alphonso Lingis (Dordrecht: Martinus Nijhoff, 1987), 54 (translation modified).

27. Ibid.

28. Derrida, *Writing and Difference*, 315 n. 42.

29. Weil, *Logique de la philosophie*, 61.

30. Derrida, *Writing and Difference*, 152.

31. Ibid., 313 n. 21. 32. Ibid., 146–47.

33. Ibid. 34. Ibid., 147–48.

35. Ibid., 148. 36. Ibid., 117.

37. See my "Adieu, à dieu, a-dieu," in A. Peperzak, ed., *Ethics as First Philosophy* (London: Routledge, 1995) 211–20.

38. J. Wahl, "Introduction," S. Kierkegaard, *Crainte et tremblement: Lyrique-dialectique par Johannès de Silentio*, trans. P.-H. Tisseau (Paris: Aubier Montaigne, 1984), viii.

39. Ibid., ix. Later in the text, Wahl reminds us that at one point Kierkegaard had considered explaining the sacrifice demanded of Abraham on the basis of some fault or prior sin. The reason he renounces this idea, Wahl notes, following the study by Geismar (*Sören Kierkegaard* [Göttingen, 1929]), is that the *mysterium tremendum* that forms the "element" of all fear and trembling is here taken to reveal God's "*grandeur*" rather than our limitation. Sin will be the subject of *The Concept of Anxiety* and *The Sickness unto Death*. In *Fear and Trembling*, Wahl concludes, it is suggested that to locate the terrible flipside of our condition—and, indeed, of all faith—in an original sin is somehow "facile" (xviii n. 1). Kierkegaard's reasoning at this point demonstrates at least a formal resemblance to the Kantian doctrine of radical evil, whose nature is also incommensurable with any previous trespass. Yet for Kant the *tremendum* is neither a quality nor an aspect of God's *grandeur*. It is not so much the other side of God but God's other, albeit a counterpart which is at least equally inscrutable.

40. Ibid., xiv.

41. Ibid., xvii–xviii.

42. Ibid., xii; cf. ibid., xvi–xvii: "L'instant qui commence l'éternité prend place dans un processus long et douloureux. Durée et instant éternels sont intimement mêlés l'un à l'autre."

43. Jacques Derrida, *The Gift of Death*, trans. David Wills (Chicago: University of Chicago Press, 1995), 65.

44. Wahl, "Introduction," xxiv.

45. Ibid., xxv.

46. Ibid., xix–xx.

47. *Totalité et Infini*, xiii.

48. Jean-Luc Nancy, *The Experience of Freedom*, trans. Bridget McDonald (Stanford: Stanford University Press, 1994), 204, n. 2.

49. Emmanuel Levinas, *De dieu qui vient à l'idée* (Paris: Vrin, 1982), 111.

50. Emmanuel Levinas, *Autrement qu'être ou au-delà de l'essence* (The Hague: Martinus Nijhoff, 1974), 143.

51. Levinas, *De dieu qui vient l'idée*, 110.

52. Levinas, *Collected Philosophical Papers*, 176.

53. Levinas, *En découvrant l'existence avec Husserl et Heidegger*, 215.

54. If Kierkegaard's discussion is less a critique of Kant than of Hegel, responding to the section on "the good and conscience" in the *Philosophy of Right*, we should not forget that for Hegel the moment of ethical decision also comes to pass in a transition from mere violence to legitimate force, in particular, in the sublation of subjective violence in objective *Gewalt*. One is reminded here of the trajectory whose telos is the paragraphs devoted to the State, notably the staggering affirmation that for modern subjects "sacrifice for the individuality of the state is the substantial relation of everyone and therefore a *universal duty*," *Elements of the Philosophy of Right*, trans. H. B. Nisbet, ed. Allen W. Wood (Cambridge: Cambridge University Press, 1991), 363.

55. Derrida, *The Gift of Death*, 63.

56. Jacques Derrida, *Aporias*, trans. Thomas Dutoit (Stanford: Stanford University Press, 1993), 16–17.

57. Kierkegaard, *Fear and Trembling*, ed. and trans. Howard V. Hong and Edna H. Hong (Princeton: Princeton University Press, 1983), 35–36.

58. Ibid., 46.

59. Ibid.

60. Ibid., 47.

61. Derrida, *The Gift of Death*, 66.

62. Kierkegaard, *Fear and Trembling*, 47.

63. Ibid.

64. Ibid., 52.

65. Ibid., 53.

66. Ibid., 23; cf. Plato, *Phaedrus*, 244–45 c, 265 b.

67. Levinas, "La mort et le temps," 26; cf. *Autrement qu'être ou au-delà de l'essence*, 49–55.

68. Derrida, *The Gift of Death*, 82.

69. Ibid., 76.

70. Ibid., 78.

71. Ibid., 68.

72. Emmanuel Levinas, *Autrement qu'être ou au-delà de l'essence*, (The Hague: Martinus Nijhoff) 145.

73. Derrida, *The Gift of Death*, 61.

74. Ibid., 70.

75. Ibid., 68; see also Jacques Derrida, *Spectres de Marx* (Paris: Galilée, 1993), 273.

76. Derrida, *The Gift of Death*, 78.

77. Cf. ibid., 29–30: "a gift that could be recognized as such in the light of day, a gift destined for recognition, would immediately annul itself. The gift is the secret itself, if the secret *itself* can be told. Secrecy is the last word of the gift which is the last word of the secret."

78. Ibid., 78–79. Along different lines, Levinas continues to insist on a difference between the Other as God and the Other as *autrui*, as neighbor (the difference between "us" and God seems to be beyond question here): "Je ne peux pas décrire la relation à Dieu sans parler de ce qui m'engage à l'égard d'autrui. Je cite toujours, quand je parle à un Chrétien, *Matthieu 25*: la relation à Dieu y est présentée comme une relation à l'autre homme. Ce n'est pas une métaphore: en autrui il y a présence réelle de Dieu. Dans ma relation à autrui j'entends la Parole de Dieu . . . c'est vrai à la lettre. Je ne dis pas qu'autrui est Dieu" (*Entre nous: Essais sur le penser-à-l'autre* [Paris: Grasset, 1991], 128). The circumstance that the Other as God leaves only his trace in the face of the other Other that is the visage of *autrui* gives rise to a paradox. On the one hand, the difference in the analogy between the in-finite and Other as God and the ab-solute as *autrui* explains why there can be no strict or absolute distinction between the ethical in general (or, for that matter, the ethical as the general) and the religious, as *Fear and Trembling* suggests. On the other hand, Derrida observes that since Levinas wishes to uphold a certain indelible difference between the two Others— God, the Infinite, the Illeity "is" neither a Thou nor a grand *Autrui*—he cannot say or write something that is completely different from what Kierkegaard intends (*The Gift of Death*, 83–84). As a consequence, the relation to the Other can no longer be seen as simply or exclusively ethical. As long as one holds God and the Other, *autrui*, at a distance from each other, ethics and religion, as relations to the totally other, cannot coincide totally. Nor, for that matter, can they be separated totally.

79. Derrida, *The Gift of Death*, 80.

80. Ibid.

81. Cf. Levinas, *Autrement qu'être ou au-delà de l'essence*, 136: "Indicible et, par là même, unjustifiable."

82. *Autrement qu'être ou au-delà de l'essence*, 143; cf. Emmanuel Levinas, *De dieu qui vient à l'idée* (Paris: Vrin, 1982), 120: "la fission du sujet est une croissance de l'obligation au fur et à mesure de mon obéissance, l'augmentation de la culpabilité avec l'augmentation de la sainteté, accroisement de la distance au fur et à mesure de mon approche."

83. Emmanuel Levinas, "Diachrony and Representation," *Time and the Other*, trans. Richard A. Cohen (Pittsburgh: Duquesne University Press, 1987), 97–120, 110 (translation modified).

84. *Transcendence et intelligibilité* (Geneva: Labor et Fides, 1984), 26.

85. Cf. Derrida, *The Gift of Death*, 73.

86. Derrida, *Aporias*, 64.

87. Derrida, *The Gift of Death*, 66.

88. See ibid., 70.

89. Ibid., 47.

90. Ibid., 49.

91. Ibid.

92. Ibid.

93. Ibid.

94. Cf. ibid., 25–26: "We must continually remind ourselves that some part of irresponsibility insinuates itself wherever one demands responsibility without sufficiently conceptualizing and thematizing what 'responsibility' means; *that is to say everywhere*. One can say *everywhere* a priori and nonempirically, for if the complex linkage between the theoretical and practical . . . is, quite clearly, irreducible, then the heterogeneity between the two linked orders is just as irreducible."

95. Ibid., 64.   96. Ibid.

97. Ibid., 69.   98. Ibid., 70.

99. Sacrifice and the secret of the *mysterium tremendum* figure in the thought of "the incineration, of the holocaust, of cinders," that runs through several of Derrida's texts, and this, he stresses, "well before *Of Spirit*, which speaks exclusively of this, and well before *Shibboleth*, whose sole theme it is" ("Canons and Metonymies: An Interview with Jacques Derrida," in Richard Rand, ed., *Logomachia: The Conflict of the Faculties* [Lincoln: University of Nebraska Press, 1992], 211). One could think not only of *Glas* and *Feu–la cendre*, which address the "all-burning," the *brûle-tout*, but of how, in *The Gift of Death*, Derrida rewrites as "the instant of Abraham's renunciation" his earlier quasi-psychoanalytic definition or, rather, figuration of "dissemination" as "that which doesn't come back to the father [*ce qui ne revient pas au père*]" (*The Gift of Death*, 96; cf. *Positions*, trans. Alan Bass [Chicago: University of Chicago Press, 1981], 113 n. 47).

100. Cf. Jean-Luc Nancy, *Une pensée finie*, (Paris: Galilée, 1990), 94ff.

101. Martin Heidegger makes this clear: "In being toward its death, Dasein is dying factically and indeed constantly, as long as it has not yet come to its demise. When we say that Dasein is factically dying, we are already saying that in its Being-towards-death Dasein has always decided itself in one way or another" (*Being and Time*, trans. John Macquarrie and Edward Robinson [New York: Harper and Row, 1962], 303).

102. Derrida, *The Gift of Death*, 81, 83.

103. Jacques Derrida, *The Other Heading*, trans. Pascale-Anne Brault and Michael B. Naas (Bloomington: Indiana University Press, 1992), 6.

104. Geoffrey Bennington, in Geoffrey Bennington and Jacques Derrida, *Jacques Derrida*, trans. Geoffrey Bennington (Chicago: University of Chicago Press, 1993), 271.

105. Nancy, *Une pensée finie*, 93.

106. Nancy, *The Experience of Freedom*, 123, cf. 155: "evil [the fury of evil] does not exist as a dialectical moment; it is an absolute possibility of freedom."

107. Kierkegaard, *Fear and Trembling*, 31.

108. Nancy, "L'insacrifiable," in *Une pensée finie* (Paris: Galilée, 1990), 77, recalls Pascal's words in the *Pensées*: "Circumcision of the heart, true fasting, true sacrifice, true temple; the prophets showed that all this must be spiritual. Not the flesh that perishes, but that which does not perish (Blaise Pascal, *Pensées*, trans. A. J. Krailsheimer [Harmondsworth, Middlesex: Penguin Books, 1966], 109.

109. Emmanuel Levinas, "Damages Due to Fire," *Nine Talmudic Read-*

ings, trans. and introd. Annette Aronowicz (Bloomington: Indiana University Press, 1990), 192–93.

110. Ibid., 179.

111. Ibid., 180.

Pranger, "Monastic Violence"

1. Robert Musil, *The Man Without Qualities*, Vol. 2, trans. Eithne Wilkins and Ernst Kaiser (London: Secker and Warburg, 1967), 336.

2. For a discussion of the "bookish" nature of Benedictine monastic life and its relation to history, see M. B. Pranger, *Bernard of Clairvaux and the Shape of Monastic Thought: Broken Dreams* (Leiden: Brill, 1994). Bernard of Clairvaux and his Cistercian order lived according to the Rule of St. Benedict, which dates from the sixth century and was predominant until the beginning of the thirteenth century. It governed monastic life, dividing a monk's day into set hours of prayer, reading, and manual work. The Cistercian order, founded in the beginning of the twelfth century, was one of the many attempts at reformation, which, in the case of monastic reform, always meant a return to the Rule. The Cistercians emphasized the ascetic nature of monastic life. This asceticism showed in the austerity of their buildings, among other things.

3. Bernard of Clairvaux, Epistola 64, *Sancti Bernardi Opera*, ed. J. Leclercq, C. H. Talbot, and H. M. Rochais (Rome: Editiones Cistercienses, 1957–77) 7: 157–58.

4. See M. Diers, *Bernhard von Clairvaux: Elitäre Frömmigkeit und begnadetes Wirken*. Beiträge zur Geschichte der Philosophie und Theologie des Mittelalters. n.s. 34 (Münster: Aschendorff, 1991), 351.

5. See Janet Coleman, *Ancient and Medieval Memories: Studies in the Reconstruction of the Past* (Cambridge: Cambridge University Press, 1992), 129–36.

6. Historians disagree over why Bernard preached the crusade at all. Recently Michaela Diers, in *Bernhard von Clairvaux: Elitäre Frömmigkeit und begnadetes Wirken* (Münster: Aschendorf, 1991), 349–92 has argued that Bernard, by preaching the crusade, intended to monasticize the extramural world. In my view, Bernard engaged in his extra-mural activities in order to be able to withdraw from them, thus intensifying the monastic experience. (Pranger, *Bernard of Clairvaux and the Shape of Monastic Thought*, 32–44).

7. Bernard of Clairvaux, Epistola 256, *Sancti Bernardi Opera*, 8: 164.

8. Bernard of Clairvaux, "De consideratione," II, 14, *Sancti Bernardi Opera*, 3: 410–11.

9. Michel de Certeau, *La fable mystique* (Paris: Gallimard, 1982), esp. chap. 5, pp. 216–42.

10. Jacques Derrida, "Nombre de Oui," in *Psyché: Inventions de l'autre* (Paris: Galilée, 1987): 639–50.

11. Hent de Vries, "Anti-Babel: The 'Mystical Postulate' in Benjamin, de Certeau and Derrida," *MLN* 107 (1992): 441–77.

12. Ibid., 449.

13. Ibid., 452.

14. Cf. my discussion of Certeau's view: M. B. Pranger, "Quelques remarques historiographiques concernant le principe d'individuation," *Nederlands Theologisch Tijdschrift* 35 (1981): 7–31.

15. De Certeau, *La fable mystique*, 242.

16. Ibid., 231.

17. Richard of St. Victor, *Tractatus de quattuor gradibus violentae charitatis, Patrologiae cursus completus, series latina*, ed. J. P. Migne (Paris, 1841–64), 196: 1207–24.

18. Ibid., 1213B.

19. Ibid., 1214C.

20. Bernard of Clairvaux, "Sermo in nativitate beatae Mariae," *Sancti Bernardi Opera*, 5: 286.

Hobson, *"Characteristic Violence"*

1. Immanuel Kant, *Anthropologie in pragmatischer Hinsicht*, vol. 10 of *Werke in zehn Bänden*, ed. Wilhelm Weischedel (Darmstadt: Wissenschaftliche Buchgesellschaft, 1983), 690.

2. "Fixing the human personality, giving to each human being an identity and a certain individuality, lasting, invariable, always recognizable and easily provable," said Bertillon in a lecture given in 1866 to an international conference on prisons, "Les signalements anthropométriques: Méthode nouvelle de détermination de l'identité individuelle" (quoted in Martin Stingelin, "Der Verbrecher ohnegleichen: Die Konstruktion 'anschaulicher Evidenz' in der Criminal-Psychologie, der forensischen Physiognomik, der Kriminalanthropometrie und der Kriminalanthropologie," in W. Groddeck and U. Stadler, eds., *Physiognomie und Pathognomie: Zur literarischen Darstellung von Individualität* [Berlin: Walter de Gruyter, 1994], 114). All translations from this article are mine unless otherwise stated.

3. See R. Villa, "Scienza medica e criminalità nell'Italia Unita," in F. Della Peruta, ed., *Mallattia e medicina*, no. 7 of *Storia d'Italia* (Turin: Einaudi, 1984). Cesare Lombroso, *L'anthropologie criminelle et ses récents progrès* (Paris: F. Alcan, 1890), contains at its outset a long discussion of types and "subspecies of *Homo criminalis*" (33).

4. J. Kagan and D. Arcus, "Temperament and Craniofacial Variation in the First Two Years," *Child Development* 66 (1995): 1529–41.

5. Kant, *Anthropologie*, 640.

6. The anecdote occurs in G. C. Lichtenberg, "Über Physiognomik," in *Gesammelte Werke*, ed. W. Grenzmann, 2 vols. (Frankfurt a. M.: Holle, 1949), 2: 67.

7. Kant, *Anthropologie*, 623. This is a marginal correction in the Rostock manuscript of the *Anthropologie*.

8. G. C. Lavater, *Essays on Physiognomy: Designed to Promote the Knowledge and Love of Mankind*, trans. Henry Hunter (London, 1789), 1: 20.

9. Kant, *Anthropologie*, 625, 633.

10. Ibid., 673.

11. Lavater, *Physiognomy*, 1: 14–15.

12. Ibid., 1: 16.

13. Lavater's publication of the physiognomical material was spurred by the fact that in 1772 his friend Zimmerman published in *Hanoverisches Magazin*, without Lavater's knowledge, a piece Lavater had sent him. Lavater filled this piece out as *Von der Physiognomik* (1772) and further as *Physiognomical Fragments*, published from 1775 on, which gave physiognomy European currency. There were five publications of Lavater's work in the 1770's, four in the 1780's—by the 1790's there were twelve English versions in five different translations. The figures are similar for France; see John Graham, "Lavater's Physiognomy in England," *Journal of the History of Ideas* 22 (1961): 561–72.

14. Anonymous, *Briefe von Johann Caspar Lavater und an Ihn und seine Freunde* (Bremen, 1787), 2.

15. Lavater, *Physiognomy*, 1: 113.

16. For the complexity of the actual practice, see Siegrist's comment in Lavater, *Physiognomische Fragmente*, ed. C. Siegrist (Stuttgart: Reklam, 1984), 379, on Lavater's rendering an example—an engraving—unique by writing verses on it, for which rich admirers paid. Forgeries existed, no doubt made easier because he allowed his secretaries to imitate his handwriting.

17. Lavater, *Physiognomy*, 1: 14; 1: 25.

18. Ibid., 1: 34–35.

19. G. C. Lavater, *Aussichten in die Ewigkeit* (Zurich: Orell, Füßli, und Compagnie, 1841; orig. pub. 1773), 229.

20. Ibid., 230.

21. E. Benz, "Swedenborg und Lavater: Über die religiösen Grundlagen der Physiognomik," *Zeitschrift für Kirchengeschichte* 57 (1938): 153–216. For Frege, too, there may have been beings who grasped thoughts without language; see M. Dummett, *The Origins of Analytical Philosophy* (London: Duckworth, 1993), 10–11.

22. Lavater, *Physiognomy*, 1: 34.

23. Ibid., 1: 20.

24. Ibid., 1: 69.

25. G. C. Lavater, letter to Charles Bonnet of August 21, 1778, Bibliothèque publique et universitaire, Geneva, Ms. Bonnet 34, no. 196.

26. Lavater, *Physiognomy*, 2: 297–98.

27. Ibid., 3: 317.

28. Jane Austen's Elinor Dashwood, in *Sense and Sensibility*, is an accomplished draughtswoman; subjects as drawn by the sister of the hero of *Pride and Prejudice* are more comprehensible than most of the paintings in the family picture gallery.

29. Foreword to Lavater, *Physiognomy*, n. p. All later Fuseli quotes in this paragraph are from this source.

30. Fuseli is critical of the English style of historical painting, which under pressures from naval and commercial expansion ("the discoveries of Navigation, the speculations of Commerce, connexions in every direction of the globe and above all, national pride") has aimed at accurate depiction of the faces and clothing of foreign climes, but which has produced paint-

ings with little grandeur and less significance, merely resembling prints from travel books.

31. Lavater, *Physiognomy*, 1: 27.

32. Denis Diderot, "Essais sur la peinture," in *Oeuvres esthétiques*, ed. P. Vernière (Paris: Garnier, 1959), chap. 1.

33. Denis Diderot, *Salon de 1767*, ed. J. Seznec and J. Adhémar (Oxford: Oxford University Press, 1963), 60.

34. Ibid., 57.

35. Ibid., 60.

36. The description of the hunchback, for instance, which nature recognizes from his feet alone, is chronologically complex: it is partly the order of deformation of other limbs, but partly the order of discovery by the onlooker, ending with a constrained facial expression, which registers the emotion of muscular effort (Diderot, 'Essais sur la peinture," 665–66). The account of the development of the "ideal line" is rhythmically a set of chained repetitions which keep the object discussed in play by giving it a further tap each time it seems to settle (Diderot, *Salon de 1767*, e.g., 60).

37. Diderot, "Essais sur la peinture," 665–66.

38. Diderot, *Le Neveu de Rameau*, ed. J. Fabre (Geneva: Droz, 1950), 103–4.

39. Lavater, *Physiognomy*, 2: 100; text not by Lavater.

40. "The exterior forms marking the nature of each animal, the physiognomists say that if it happens that a man has some body part similar to that of a beast, then there must be made conjectures from this part about his inclinations, which is what one calls physiognomy" (Charles Le Brun, "L'expression des passions, et autres conférences," presentation by Julien Philipe [Paris: Dédale, Maisonneuve, et Larose, 1994], 124; the lecture dates from 1668).

41. Ibid., 128.

42. Ibid., 125.

43. Lavater, *Physiognomy*, 2: 125.

44. Ibid., 2: 119.

45. Ibid., 2: 423.

46. Ibid., 1: 16. Compare: "In the face there is a character of nobleness observable, depending on the developement of certain organs which indicate the prevalence of the higher qualities allied to thought, and therefore human" (Sir Charles Bell, *The Anatomy and Philosophy of Expression as Connected with the Fine Arts*, 3d ed. [London: John Murray, 1844], 31). The human nose and mouth then exist for speaking, and for the resonance of the human voice, rather than as indications of propensities to groveling or ferocity. By contrast, for Le Brun, the head was not merely the "microcosm" (*raccourci*) of the whole body, but man was the microcosm of the world (Le Brun, "L'expression," 128).

47. Bell, *Anatomy and Philosophy*, 30.

48. Jean-Jacques Rousseau, *Contrat social*, 1st version, vol. 3 of *Oeuvres complètes* (Paris: Pléaide, 1995), 284. Cf. Jean-Pierre Marcos, *La société générale du genre humain*, Papiers du Collège International de Philosophie, 28 (Paris: Collège International de Philosophie, 1996), 8.

49. Diderot, "Essais sur la peinture," 668.
50. Diderot, *Salon*, 59.
51. Sir Joshua Reynolds, *Seven Discourses Delivered in the Royal Academy by the President* (Menston: Scolar Press, 1971; orig. delivered 1778), 79.

52. Ibid., 80–82.   53. Ibid., 76.
54. Ibid., 277–78.   55. Ibid., 91.
56. Ibid., 222.

57. The same argument, with a great deal more amplitude, could be mounted apropos Hegel's *Phenomenology*.
58. Michael Frede and Lorenz Krüger, "Über die Zuordnung der Quantitäten des Urteils und der Kategorien der Grösse bei Kant," *Kantstudien* 61 (1970): 28–49.
59. William Blake, *The Complete Writings*, ed. Geoffrey Keynes (Oxford: Oxford University Press, 1974), 459.
60. Cf. Diderot, *Satire première: Sur les caractères et les mots de caractère, de profession, etc.*, in Diderot, *Oeuvres complètes*, ed. R. Lewinter (Paris: Le Club Français du Livre, 1963–73), 10: 275–86.
61. Hegel, *Aesthetics: Lectures on Fine Art*, trans. T. M. Knox (Oxford: Oxford University Press, 1988; orig. pub. 1835), 1: 17. Hegel is quoting Aloys Hirt, "Versuch über das Kunstschöne," *Die Hören*, 1797, 34–35.
62. Ibid., trans. modified.
63. Ibid., 17–18.
64. Ibid., 19.
65. This text accompanies his engraving *Characters and Caricaturas*.
66. Immanuel Kant, *Critique of Judgement*, trans. J. H. Bernard (New York: 1966; orig. pub. 1790), section 17.
67. Hegel, *Aesthetics*, 19.
68. Kant, *Critique of Judgement*, section 17.
69. The vocabulary of this paragraph is particularly problematic in relation to contemporary aesthetics: Polycletus's statue is called "the rule" but is not for Kant, as it was for many of his immediate predecessors, an embodiment of the set of proportions which made for perfect beauty.
70. Kant, *Critique of Judgement*, section 17.
71. Jacques Derrida, *The Truth in Painting*, trans. Geoff Bennington and Ian McLeod (Chicago: University of Chicago Press, 1987), 104–18.
72. Lavater, *Physiognomy*, 1: 132.
73. Ibid., 1: 119–20.
74. Kant, *Anthropologie*, 638.
75. An English woman cannot help noting that in the preceding chapter the English people—who are said to have no character by nature, since they are a product of immigrations from Germany and France—get themselves one (*sich anschaffen*, or, of humans, *sich schaffen*). The Rostock manuscript adds that, being a commercial people, they have no character but what they get for themselves. It is their character to stay in a rigid frame of mind, following a freely accepted principle, so that at least one knows where one stands with them. This English character seems a satirical version of the character of man, and in the satire the eighteenth-century connection between commerce, liberty, and John Bull peeps through, thus

revealing the anchorage of this particular slant on self-determination. (Ibid., 663.)

76. Kant, *Anthropologie*, 673.

77. Ibid., 674. The threefold pattern is related to Kant's readings of Rousseau: a natural duality exists; out of reason develops unity; though the unity is indeed the purpose of the idea, the duality is, according to nature's plan, the means of producing an "unfathomable" wisdom of progress through sacrifice. The tragic rhythm of self-denial within culture, defined as the characteristic of man, occurs immediately after the account of human autonomy. The relation to the Freud of *Civilization and Its Discontents* seems clear.

78. Ibid., 685.

79. E.g., Jean-Jacques Rousseau, *Emile, Oeuvres complètes*, 4: 841.

80. Kant, *Anthropologie*, 690. The date of the text, 1798, after the Terror, is no doubt relevant.

81. Ibid., 687–89.

82. Immanuel Kant, *The Critique of Judgement*, section 90.

83. Ibid., section 16; cf. Derrida, *The Truth in Painting*, 117.

84. Lavater, *Physiognomy*, 1: 28, 29.

85. Ibid., 29.

86. G. C. Lichtenberg, "Wider Physiognomik," in *Schriften und Briefe*, ed. F. Mautner, 5 vols. (Frankfurt: Insel, 1983), 2: 123–38.

87. See, e.g., Jean-Jacques Rousseau, "Essai sur l'origine des langues," *Oeuvres complètes*, 5. Cf. my "'Nexus Effectivus' and 'Nexus Finalis': Causality in the 'Inégalité' and in the 'Essai sur l'origine des langues," in M. Hobson, J. Leigh, and R. Wokler, eds., *Rousseau and the Eighteenth Century: Essays in Memory of R. A. Leigh* (Oxford: Voltaire Foundation, 1992).

88. Lichtenberg, "Über Physiognomik," 58.

89. Ibid., 85.

90. Ibid., 86.

91. Ibid., 78. Lichtenberg allows instead the value of *pathognomy*: the face can express emotion, which can be "read off," but not character in any reliable way.

92. Ibid., 73.

93. G. C. Lavater, "Zwei Freunde der Wahrheit: Ein Briefwechsel zwischen Ch. Garve und J. C. Lavater," ed. G. Schultz, in *Jahrbuch der schlesische Friedrich-Wilhelms Universität zu Breslau*, vol. 8 (1963): 71. This letter of September 2, 1784, is referred to by J. G. Hamann, in *Sämtliche Werke*, ed. J. Nadler, 7 vols. (Vienna: Thomas-Morus-Press im Verlag Herder, 1957), 4: 459.

94. J. G. Hamann, letter to Herder of December 20, 1774, in *Briefwechsel*, ed. Walter Ziesemer and A. Henkel, 7 vols. (Frankfurt a. M.: Insel, 1955–59), 3: 129–34, letter 424.

95. Hamann, "Versuch über eine akademische Frage," *Sämtliche Werke*, 2: 122.

96. Ibid., 2: 123.

97. Arguing against Kant's treatment of language as if it were merely a question of usage, Hamann writes: "This meaning and its determination derive, according to knowledge of the world, from the combination

of a word-sign, which is *a priori* arbitrary and indifferent, but *a posteriori* necessary and indispensable, with the perception of the object itself. And through this repeated bond the concept is communicated to, engraved upon, and embodied in the understanding by means of the word-sign rather than by means of the perception itself" ("Metakritik über den Purismus der Vernunft," *Sämtliche Werke*, 3: 288; cf. K. Gruender, "Langage et histoire: Perspectives de la Métacritique sur le purisme de la Raison de J. G. Hamann," *Archives de philosophie* 24 (1961): 414–25).

98. I leave aside the "physiognomical" connection of national language and of national "character" developed by Herder and Humboldt. Herder writes, "The idiotisms of each tongue are impressions of their land, their people, their history" (J. G. Herder, *Sämtliche Werke*, ed. B. Suphan, 33 vols. [Berlin: Weidmannsche Buchhandlung, 1877–1913], 2: 49), whereas Humboldt says: "But the individualities to be found in the same nation fall within the *national uniformity*, which again distinguishes each particular turn of thought from those that resemble it in another people. From this uniformity, and that of the special stimulus peculiar to every language, the *character* of that language arises. Every language receives a specific individuality through that of the nation, and has on the latter a uniformly determining reverse effect" (W. von Humboldt, *The Diversity of Human Language-Structure and Its Influence on the Mental Development of Mankind*, trans. P. Heath, introd. H. Aarsleff [Cambridge: Cambridge University Press, 1988], 152). Behind national character is likeness, explicable by descent, but language too may be at work in linking mental processes to the body, so that "in their most primal relation to the nature of individuality, therefore, language and the basis of all nationality have a direct resemblance to one another" (ibid., 152–53).

99. Lavater, *Physiognomische Fragmente*, ed. Siegrist, 167.

100. Ibid., 166.

101. Lavater, *Physiognomy*, 1: 104.

102. Ibid., 2: 100.

103. At the level of vocabulary, then, fixed repertoires are necessary, even if the very act of classification is unjust. The openness thus lost might seem to be regained in the form of Lavater's work—fragments which can be revised and added to—and in the style, the sense of individual voices he is at pains to produce in his own writing and to preserve in the fragments authored by others. Yet in his writing, an assumption of quirky originality is accompanied by a willingness to hand out judgments on the moral qualities of those whose portraits he is discussing; the assumed daring of the sentences belies his claimed humility.

104. G. W. F. Hegel, *The Phenomenology of Spirit*, trans. A. V. Miller (Oxford: Oxford University Press, 1977; orig. pub. 1807), sections 319–20.

105. Cf. Jacques Derrida, "Violence and Metaphysics," in *Writing and Difference*, trans. Alan Bass (Chicago: University of Chicago Press, 1978), 114.

106. Emmanuel Levinas, *Totality and Infinity*, trans. A. Lingis (Pittsburgh: Duquesne University Press, n. d.), 59.

107. Ibid., 50–51.

108. Ibid., 66.

109. Ibid., 47.
110. Ibid., 66–67.
111. Ibid., 206.
112. Ibid., 201.
113. Rousseau, *Dictionnaire de musique, Oeuvres complètes*, 5: 928.
114. Levinas, *Totality and Infinity*, 69.
115. Ibid., 204.
116. Derrida, "Violence and Metaphysics," 114.
117. In *Writing and Difference*, 31–63.
118. Derrida, "Violence and Metaphysics," 147–48.
119. Cf.: Derrida, *Of Grammatology*, trans. G. C. Spivak (Baltimore: Johns Hopkins University Press, 1974), 132; Marian Hobson, *Jacques Derrida: Opening Lines* (London: Routledge, 1997), chap. 1.
120. Derrida, "Violence and Metaphysics," 149.
121. Derrida here refers to—but also, in my view, silently departs from—the last part of Heidegger's *Introduction to Metaphysics* and *The Origin of the Work of Art*, where the violence of language is not of a different order from political violence.

Weber, "Wartime"

1. Plato, *The Laws*, trans. A. E. Taylor, in Plato, *Collected Dialogues*, ed. Edith Hamilton and Huntington Cairns (Princeton: Princeton University Press, 1961), x, 884, p. 1440.
2. Ibid., 886d, p. 1442.
3. Ibid., 887e, p. 1443.
4. Sigmund Freud, "Thoughts for the Times on War and Death," *The Standard Edition of the Complete Psychological Works of Sigmund Freud*, ed. James Strachey, vol. 14 (London: Hogarth, 1953–74), 288. (Hereafter, *SE*.)
5. Ibid., 279.
6. Ibid.
7. Ibid., 276.
8. Ibid.
9. Ibid., 287.
10. My translation here diverges considerably from the published one. It is an attempt to render Freud's syntax as literally as possible. Here is the German text: "Von dem Wirbel dieser Kriegszeit gepackt, einseitig unterrichtet, ohne Distanz von den großen Veränderungen, die sich bereits vollzogen haben oder zu vollziehen beginnen, und ohne Witterung der sich gestaltenden Zukunft, werden wir selbst irre an der Bedeutung der Eindrücke, die sich uns aufdrängen, und an dem Werte der Urteile, die wir bilden (*Gesammelte Werke* [Frankfurt a. M., Fischer, 1947], 10: 324).
11. Freud, "Thoughts," 275.
12. Friedrich Nietzsche, *Unzeitgemäße Betrachtungen*, in *Werke*, ed. Karl Schlechta (Hanser: Munich, 1960), 1: 210. My translation.
13. Ibid., 1: 137.
14. Freud, "Thoughts," 280.
15. "In the last resort it may be assumed that every internal compulsion which makes itself felt in the development of human beings was originally—that is in the history of mankind—only an external one" (ibid., 282).
16. Ibid., 281.
17. See Jacques Derrida's discussion of Hamlet's formulation in *Specters of Marx*, trans. Peggy Kamuf (New York: Routledge, 1994).

18. Freud, "Thoughts," 337.
19. Sigmund Freud, "Instincts and Their Vicissitudes," in *General Psychological Theory* (New York: Collier, 1972), 95.
20. Freud, "Thoughts," 300.   21. Ibid., 289.
22. Ibid., 291.   23. Ibid., 292.
24. Ibid., 293.   25. Ibid., 297.
26. Ibid., 294.   27. Ibid.
28. Sigmund Freud, "Negation," *SE*, 19: 235–36.
29. Sigmund Freud, *Inhibitions, Symptoms and Anxiety*, trans. Alix Strachey (New York: Norton, 1989), 48.
30. Freud, "Thoughts," 298 n. 30.
31. The Pléiade edition comments on the matter as follows. "Following previous commentators on *Père Goriot*, we have searched in vain for this text on the Mandarin in the work of Rousseau. P. Ronaï, 'Tuer le mandarin,' *Revue de littérature comparée* (July–September 1930), sees the following text of Chateaubriand as the sole source of the passage: 'Oh conscience! Could you only be a phantom of the imagination, or the fear of human punishment? I ask myself, I pose this question: "If, by your sole desire, you could kill a man in China and inherit his fortune in Europe, with the natural conviction that no one would ever know anything about it, would you agree to form such a desire?" Even if I exaggerate my poverty; even if I seek to attenuate this homicide by supposing that, through my wish, the China-man would die suddenly without pain, that he has no heir, that even at his death his possessions will be lost to the State; even if I imagine this foreigner as overcome with illness and chagrin; even if I tell myself that death is a blessing for him, that he calls out for it himself, that he doesn't have a moment longer to live—despite my vain subterfuges, I hear at the bottom of my heart a voice that protests so loudly against such a supposition that I cannot doubt for an instant the reality of conscience' (*The Genius of Christianity*, 1.6.2)" (Balzac, *La comédie humaine*, Editions de la Pléiade, ed. Pierre-Georges Castex [Paris: Gallimard, 1976], 3: 1280. My translation).
32. See Jacques Derrida, ". . . and pomegranates," the concluding essay of this volume.

Agamben, *"The Camp as* Nomos *of the Modern"*

1. In English in the original—Trans.
2. Klaus Drobisch and Günter Wieland, *System der NS-Konzentrationslager 1933-39* (Berlin: Akademie Verlag, 1993), 26.
3. Ibid., 28.
4. "Order" renders the word *ordinamento*, which is the Italian translation of Carl Schmitt's *Ordnung* and carries the sense not only of order, but of political and juridical rule, regulation, and system—Trans.
5. Ibid., 27.
6. Ibid., 30.
7. In archaic Roman law, *homo sacer* was a man whom anyone could kill without committing homicide, but who nevertheless could not be put to death according to any ritual form. In the larger work from which this essay is drawn, it is argued that the life of *homo sacer*, which is thus in-

cluded in the order of profane and religious law in the form of its exclusion (that is, of its absolute killability), constitutes the originary element and hidden presupposition of the Western political tradition. See Giorgio Agamben, *Homo Sacer: Sovereign Power and Bare Life*, trans. Daniel Heller-Roazen (Stanford: Stanford University Press, forthcoming)—Trans.

8. Carl Schmitt, "Staat, Bewegung, Volk," in *Die Dreigliederung der politischen Einheit* (Hamburg: Hanseatische Verlagsanstalt, 1933).

9. Walter Benjamin, *Ursprung des deutschen Trauerspiels*, in *Gesammelte Schriften*, ed. Rolf Tiedemann and Hermann Scweppenhäuser (Frankfurt a. M.: Suhrkamp, 1974), 1.1.249–50.

10. Jesper Svenbro, *Phrasicleia, anthropologie de la lecture en Grèce ancienne* (Paris: Découverte, 1988), 128.

11. Schmitt, "Staat, Bewegung, Volk."

12. Ibid.

13. Hannah Arendt, *On Revolution* (New York: Viking Press, 1963), 70.

14. In thirteenth-century Florence, *popolo minuto* referred to the class of artisans and tradespeople and *popolo grasso* referred to the business classes and bourgeoisie—Trans.

Gourgouris, *"Enlightenment and* Paranomia*"*

1. Harold J. Berman, *Law and Revolution: The Formation of the Western Legal Tradition* (Cambridge: Harvard University Press, 1983).

2. Ibid., 8.

3. The terminology here belongs to Cornelius Castoriadis. (See *The Imaginary Institution of Society*, trans. Kathleen Blamey [Cambridge: MIT Press, 1987].) Following Castoriadis, I should add that the allegedly natural antinomy between individual and society, which in all essence does not exist (society is a community of individuals and the individual is always a social entity) surfaces along with this particular social-imaginary institution.

4. I am not ignoring the relation between *logos* and *nomos*, encapsulated by the double meaning of the Latin *lex*. But I choose to bracket this particular reduction of the legal to the *logos*, which has nothing to do with Greek thought and is altogether due to the writing of a Christian metaphysics (a writing that was inaugurated in the Greek language but preempted its philosophical idiom). This resolutely un-Greek metaphysics institutes a new notion of *nomos* by the bizarre conception of an impregnated *logos*: *lex animata*, the peculiar law of the Word become flesh. What matters here instead is to trace Enlightenment law, in all its ambivalence and duplicity, to the mythic framework that animates its existence.

5. Consider Horkheimer and Adorno's famous phrase: "The program of the Enlightenment was the disenchantment of the world [*Entzauberung der Welt*]; the dissolution of myths and the substitution of knowledge for fancy" (*Dialectic of Enlightenment*, trans. John Cumming [New York: Seabury Press, 1972]), 3. The notion literally suggests the abandonment of magic as the operational force of the universe, and it reflects the rather standard Enlightenment view of religion as superstition and fanaticism. It does not mean the abolition of myth; if anything, Horkheimer and

Adorno's essay contemplates precisely the repressed mythological power of Reason (and all the destructive energies this repression entails). That this disenchantment of the world, which in effect constitutes the particularity of our modernity, established itself with such enormous enchanting power is another way to register the history of the problem raised here. (See also Marcel Gauchet, *Le désenchantement du monde* [Paris: Gallimard, 1985]).

6. Immanuel Kant, *Groundwork of the Metaphysics of Morals* and *What is Enlightenment?*, trans. Lewis White Beck (New York: Macmillan, 1985), 86.

7. Kant's notion of public and private is the opposite of how we conceive these today: "The public use of one's reason must always be free, and it alone can bring enlightenment among men. The private use of reason, on the other hand, may often be very narrowly restricted without particularly hindering the progress of enlightenment. By the public use of one's reason I understand the use which a person makes of it as a scholar before the reading public. Private use I call that which one may make of it in a particular civil [*bürgerlichen*] post or office which is entrusted to him" (ibid., 87). In other words, one's private (individual) thought should enter the public domain unhindered, while one's civic duty (in effect, the duty to one's class) is conceived as the State's private domain and is to be strictly administered.

8. Etienne Balibar, "Citizen Subject," trans. James B. Swenson, in Eduardo Cadava, ed., *Who Comes After the Subject?* (New York: Routledge, 1991), 33–57.

9. Etienne Balibar, *Masses, Classes, Ideas: Studies on Politics and Philosophy Before and After Marx*, trans. James Swenson (New York: Routledge, 1994), 39–60.

10. See: Marcel Gauchet, *La révolution des droits de l'homme* (Paris: Gallimard, 1989); Brian Singer, *Society, Theory, and the French Revolution* (London: Macmillan, 1986); Peter Fitzpatrick, " 'The Desperate Vacuum': Imperialism and Law in the Experience of Enlightenment," in Anthony Carty, ed., *Post-Modern Law: Enlightenment, Revolution, and the Death of Man* (Edinburgh: Edinburgh University Press, 1990), 90–106.

11. I discuss in detail the permutations of the national imaginary and its relation to the Enlightenment in *Dream Nation: Enlightenment, Colonization, and the Institution of Modern Greece* (Stanford: Stanford University Press, 1996).

12. Garry Wills, *Inventing America: Jefferson's Declaration of Independence*, (New York: Vintage, 1979).

13. Ibid., 181–92.

14. For an incisive discussion of this imitation of divine naming, in relation particularly to Rousseau's attempt to theorize it in *The Social Contract*, see Samuel Weber, "In the Name of the Law," in Drucilla Cornell, Michel Rosenfeld, and David Gray Carlson, eds., *Deconstruction and the Possibility of Justice* (New York: Routledge, 1992), 232–53.

15. This is evidence of a long and contradictory history that hinges on the notion of dechristianization, which first led to the Goddess Reason being worshiped inside the walls of Notre Dame and soon after, with the official decrees of Year 2, to the cult of the Supreme Being. This history testifies to the profound ambiguity between secular and theological thought

at the heart of the Enlightenment project, of which the French Revolution is a paradigmatic case. It is difficult to separate the domains. On the one hand, for example, next to the National Assembly's decreed dechristianization existed a popular movement for emancipation from Christian worship (which even raises the question of how effectively Christianization had ever been implemented in the provinces). On the other hand, while France remains culturally a Catholic country, the revolutionary experience of dechristianization is profoundly embedded in its contemporary social and cultural framework. See Michel Vovelle, *The Revolution Against the Church*, trans. Alan José (Cambridge: Polity Press, 1991).

16. Peter Fitzpatrick argues the same matter in different terms: "[with] the embodiment of the Enlightenment domestication of the Deity, law's range of determination becomes infinite" (" 'The Desperate Vacuum,' " 93). See also Stéphane Lojkine's notion of the cannibalization of divine law and violence in Voltaire's *Dictionnaire philosophique* ("Langages et poétique du *Dictionnaire* voltairien," *Littératures* 32 [Spring 1995]: 35–59).

17. Here and for much of this section, I am merely outlining Jacques Derrida's position in "Force of Law: 'The Mystical Foundation of Authority,' " in Drucilla Cornell, Michel Rosenfeld, and David Gray Carlson, eds., *Deconstruction and the Possibility of Justice* (New York: Routledge, 1992), 3–67.

18. See Walter Benjamin, "Critique of Violence," in *Reflections*, trans. Edmund Jephcott (New York: Harcourt, Brace, and Jovanovich, 1978), 277–300. The translation will occasionally be modified, with the original German cited in brackets.

19. Ibid., 287.

20. Robert Cover, "The Bonds of Constitutional Interpretation: Of the Word, the Deed, and the Role" *Georgia Law Review* 20, no. 4 (1986): 820.

21. Ibid., 819–20. See also Robert Cover, "Violence and the Word," *The Yale Law Journal* 95, no. 8 (1986): 1610.

22. There is much to learn from Pierre Clastres's brilliant observations, not only in his monumental *Society Against the State*, trans. Robert Hurley and Abe Stein (New York: Zone Books, 1989), but also in one of his last writings before his untimely death: "Archéologie de la violence: La guerre dans les sociétés primitives" (*Libre* no. 1, 1977). Clastres argues that primitive society is characterized by an immanent centrifugal logic that prevents "the externalization of a unifying law," the unifying logic of the One that eventually takes over the reins of representation. For a primitive society, the discourse of the One is the power of the Other, the radical annihilating alterity that eventually becomes the State. Civilization takes place when this alterity (*exonomy*) becomes an institution.

23. See Robert Cover, "Violence and the Word," 1604, and Jacques Derrida, "Force of Law," 33–36.

24. Surely, my argument itself betrays a certain kind of formalism. I acknowledge that from the standpoint of the individual policeman the daily experience is like any other job, differing only in the radical unpredictability of a gamut of emotions from boredom to fear for one's life. Nonetheless, like any other job, this job has its own unique social nature, in which individual experience is ultimately subsumed. Understanding

the symbolic relation between the police and the law would not be any better achieved by focusing on the individual experience than it would by focusing on the phenomenon of mass police corruption (that is, criminal behavior in a strict sense).

25. Benjamin, "Critique of Violence," 287.

26. In addition to Cover's "Violence and the Word," see his "Nomos and Narrative," *Harvard Law Review* 97, no. 1 (1983): 4–68. For insightful commentary on Robert Cover's problematic, see Austin Sarat and Thomas R. Kearns, "A Journey Through Forgetting: Toward a Jurisprudence of Violence," in Sarat & Kearns, eds., *The Fate of the Law* (Ann Arbor: University of Michigan Press, 1991), 209–73, and Douglas Hay, "Time, Inequality, and Law's Violence," in Sarat & Kearns, eds., *Law's Violence* (Ann Arbor: University of Michigan Press, 1992), 141–73.

27. One recent name with an overwhelming *Wanted!* sign addressed to it would have to be O. J. Simpson, although it is unlikely that his current legend will outlast its immediate historical context. This is because his outlaw status is not generated by the crime to which he was linked (in which his status as guilty or not guilty has been forever conflated by the equally doubtful antithetical verdicts in his two trials). Rather, he draws to himself the magnetic force of the outlaw because he had already been marked with the magnetism of an American hero. The public's exuberant turnout to cheer O.J. on his last run from the law demonstrates how the status of the American hero, not only is *not* challenged by, but actually benefits from the mark of the outlaw. (In many ways, the famous slow chase scene is much more revealing of the social imaginary at work than the orchestrated video staging of the subsequent trial. This instant media event did not hesitate to devour its own media persona: a live chase scene where O.J.'s partner in sports commentary provided on-the-spot coverage and commentary on his friend's sad demise.) Yet there is an inevitable residual racism in all those who cheered O.J.'s fall from grace: resentment for the fact that O.J., the perfect image of the assimilated, bourgeoisified black, betrayed his cultural training, which means none other than an implicit confirmation as to the untrainable nature of those who lack culture. Thus, the brutally antagonistic popular sentiment, encapsulated by the institution's own ambivalence in the two trials and the two opposite verdicts, is now the new content of the name O. J. Simpson: a coincidence between the allure of the outlaw and the racist cheer for the failed project of emancipation.

28. Derrida, "Force of Law," 40.

29. See Lawrence Rickels, "Kafka and the Aero-Trace," in Alan Udoff, ed., *Kafka and the Contemporary Critical Performance* (Bloomington: Indiana University Press, 1987), 111–27.

30. Slavoj Žižek, "Beyond Discourse-Analysis," appendix in Ernesto Laclau, *New Reflections on the Revolution in Our Time* (London: Verso, 1990), 257.

31. Jacques Derrida, "Devant la loi," trans. Avital Ronell, in Alan Udoff, ed., *Kafka and the Contemporary Critical Performance* (Bloomington: Indiana University Press, 1987), 141.

32. Ibid., 146.

33. On another occasion, this deserves to be reread at length in the

terms of Gillian Rose's remarkable *The Broken Middle* (Oxford: Black-well, 1992).

34. Benjamin, "Critique of Violence," 297.

35. See Tom McCall, "Momentary Violence," in David S. Ferris, ed., *Walter Benjamin: Theoretical Questions* (Stanford: Stanford University Press, 1996), 188, 192. McCall's reading of Benjamin is not too distant from mine, although paradoxically our understanding of myth is antithetical. While he considers myth to be the speech act that "sutures experience seamlessly" as "the authority to name the 'real,'" I see it as a profoundly ambiguous, indeed undeconstructible, performance of the allegorical as real.

36. Georges Sorel, *Reflections on Violence*, trans. T. E. Hulme (New York: Peter Smith, 1941), 19.

37. Ibid., 23.

38. Ibid., 31.

39. Henri Bergson, *Time and Free Will*, quoted in ibid., 30.

40. In Marxist terms, this might be a way to reconceive (and revolutionize) Lenin's idea of the revolutionary moment, so as to extract from it the disastrous metaphysics of the once-and-for-all, the unreturnable nature of the potential event in time, which makes any political failure tantamount to historical death.

41. Sorel, *Reflections on Violence*, 135.

42. Ibid., 137.

43. Ibid., 133.

44. Kant, *Groundwork of the Metaphysics of Morals*, 19.

45. J. Hillis Miller, *The Ethics of Reading* (New York: Columbia University Press, 1987).

46. Weber, "In the Name of the Law," 246–47.

47. For the full range of the psychoanalytic implications of this issue, I defer to Renata Salecl's incisive argument in "Democracy and Violence," *New Formations* 14 (1991): 17–26.

48. See Costas Douzinas and Ronnie Warrington, *Justice Miscarried: Ethics, Aesthetics, and the Law* (London: Harvester, 1994), for an exceptional reading of Antigone's mark in the history of philosophy.

49. See, especially, Paul Veyne, *Did the Greeks Believe in Their Myths?*, trans. Paula Wissing (Chicago: University of Chicago Press, 1988), and Odo Marquard, "In Praise of Polytheism (On Monomythical and Polymythical Thinking)," in *Farewell to Matters of Principle*, trans. Robert M. Wallace (Oxford: Odéon, 1989), 87–110.

50. See Derrida, "Devant la loi," 140–41.

Shell, "Cannibals All"

1. Peter Fenves, "Testing Right—Lying in View of Justice," *Cardozo Law Review* 13, no. 1 (December 1991): 1081–114.

2. *Uber den Gemeinspruch: Das mag in der Theorie richtig sein, taugt aber nicht für die Praxis*, in *Kant's Gesammelte Schriften* (Berlin: [Royal] Prussian Academy, 1911–), VIII 297; translated as *On the Common Saying: This may be true in theory, but it does not apply in practice*, in *Political*

Writings, ed. Hans Reiss, 2d ed. (Cambridge: Cambridge University Press, 1991), 79. All subsequent references to Kant's work cite the Academy edition, followed where possible by an available English translation.

3. See Kant, *Kritik der Urteilschaft*, v 375; *Critique of Judgment*, trans. Werner Pluhar (Indianapolis: Hackett, 1987), 254.

4. Kant, *Die Metaphysik der Sitten*, vi 320n.; *The Metaphysics of Morals*, trans. Mary J. Gregor (Cambridge: Cambridge University Press, 1991), 132n.

5. Kant, *Der Streit der Facultäten*, vii 92n.; *Conflict of the Faculties*, trans. Mary J. Gregor (New York: Abaris Books, 1979), 167n.

6. See, e.g., Kant, *Metaphysics of Morals*, Part One, vi 359–60; 166.

7. The Dutch innkeeper's sign (from Leibniz by way of Fontenelle) was already something of a stalking horse.

8. Kant, *Zum Ewigen Frieden*, viii 343; *Toward Perpetual Peace*, in *Kant's Political Writings*, ed. Hans Reiss, 2d ed. (Cambridge: Cambridge University Press, 1991), 93.

9. Cf. Kant, *Reflexion* no. 936, xv 415–16.

10. Authors traditionally used a *clausula salvatoria* to disavow in advance any unintended heresy.

11. Cf. Kant, *Metaphysics of Morals*, Part One, vi 345; 152.

12. See Michael W. Doyle, "Liberalism and World Politics," in *American Political Science Review* 80, no. 4 (December, 1986): 1151–69.

13. *Konx Ompax* is an expression associated with the Greek mysteries and traceable, according to Kant, to a more ancient Tibetan term meaning, roughly, the divine lawgiver pervading the whole of nature. Cf. Johann G. Hamann, *Konxompax*: "This unity of the head together with the division of the body into its members and their *differentia specifica* is the mystery of the kingdom of heaven from its genesis to its apocalypse—the burning point of all parables and types in the whole universe" (*Werke*, ed. J. Nadler [Vienna: Herder, 1949–57], 3: 226).

14. As in *generatio equivoca*, or "spontaneous generation."

15. The older meaning of *Schelm* is "skeleton" or "corpse."

16. Kant, *Verkündigung des nahen Abschlusses: Eines Tractats zum ewigen Frieden in der Philosophie*, viii 113; *Announcement of a Near Conclusion for a Treaty of Eternal Peace in Philosophy*, trans. Peter Fenves in *Raising the Tone of Philosophy: Late Essays by Immanuel Kant, Transformative Critique by Jacques Derrida*, (Baltimore: Johns Hopkins University Press, 1993), 90.

17. Ibid.

18. For Kant's views concerning the life-promoting effects of gambling, see *Anthropologie in pragmatischer Hinsicht*, vii 275; *Anthropology from a Pragmatic Point of View*, trans. Mary J. Gregor (The Hague: Nijhoff, 1974), 141.

19. See Kant, *Metaphysics of Morals*, vi 339; 147–48.

20. Kant points to an analogy between the bodily separation of human individuals and the "natural diversity of language and religion" separating nations. Yet such diversity is "progressively weakened as culture develops," suggesting the special fragility of national boundaries, whose natural foundation is undermined by the very process that juridically secures them.

Dillon, "Otherwise than Self-Determination"

1. For an extended account of this thesis and a more extensive reading of *Oedipus Rex*, see Michael Dillon, *Politics of Security: Towards a Political Philosophy of Continental Thought* (London: Routledge, 1996).

2. This point is prompted by Heidegger's reading of the opening chorus of *Antigone*. See *An Introduction to Metaphysics*, trans. Ralph Mannheim (New Haven: Yale University Press, 1959), 148.

3. Line 39. The Greek is taken throughout from *Sophocles*, trans. F. Storr (Cambridge: Harvard University Press, 1962). Throughout the remainder of this paper, line numbers will be given in the text.

4. *Asphaleia* means "security"; *sphalo*, "to limp or stumble" and also "to mistake the truth, to err"; *orthos*, "to stand"; and *orthotes*, truth as correspondence.

5. See also the translation by Stephen Berg and Diskin Clay, *Oedipus the King* (New York: Oxford University Press, 1978): "Here? Now? In front of all these people? Or inside privately?" (27).

6. See Friedrich Nietzsche, *Untimely Meditations*, trans. R. J. Hollingdale (Cambridge: Cambridge University Press, 1989).

7. Claude Lefort, *Democracy and Political Theory* (Cambridge: Polity Press, 1988), 223.

8. See, by contrast, Fred Dallmayr's description of it as "a broadly ontological perspective . . . in which different elements or modalities of being are related without mutual intrusion and by granting each other space in the interstices of presence and absence, arrival and departure" (Dallmayr, *The Other Heidegger* [Ithaca: Cornell University Press, 1993], 10). This seems to capture very well what is going on at this point in the play.

9. Derrida, of course, explores in detail how this structure continuously operates: "Repetition and first time, but also repetition and last time, since the singularity of any first time makes of itself also a last time. Each time it is the event itself, a first time is also a last time" (*Specters of Marx* [London: Routledge, 1994], 10).

10. "A mimesis opens the fiction of tone. It is the tragedy of 'Come' that it must be repeatable (*a priori* repeated in itself) in order to resonate" (a remark by Jacques Derrida quoted in "Introduction: The Topicality of Tone" to Peter Fenves, ed., *Raising the Tone of Philosophy: Late Essays by Immanuel Kant, Transformative Critique by Jacques Derrida* (Baltimore: The Johns Hopkins University Press, 1993), p. 48 n. 55.)

11. Martin Heidegger, *Nietzsche*, trans. David Farrell Krell (San Francisco: Harper Collins, 1991) 1: 311.

12. Heidegger, *Nietzsche*, vol. 1, quoted in Peg Birmingham, "The Time Of The Political," *Graduate Faculty Philosophy Journal*, special issue *Heidegger and the Political*, vol. 14, no. 2 and vol. 15, no. 1 (1991), p. 34. I have relied heavily on Peg Birmingham's excellent essay in the preceeding analysis.

13. Hannah Arendt, "What Is Freedom?," *Between Past and Future* (Harmondsworth, Middlesex: Penguin Books, 1977), 169.

14. Ibid.

15. Hannah Arendt, "Freedom and Politics," in A. Hunold, ed., *Freedom and Serfdom* (Dordrecht: Reidel, 1961), 192.

16. Hannah Arendt, *Willing*, vol. 2 of *The Life of the Mind* (New York: Harcourt Brace Jovanovich, 1977).

17. Perhaps this is why Creon is so ambivalent about Oedipus' exile at the end of the play.

18. Birmingham, "The Time of the Political," 40.

19. Ibid., 41.

20. Antigone shows in a later play how she can, in a sense, stand up for herself, too. The issue of male and female is relevant here but falls outside the compass of this essay.

21. Sophocles, *Oedipus the King*, trans. Robert Fagles (Harmondsworth, Middlesex: Penguin, 1984), 249.

22. This is Heidegger's summary of Schelling's thought, which, as Dallmayr says, "is not alien to Heidegger's thought" (Heidegger, *Schelling's 'Abhandlung'*, quoted in Dallmayr, *The Other Heidegger*, 117).

23. I trust Peg Birmingham will forgive my weaving her into my own text throughout the preceding section without always acknowledging precisely where and how. My debt to her essay must, however, be very evident.

24. Heidegger, *Schelling's 'Abhandlung'*, quoted in Dallmayr, *The Other Heidegger*, 128.

25. The theme of love and friendship is discussed in Hannah Arendt, *Men in Dark Times* (New York: Harcourt Brace, 1965), especially the essay on Lessing, and in Jacques Derrida, "The Politics of Friendship," *The Journal of Philosophy* 85, no. 11 (November 1988): 632–48. See also John M. Cooper, "Aristotle on the Forms of Friendship," *Review of Metaphysics* 30, no. 4 (June 1970): 619–48.

26. Derrida, *Specters of Marx*, 16.

27. "That which we *are* as having been," Heidegger explains, "has not gone by, passed away, in the sense in which we say that we could shuffle off our past like a garment. The *Dasein* can as little get rid of its bygones as escape its death. In every sense and in every case everything we have been is an essential determination of our existence" (*The Basic Problems of Phenomenology* [Bloomington: Indiana University Press, 1982], 265–66).

28. Derrida, *Given Time: 1. Counterfeit Money*, trans. Peggy Kamuf (Chicago: University of Chicago Press, 1992), 57.

29. Quoted in Jean-François Lyotard, *The Inhuman: Reflections on Time* (Stanford: Stanford University Press, 1991), 114.

30. "A masterpiece," Derrida reminds us, "always moves by definition in the manner of a ghost" (*Specters of Marx*, 53).

31. Again I am indebted to Peg Birmingham, especially to "Ever Respectfully Mine: Heidegger on Agency and Responsibility," in Arleen B. Dallery and Charles E. Scott, with P. Holley Roberts, eds., *Ethics and Danger: Essays on Heidegger and Continental Thought* (Albany: State University of New York Press, 1992), 121.

32. Bernard Knox, *Oedipus at Thebes* (New Haven: Yale University Press, 1957), 116.

33. Girard, *Violence and the Sacred* (Baltimore: The Johns Hopkins University Press, 1977), 74–75.

34. Froma Zeitlin, "Theater of Self and Society in Ancient Athenian Drama," in J. Peter Euben, ed., *Greek Tragedy and Political Theory* (Berkeley: University of California, 1986), 101–41.

35. Girard, *Violence and the Sacred*, 74.

36. J. Peter Euben, *The Tragedy of Political Theory* (Princeton: Princeton University Press, 1990), 98.

37. Ibid.

38. In Emmanuel Levinas, the beyond which is always integral to the present of human being is the unlimited ethical call of the other, which summons the self to be a self. See, especially, *Totality and Infinity*, trans. Alphonso Lingis (Dordrecht: Kluwer, 1991) and *Otherwise than Being*, trans. Alphonso Lingis (Dordrecht: Kluwer, 1991).

39. As Euben notes: "Greek tragedy was about boundaries of space, time and place, about being inside and outside. It was also about how such boundaries, divisions, and oppositions are born, maintained and justified" (Introduction to Euben, ed., *Greek Tragedy and Political Theory*, 37).

40. Euben makes the interesting point that the Sphinx is in its own way like Oedipus: part human, part beast (*The Tragedy of Political Theory*, 113n).

41. Herbert Musurillo, *The Light and the Darkness* (Leiden: E. J. Brill, 1967), 81–82.

42. See Bernard M. Knox, "The Last Scene," in Michael J. O'Brian, ed., *Twentieth-Century Interpretations of 'Oedipus Rex'* (Englewood Cliffs, N. J.: Prentice Hall, 1968), and the last chapter of Knox's classic *Oedipus at Thebes*. The same point is emphasized in Joel Schwartz, "Action in *Oedipus Tyrannos*," in J. Peter Euben, ed., *Greek Tragedy and Political Theory*, 183–209.

43. Girard, *Violence and the Sacred*, 55. In the play the plague is sent by the gods, but that is consistent with my reading because human being also arrives from what is beyond it.

44. Ibid., 195.

45. Martin Heidegger, *An Introduction to Metaphysics*, 152–53.

46. For Heidegger not man or even human being but the event of presencing is saved in the turn made possible by the advent of the age of technology. This is why he appears so uninterested in the concrete future of humankind. But that neither dismisses nor resolves the question of the relationship between *Dasein* and the saving turn which he detects in technology. Rather, it poses it in a certain way, which is why he calls for a different sort of thought: "Neither the political, nor the economical, nor the sociological, nor the technical and scientific, nor even the religious or metaphysical perspectives are adequate to thinking what is happening in this age of the world" (Heidegger, "The Word of Nietzsche," in *The Question Concerning Technology and Other Essays*, trans. William Lovitt [New York: Harper and Row, 1977], 111).

47. Ibid., 48–49.

48. This is one way of describing what Arendt addresses in "Philosophy and Politics," *Social Research* 57 (1990): 73–103.

49. Gerald Segal, *Tragedy and Civilization* (Cambridge: Harvard University Press, 1981), 241. "No figure in Greek drama more powerfully and

tragically embodies the paradoxes of man's civilizing power than Oedipus. . . . Oedipus sums up all that man can attain by mind alone. And yet this solver of riddles does not know the most fundamental thing about himself. He lacks the basic information about his origins that gives man his human identity and sets him apart from the undifferentiated realm of nature and the anonymous, undifferentiated realm of the beasts" (Ibid., 207).

50. The advice comes once from the shepherd, once from Teiresias, and twice from Jocasta (Knox, *Oedipus at Thebes*, 12).

51. Segal, *Tragedy and Civilization*, 208.

52. For a stimulating collection of essays on the theme of inside/outside as it arises in international political theory, see R. B. J. Walker, *Inside/Outside: International Relations as Political Theory* (Cambridge: Cambridge University Press, 1993).

53. Of course, Sophocles explores these issues further in the other two Theban plays, *Oedipus at Colonus* and *Antigone*.

van der Veer, "The Victim's Tale"

NOTE: Portions of this article were originally published as "Writing Violence," in *Contesting the Nation*, ed. David Ludden, © 1996 by the University of Pennsylvania Press. Reprinted with permission. I want to thank Hent de Vries and Sam Weber for their willingness to let an anthropologist join the conversation of the "philosophers," both in Amsterdam and in La Baule. And I am grateful to Helen Tartar for her editorial comments.

1. Gyanendra Pandey, "In Defence of the Fragment: Writing About Hindu-Muslim Riots in India Today," *Economic and Political Weekly*, annual number (March 1991): 559–72. This essay has been reprinted in *Representations*, no. 37 (1992): 27–55.

2. Pierre Nora, "Between Memory and History: *Les Lieux de Mémoire*," *Representations*, no. 26 (1989): 1–25.

3. See J. H. Plumb, *In the Light of the Past* (London: Allen Lane, 1972); J. G. A. Pocock, *Politics, Language and Time* (New York: Atheneum, 1971), N. Dirks, "History as a Sign of the Modern," *Public Culture* 2 (1990): 25–33.

4. See esp. James Mill, *The History of British India* (London, 1817).

5. See the critical discussion of the absence of colonialism in Foucault's writing in Ann Stoler, *Race and the Education of Desire: Foucault's History of Sexuality and the Colonial Order of Things* (Durham: Duke University Press, 1995).

6. Marcel Mauss, "La Nation," *Oeuvres* (Paris: Minuit, 1969), 3: 592, 593; see also my discussion of these issues in "The Moral State: Religion, Nation and Empire in Victorian Britain and British India," in Peter van der Veer and Hartmut Lehmann, eds., *The Religious Morality of the Nation-State* (Princeton: Princeton University Press, forthcoming).

7. Ernest Renan, "Qu'est ce que c'est une nation?" In *Oeuvres Completes* (Paris: Callman-Levy, 1947–61; orig. pub. 1882), 1: 887–906.

8. Benedict Anderson, *Imagined Communities* (London: Verso, 1991).

9. Salman Rushdie, *The Satanic Verses* (London: Viking, 1988), 210.

10. Arjun Appadurai, "Number in the Colonial Imagination," in Carol A. Breckenridge and Peter van der Veer, eds., *Orientalism and the Postcolo-*

nial Predicament (Philadelphia: University of Pennsylvania Press, 1993), 314–41.

11. See Ranajit Guha and Gayatri Spivak, eds., *Selected Subaltern Studies* (New York: Oxford, 1988).

12. Mark Tully, *No Full Stops in India* (London, 1991).

13. Ibid., p. 267.

14. Ashis Nandy, "The Politics of Secularism and the Recovery of Religious Tolerance," in Veena Das, ed., *Mirrors of Violence* (Delhi: Oxford, 1990).

15. Timothy Mitchell, "The Limits of the State: Beyond Statist Approaches and Their Critics," *American Political Science Review* 85, no. 1 (1991): 95.

16. Ibid., 77.

17. Rajni Kothari, "State and Statelessness in Our Time," *Economic and Political Weekly*, annual number (March 1991): 553.

18. Ibid.

19. Ibid., 554.

20. Jan Breman, "Anti-Muslim Pogrom in Surat," *Economic and Political Weekly*, April 17, 1993, 741.

21. Michel Foucault, "Governmentality," in Graham Burchell, Colin Gordon, and Peter Miller, eds., *The Foucault Effect: Studies in Governmentality* (Chicago: University of Chicago Press, 1991).

22. See, for a Weberian understanding of this teleology, Ernest Gellner, *Nations and Nationalism* (Ithaca: Cornell University Press, 1983).

23. Cf. Partha Chatterjee, *The Nation and Its Fragments* (Princeton: Princeton University Press, 1993).

24. Immanuel Kant, *Political Writings*, ed. H. Reiss (Cambridge: Cambridge University Press, 1991). See also Jürgen Habermas's reading of Kant in his classic account of the public sphere: *The Structural Transformation of the Public Sphere* (Cambridge: MIT Press, 1989). Peter Gay is eloquent about the Enlightenment's distaste for "unhealthy religion"; see Peter Gay, *The Enlightenment: An Interpretation; The Science of Freedom* (New York: Norton, 1969), 16. The famous separation of State and Church in the French and American constitutions is the political institutionalization of the thought of the "philosophers."

25. Peter van der Veer, *Religious Nationalism: Hindus and Muslims in India* (Berkeley: University of California Press, 1994).

26. Talal Asad, *Genealogies of Religion: Discipline and Reasons of Power in Christianity and Islam* (Baltimore: Johns Hopkins University Press, 1993).

27. See Jose Casanova, *Public Religions in the Modern West* (Chicago: University of Chicago Press, 1994).

28. This large topic is discussed at length in my essay "Syncretism, Multiculturalism and the Discourse of Tolerance," in Charles Stewart and Rosalind O'Hanlon, eds., *Syncretism/Anti-Syncretism* (London: Routledge, 1994), 196–211.

29. Quoted in Wilhelm Halbfass, *India and Europe* (Albany: State University of New York Press, 1988), 409.

30. See my discussions of Hindu and Sufi ritual in: *Gods on Earth* (Lon-

don: Athlone, 1988); "Playing or Praying: A Saint's Day in Surat," *Journal of Asian Studies* 51, no. 3: 545–65; "Riots and Rituals," in Paul Brass, ed., *Riots and Pogroms* (New York: NYU Press, 1996), 154–77.

31. Georges Bataille, *Literature and Evil* (New York: Orisen, 1973).

32. See Pradip Kumar Datta, " 'Dying Hindus': Production of Hindu Communal Common Sense in Early 20th Century Bengal," *Economic and Political Weekly*, June 19, 1993, 1305–19; see also Sumit Sarkar, "Indian Nationalism and the Politics of Hindutva," in David Ludden, ed., *Contesting the Nation: Religion, Community, and the Politics of Democracy in India* (Philadelphia: University of Pennsylvania Press, 1996), 270–93.

33. See Peter van der Veer, "Playing or Praying: A Saint's Day in Surat," *Journal of Asian Studies* 51, no. 3 (1992): 545–65.

34. Sandria Freitag, *Collective Action and Community: Public Arenas and the Emergence of Communalism in North India* (Berkeley: University of California Press, 1989).

35. Sudhir Chandra, "Of Communal Consciousness and Communal Violence: Impressions from Post-Riot Surat," *Economic and Political Weekly*, September 4, 1993, 1883–87; Asghar Ali Engineer, "Bastion of Communal Amity Crumbles," *Economic and Political Weekly*, February 13, 1993, 262–64.

36. Marcel Mauss, *The Gift* (London: Routledge, 1974), 76.

37. Pandey, *Representations*, 55.

Behdad, "Eroticism, Colonialism, and Violence"

NOTE: I wish to thank Samuel Weber for inviting me to participate in this stimulating project and for his insightful remarks on the first draft of my essay.

1. Edward W. Said, *Culture and Imperialism* (New York: Knopf, 1993), 9.

2. Abdul R. JanMohamed, "The Economy of Manichean Allegory: The Function of Racial Difference in Colonialist Literature," in Henry Louis Gates, Jr., ed., *"Race," Writing, and Difference* (Chicago: University of Chicago Press, 1985), 80.

3. J. M. Coetzee, *Waiting for the Barbarians* (Harmondsworth, Middlesex: Penguin Books, 1980). All page references will be given parenthetically in the text. I wish to emphasize at the outset that I do not intend to offer an interpretation of this novel, but to think in general terms about what I have called "the erotics of colonial dissolution" and, in a fragmented fashion, about the particular question of colonial violence at the heart of this form of eroticism. The novel provides me with a discursive site to anchor my reflections. I am hesitant to offer an interpretation because interpretation always involves exclusion and claims of authority. Teresa Dovey is right to point out that Coetzee's novel anticipates the danger of allegorical interpretation to "reinstate itself in the position of authority"; she goes on to argue that the novel "circumvents it by a 'double-sided' allegorical structure, which involves both the allegorical readings of a prior mode of discourse, and a self-reflexive allegory of the way in which the novelistic discourse inevitably works to erect an identity for the speaker, an identity which ultimately would be divested of authority by the authority of the dis-

cursive context in which the novel is read" ("Allegory vs. Allegory: The Divorce of Different Modes of Allegorical Perception in Coetzee's *Waiting for the Barbarians*," *Journal of Literary Studies* 4, no. 2 (June 1988): 141). This is the rationale behind this essay's open-ended and fragmentary structure.

4. The end of the novel in fact echoes the last lines of the poem:

> Because night has fallen and the barbarians haven't come
> And some of our men just in from the border say
> There are no barbarians any longer.
> Now what's going to happen to us without barbarians?
> Those people were a kind of solution.

(Constantin Cavafy, *Collected Poems*, trans. Edmund Keeley and Philip Sherrard, ed. George Savadis [Princeton: Princeton University Press, 1975], 33.)

5. Georges Bataille, *Erotism: Death and Sensuality*, trans. Mary Dalwood (San Francisco: City Lights Books, 1986), 42; Sigmund Freud, *Totem and Taboo* (London: Hogarth Press, 1955).

6. Eric Weil, *Logique de la philosophie* (Paris: Vrin, 1951).

7. Bataille, *Erotism*, 64.

8. Ibid., 63.

9. Bataille distinguishes three forms of eroticism: "l'érotisme des corps," "l'érotisme des coeurs," and "l'érotisme sacré." All three categories involve a movement toward dissolution as the ultimate state of continuity, having initially posited a sense of separatedness, but the locus of such a movement can be the body, the heart (emotions), and the spirit (or sacred practices). These categories also suggest a hierarchical structuration of the notion of eroticism in Bataille. Whereas the eroticism of the body is more "cynical" and "sinister," the eroticism of hearts and sacred eroticism are, respectively, less constrained and more "intellectual." For further illumination of these distinctions, see *Erotism*, 19–23.

10. Bataille, *Erotism*, 19.

11. Homi K. Bhabha, "Signs Taken for Wonders: Questions of Ambivalence and Authority Under a Tree Outside Delhi, May 1817," in Henry Louis Gates, Jr., ed., *"Race," Writing, and Difference* (Chicago: University of Chicago Press, 1985), 171.

12. Debra A. Castillo, "The Composition of the Self in Coetzee's *Waiting for the Barbarians*," *Critique* 27, no. 2 (Winter 1986).

13. Bataille, *Erotism*, 17.

14. See Walter Benjamin, "Theses on the Philosophy of History," *Illuminations*, trans. Harry Zohn, ed. Hannah Arendt (New York: Schocken Books, 1969).

Caruth, "Traumatic Awakenings"

NOTE: A longer version of this essay appears in my *Unclaimed Experience: Trauma, Narrative, and History*. © 1996. The Johns Hopkins University Press.

1. Lacan's study of the dream of the burning child constitutes the core

of the first section of *The Four Fundamental Concepts of Psychoanalysis*, ed. Jacques Alain Miller, trans. Alan Sheridan (New York: Norton, 1981), entitled "The Unconscious and Repetition." In this section, a large portion of chapter 5, entitled "Tuché and Automaton," is consecrated to Lacan's re-reading of the dream. Sporadic references to and reflections on the dream can also be found in chapters 3 and 6.

2. Sigmund Freud, *The Standard Edition of The Complete Psychological Works of Sigmund Freud*, trans. and ed. James Strachey (London: The Hogarth Press, 1953), 5: 509–10; hereafter cited as *SE*.

3. *SE*, 5: 509.

4. On the relation between the dream of the burning child and Freud's dream of his own father, see Jane Gallop, *Reading Lacan* (New York: Cornell, 1985). Peter Gay suggests that the dream may be Freud's own; see Peter Gay, *Freud: A Life for Our Time* (New York: Doubleday, 1988).

5. *SE*, 5: 570–71.

6. *SE*, 4: 233–34; translation modified.

7. Jacques Lacan, *Four Fundamental Concepts*, 57–58. I have slightly modified Sheridan's translation of Lacan's quotations of Freud in order to make them correspond to Strachey's translation.

8. Freud describes trauma as the response to a sudden or unexpected threat of death that happens too soon to be fully known and is then endlessly repeated in reenactments and nightmares that attempt to relive, but in fact only miss again, the original event.

9. Leonard Shengold provides a reading of the burning as highly symbolic and as essentially linked to desire in *"Father, Don't You See I'm Burning?" Reflections on Sex, Narcissism, Symbolism, and Murder: From Everything to Nothing* (New Haven: Yale University Press, 1991). I believe that Lacan's text resists an overly symbolic reading, although Lacan does link the figure of the burning to desire in chapter 4 of the seminar and in the final comments in chapter 5.

For psychoanalytic readings of traumatic nightmares that focus on their unconscious meaning, see Theodor Lidz, "Nightmares and the Combat Neuroses," John Mack, "Toward a Theory of Nightmares," and Melvin R. Lansky, "The Screening Function of Post-Traumatic Nightmares," all in Melvin R. Lansky, ed., *Essential Papers on Dreams* (New York: New York University Press, 1993). Interestingly, one of the difficulties that interpretations of traumatic nightmares face is the problem of awakening, which, as far as I am aware, is always acknowledged as an important aspect of the traumatic nightmare. A review of different kinds of nightmares, which doesn't focus as much on traumatic nightmares, can be found in Ernest Hartmann, *The Nightmare: The Psychology and Biology of Terrifying Dreams* (New York: Basic Books, 1984). For nonpsychoanalytic approaches to the problem of the traumatic nightmare, in studies undertaken by clinicians and researchers concerned specifically with trauma, see, e.g.: Abram Kardiner with Herbert Spiegel, *War Stress and Neurotic Illness*, 2d ed. (New York: Paul B. Hoeber, 1947); Bessel van der Kolk et al., "Nightmares and Trauma: A Comparison of Nightmares After Combat with Lifelong Nightmares in Veterans," *American Journal of Psychiatry* 141 (1984); and, in the context of general issues concerning traumatic imagery, Elizabeth A. Brett and Robert Ostroff, "Imagery and Posttraumatic Stress Disorder: An Overview," *American Journal of Psychiatry* 142, no. 4 (1985).

Lacan's text suggests, I believe, that it would be necessary to rethink the drive through the curious resistance of trauma to symbolism, rather than through a conventional interpretation of the traumatic nightmare in terms of the established concept of repression and the traditional Oedipal theory of received psychoanalysis. One notion that such a rethinking would have to engage would be that of ambivalence, and specifically the possibility of the father's ambivalence toward the child, an interpretation that Freud allows when he suggests that the father may feel some guilt at having left a man who was not up to the task of watching over his child. Rather than address this ambivalence in terms of the individual father in a father-son antagonism, Freud seems to incorporate it into a larger problem of consciousness as such when he says that it is consciousness itself that does not wish to wake up: for in this case the wish to keep the child alive, which Freud originally reads as the motivation of the dream, indeed becomes secondary to the wish of consciousness to sleep and may only serve the wish of consciousness, even in the face of the death of a child, to protect its own sleep.

On the inherent relation between burning and the notion of trauma, see Jean Laplanche (writing about Bachelard), "Le traumatisme incitateur," in *Problématiques III, La Sublimation* (Paris: Presses Universitaires de France, 1980).

10. See the examples of the accident nightmare in *Beyond the Pleasure Principle* (chapter 2) and the comparison of the trauma of the Jews with that of a train accident survivor in *Moses and Monotheism* (pt. 3, sec. 1, chapter 3). See also my detailed discussion of the train collision in chapter 1 of *Unclaimed Experience: Trauma, Narrative, and History* (Baltimore: The Johns Hopkins University Press, 1996). The resonances of the burning of the body of the child in the dream with the burning corpses of the Holocaust remain unspoken, but suggestive in Lacan's text. On the experiences of nightmare and awakening as they appeared from within the concentration camps, see Terence Des Pres, "Nightmare and Waking," in *The Survivor: An Anatomy of Life in the Death Camps* (New York: Oxford University Press, 1976).

11. Lacan, *Four Fundamental Concepts*, 55.

12. Ibid., 69.

13. Shoshana Felman evocatively reads Lacan's interpretation of the dream in terms of the "encounter between sleep and waking" in "Don't You See I'm Burning?, or Lacan and Philosophy," in *Writing and Madness* (Ithaca: Cornell University Press, 1985), pp. 143–60. It should be noted that the relation between sleeping and waking, analyzed in my essay in terms of father and child, involves another character, the *Wächter*, who has fallen asleep next to the child and remains asleep even when the father awakens. Lacan also describes the moment between sleeping and waking in terms of this split between father and *Wächter*, and picks up on this notion of splitting in the third section of "Tuché and Automaton." He thus touches on another dimension of trauma that, in the history of psychiatry and psychoanalysis, goes alongside the temporal understanding of

trauma as experiencing too late: the notion of dissociation of the psyche around the event—the splitting off of a "traumatic memory" from the rest of consciousness (and unconsciousness, for that matter). This notion was developed at length by Pierre Janet, and in contemporary trauma theory there is a certain division around the Freudian understanding of trauma as repetition and reenactment (which, whether acknowledged or not, has a constitutively temporal basis) and dissociation theories, which are often identified with Janet (although Freud also wrote on splitting). (It is interesting that Janet uses the language of sleep and waking to describe the difference between hypnotic and nonhypnotic states in his discussion of dissociation in hysterics; see, e.g., "L'amnésie et la dissociation des souvenirs par l'émotion," in *L'evolution de la mémoire et la notion du temps* [Paris: Cahine, 1928]. This terminology also passes into Freud and Breuer's discussion of hysteria in "On the Psychical Mechanism of Hysterical Phenomena: Preliminary Communication," [*SE*, vol. 2].) On Janet and Freud, see Bessel A. van der Kolk and Onno van der Hart, "The Intrusive Past: The Flexibility of Trauma and the Engraving of Memory," in Cathy Caruth, ed., *Trauma: Explorations in Memory* (Baltimore: The Johns Hopkins University Press, 1995), and Ruth Leys, "Traumatic Cures: Shell Shock, Janet, and the Question of Memory," *Critical Inquiry* 20 (Summer 1994): 623–62. For a fascinating contemporary reading of Holocaust trauma in terms of a dissociative splitting of discourse, see Lawrence L. Langer, *Holocaust Testimonies: The Ruins of Memory* (New Haven: Yale University Press, 1991). It is interesting to note (and may be behind Lacan's own reading) that the *Wächter*—the watchman—in the dream of the burning child resonates with Freud's own general definition of the dream, in *The Interpretation of Dreams*, as the watchman or guardian of sleep, "der Wächter des Schlafens."

14. My reading of chapter 5 of *The Four Fundamental Concepts of Psychoanalysis* can be in part understood as a reading of Lacan's comments in chapter 3:

> The status of the unconscious, which, as I have shown, is so fragile on the ontic plane, is ethical. In his thirst for truth, Freud says, *Whatever it is, I must go there*, because, somewhere, this unconscious reveals itself. . . . Freud said, *There is the country where I shall take my people*. . . . I am not being impressionistic when I say that Freud's approach here is ethical . . .
>
> Freud shows that he is very well aware how fragile are the veils of the unconscious where this register is concerned, when he opens the last chapter of *The Interpretation of Dreams* with the dream which, of all those that are analysed in the book, is in a category of its own—a dream suspended around the most anguishing mystery, that which links a father to the corpse of his son close by, of his dead son. (33–34)

Slavoj Žižek suggests that the awakening in Lacan's reading of the dream is a precise reversal of the usual understanding of dream as fiction and of awakening as reality: he argues that the awakening of the father, in Lacan's reading, is an "escape" from the real into ideology. Aside from the difficulty of accepting that awakening to a child's dead corpse could ever be understood as an escape, the force of Lacan's reading, in the way that I understand it, clearly suggests that the encounter with the real cannot be located simply either inside or outside the dream, but has to be located in the very moment of the transition between the two, in the movement from one to the other. This is what Lacan calls "the gap that constitutes awakening" (57). See Slavoj Žižek, *The Sublime Object of Ideology* (London: Verso, 1989).

15. Lacan, *Four Fundamental Concepts*, 58.

16. One can also understand Freud's description of the death drive in this context in terms of the very specific death described in the dream of the burning child, the death, that is, of a child. For what Freud defines as the death drive—the originating and repeated attempt by the organism to return to the state of the inanimate, the awakening into life that immediately entails an attempt to return to death—could be seen generally as a sense that death is late, that one in fact dies only *too late*. And what could it mean to die *too late*, except to die *after one's child*?

It is important to note, here, a crucial shift that is not explicitly articulated in Freud's text but is implied and underscored by Lacan's reading: from the notion of trauma as a relation to one's own death to the notion of trauma as primarily a relation to another's death. Freud's own shift from *Beyond the Pleasure Principle* to *Moses and Monotheism* may suggest, as I have noted elsewhere, that the death of the other was always inseparable from his notion of one's "own" death. The peculiar temporality of trauma and the sense that the past it foists upon one is not one's own may perhaps be understood from this perspective in terms of a temporality of the other (of the other's potential death). In emphasizing the potentiality in this temporality, my reading differs from Ellie Ragland's interpretation of the dream of the burning child, in particular her suggestion that the death drive "is a traumatic knowledge we all possess," as opposed to my suggestion and my understanding that we could all potentially be traumatized, a point that I believe is closer to the paradoxical temporality of the death drive. See Ellie Ragland, "Lacan, the Death Drive and the Burning Child Dream," in Sarah Webster Goodwin and Elisabeth Bronfen, eds., *Death and Representation* (Baltimore: The Johns Hopkins University Press, 1993).

17. The description of the foundational moment of consciousness as a responsibility toward others in their death (or potential death), as indeed the response to a call from those (potential) deaths, resonates with the ethical thinking of Emmanuel Levinas. Levinas writes about the awakening— the "éveil à partir de l'autre"—that is linked to a foundational moment also associated with trauma in "La philosophie et l'Éveil" (*Entre Nous: Essais sur le Pense-à-l'Autre* [Paris: Grasset, 1991], pp. 93–106). The ethical resonances of the problematics of trauma were first brought to my attention by Jill Robbins, whose brilliant work on Levinas and whose discussions with me about the intersection between the two fields have been invaluable. See esp. "*Visage, Figure*: Speech and Murder in Levinas's *Totality and Infinity*," in Cathy Caruth and Deborah Esch, eds., *Critical Encounters: Reference and Responsibility in Deconstructive Writing* (New Brunswick, N.J.: Rutgers University Press, 1994), 275–98, and her forthcoming *Ethics and the Literary Instance: Reading Levinas*. On the specific appearance of the

notion of trauma in Levinas, see Elisabeth Weber, *Verfolgung und Trauma: Zu Emmanuel Lévinas' 'Autrement qu'être ou au-delà de l'essence'* (Vienna: Passagen-Verlag, 1990).

18. This insight would indeed resurface in the history of trauma research in the ongoing dilemma of "survivor guilt," most notably remarked by Robert Jay Lifton as a paradoxical guilt frequently attending survivor experience: "In all this, self-condemnation strikes us as quite unfair. . . . This guilt seems to subsume the individual victim-survivor rather harshly to the evolutionary function of guilt in rendering us accountable for our relationship to others' physical and psychological existence. This experience of guilt around one's own trauma suggests the moral dimension inherent in all conflict and suffering" (Robert Jay Lifton, *The Broken Connection* [New York: Basic Books], 172).

19. Lacan, *Four Fundamental Insights*, 53.

20. Ibid., 58, 59.   21. Ibid., 61.

22. Ibid., 59.   23. Ibid., 54.

24. Ibid., 55.

25. Jacques Derrida suggests, in a reading of *Beyond the Pleasure Principle*, that the passing-on of psychoanalysis must be understood through the survival of the father past his children (see Jacques Derrida, *The Post Card: From Socrates to Freud and Beyond*, trans. Alan Bass [Chicago: University of Chicago Press, 1987]. Derrida moves between the notion of trauma and the notion of responsibility in "Passages—from Traumatism to Promise," in his interview with Elisabeth Weber in *Points . . . : Interviews, 1974–1994* (Stanford: Stanford University Press, 1995), 372–95. To take up the matter of survival in the seminar fully, one would want also to include a reading of the "knocking dream" with which Lacan introduces his discussion of the dream of the burning child. In a prospectus for a dissertation submitted to the Department of Comparative Literature at Yale University, entitled "Waking Dreams," which includes a proposed chapter on the dream of the burning child, Mary Quaintance discusses the allusion to Macbeth in the knocking dream and points to the text by de Quincey on this play. I was interested to find (in the context of chapter 3 of my *Unclaimed Experience: Trauma, Narrative, and History* [Baltimore: The Johns Hopkins University Press, 1996]) that de Quincey suggests that the figure of the knocking in Macbeth (to which Lacan alludes) signifies not, as one might expect, the imminence of death, but rather the return to life. The crisis, that is, is the survival. This reflection and association in Lacan's texts constitutes a striking introduction, indirectly, to the problem of survival and of the death drive in the dream of the burning child (see Thomas de Quincey, "On the Knocking at the Gate in Macbeth," in *Miscellaneous Essays* [Boston: Ticknor and Fields, 1857]). As Marjorie Garber has pointed out to me, the *Macbeth* resonances in Lacan's story of the knocking dream might be read also in the dream of the burning child through the emphasis on the burning candle.

An exploration of the meaning and the force of the literary allusion in Lacan's text might open onto other questions concerning the literary dimension of the writing of the drama of the dream in both Freud and Lacan. One might consider, for example, the possible resonance between Freud's description of the child's words in the dream of the burning child and the words of the child in Goethe's "Erlkönig."

26. On the possibilities for change opened up by the death drive (as a dislocation of the inside-outside opposition) in a feminist context, see Jacqueline Rose, "Where Does the Misery Come From? Psychoanalysis, Feminism and the Event," in Richard Feldstein and Judith Roof, eds., *Feminism and Psychoanalysis* (Ithaca: Cornell University Press, 1989), reprinted in Jacqueline Rose, *Why War? — Psychoanalysis, Politics, and the Return to Melanie Klein* (Oxford: Blackwell, 1993).

27. Elisabeth Roudinesco tells of the death of Lacan's daughter Caroline in *Jacques Lacan: Esquisse d'une vie, histoire d'un système de pensée* (Paris: Fayard, 1993).

28. Jacques Lacan, "Tuché et automaton," in *Le séminaire, livre XI: Les quatre concepts fondamentaux de la psychanalyse* (Paris: Seuil, 1973), 57.

Haverkamp and Vismann, "Habeas Corpus: The Law's Desire to Have the Body"

1. The present essay follows in the wake of Jacques Derrida's seminal "The Force of Law," trans. Mary Quaintance, *Cardozo Law Review* 11 (1990): 919–1045. See the discussions in *Gewalt und Gerechtigkeit: Derrida-Benjamin*, ed. Anselm Haverkamp (Frankfurt a. M.: Suhrkamp, 1993), as well as the review article by Cornelia Vismann, "Das Gesetz der Dekonstruktion," *Rechtshistorisches Journal* 11 (1992): 250–64.

2. Walter Benjamin, "Critique of Violence," trans. Edmund Jephcott, in *Reflections* (New York: Schocken, 1979), 286; throughout this essay, the translation has frequently been modified.

3. Robert Cover, "Violence and the Word," *Yale Law Review* 95 (1985): 1628–29.

4. For the dialectics of the literal and the metaphorical, see Nelson Goodman, *Languages of Art* (Indianapolis: Bobbs-Merrill, 1968), 68–70.

5. In our use of speech-act theory we are indebted to Ted Cohen's account and amendments in "Figurative Speech and Figurative Acts," *Journal of Philosophy* 72 (1975): 669–84.

6. Owen Barfield, "Poetic Diction and Legal Fiction" (1947), a unique essay in the metaphorology of law, reprinted in Max Black, ed., *The Importance of Language* (Ithaca: Cornell University Press, 1962), 64.

7. See, for the locus classicus, J. L. Austin, *How to Do Things with Words* (Cambridge: Harvard University Press, 1962), 99, as well as the famous critique by Jacques Derrida, "Signature Event Context" in *Limited Inc* (Evanston: Northwestern University Press, 1988), 14.

8. Edward Jenks, "The Story of the Habeas Corpus," *Law Quarterly Review* 18 (1902): 67. See the specimen writ in J. H. Baker's *Introduction to English Legal History*, 3d ed. (London: Butterworths, 1990), 626–27.

9. References here and throughout this essay, if not otherwise attributed, are from Baker, *Introduction to English Legal History*, 165 ("the rule

of law"), 168–69, 537–40 (habeas corpus). We restrict ourselves to the exemplary English development—an example highly acclaimed, though most complicated.

10. M. T. Clanchy, *From Memory to Written Record: England, 1066–1307* (Cambridge: Harvard University Press, 1979), 220. Cf. Theodor Mommsen, *Römisches Staatsrecht* (Darmstadt: Wissenschaftliche Buchgesellschaft, 1955), 324.

11. Baker, *English Legal History*, 112–13, citing the prominent *Case of Prohibitions del Roy* (1608).

12. Ernst H. Kantorowicz, *The King's Two Bodies: A Study in Medieval Theology* (Princeton: Princeton University Press, 1958), 140, 146 (chapters on Frederick and Bracton).

13. As, most recently, in Martha Nussbaum's impressive attempt to restitute mercy as a principle of justice in her article "Equity and Mercy," *Philosophy and Public Affairs* 22 (1993): 83–125. Despite her own emphasis on Seneca, Nussbaum finally succumbs to the Christian reading of mercy as primarily motivated, and justified, by sympathy; she gives away Seneca's point but may have a rhetorical point of her own with respect to what counts as an argument in today's legal debate.

14. As far as the procedure is concerned, habeas corpus belongs with another writ, the certiorari, another means of removing the proceedings from an inferior to a higher court, finally to the king. See Naomi Hurnard, *The King's Pardon for Homicide before A.D. 1307* (Oxford: Blackwell, 1969), 47, and Baker, *English Legal History*, 170.

15. Besides Hurnard, *The King's Pardon*, see Thomas Andrew Green, *Verdict According to Conscience: Perspectives on the English Criminal Jury 1200–1800* (Chicago: University of Chicago Press, 1985), 72ff, 97ff. Cf. Natalie Zemon Davis, *Fiction in the Archives: Pardon Tales and Their Tellers in Sixteenth-Century France* (Stanford: Stanford University Press, 1987).

16. Michel Foucault, *Discipline and Punish: The Birth of the Prison*, trans. Alan Sheridan (New York: Random House, 1979), 29.

17. Baker, *English Legal History*, 168, citing from *R. v. Lord Warden of the Cinque Ports* (1619).

18. Jenks, "The Story of the Habeas Corpus," 64.

19. *Habeas Corpus Act*, cited after William Stubbs, *Select Charters and Other Illustrations of English Constitutional History*, 4th ed. (Oxford: Oxford University Press), 518.

20. F. M. Maitland, *Justice and Police* (London: MacMillan, 1885), 130.

21. Stubbs, *Select Charters*, 518.

22. Maitland, *Justice and Police*, 132.

23. See, if only in the most general manner, Alan Hunt and Gary Wickhamm, *Foucault and Law: Towards a Sociology of Law and Governance* (London: Pluto, 1994), 61–64.

24. Baker, *English Legal History*, 589.

25. Stanley Fish, "The Law Wishes to Have a Formal Existence," in Austin Sarat and Thomas Kearns, eds., *The Fate of Law* (Ann Arbor: University of Michigan Press, 1991), 159. See Anselm Haverkamp, "Rhetoric, Law, and the Poetics of Memory," *Cardozo Law Review* 13 (1992): 1641.

26. Derrida, "The Force of Law," 971; John Rawls, *Justice as Fairness: A Guided Tour* (Harvard and New York universities, Fall 1990). See also Stanley Cavell, "The Conversation of Justice: Rawls and the Drama of Consent," in *Conditions Handsome and Unhandsome* (Chicago: University of Chicago Press, 1990), 113.

27. See, most characteristically, this use of the term by Paul Virilio, "Metémpsychose du passager," *Traverses* 8 (1977).

28. *Encyclopedia Britannica* (1910), s.v. "Habeas Corpus," 784–85.

29. See H. L. A. Hart, "Legal Powers," in *Essays on Bentham* (Oxford: Oxford University Press, 1982), 217.

30. Foucault, *Discipline and Punish*, 29.

31. Georg Wilhelm Friedrich Hegel, *Hegel's Philosophy of Right*, trans. T. M. Knox (Oxford: Oxford University Press, 1952), 186. See Jean-Luc Nancy, "The Jurisdiction of the Hegelian Monarch," trans. Mary Ann and Peter Caws, *Social Research* 49 (1982): 486.

32. See Kenley R. Dove, "Logik und Recht bei Hegel," *Neue Hefte für Philosophie* 17 (1979): 96.

33. See Chiara Frugoni, *La citta lontana* (Turin: Einaudi, 1983), 147; as well as Anselm Haverkamp, "Die Gerechtigkeit der Texte," *Poetik und Hermeneutik* 15 (1994): 17–27.

34. Francis Barker, "A Wilderness of Tigers," *The Culture of Violence* (Chicago: University of Chicago Press, 1993), 170.

35. Benjamin, "Critique of Violence," 286; for the connection of this motif with Benjamin's later work *Origin of the German Mourning Play*, see Anselm Haverkamp, "How to Take It (and Do the Right Thing): Violence and the Mournful Mind in Benjamin's Critique of Violence," *Cardozo Law Review* 13 (1991): 1159.

36. Robert Cover, "Nomos and Narrative"—Foreword, The Supreme Court, Term 1982, *Harvard Law Review* 97 (1983–84): 4–68. See, in defense of Cover's counterpart Ronald Dworkin—notably *Law's Empire* (Cambridge: Harvard University Press, 1986)—Klaus Günther, *Der Sinn für Angemessenheit: Anwendungsdiskurse in Moral und Recht* (Frankfurt a. M.: Suhrkamp, 1988).

37. Hegel, *Hegel's Philosophy of Right*, 145 (our paraphrase).

38. See, e.g., Peter Goodrich, *Languages of Law* (London: Weidenfeld, 1990), 265.

39. We borrow this phrase from Stanley Cavell, *Disowning Knowledge in Six Plays of Shakespeare* (Cambridge: Cambridge University Press, 1987), 191.

Hanssen, "On the Politics of Pure Means"

NOTE: This essay is part of a longer study on the phenomenon of violence, ranging from the recent rise in neo-nationalism to postmodern and feminist strategies of violence. The study includes: "Violence and Interpretation: Enzensberger's *Civil Wars*," published in Marjorie Garber et al., *Field Work: Sites in Literary and Cultural Studies* (New York: Routledge, 1996), 67–76, and "Elfriede Jelinek's Language of Violence," in *New German Critique* 68 (Spring/Summer 1996): 79–112.

1. Gershom Scholem, *Walter Benjamin: The Story of a Friendship*, trans. Harry Zohn (New York: Schocken, 1981), 93.

2. Walter Benjamin, *The Correspondence of Walter Benjamin, 1910–1940*, ed. Gershom Scholem and Theodor W. Adorno, trans. Manfred R. Jacobson and Evelyn M. Jacobson (Chicago: University of Chicago Press, 1994), 174, trans. mod.

3. Scholem, *Friendship*, 80.

4. Its second part, entitled "Die wahre Politik" ("True Politics") was to comprise two chapters, "Abbau der Gewalt" ("Dismantling Power") and "Teleologie ohne Endzweck" ("Teleology Without a Final Goal"), now widely held to be the "Theologico-Political Fragment." See Benjamin, *Correspondence*, 168–69 and Scholem, *Friendship*, 93.

5. See Oskar Negt, "Rechtsordnung, Öffentlichkeit und Gewalt," in Heinz Grossmann and Oskar Negt, *Die Auferstehung der Gewalt: Springerblockade und politische Reaktion in der Bundesrepublik* (Frankfurt a. M.: Europäische Verlagsanstalt, 1968), 168–85.

6. Jürgen Habermas, "Walter Benjamin: Consciousness-Raising or Rescuing Critique," in Gary Smith, ed., *On Walter Benjamin: Critical Essays and Recollections* (Cambridge: MIT Press, 1988), 118–19.

7. Jürgen Habermas, "The Horrors of Autonomy: Carl Schmitt in English," in *The New Conservatism: Cultural Criticism and the Historians' Debate* (Cambridge: MIT Press, 1989), 137. On Schmitt, see further Stephen Holmes's *The Anatomy of Antiliberalism* (Cambridge: Harvard University Press, 1993), which offers a genealogy of conservative antiliberalism, from de Maistre via Schmitt to Leo Strauss and Christopher Lasch, among others. I am grateful to Andreas Huyssen for emphasizing the importance of this study.

8. Walter Benjamin, "Für die Diktatur: Interview mit Georges Valois," in Walter Benjamin, *Gesammelte Schriften*, ed. Rolf Tiedemann and Hermann Schweppenhäuser (Frankfurt a. M.: Suhrkamp, 1974–) vol. 4.1.2, pp. 487–92. See also Michael Rumpf, "Radikale Theologie: Benjamins Beziehung zu Carl Schmitt," Peter Gebhardt et al., *Walter Benjamin—Zeitgenosse der Moderne* (Kronberg: Scriptor, 1976), 37–50.

9. Benjamin, "Diktatur," 489.

10. Ibid., 491.

11. As Derrida has argued in "Force of Law," "Critique of Violence" participates in a Kantian tradition in that it announces itself as a "judgment, evaluation, examination that provides itself with the means to judge violence." As such, it presents "an attitude that permits us to choose (*krinein*) and so to decide and to cut decisively in history and on the subject of history" (Jacques Derrida, "Force of Law: The Mystical Foundation of Authority," *Cardozo Law Review* 11, no. 5–6 [1990]: 1031). On Benjamin's connections to Kant, see also Michael W. Jennings, *Dialectical Images: Walter Benjamin's Theory of Literary Criticism* (Ithaca: Cornell University Press, 1987); Gary Smith, "Thinking Through Benjamin: An Introductory Essay," *Benjamin: Philosophy, History, Aesthetics* (Chicago: University of Chicago Press, 1989), vii–xlii, as well as my *Walter Benjamin's Other History: Of Stones, Animals, Humans, and Angels* (Berkeley: University of California Press, 1997).

12. For a related discussion of this "diacritical principle," which informs many discussions of violence, including feminist and postmodern appropriations of violence, see also my "Elfriede Jelinek's Language of Violence," *New German Critique* no. 68 (Spring-Summer 1996), 89–90.

13. See the entry "Mittel" ["Means"] in *Historisches Wörterbuch der Philosophie* (Darmstadt: Wissenschaftliche Buchgesellschaft, 1971).

14. Hannah Arendt, *On Revolution* (Harmondsworth, Middlesex: Penguin, 1990), 19.

15. This issue has become topical again in the recent multiculturalism and immigration debates, insofar as nonliberal modes of socialization fundamentally question the assumed cohesiveness and uniformity of the liberal community. See especially Habermas's contribution to these debates in Charles Taylor et al., *Multiculturalism* (Princeton: Princeton University Press, 1994).

16. Legal positivism also forms the target of Schmitt's *The Crisis of Parliamentary Democracy*; see Ellen Kennedy, "Introduction: Carl Schmitt's *Parlamentarismus* in Its Historical Context," *The Crisis of Parliamentary Democracy* (Cambridge: MIT Press, 1988), xxxv.

17. Walter Benjamin, "Critique of Violence," *Reflections: Essays, Aphorisms, Autobiographical Writings*, trans. Edmund Jephcott (New York: Schocken, 1986), 279. In the original, the phrase appears as *geschichtsphilosophische Rechtsbetrachtung*.

18. See the entry "Gewalt" in *Historisches Wörterbuch der Philosophie* (Darmstadt: Wissenschaftliche Buchgesellschaft, 1971–).

19. Horst Folkers, "Zum Begriff der Gewalt bei Kant und Benjamin," in Günter Figal and Horst Folkers, eds., *Zur Theorie der Gewalt und Gewaltlosigkeit bei Walter Benjamin* (Heidelberg, F.E.S.T., 1979), 25–57.

20. Benjamin, *Reflections*, 300.

21. On the means-end relation, see the entry "Mittel" in *Historisches Wörterbuch der Philosophie*.

22. Benjamin, *Reflections*, 285.

23. See Günter Figal, "Die Ethik Walter Benjamins als Philosophie der reinen Mittel," in Günter Figal and Horst Folkers, eds., *Zur Theorie der Gewalt und Gewaltlosigkeit bei Walter Benjamin* (Heidelberg: F.E.S.T., 1979), 4ff.

24. Benjamin, *Reflections*, 287.

25. Ibid., 293.

26. Ibid., 292.

27. On Sorel, see Ernesto Laclau and Chantal Mouffe, *Hegemony and Socialist Strategy: Towards a Radical Democratic Politics* (London: Verso, 1985), 36–42.

28. Schmitt, *Crisis*, 69.

29. The passage from Schmitt's *Concept of the Political* reads as follows: "The political entity is by its very nature the decisive entity, regardless of the sources from which it derives its last psychic motives. It exists or does not exist. If it exists, it is the supreme, that is, in the supreme case, the authoritative entity. That the state is an entity and in fact the decisive entity rests upon its political character." (Carl Schmitt, *The Concept of the Political*, trans. George Schwab [Chicago: University of Chicago Press,

1996], 43–44.) Schmitt's notion of the extreme situation is homologous to his concept of the *Ausnahmezustand*, developed in his *Political Theology*, for sovereign is the one who decides on the exception. In his *Concept of the Political*, Schmitt invoked the thesis first formulated in *Political Theology* that "juridic formulas of the omnipotence of the state are, in fact, only superficial secularizations of theological formulas of the omnipotence of God" (42).

30. Schmitt, *Concept of the Political*, 28.

31. Carl von Clausewitz, *On War*, ed. Michael Howard and Peter Paret (Princeton: Princeton University Press, 1984), 87. As Clausewitz observes: "The political object is the goal, war is the means of reaching it, and means can never be considered in isolation from their purpose."

32. Schmitt, *Concept of the Political*, 35.

33. For a discussion of Benjamin's theory of means in relation to the "Theologico-Political Fragment," see Werner Hamacher, "Afformative, Strike: Benjamin's 'Critique of Violence,'" in Andrew Benjamin and Peter Osborne, eds., *Walter Benjamin's Philosophy: Destruction and Experience* (London: Routledge, 1994), 110–38.

34. Going even further, Derrida has argued that Benjamin's "bloodless revolution" could not be demarcated from the technological extermination of the Holocaust.

35. For a related discussion of Benjamin's film theory, see Samuel Weber, *Mass Mediauras: Form, Technics, Media*, ed. Alan Cholodenko (Stanford: Stanford University Press, 1996).

36. Hannah Arendt, *On Violence* (San Diego: Harcourt Brace Jovanovich, 1970), 9.

37. Ibid.

38. Ibid., 5.

39. Ibid., 54.

40. Ibid., 36 and 37n.

41. Ibid., 37.

42. Ibid., 38.

43. Ibid., 56.

44. Ibid., 4.

45. Ibid., 46.

46. Ibid., 79.

47. Ibid., 51.

48. Ibid.

49. On peace as an absolute, see Arendt, *On Violence*, 51.

50. Arendt, *On Revolution*, 18 and 19.

51. Jürgen Habermas, "Hannah Arendt: On the Concept of Power," in *Philosophical-Political Profiles* (Cambridge: MIT Press, 1983), 174.

52. Ibid., 172.

53. Ibid., 173.

54. Ibid., 179.

55. This is corroborated by Habermas when he states that, following the Greek model, the "conduct of war is the classic model of strategic action. For the Greeks, strategic action took place outside the city's walls; for Arendt, too, it is essentially apolitical, an affair for experts."

56. Arendt, *On Revolution*, 19.

57. See Negt's comments on Marcuse in his 1968 "Rechtsordnung, Öffentlichkeit und Gewalt."

58. Arendt, *On Violence*, 56.

59. Ibid., 30–31.

60. Arendt, *On Revolution*, 98, 99.

61. See Jean-Paul Sartre, Preface to Frantz Fanon, *The Wretched of the Earth*, trans. Constance Farrington (New York: Grove Press, 1963), 7–31. On Fanon's critique of Hegel, see his "The Negro and Recognition," in *Black Skin, White Mask*, as well as my "Violence and Interpretation: Enzensberger's *Civil Wars*," in Marjorie Garber et al., *Field Work: Sites in Literary and Cultural Studies* (New York: Routledge, 1996), 67–76.

62. See Gayatri Chakravorty Spivak's discussion of Foucault's notion of epistemic violence, in her "Can the Subaltern Speak?," in Cary Nelson and Lawrence Grossberg, eds., *Marxism and the Interpretation of Culture* (Chicago: University of Illinois Press, 1988), 280–81.

63. Michel Foucault, *The History of Sexuality, Volume I: An Introduction*, trans. Robert Hurley (New York: Vintage Books, 1978), 93.

64. Ibid., 96.

65. Ibid., 102.

66. Michel Foucault, "Politics and Ethics: An Interview," in Paul Rabinow, ed., *The Foucault Reader* (New York: Pantheon, 1984), 378–80.

Fenves, "Marx, Mourning, Messianicity"

1. Jacques Derrida, *Specters of Marx: The State of Debt, the Work of Mourning, and the New International*, trans. Peggy Kamuf (New York: Routledge, 1994), 53; Derrida's italics.

2. Ibid., 59.

3. Karl Marx, "Critique of the Gotha Program," in *The First International and After*, ed. and intro. David Fernbach (New York: Vintage, 1974), 347.

4. Gottfried Wilhelm Leibniz, "Discourse on Metaphysics," in *Philosophical Papers and Letters*, ed. and trans. Leroy Loemker (London: Reidel, 1969), 308; trans. mod.

5. Leibniz, "Leibniz and Clarke Correspondence," sixth letter, *Philosophical Papers*, 687. Marx's dissertation, *Differenz der demokratischen und epikurischen Naturphilosophie* (1841), clarified the difference between these two versions of ancient atomism and their respective conception of "natural philosophy" by referring to the philosophy of Leibniz, for the latter is the only modern "natural philosophy" to take its orientation from the thought of the undivided, the perfectly individuated, the "atomic." In 1837 Feuerbach had devoted an entire volume of his history of modern philosophy to the "presentation, development, and critique of Leibnizian philosophy," and this exegesis exerts its sway not only over Marx's dissertation but also over his reinterpretation of Feuerbach's concept of the *Gattungswesen* ("species-being"). For a discussion of the young Marx's use of Leibnizian categories, see my "Marx's Doctoral Dissertation on Two Greek Atomists and the Post-Kantian Interpretations," *The Journal of the History of Ideas* 46 (July–September 1986): 433–52. The effects of Marx's doctoral dissertation on his later thought is occasionally discernible. He attacks Stirner's *Der Einzige und sein Eigentum* for claiming to have arrived at a new philosophical position, whereas it is in fact, according to Marx, nothing more than an expression of the principle of the identity of indiscernibles; see Marx and Engels, *The German Ideology* (Moscow: Progress

Press, 1976), 468. One of the few interpretations of Marx's work that, like Derrida's *Specters of Marx*, stresses the significance of his encounter with Stirner is the massive exegesis undertaken by Michel Henry. (See, in particular, M. Henry, *Marx* [Paris: Gallimard, 1976], 2:9–56). But as Derrida notes, the primary category of Henry's interpretation is not individuality but "life" (see *Specters*, 186–89). This category must be primary for Henry's *systematic* reconstruction of Marx's "philosophy" because individuality is as such paradoxical and therefore unreconstructable in a systematic fashion. As Marx asserts in the passage from the *German Ideology* mentioned above, to the extent that Stirner presents himself as an individual, he is no different from anything else in the world, including every "louse" and every "grain of sand." The allure of "life"—and especially of "immanent life"—is that it grants a *principle* of difference: the living are to be distinguished from the nonliving (grains of sand), and each living thing can distinguish itself by its degree of aliveness (louse, human being).

6. See especially Marx's use of this Feuerbachian term in the section of the Paris Manuscripts titled "Estranged Labor," in *Economic and Philosophical Manuscripts of 1844*, trans. Martin Milligan (Buffalo, N.Y.: Prometheus Books, 1987), 75–78. A fuller discussion of this term in Feuerbach and Marx is outside the scope of the present essay.

7. Frederick Engels, *Anti-Dühring*, rev. trans. (Peking: Foreign Languages Press, 1976), 135. Marx haunts the pages of *Anti-Dühring*, just as Engels haunts every text signed by Marx beginning in his youth: "I read the whole manuscript to him before it was printed, and the tenth chapter of the part on economics . . . was written by Marx," Engels writes in the preface to *Anti-Dühring* (9). But to speak of Engels "haunting" Marx and Marx "haunting" Engels is doubtless an error, especially if one understands haunting from the perspective of Marx's encounter with Stirner in the *German Ideology* (large parts of which were written in Engels's hand and yet are generally attributed to Marx's voice). As an *Engel* ("angel"), Engels does not "visit" Marx but, instead, erases himself to make him—or his work—visible. On this point Engels is never ambiguous, even if he remains discrete about his self-erasure: "I must note in passing that . . . the outlook expounded in this book was founded and developed in far greater measure by Marx, and only in an insignificant degree by myself" (*Anti-Dühring*, 8–9). For this reason, any discussion of Marx's "hauntology" (Derrida's term) should pay some attention to the phenomenon, if it is a phenomenon in any rigorous sense, of the angel. The peculiar circumstance that angels are everywhere in America today—in the theater, on television, in movies, at the bookstore—is another reason to reconsider the terms in which Derrida casts *Specters of Marx*. Perhaps the appearance of angels en masse indicates something about the future of Engelism.

8. Walter Benjamin, *Der Ursprung des deutschen Trauerspiels*, in *Gesammelte Schriften*, ed. Rolf Tiedemann and Hermann Schweppenhäuser (Frankfurt a. M.: Suhrkamp, 1977–85), 1: 350. All further references to Benjamin's writings are in the text.

9. See Samuel Weber, "Taking Exception to Decision: Walter Benjamin and Carl Schmitt," *diacritics* 22, no. 3 (Fall–Winter, 1992): 5–18.

10. A more thorough account of Benjamin's exposition of *Hamlet*

would have to take into consideration the primary idea of *Der Ursprung des deutschen Trauerspiels*, namely, the Idea itself. This would, in turn, demand an explication of Benjamin's theory of genre. *Hamlet* is an important point of reference for this explication, for within the context of the treatise it can be seen both to complete and to destroy the genre to which it belongs and thus to participate in an Idea. For Benjamin, artworks—as the most phenomenal of phenomena—participate in Ideas. By emphasizing the term "participation" over that of "belonging," Derrida joins Benjamin in displacing traditional questions of genre toward a certain experience of the ungeneric, the nongeneric, perhaps even "the individual." See Jacques Derrida, "La loi du genre" in *Parages* (Paris: Galilée, 1986), 251–87.

11. Friedrich Nietzsche, *Der Geburt der Tragödie*, §7, in *Sämtliche Werke*, ed. Giorgio Colli und Mazzino Montinari (Berlin: de Gruyter, 1967–77), 1: 56–57.

12. See, for example, Marx's early but still in many ways decisive "Contribution to the Critique of Hegel's *Philosophy of Right*: Introduction," in *Critique of Hegel's "Philosophy of Right,"* trans. A. Jolin and J. O'Malley (Cambridge: Cambridge University Press, 1970), 134. More famous, of course, is the opening of the *18th Brumaire of Louis Bonaparte*, which Derrida discusses at length in chapter 4 of *Specters of Marx*.

13. For some aspects of this phenomenon in relation to Benjamin's decision to concentrate on the mourning-play as it returns to Germany, see my "Tragedy and Prophecy in Benjamin's *Origin of the German Mourning Play*," *Jewish Studies Quarterly* (forthcoming).

14. See, above all, Kierkegaard's analysis of the power of farce in—what else?—*Repetition*, included in *Fear and Trembling*, trans. and ed. Howard and Edna Hong (Princeton: Princeton University Press, 1983), 158–67. Adorno makes use of Kierkegaard's conception of farce in the final, "revolutionary" section of his *Habilitationsschrift*, which is not so much "influenced" by Benjamin's as dominated by it; see Theodor W. Adorno, *Kierkegaard* (Frankfurt a. M.: Suhrkamp, 1974), 183–85.

15. See Franz Rosenzweig, *Der Stern der Erlösung* (Frankfurt a. M.: Suhrkamp, 1988), 67–90, esp. 83–87 (The section entitled "The Meta-Ethical").

16. The opening scene of "swearing" (or conjuration) is the point of departure for Derrida's reading of Hamlet in relation to the "injunction" and "promise" of Marx; see the first chapter of *Specters of Marx*.

17. These words are enigmatic in an eminent sense, for they may very well correspond to the secret of a particularly intimate and in a sense impossible correspondence—that between Benjamin and Florens Christian Rang. Although Benjamin doubtless repeats a commonplace when he presents the end of *Hamlet* in terms of a certain "Christianness," it is also, and perhaps for this very reason, an esoteric thesis whose meaning and doctrinal position are impossible to determine from the written text alone. There is good reason to consider this one of the esoteric moments in *The Origin of the German Mourning Play*, for Benjamin is repeating in his own fashion the words of Rang, who had given him his essay on Shakespeare for inclusion in *Angelus Novus*, the journal Benjamin wanted to found with his friends. The "angel" of this journal, whom Benjamin would occa-

sionally invoke in his letters to Scholem, passes the following judgment on Rang's contribution: "He (the angel) does not think nearly as much of another manuscript, recently dedicated to him, and he is once again embarrassing me by making me lend my voice to his most secret thoughts. I refer to Rang's Shakespeare study, or better, an excerpt from it that consists of eight translations with commentary. The few sections I sampled seemed to me to be in such urgent need of categorical judgment, or at least, a more open exchange of views, that I have still not summoned the courage to study it more thoroughly" (*Correspondence of Walter Benjamin*, trans. M. Jacobsen and E. Jacobsen [Chicago: University of Chicago Press, 1994], 197–98). According to Benjamin, Rang's essay on Shakespeare has the same outcome as his dialogue on Goethe's "Selige Sehnsucht": everything comes down to "Christus" (*Correspondence*, 195). It is even possible to read the section of the *Trauerspiel* book entitled "Hamlet" according to the terms set down in the above letter to Scholem: Benjamin "lends his voice" to the "most silent thoughts" of the Angelus, and these thoughts are of a Hamlet who has been lent a life so that he may finally speak—of silence.

In a letter written to Hugo von Hofmannsthal after Rang's death, Benjamin explains how much he owed to Rang in all matters related to Shakespeare: "I cannot act immediately on your suggestion that I expound for you my ideas about Shakespeare's use of metaphor. . . . I am not actually all that familiar with Shakespeare, but have confronted him only sporadically. On the other hand, of course, I learned what it means really to know Shakespeare through my contact with Florens Christian Rang" (*Correspondence*, 286). The section on *Hamlet* could be understood, finally, as a moment in which Benjamin mourns for Rang, whom he always called "Christian." The same is true of the conclusion to his review of Hofmannsthal's *Tower*, where he cites Hamlet's closing words (4:100).

18. See Benjamin, *Correspondence*, 262: "Strictly speaking and just between us, with Rang's death it has lost its authentic reader [*eigentlichen Leser*]" (trans. mod.).

19. One of the terms favored by Florens Christian Rang in his study of Shakespeare is in fact *Christlichkeit*. This term not only lets him present Shakespeare on the hitherside of the Catholic-Protestant divide but also allows him to distinguish another mode of Christianity, one that is no longer "pneumatic" and not merely "spiritual" (*geistlich*), but thoroughly "Christic." The importance of Rang's work for the plan of the *Trauerspiel* book can perhaps be gauged by the titles of its first and last chapters: "Vom Weg messianischer Deutung" ("On the Way of Messianic Interpretation") and "Vom Sinn der Allegorie" ("On the Meaning of Allegory"), respectively. The way of messianic interpretation passes through translation and critique until it reaches allegory. The critical moment, as Rang explains in the opening paragraph, does not consist in the elucidation of obscure moments in a text but in the exposition of an artwork's "light": "For the critical hour is placed closer, since world critique directs itself toward the highest: we must interpret messianically, when the latter [i.e., classical-romantic critique] still interprets pneumatically. We are christic [*Christisch*]—which is fundamentally different from Christian! Messianic elucidation is redelivering death [*wiedergebärender Tod*]. In it the child departs from the

mother who lives higher in him" (*Shakespeare der Christ: Eine Deutung der Sonette*, ed. Bernhard Rang [Heidelberg: Schneider, 1954], 14). Critique means, for both Benjamin and Rang, scission and decision. Every critique thus takes place at a moment of crisis and anticipates its resolution on the day of judgment: "Indeed, the hour is so critical that the critical spirit simply does not know whether that one [i.e., the messiah] will show himself at all. Our spirit is not allowed to enjoy itself as it constructs the future [or] console itself by developing form upon form; rather, without guarantee, it must reach something higher, do away with all its images as too lowly, and de-form itself of all forms. . . . Messianic critique of art is only a particular case of messianic world critique, of the judgment of the world. The latter allows no image, no construct, to stand; even the form of art and the work of art must again be destroyed [*zerschlagen*] along with earlier concepts of art" (*Shakespeare*, 15). Not only is this *Zerschlagen* intimately related to Benjamin's concept of *Destruktion*, but it gives an indication of why Benjamin considered Rang his "authentic reader." Benjamin does not, however, follow Rang's next directive: he does not set out to replace the defunct and destroyed work of art with another kind of work, namely "faith work" (*Glaubenswerk*): "To us, the workless, this is given as the last—and also the first—work of faith" (*Shakespeare*, 17). Rang's discussion of *Hamlet*, like Benjamin's, centers around melancholic self-recognition: "He [Hamlet] is the figure of melancholia . . . in which Shakespeare presented the consciousness of being an insufficient expression of man as the man that therein supersedes himself [*sich aufhebt*]" (*Shakespeare*, 166). This *Aufhebung* of Hamlet corresponds to what Benjamin called the overcoming (*Überwindung*) of his melancholic features. The transcendence of melancholia, according to Rang, allows us to see the mood in which the "fluctuating prophetic form" of Shakespeare's work speaks and remains silent (ibid.).

20. See Carl Schmitt, *Hamlet oder Hekuba: Der Einbruch der Zeit in das Spiel* (Düsseldorf: Diederich, 1956). Schmitt's decision to publish a book in which he had an opportunity to discuss Benjamin's treatise may have been motivated by a desire to reclaim an old debt, since Adorno and Scholem had eliminated Schmitt's name from the notes to *The Origin of the German Mourning Play* in the edition of Benjamin's writings they edited and published in 1955. In Schmitt's excursus on Benjamin's book, which was still largely unknown, he not only could reclaim Benjamin's debt but could also state for the record that Benjamin had sent him a copy in appreciation of his work.

21. See the first chapter of Schmitt's *Hamlet*, "Das Tabu des Königen," 13–21, as well as Derrida's note concerning the significance of Schmitt's treatise and, in particular, of his quotation of Freiligrath's line "Deutschland ist Hamlet!" in *Politiques de l'amitié* (Paris: Galilée, 1994), 180.

22. See Schmitt, *Hamlet*, esp. 62–67 (excursus 2). For an analysis of Hamlet's final words that draws strength from both Benjamin's *Origin of the German Mourning Play* and Schmitt's *Hamlet or Hecuba*, see Franco Moretti's extraordinarily insightful "The Great Eclipse," trans. David Miller, in *Signs Taken for Wonders* (New York: Verso, 1983), 55. Moretti reads the line "the rest is silence" as an injunction, no different in principle

from the old Hamlet's demand for silence: "With the mediocre conscientiousness that characterizes him, Horatio will tell Fortinbras 'of carnal, bloody, and unnatural acts. . . .' In short, he [Horatio] will offer him [Fortinbras] a plot summary. But what of the 'rest,' which is nothing if not the meaning of what happened? On that falls Hamlet's prohibition: let no one presume to confer meaning on it." But it is only Horatio's "mediocre conscientiousness" that interprets "the rest" in a univocal manner and concomitantly converts the statement "the rest is silence" into a prohibition.

23. The young Benjamin also counted Shakespeare among the romantics and, like the early romantics, presented him as the supreme representative of romantic art; see Benjamin's short essay on *As You Like It*, 2: 610–11. In "Sleeping Beauty," the earliest writing of Benjamin to find its way into the *Gesammelte Schriften*, Benjamin, like Derrida, takes his orientation for a consideration of "the times" from Hamlet's statement "the time is out of joint" ("Die Zeit ist aus den Fugen," 2: 9).

24. The term *Christisch* was invented by Florens Christian Rang as a translation of "messianic," as discussed in note 19 above.

25. The convergence of good conscience and scientism is one of the most distinctive features of Francis Fukuyama's *The End of History and the Last Man* (New York: The Free Press, 1992). Derrida's analysis of this book concentrates, for the most part, on its "good conscience," especially when it expresses itself in an "evangelic" spirit. For a consideration of what is at stake in Fukuyama's depiction of a scientific-technological "mechanism" which makes it impossible for history to repeat itself, see my "The Tower of Babel Rebuilt: Some Remarks on 'The End of History,'" in *After History?: Francis Fukuyama and His Critics*, ed. Timothy Burns (Lanham, Md.: Rowan and Littlefield, 1994), 217–37.

26. Derrida, *Specters*, 167–69.

27. Paul de Man, "Anthropomorphism and Trope in Lyric," in *The Rhetoric of Romanticism* (New York: Columbia University Press, 1983), 262. See also Derrida's response to these enigmatic closing lines, *Memoires —for Paul de Man* (New York: Columbia University Press, 1986), 30–39.

28. See Benjamin, "Politico-Theological Fragment," esp. 2: 204.

29. This is Albert Ludwig's contention, which Benjamin reiterates (1: 315).

30. This word "rotten" is used, of course, by Hamlet to describe the state of Denmark, and it is also used by Benjamin to describe the State as such: "For in the exercise of violence over life and death the State [*das Recht*] affirms itself [*bekräftigt sich selbst*] more than in any other legal action [*Rechtsvollzug*]. Something rotten in the State [*etwas morsches im Recht*] at the same time announces itself to the finer feeling in precisely this exercise" (2: 188). Benjamin may not have had Hamlet in mind when he wrote this sentence, since the Schlegel-Tieck edition of Shakespeare translates "rotten" in the line "Something's rotten in the state of Denmark" as *faul*. But something in the very act of translation betrays the same foulness, for it reveals, according to Benjamin, the "rotten limits of one's own language [*morsche Schranken der eigenen Sprache*]" (4: 19). Nations share with native languages at least one property: rottenness. A disclosure of this rottenness of nations and native languages does not serve to justify,

for Benjamin, the project of making a more perfect state or a more perfect language.

31. Marx, *The 18th Brumaire of Louis Bonaparte*, in *Surveys from Exile*, ed. and intro. David Fernbach (New York: Vintage, 1974), 149 (trans. mod.).

32. See Benjamin, 1: 398. This section of the *Trauerspiel* book repeats the closing paragraphs of "Über Sprache überhaupt und über die Sprache des Menschen," esp. 2: 155.

33. Derrida, *Specters*, 59.

Kamuf, "Violence, Identity, Self-Determination, and the Question of Justice"

1. Jacques Derrida, *Specters of Marx: The State of the Debt, the Work of Mourning, and the New International*, trans. Peggy Kamuf (New York: Routledge, 1994).

2. Frances Fukuyama, *The End of History and the Last Man* (New York: The Free Press, 1992), as quoted in Derrida, *Specters*, 72.

3. Jacques Derrida, "Foi et savoir, les deux sources de la 'religion' aux limites de la simple raison," in Jacques Derrida and Gianni Vattimo, eds., *La religion* (Paris: Seuil, 1996), see esp. n. 13, pp. 35–36.

4. See Jacques Derrida, "Force of Law: 'The Mystical Foundation of Authority,' " in Drucilla Cornell, Michel Rosenfeld, and David Gray Carlson, eds., *Deconstruction and the Possibility of Justice* (New York: Routledge, 1992), 3–67.

5. This translation has been slightly modified from the published version. Specifically, the phrase set off by dashes, "and the most ontological, the most critical, and the most risky of all questions," revises my own earlier translation, which missed this sense of a critique of the question in general.

Hamacher, "One 2 Many Multiculturalisms"

NOTE: Composed between January 24 and February 10, 1994.

1. Friedrich Nietzsche, *Human, All Too Human: A Book for Free Spirits*, trans. Marion Faber with Stephen Lehmann (Lincoln: University of Nebraska Press, 1984), 153–54, trans. mod.

2. Ibid., 153.

3. On the further development of the structure or di-structure of this "diaporia," see my *Pleroma—Reading Hegel*, trans. Nicholas Walker and Simon Jarvis (Stanford: Stanford University Press, forthcoming).

4. Sigmund Freud, *The Future of an Illusion*, in James Strachey, ed., *The Standard Edition of the Complete Psychological Works of Sigmund Freud*, 24 vols. (London: Hogarth, 1953–74), 21: 5–6, trans. mod. Hereafter referred to as *SE*.

5. Ibid., 21: 7.

6. Ibid., 21: 9.

7. Freud, "Why War?" *SE*, 22: 203–9.

8. Ibid., 22: 214.

9. Ibid., 22: 213, trans. mod.

10. Freud, "The Future of an Illusion," *SE*, 21: 13, trans. mod.

11. Ibid.

12. See, e.g., Sigmund Freud, *Gesammelte Werke* (Frankfurt a. M.: Fischer, 1947), 16: 22.

13. Theodor W. Adorno, *Negative Dialectics*, trans. E. B. Ashton (New York: Continuum, 1983), 366, trans. mod.

14. Herman Melville, *Redburn: His First Voyage*, chap. 33, in vol. 4 of *The Writings of Herman Melville* (Evanston and Chicago: Northwestern University Press and The Newberry Library, 1969), 169. A very rich text by Marc Shell, "The Politics of Language Diversity," sketches the history of the discussions regarding languages in the United States and in Canada, the history of an often violently suppressed diversity. Shell cites, among other things, an astonishing pronouncement by Benjamin Franklin dating from 1751 in which the linguistic racism concealed by Melville in his biblical imagery blatantly comes to the fore. Upon the failure of a German-language newspaper published by Franklin, due to pressure from the competition, he writes: "Why should Pennsylvania, founded by the English, become a Colony of Aliens, who will shortly be so numerous as to Germanize us instead of our Anglifying them, and will never adopt our *Language or Customs* any more than they can acquire our *Complexion?*" (*Critical Inquiry* 20, no. 1 (Autumn 1993): 109; my emphasis).

15. Ibid., 165.

16. David Rieff, "Multiculturalism's Silent Partner," in *Harper's* (August 1993), 67.

17. Karl Marx and Friedrich Engels, *Collected Works* (New York: International Publishers, 1976), 5: 60.

18. Ibid., 5: 73–74. In the same context, one example among many, Marx indicates that the precondition of the victory of the merchant town over the country is "the automatic system."

19. Karl Marx, in Marx/Engels, *Collected Works*, 4: 81–82, trans. mod.

20. The structure of the idea's "ideal" advantage over interest is analogous to the one described by Marx in *Capital* as the structure of primitive accumulation: it consists, among other things, of credit. "Public credit becomes the *credo* of capital" (Karl Marx and Friedrich Engels, *Capital*, vol. 1, trans. Ben Fowkes [New York: Vintage Books, 1977], 919). For more on the structure of credit, see my "Faust, Geld" in *Athenäum* 4 (1994).

21. Benedict Anderson impressively describes the preparation of such a touristic mausoleum culture in the era of colonialism in his *Imagined Communities* (London: Verso, 1991), 163–86.

22. One might call this argument that of the reversion of terrorism. Its strongest proponent is Frantz Fanon, who demonstrates in *Les damnés de la terre* that the humiliating image imposed upon Africans by their colonial rulers led to clinical forms of psychosis and made self-esteem impossible for them, leaving them only one way out: a kind of cathartic reversion to the violence that had been perpetrated against them. The violence of an image or of a glance, the violence of an ideal—this is, according to Fanon, the actual colonizing violence, and its effect lies not so much in the imposition of an image as in the destruction of any possibility of an image,

the traumatization and the ruin of any possible identity. The violence of the glance or of the ideal—of a *particular* glance and a *particular* ideal—is described by Ralph Ellison in a scene in *Invisible Man* in which his protagonist, his "I," is able to keep himself back from murdering a white man by noticing that "the man had not *seen* me, actually" (New York: Random House, 1992), 4. The violence of the glance is not one that gives, or renders visible, a face; still less does it make room for a face, allowing it to persevere. Rather, it is a violence that extinguishes the face, brings about its disappearance, renders it invisible. It is the violence of a glance that no longer sees anything—and not because it is consumed by what it sees, but because it *shows* its power of vision. This is the violence of the ostentation of staring, for which there is no other phenomenon but itself: an imperial subjectivity that posits itself and itself alone. Ellison's "I" holds itself back from the reversion of violence—and this is the ethical moment par excellence, the moment of interruption, the opening in the historical system of violences and counterviolences—because it sees through precisely this structure of the glance: it is not meant for him, it is meant for nobody and for nothing and is therefore as void as it is annihilating.

23. The motif of self-invention can be found, along with all of its accompanying paradoxes, throughout the work of Gayatri Chakravorty Spivak, for example. Cf. her *In Other Worlds* (London: Routledge, 1987) and "Questions of Multiculturalism," in Simon During, ed., *The Cultural Studies Reader* (London: Routledge, 1993), 193–202.

24. Charles Taylor, *Multiculturalism and "The Politics of Recognition"* (Princeton University Press, 1992).

25. Taylor, *Multiculturalism*, 25, 65–66.

26. Ibid., 32, 47.

27. Ibid., 50.

28. Jean-Jacques Rousseau, "The Letter to M. d'Alembert on the Theatre," trans. Allan Bloom, in *Politics and the Arts* (Ithaca: Cornell University Press, 1991), 126, trans. mod. Taylor discusses this in *Multiculturalism*, 47–48.

29. Rousseau, "Letter to d'Alembert," 126, trans. mod. See Taylor, *Multiculturalism*, 47.

30. Ibid., 50.   31. Ibid., 51.

32. Ibid., 44.   33. Ibid., 41.

34. Ibid.

35. Immanuel Kant, *Groundwork of the Metaphysic of Morals*, trans. H. J. Paton (New York: Harper & Row, 1964), BA 77. The abbreviation BA refers to the pagination of Kant's second edition.

36. Ibid., BA 78.

37. Taylor, *Multiculturalism*, 50.

38. Kant, *Groundwork*, BA 79, my emphasis.

39. Thus, proceeding from Kant, we touch upon the major motif of Emmanuel Levinas's later work, which may be characterized, in political terms, as a motif of a democracy for the other. In *Otherwise than Being* he writes in this vein (and I shall limit myself to this one reference): "The other in the same is my substitution for the other through *responsibility*, for which I am summoned as someone *irreplaceable*." And, in a state-

ment that is programmatic for this work: "The emphasis of openness is responsibility for the other to the point of substitution, where the *for-the-other* proper to disclosure, to monstration to the other, turns into the *for-the-other* proper to responsibility. This is the thesis of the present work" (*Otherwise Than Being*, trans. Alphonso Lingis [Dordrecht: Kluwer, 1991], 114, 119, trans. mod.).

40. Taylor, *Multiculturalism*, 44.

41. "And precisely here we encounter the paradox that without any further end or advantage to be attained the mere dignity of humanity, that is, of rational nature in man—and consequently that reverence for a mere Idea—should function as an inflexible precept for the will; and that it is just this freedom from dependence on interested motives which constitutes the sublimity of a maxim and the worthiness of every rational subject to be a law-giving member in the kingdom of ends; for otherwise he would have to be regarded as subject only to the law of nature—the law of his own needs" (Kant, *Groundwork*, BA 85, trans. mod.). And: "In this, we must frankly admit, there is shown a kind of circle, from which, as it seems, there is no way of escape. In the order of efficient causes we take ourselves to be free so that we may conceive ourselves to be under moral laws in the order of ends; and we then proceed to think of ourselves as subject to moral laws on the ground that we have described our will as free. Freedom and the will's enactment of its own laws are indeed both autonomy—and therefore are reciprocal concepts—but precisely for this reason one of them cannot be used to explain the other or to furnish its ground. It can at most be used for logical purposes in order to bring seemingly different ideas of the same object under a single concept (just as different fractions of equal value can be reduced to their simplest expression)" (Kant, *Groundwork*, BA 104–5). (I have developed in detail the problems of this "paradox" and this "circle," esp. with regard to language and its prestructure and thus to the promise [*Versprechen*] as a speaking-*ahead of-oneself* in "Das Versprechen der Auslegung," in N. Bolz and W. Hübner, eds., *Spiegel und Gleichnis—Festschrift für Jacob Taubes* [Würzburg: Königshausen und Neuman, 1983], further developed in *Premises: Essays on Philosophy and Literature from Kant to Celan* [Cambridge: Harvard University Press, 1996].)

42. Kant, *Groundwork*, BA 40.

43. Ibid., BA 80.

44. On the large complex of the aporia—the aporia "itself," the impossibility of a "self" of aporia, the aporia of death as the possible impossibility of *Dasein*—and of the aporias of a "culture" of death, see Jacques Derrida, *Aporias* (Stanford: Stanford University Press, 1993).

45. On this point—especially on the "argument of the argument" and the paradoxes connected with it—see Alexander García Düttmann, "Die Dehnbarkeit der Begriffe," in Jutta Georg-Lauer, ed., *Postmoderne und Politik* (Tübingen: edition diskord, 1992), and "Versuche, das Besondere zu denken," *faultline* 2 (1993).

46. Jürgen Habermas, "Anerkennungskämpfe im demokratischen Rechtsstaat," in Charles Taylor et al., *Multikulturalismus und die Politik der Anerkennung* (Frankfurt a. M.: S. Fischer, 1993), 179. Cf. the English version of the passage under discussion, Habermas, "Struggles for Recog-

nition in Constitutional States," *European Journal of Philosophy* 1, no. 2 (1993): 145–53.

47. Habermas, "Anerkennungskämpfe," 179.

48. Ibid., 182.

49. Ibid., 183, 184.

50. Ibid., 187. Habermas writes: "The limits of capacity have surely not been reached in the European societies, which are shrinking demographically and are still dependent on immigration, if for economic reasons alone." Habermas's argument, here and elsewhere in his discussion, is complicated by the fact that he seeks to counter the scandalous parties' agreement of January 15, 1993, an amendment to the Federal Republic's Basic Law which amounts de facto to its corruption. But he does so with a "rational" argument, in which both the "rationality" and the "argumentative" nature of his conception of democracy are shown in their most embarrassing aspect, in the light of national egotism: "demographically and . . . for economic reasons alone," European societies are "dependent" on immigration; and "the limits of capacity" have "not been reached." De jure, Habermas thereby concedes, these "limits of capacity"—though they may not have been reached de facto and are thus not yet an "argument" in a political debate—de jure they are not only a possible, but in principle an indispensable argument, for these "limits of capacity" are given by just those "limits" imposed by a community organized along the lines of "constitutional patriotism" in order to "preserve" its "identity . . . , which must not be affected even by immigration" (183), and in order to secure its "national consciousness based on citizenship" (194)!

Habermas's essay, which is in more than one respect symptomatic for the level of discussion concerning the "limits" of democracy and the "nation's right to assert its identity" and its "political culture," deserves a more detailed analysis. My interest here, however, is only in the conception of "rational argumentation" which he invokes in connection with the debate on immigration and asylum and which is characteristic of the compromise-based morality of his "constitutional patriotism." Just one further quote from this confused and troubling text by someone who is still readily cited, and not only in Germany, as a model of a radical democrat. Habermas writes:

> Irrespective of the angle taken [on postwar immigration to western Europe], Europe was a beneficiary of these migratory flows.—These and similar moral reasons [by which it is suggested that morality is "similar" to the interest in benefits], while they don't justify guaranteeing actionable individual legal rights to immigration [those grounds of profit "morality" indeed justify only decisions in favor of further profits], do justify the obligation to practice a liberal immigration policy which opens one's own society [how can a society still be its "own" when it participated, as did European society, in the intercontinental migratory movements between 1800 and 1960, as Habermas himself states, at the rate of 80 percent (186)? And how can it be its "own" if, as was the case in West Germany after the Second World War, a third of it consists of immigrants (190)?] to emigrants and manages the

flow of immigration in line with existing capacities [these "available capacities (*Kapazitäten*)," the same phantom as the "limits of capacity (*Belastbarkeit*)," are for Habermas the measure which "manages" his politics of "constitutional patriotism"]. The defensive slogan "the boat is full" lacks the willingness to look at things also from the other side's point of view. (187)

"Also" the other side's point of view—this "also" is the password by which Habermas secures his participation in the "rational," "argument-based" discussion with a nationalistic, nation-state-oriented, and xenophobic politicians' alliance and at the same time reserves his access to a political morality limited only by completely imaginary "capacities." But is it not "also" the point of view of the others that must be adopted—"that of those 'boat people,' for example, who sought to escape the terror in Indochina aboard unseaworthy skiffs" (ibid.)? It must be first and foremost the point of view of these suffering others that is adopted, and this means also the point of view of those who do not argue, who cannot advance arguments that measure up to the rationale of profits or capacities, but who must be spoken and acted *for* without regard for profit or compensation. A democracy that curtails the others' claims—which are always claims for democratization—by calculating its own benefits and that, along with Habermas, measures its obligations to others in terms of capacity can no longer take itself seriously, can no longer take itself to be a democracy, and has sold out the claim to unconditional autonomy for all to a fantasy of self-interest.

51. Habermas, "Anerkennungskämpfe," 181.
52. Taylor, *Multiculturalism*, 71.
53. Kant, *Groundwork*, BA 16.
54. Taylor, *Multiculturalism*, 70, 64.
55. Ibid., 71.
56. Ibid.
57. Ibid., 61.
58. Since my reflections here concern the logical, ethical, and political status of number and the countability of the many—and of the one—let me make a brief remark regarding the paradox in the logic of the classes of the one and the many formulated by Russell in his *Principles of Mathematics* (1903). Russell notes: "A class as one may be a term of itself as many. Thus the class of all classes is a class; the class of all the terms that are not men is not a man, and so on. Do all the classes that have this property form a class? If so, is it as one a member of itself as many or not? If it is, then it is one of the classes which, as ones, are not members of themselves as many, and *vice versa*. Thus we must conclude again that the classes which as ones are not members of themselves as many do not form a class or rather, that they do not form a class as one, for the argument cannot show that they do not form a class as many" [New York: Norton, n.d.] §101, p. 102). If "one" cannot be a term of itself as many, then there is no class of classes, which means that there is no extension of the concept of class, no extension of the one and thus no meaning that could be attributed to the one as a predicate. Yet if "one" is a term that belongs to itself—its class—as many; if there is thus no class that could be ascribed to the one as its extension, then again

there is no meaning of the one and thus no one. "One" must thus belong to itself as many, but at the same time it cannot belong to itself under any circumstances. It must constitute a class and at the same time cannot be one, must have an extension and cannot have one, must be one and itself but at the same time cannot be. That which is true of one is just as true of many, insofar as many must always be counted as *one* many: it too cannot be a class and must nevertheless be one, cannot and must nevertheless be many. One and many are thus inconsistent manifolds—that is, manifolds that resist counting in principle, even counting, but that nevertheless, and no less essentially, provoke such counting. They are unities that are just as necessarily unities as they are disunities.

A mathematical theory of a classless society is thus confronted with an aporia: that "classless" would still be a class—and could nevertheless not be one. Such a theory must thus become a theory of class-aporia and of the aporia of number and uncountability, and it thus dissolves the basic terms with which it operates. This theory would concern "objects" that are not *more* than one or *more* than many but *otherwise* than one and *otherwise* than many—and that are thus *otherwise* than *are*. Their ontological status determines and indetermines itself each time according to an other, *anontological* one.

59. Taylor, *Multiculturalism*, 71.

60. Ibid., 73.

61. No one saw this more clearly than the thinker to whom the theorists of the democracy of recognition appeal. In the *Metaphysics of Morals*, Kant writes, definitionally, "Reverence (*reverentia*) is . . . a feeling of a special kind, not a judgment about an object that it would be a duty to bring about or promote. For such a duty, regarded as a duty, could be presented to us only through the reverence we have for it. . . . he must have reverence for the law within himself in order even to think of any duty whatsoever" (*Metaphysics of Morals*, trans. Mary Gregor [Cambridge: Cambridge University Press, 1991], 203–4, trans. mod.). The objective notion of duty and a judgment corresponding to it must thus be preceded by a subjective—and in this context, this means an a priori—reverence, so that a duty and the urgency of a judgment may be perceived in the first place.

62. Walter Benjamin, "Theses on the Philosophy of History" (VII), in *Illuminations*, trans. Harry Zohn (New York: Schocken, 1969), 256–57, trans. mod.

Derrida, ". . . and pomegranates"

NOTE: This is the third and final part of an essay entitled "Faith and Knowledge: The Two Sources of 'Religion' at the Limits of Simple Reason" ("Foi et savoir, les deux sources de la 'religion' aux limites de la simple raison," in Jacques Derrida and Gianni Vattimo, eds., *La religion* [Paris: Seuil, 1996]; forthcoming in English from Stanford University Press). Curly brackets ({ }) have been used for translator's insertions; square brackets are the author's.

1. Let us worry {*Égrenons*} here the premises of a work to come. Let them be drawn . . . from the rich chapter of Benveniste's *Indo-European*

Language and Society, trans. Elizabeth Palmer (London: Faber and Faber, 1973), which addresses the Sacred and the Holy after having opportunely recalled several "methodological difficulties." It is true that to us these "difficulties" seem even more serious and more fundamental than to Benveniste —even if he is willing to acknowledge the risk of "seeing the object of study dissolve bit by bit" (445). Maintaining the cult of "original meaning" (religion itself, and the "sacred"), Benveniste identifies, through the enormously complex network of idioms, filiations, and etymologies studied, the recurrent and insistent theme of the "fertility" of the "strong," of the "powerful," in particular in the figure or the imaginal scheme of swelling.

Allow us the following long citation, while referring the reader to the article itself for the rest: "The adjective *sura* does not signify merely 'strong'; it is also a qualification of a number of gods, of several heroes including Zarathustra, and of certain notions such as 'dawn.' Here, comparison with related forms of the same root can lead us to the original meaning. The Vedic verb *su- sva-* signifies "to swell, grow," implying "force" and "prosperity"; whence *sura-*, "strong, valiant." The same conceptional relation joins in Greek the present *kuein*, "to be pregnant, carry in the womb," the noun *kūma*, "swelling (of waves), flood," on the one hand, and *kuros*, "force, sovereignty," *kurios*, "sovereign," on the other. This juxtaposition brings out the initial identity of the meaning of 'swell' and, in each of the three languages, a specific evolution. . . . In Indo-Iranian no less than in Greek, the meaning evolves from "swelling" to "strength" or "prosperity." . . . Between gr. *kueō*, "to be pregnant," and *kurios*, "sovereign," between Av. *sura*, "strong," and *spénta*, relations are thus restored which, little by little, make more precise the singular origin of the notion of "sacred." . . . The holy and sacred character is thus defined through a notion of exuberant and fecundating force, capable of bringing to life, of causing the productions of nature to burst forth" (448–49).

One could also inscribe under the title of the "two sources" the remarkable fact, often emphasized by Benveniste, that "almost everywhere" there correspond to the "notion of the 'sacred' not one but two distinct terms." Benveniste analyzes them, notably in Germanic (the Gothic *weihs*, "consecrated," and the Runic *hailag*, ger. *heilig*) in Latin *sacer* and *sanctus*, in Greek *hagios* and *hieros*. At the origin of the German *heilig*, the Gothic adjective *hails* translates the idea of "soundness, health, physical integrity," translation of the Greek *hygies*, *hygianion*, "in good health." The corresponding verbal forms signify "render or become healthy, heal." (One might situate here—although Benveniste does not—the necessity for every religion or all sacralization to also involve healing: *heilen*, health, hail or promise of a cure, *cura*, *Sorge*, horizon of redemption, of the restoration of the unscathed, of indemnification). The same for the English *holy*, neighbor of *whole* ("entire, intact," therefore "safe, saved, unscathed in its integrity, immune"). The Gothic *hails*, "in good health, in possession of physical integrity," carries with it a wish, as does the Greek *khaīre*, "hail!." Benveniste underscores its "religious value": "Whoever possesses 'hail' (*le 'salut'*), that is, whose physical integrity is intact, is also capable of conferring 'hail.' "To be intact" is the luck that one wishes, predicts or expects. It is natural to have seen in such perfect 'integrity' a divine grace, a sacred meaning. By its very nature, divinity possesses the gift of integrity, of being hail, of luck, and can impart it to human beings. . . . In the course of history the primitive Gothic term *weihs* was replaced by *hails, hailigs*" (451–52).

2. Elsewhere, in a seminar, I attempt to reflect in a more sustained manner on this value of the halt and on its lexical ramifications, in particular surrounding the use of *halten* by Heidegger. In addition to *Aufenthalt* ("stopover," "ethos," often involving the *heilig*), *Verhaltenheit* (modesty or respect, scruple, reserve or silent discretion, which suspends itself in and as reticence) would be only one example, albeit a major one for what concerns us here, taking into account the role played by this concept in the *Beiträge zur Philosophie* with respect to the "last god," or the "other god," the god who comes or the god who passes. I refer here, in particular regarding this last theme, to the recent study by Jean-François Courtine, "Les traces et le passage du Dieu dans les Beiträge zur Philosophie de Martin Heidegger," *Archivio di Filosofia*, 1994, nos. 1–3. When he recalls Heidegger's insistence on modern nihilism as "uprooting" (*Entwürzelung*), Courtine rightly associates it with what is said of—and always implicitly against—the *Gestell* and all "technical-instrumental manipulation of beings" (*Machenschaft*), with which he even associates "a critique of the idea of creation directed primarily against Christianity" (528). This seems to go in the direction of the hypothesis developed above (in an earlier part of the essay excerpted here): Heidegger directs suspicion at the same time against "religion" (especially Christian-Roman), against belief, and against what in technics menaces the safe and sound, the unscathed or the immune, the sacro-sanct (*heilig*). The interest of his "position" consists, simplifying considerably, in the way it tends to take its distance (*se déprendre*) from both religion and technics, or rather from what is called *Gestell* and *Machenschaft*, as though they were the same. The same, yes, as what we are trying to say here as well, modestly and in our fashion. And the same neither excludes nor effaces any of the differential folds. But once this same possibility is recognized or thought, it is not certain that it calls only for a Heideggerian "response," nor that the latter is alien or exterior to this same possibility, be it the logic of the unscathed, or the auto-immune indemnification that we are trying to approach here. We shall return to this later in this essay and elsewhere.

3. That is, of what in Western cultures remains sacrificial, up to and including its industrial, sacrificial, and "carno-phallogo-centric" implementation. On this latter concept, see " 'Eating Well,' or the Calculation of the Subject," in Jacques Derrida, *Points . . .: Interviews, 1974–1994* (Stanford University Press: Stanford, 1995), 255–87.

4. Concerning the association and disassociation of these two values (*sacer* and *sanctus*), we refer below to Benveniste and to Levinas.

5. Henri Bergson, *The Two Sources of Morality and Religion*, trans. R. Ashley Audra and Cloudesley Brereton, with W. Horsfall Carter (Notre Dame: University of Notre Dame Press, 1986), 317.

6. Although Derrida uses the English word here, elsewhere he consistently uses the French term *mondialisation* and the neologism *mondialatinisation*, which have been translated throughout as "globalization" and "globalatinization"—Trans.

7. Heidegger, *Beiträge zur Philosophie* (Frankfurt a. M.: V. Klostermann, 1987), 256. French translation and as cited by J.-F. Courtine, "Les traces et le passage de Dieu," 533. On a certain question of the future, Judaism, and Jewishness, let me refer to "Archive Fever: A Freudian Impression," trans. Eric Prenowitz, *diacritics* 25 (Summer, 1995): 9–63.

8. This letter to Löwith, dated August 19, 1921, was recently cited in French by J. Barash, *Heidegger et son siècle* (Paris: Presses Universitaires de France, 1995), 80, n. 3, and by Françoise Dastur, in "Heidegger et la théologie," *Revue philosophique de Louvain*, May–August 1994, nos. 2–3, 229. Together with that of Jean-François Courtine cited above, Dastur's study is one of the most illuminating and richest, it seems to me, to have been published on this subject in recent years.

9. I take the liberty, in regard to these questions, of referring once again to "How to Avoid Speaking: Denials," in Sanford Budick and Wolfgang Iser, eds., *Languages of the Unsayable: The Play of Literature and Literary Theory* (New York: Columbia University Press, 1989), 3–70; rpt. Stanford University Press, 1996. As to the divinity of the divine, the theion, which would thus be the theme of a theiology, distinct both from theology and from religion, the multiplicity of its meanings should not be overlooked. Already in Plato, more specifically, in the *Timaeus*, where there are no fewer than four concepts of the divine (see on this point the remarkable work of Serge Margel, *Le tombeau du dieu artisan* [Paris, Editions de Minuit, 1995]). This multiplicity does not prevent, but on the contrary commands one to return to the unitary precomprehension, to the horizon of meaning, as it is called, of the same word. Even if, in the final accounting, this horizon itself must be abandoned.

10. "The Anaximander Fragment," in Martin Heidegger, *Early Greek Thinking*, trans. David Farrell Krell and Frank A. Capuzzi (Harper: San Francisco, 1984), 57.

11. On these issues—since I am unable to develop them here—let me refer to my *Of Spirit: Heidegger and the Question*, trans. Geoffrey Bennington and Rachel Bowlby (Chicago: University of Chicago Press, 1989), 129–36. Cf. also Françoise Dastur, "Heidegger et la théologie," 233, n. 21.

12. On all these themes, the corpus to be invoked is immense, and we are incapable of doing it justice here. It is above all determined by the discourse of a conversation between the Poet (to whom is assigned the task of saying, and hence of saving the unscathed, *das Heilige*) and the Thinker, who searches for the signs of the god. On the *Beiträge*, particularly rich in this respect, I refer once again to the study of Jean-François Courtine and to all the texts that it evokes and interprets.

13. Samuel Weber has reminded me, and I thank him for doing so, of the very dense and difficult pages devoted by Heidegger to "The Thought of the Eternal Return as Belief [*als ein Glaube*]" in his *Nietzsche*, trans. David Farrell Krell (Harper: San Francisco, 1991), 121–32 {the published translation has been modified where greater literalness is helpful for following Derrida's discussion}. . . . In rereading these passages, it strikes me as impossible in a footnote to do justice to their richness, complexity, and strategy. I will try to return to this elsewhere. While waiting, however, just these two points:

(1) Such a reading would suppose a patient and thoughtful sojourn with holding (*Halt, Haltung, Sichhalten*) . . . throughout Heidegger's way of thinking.

(2) This "holding" is an essential determination of belief, at least as Heidegger interprets it in his reading of Nietzsche, notably of the question posed in *The Will to Power*: "What is a belief? How is it born? All belief is a holding-for-true (*Jeder Glaube ist ein Für-Wahr-halten*)." No doubt Heidegger remains very careful and suspensive in his interpretation of this "concept of belief" (*Glaubensbegriff*) in Nietzsche, which is to say, of Nietzsche's "concept of truth and of 'holding-himself [*Sichhalten*] in truth and for truth.'" He even declares that he abandons the task, as well as that of representing the Nietzschean grasp of the difference between religion and philosophy. Nevertheless, he multiplies preliminary indications in referring to sentences dating from the period of Zarathustra. These indications reveal that in his eyes, if belief is constituted by "holding-for-true" and by "holding-oneself in truth," and if truth signifies for Nietzsche the "relation to being in its totality," then belief, which consists in "taking for true something represented [*ein Vorgestelltes als Wahres nehmen*]," remains therefore metaphysical, in some way and therefore unequal to what in thought should exceed both the order of representation and the totality of the entity. This would be consistent with the affirmation cited above: "Der Glaube hat im Denken keinen Platz." Of the Nietzschean definition of belief (*Für-Wahr-halten*), Heidegger declares first that he retains only one thing, but "the most important," which is to say, "holding to what is true and maintaining oneself in it" ("das Sichhalten an das Wahre und im Wahren"). A little further on he adds: "If maintaining-oneself in the true constitutes a modality of human life, then no decision concerning the essence of belief and Nietzsche's concept of belief in particular can be made before his conception of truth as such and its relation to 'life' has been elucidated, which is to say, for Nietzsche: its relation to the entity in its totality [*zum Seienden im Ganzen*]. Without having acquired a sufficient notion of the Nietzschean conception of belief, we would not attempt to say what the word 'religion' signifies for him" (124).

14. E. Benveniste, *Indo-European Language*, esp. 449, 453–56, 468.

15. *Plus d'un* can mean both "more than one" and "one no more." See Jacques Derrida, *Specters of Marx*, trans. Peggy Kamuf (New York: Routledge, 1994).

Library of Congress Cataloging-in-Publication Data

Violence, identity, and self-determination / edited by Hent de Vries
and Samuel Weber.
    p.   cm.
  "Proceedings of an international workshop held during the
summer of 1995 in Amsterdam."
  Includes bibliographical references.
  ISBN 0-8047-2995-6 (cloth). — ISBN 0-8047-2996-4 (pbk.)
  1. Violence—Philosophy—Congresses. 2. Political violence—
Congresses. 3. Self-determination, National—Congresses.
4. Autonomy (Psychology)—Congresses. I. Vries, Hent de.
II. Weber, Samuel.
HM281.V4923   1997
303.6'01—dc21   97-13450
                                                    CIP

⊗   This book is printed on acid-free, recycled paper.

Original printing 1997
Last figure below indicates year of this printing:
06 05 04 03 02 01 00 99 98 97